P9-ELR-262

THE
GREAT MERCHANTS

BOOKS BY TOM MAHONEY

The Great Merchants (*with Leonard Sloane*)

The Story of George Romney

I'm a Lucky One (*with Barry Sadler*)

The Longest Auto Race (*with George Schuster*)

The Merchants of Life

The Story of Jewelry (*with Marcus Baerwald*)

THE
GREAT MERCHANTS

**AMERICA'S FOREMOST RETAIL INSTITUTIONS
AND THE PEOPLE WHO MADE THEM GREAT**

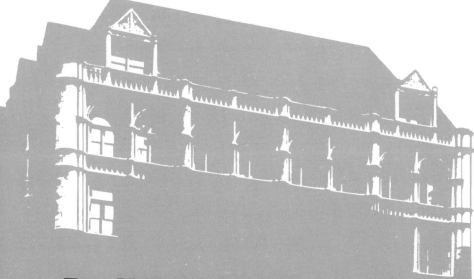

Tom Mahoney & Leonard Sloane

Updated and Enlarged Edition

HARPER & ROW, PUBLISHERS
NEW YORK, EVANSTON, SAN FRANCISCO, LONDON

Again, for Caroline and Annette

THE GREAT MERCHANTS—Updated and Enlarged Edition. Copyright ©
1966, 1974 by John Thomas Mahoney and Leonard Sloane. Copyright
© 1949, 1955 by John Thomas Mahoney. Copyright 1947, 1950, 1951 by
The Reader's Digest Association, Inc. Printed in the United States of
America. All rights reserved. No part of this book may be used or reproduced in any manner whatsoever without written permission except in the
case of brief quotations embodied in critical articles and reviews. For
information address Harper & Row, Publishers, Inc., 10 East 53rd Street,
New York, N.Y. 10022. Published simultaneously in Canada by Fitz-
henry & Whiteside Limited, Toronto.

Designed by Janice Stern

Library of Congress Cataloging in Publication Data
Mahoney, Tom.

The great merchants.
Includes bibliographical references.

1. Retail trade—United States. 2. Merchants—
United States. I. Sloane, Leonard, joint author.
II. Title.
HF5429.3.M26   1974   658.8'7'00973   73-14065
ISBN 0-06-012739-2

Contents

Preface to the Updated and Enlarged Edition

This book presents in one volume and in some detail accounts of twenty-six remarkable American retail institutions and the merchants who built them from small beginnings. They are leaders in their fields and represent the wide range of retailing in the second half of the twentieth century. Scores of others are mentioned at least briefly.

It is an enlargement of a work first published in 1955, revised in 1966 and reprinted many times. It has been translated into German, Spanish, Japanese and Korean and some parts into Russian and Polish as well. Several groups of overseas retailers have followed the table of contents in touring America. The Brand Names Foundation in 1973 based its silver anniversary convention program on the book. Many schools use it as a text.

In the preparation of this new edition, the original author is fortunate in again having the collaboration of Leonard Sloane of the business-news staff of the *New York Times*. He is one of the foremost reporters of retailing. Several chapters are entirely new. All others have been rewritten and updated to include the many changes and developments of recent years.

Included in the chronological order of their start are the world's largest department store, the largest specialty shop, the largest mail-order house, the largest variety chain, the largest apparel chain, the largest drugstore and others that dominate their sections or their particular fields. The smallest of them is a fifteen-million-dollar business. Eight have sales of more than a billion dollars a year, three more than five billion and one more than eleven billion.

All have definite personalities and distinctions other than size. Though widely diverse in their operations, all have many qualities in common that will interest any student of retailing or of business in general. Several have pioneered important innovations and their founders are in the Retailing Hall of Fame at the Chicago Merchandise Mart. All are persistent advertisers, most of them on a large scale.

All have made important contributions to the communities in which they operate, and some to the nation as well. All have adapted themselves to change and have survived the deaths of founders, wars, business depressions, population shifts and the rivalry of numerous competitors.

Small parts of the Singer, Filene's and Lane Bryant chapters appeared in the *Reader's Digest,* and the material is included here with the permission of that publication. Part of the Rich's chapter was published in the *Saturday Evening Post* and is similarly acknowledged. Ralph McGill, Atlanta editor, and Mort Weisinger, New York writer, collaborated on the original accounts of Rich's and Tiffany's. Grace Graves, Helen Brattrund, Marjorie Godfrey and Esther Vail helped on the manuscript.

In addition to the sources listed in the text and notes, the authors are indebted for information, among others, to the following:

George Anderson, Ernest L. Arms, Edith Asbury, Marcus Baerwald, Letitia Baldrige, Kurt Barnard, Anna Poland Berg, Leslie Bergesch, David Brous, Mrs. Eleanor H. Bruce, Lester A. Burcham, Joseph A. Burnham, Edward W. Carter, Marvin A. Chatinover, Kermit Claster, Arthur G. Cohen, Elisa Daggs, Arthur A. Davidson, Bruce B. Dayton, K. N. Dayton, Dorothy E. Demmy, Ernest Downing, Daniel L. Fapp, Eugene Ferkauf, Margo Fischer, James Freeman, Lillian Friedman.

Also Mel Garber, Duane Garrison, William Gekle, John W. Gerber, Harold Goldberg, Andrew Goodman, Leon A. Gorman, John Graham, E. M. Graves, Marilyn Greenbaum, Jess Gregory,

Richard Groberg, Leonard J. Hankin, Sam J. Harrington, Walter Hauser, Harold D. Hodgkinson, William Hollaender, Pamela Hollingsworth, Stacy Holmes, Charlotte Horn, Walter Hoving, A. R. Huband, Joseph L. Hudson, Jr., Russell J. Huff, William Inglis, Crosby M. Kelly, Robert C. Kirkwood, Mark Klauser, Jerome Klein, Tom Langenfeld, Fred Lazarus, Jr., Godfrey M. Lebhar, Maude Lennox, Mrs. Kitty Leslie, Raymond Loewy, Regina M. Longo, Robert G. Luckie, Jr.

Also Raphael Malsin, Stanley Marcus, David Marks, Paul Mazur, Donald S. McGiverin, Marge McLean, Mac Meconis, William Miller, M. Robert Moss, Thomas J. Noonan, James O'Gara, George R. Pfeiffer, Betty Reese, Richard Rich, George G. Rinder, Marshall Rose, Leonard Schwartz, Herbert L. Seegal, Edie Shepherd, Sidney Shore, Donald B. Smiley, Shirlee A. Smith, Mrs. Antoinette Stapper, Walter B. Stevens, Jack I. Straus, Albert Sussman, Stanley Thea, Bogart Thompson, T. C. Thomsen, Kendall L. Tolle, Russell H. Tucker, David Verlen, Rebecca Wright Wallio, E. B. Weiss, Mrs. Betsy Wells, Jess Wolf, Ann C. Wolff, Robert W. Wood, Joseph R. Wright, Morris Zale.

TOM MAHONEY

New York City

I

Peddlers to Palaces

The Evolution of American Retailing

Retailing continues to be the biggest field of business. In many ways it is the most important. Research-laboratory discoveries and the production miracles of factory and farm are meaningless until retailers place them in the hands of consumers. Nearly half of all American enterprises are retail businesses. In 1972, they had sales of $448,379,000,000—about double the figure of a decade earlier.

It is a field of infinite variety that has been growing in importance ever since primitive folk began to trade products of the field, the hunt or their own handiwork for others that they did not have but desired. As civilization developed, it became easier to do this through merchants, who often traveled from country to country, than by face-to-face exchange. From the shops of early craftsmen, who sold their own wares, and from the stalls of itinerant merchants at medieval fairs, modern stores and modern retailing have evolved.[1]*

America leads the world in retailing but every nation boasts notable stores. In some places, the oldest and newest forms of retailing exist side by side. In Baghdad, a Sindbad supermarket and the modern Orosi-Back department store sell goods from everywhere at fixed prices while native traders a few yards away haggle with their customers as in the time of *The Arabian Nights*.

Moscow took pride in Muir & Mirrieless, a fine department store run by Scotsmen until the Revolution, and now boasts

---

* Notes to the chapters begin on p. 381.

GUM (State Department Store), an enormous government-owned gray baroque establishment facing the Kremlin on Red Square. It offers fashion shows five afternoons a week with new styles in overalls for factory girls among the garments modeled. It has 7,000 employees and attracts as many as 300,000 customers a day.[2]

France has contributed the great Bon Marché, founded in Paris in 1852 by Aristide Boucicaut and in some respects the first department store; La Ville de Paris; the original Maison Blanche; and more recently the Galeries Lafayette, whose stores are visited regularly by retailers from all over the world in search of ideas. Its big Paris department store has five branches and it also has a chain of 153 smaller stores. A distinction of the Paris store is a day nursery for the care of children of employees. La Samaritaine is the biggest Paris store in area, and with $110 million a year is perhaps third in sales. It dates from 1870 and grew romantically from the marriage of Ernest Cognacq and Louise Jay, a saleswoman at Bon Marché. They died childless but the Cognacq-Jay Museum and Rue Cognacq-Jay on the Left Bank bear their names.[3]

Harrods, Ltd., of London, founded in 1849 by a grocer named Henry Charles Harrod and managed for many years by the late Sir Richard Burbidge, is the greatest store in the British Isles. Harrods' business is largely food and clothing but it also arranges funerals, deals in real estate, sells insurance and theater tickets, hires out servants and provides entertainment. Three generations of Burbidges headed Harrods until 1960, when Sir Hugh Fraser, a drapery millionaire, bought the firm for $100 million. Harrods has a basement kennel for customers' dogs, accepts American Express credit cards and is establishing branches in other countries.

The main Mitsukoshi store in Tokyo, dedicated to the Goddess of Sincerity, is even more remarkable. It dates from 1673 and was the foundation of the fortune of the Mitsui family. It introduced cash down, *Gen-Gin*, and the fixed price, *Kakene-*

Nashi, in Japan when few but Quakers practiced the latter in the Western world. From a dry-goods store selling silks and brocades, it became a full-line department store.

In addition to complete wedding outfits, since 1944 it has also been supplying brides and grooms. There is a government marriage bureau on the first floor. Men and women seeking mates leave their photographs, vital statistics and a list of qualifications they seek in a spouse. Marriage ceremonies are performed in a neighborhood chapel. Mitsukoshi offers couples a bargain in services for 700 yen. This sum borrows a trousseau for the bride, pays for maid service to dress her, the rent of a banquet hall and tea and cakes for guests. Many Japanese literally owe everything to Mitsukoshi.

With sales of more than $300 million a year, the ten Mitsukoshi stores, four of them in Tokyo, do a tenth of Japan's department-store business, some of it in $5,000 watches. But there are huge rivals. These include Daimaru, Matsuzakaya, Takashimaya, Seibu, Isetan and Sogo. All operate similarly. At each ascending escalator, a pretty girl bows and welcomes customers. At the foot of descending escalators other pretty girls thank them for coming. The girls used to be in kimonos but now wear miniskirts or hot pants. Daimaru has branches in Hong Kong and Bangkok. Mitsukoshi has a Paris branch. Takashimaya has two in New York City, one on Fifth Avenue.[4]

But nowhere has retailing become so important as in the United States. On its success in distributing the fruits of mass production, the prosperity of our entire economy very largely depends. Retailing is literally the biggest business in the country. It is a hard, competitive field, with one out of three new ventures failing within the first year, but in no other country have so many stores become vast enterprises.

Why have American retailing institutions grown so hugely? One obvious reason is that never before have there been such quantities of goods and so many customers able to afford them. American stores also have led the world in advertising, the use of electric lights, plate glass, packaging, air conditioning, self-service, refrigeration, credit, parking lots and other devices for painlessly bringing together buyers and sellers, and causing yesterday's luxuries to become today's necessities. Nowhere else have retailers of every kind gone to such lengths to guarantee satisfaction to every customer. When an American consults his doctor or his lawyer, he must pay regardless of whether he likes the outcome of his case, while in virtually any store he is assured of happiness or his money back.

Also important is the wide freedom that the retailer enjoys as to what and how he sells in the United States and the consumer's equally glorious freedom as to how and where he will spend his money. In medieval Europe, a man risked his soul as well as his capital when he attempted to sell at a profit goods that he had not made: "The man who buys it in order that he may gain by selling it again unchanged and as he bought it, that man is of the buyers and sellers who are cast forth from God's temple," warned St. Thomas Aquinas. American retailing has never had such restrictions.

By custom and sometimes by law, for tobacco is often a state monopoly, cigarettes are purchased in Europe from the tobacconist. In the United States, you can buy cigarettes from the American equivalent of the tobacconist. You can also buy them at the drugstore, delicatessen, restaurant, gasoline filling station and perhaps from a vending machine. Sears, Roebuck and Co. will sell you a simple outfit for making your own cigarettes. A person must be a registered pharmacist to sell prescription drugs, but almost anything else can be retailed by anybody.

A consumer may live in a community with only one store, but even this does not make him a captive customer of that store. If he has an automobile, as more and more Americans have, he can shop many miles away if he likes. Or he may shop by telephone or by mail and what he wants will come to him even though his post office may be in the local store he is not patronizing.

The first retail selling in most of America was done by peddlers. At the outset they walked. Those of more stature rode horseback and the even more prosperous rode in wagons or carriages. The father of the first John D. Rockefeller was a carriage peddler of patent medicines. If the peddler did not plan to return to the community, there was no limit to his chicanery, but many of them were responsible men who sold New England wares of good quality repeatedly to the same customers. The espionage of a peddler named Enoch Crosby in behalf of General Washington during the Revolution was the basis of *The Spy*, James Fenimore Cooper's first successful novel.

A peddler's life was strenuous, lonely and hazardous. When the opportunity arose or "when they found the right place or the right girl," many were happy to settle down as storekeepers. Many dry-goods stores (so called to distinguish them from those which sold liquor or "wet" goods) were started in this way. As soon as he was established as a storekeeper, a peddler began to take a dim view of his former vocation and, as often as not, would contrive to have laws passed requiring exorbitant license fees from peddlers or even banning them entirely.

The many antipeddler efforts culminated in a Green River, Wyoming, ordinance making it a misdemeanor for a salesman to call at a home without having been previously "invited" to do so by the occupant. This was upheld by the United States Supreme Court in 1951. But despite all obstacles, house-to-house selling endures and more than three thousand companies were engaged in it in 1973.

Avon Products, Inc., the leader in the field, had earnings of $124,900,000 on record sales of $1,005,300,000 in 1972 and was hailed by *Forbes* as the best managed of all major retail firms.[5] It opens doors for its women with an effective musical-chime "Avon calling" television commercial. The Fuller Brush Company and Stanley Home Products also have effective direct selling operations.

As money was scarce in rural America early in the nineteenth century, the country general store of nostalgic memory did a lot of its business by barter. Phineas T. Barnum, the great circus man, in his youth learned about human nature while clerking in such a store at Bethel, Connecticut. He wrote later in his autobiography:

Like many greenhorns before me this was the height of my ambition. Ours was a cash, credit and barter store; and I drove many a sharp trade with old women who paid for their purchases in butter, eggs, beeswax, feathers, and rags, and with men who exchanged for our commodities, hats, axe-helves, oats, corn, buckwheat, hickory-nuts, and other commodities. It was something of a drawback upon my dignity that I was compelled to sweep the store, take down the window-shutters, and make the fire; nevertheless the thought of being a "merchant" fully compensated me for all such menial duties.

There is something to be learned even in a country store. We are apt to believe that sharp trades, especially dishonest tricks and unprincipled deceptions, are confined entirely to the city, and that the unsophisticated men and women of the country do everything on the square. I believe this to be measurably true, but know that there are many exceptions to this rule. Many is the time I cut open bundles of rags, brought to the store by country women in exchange for goods, and declared to be all linen and cotton, that contained quantities of worthless trash in the interior, and sometimes stones, gravel, ashes, etc. . . .[6]

Craftsmen of various kinds, also importers, tailors and apothecaries, as well as peddlers, were among America's earliest merchants. Caswell-Massey, America's oldest chemists and perfumers, was begun in Newport, Rhode Island, in 1780 and later moved to New York. One of its employees became Sir Henry Wellcome, a founder of Burroughs Wellcome, the British pharmaceutical firm. Schieffelin & Co., a New York drug house, dates from 1794.

R. C. Williams & Co., Inc., the wholesale grocers identified with the Royal Scarlet brand, began with a fleet of packet ships in 1811. J. H. Thorp & Co., Inc., a New York fabric house, started in 1819. The Gunther Jaeckel, Inc., fur business began in 1820. John Jacob Astor was once associated with it. Hager & Bro., Inc., was founded by Christopher Hager as a general store at Lancaster, Pennsylvania, in 1821. It is now a department store run by the fourth and fifth generations of the Hager family. William Mills & Son, Inc., New York dealers in fine fishing tackle, and Browning, King & Company, clothiers (whose name was later changed to Browning Fifth Avenue), dates from 1822. Jacob Reed's Sons, Philadelphia clothiers famous for their uniforms, began in 1825.

Arnold Constable, the oldest New York specialty shop, was founded as a dry-goods store in that year by Aaron Arnold, an immigrant from the Isle of Wight. A century later it was joined with Stewart & Co., and Isaac Liberman, head of the latter, became president. Only a few months junior is Lord & Taylor, founded in 1826 by Samuel Lord and George Washington Taylor. It led fashion stores to Fifth Avenue. An Associated Dry Goods property, headed by William Lippincott and Harry Murray, its fifteen units have sales of more than $132 million a year. Another man from the Isle of Wight, George Arnold Hearn, founded Hearn's, the Manhattan—and later Bronx— department store in 1827. The S. S. Pierce Co., Boston's fancy grocers, began in 1831. McKesson & Robbins, the wholesale drug firm, dates from 1833.

Gimbel Brothers, Inc., was founded in 1842 in the then frontier town of Vincennes, Indiana, by Adam Gimbel, a peddler from Bavaria. He advertised: "Fairness and Equality of All Patrons, whether they be Residents of the City, Plainsmen, Traders or Indians." The first of the modern Gimbel stores opened in Milwaukee in 1887. A Philadelphia store, since grown to many acres of space, was opened in 1894, and New York was invaded in 1909. The Saks Company was absorbed in 1923, Saks Fifth Avenue was opened the next year and the Kaufmann and Baer Company of Pittsburgh purchased in 1925. Under the dynamic Bernard F. Gimbel, one of the founder's grandsons, who became president in 1927 and board chairman in 1953, the firm developed forceful advertising and promotion. Expansions carried it into Chicago, Detroit, Beverly Hills, Miami Beach, San Francisco and elsewhere. Bruce Alva Gimbel of the fourth generation succeeded his father as president. In 1973 he became chairman and Richard Shapiro, formerly of Filene's and Lord & Taylor, became president. The thirty-six Gimbels and twenty-nine Saks units had sales of $812,184,000 in 1973. The firm is now owned by the British-American Tobacco Company.

Thalhimer Brothers, Inc., began in Richmond, Virginia, and D. H. Holmes in New Orleans in 1842. The former boasts the first aluminum-clad store and provides showers for women shoppers. The latter was the first big store in the South to hire women and one of the first to provide free delivery service for customers. Free delivery, by wheelbarrow, was the boast also of the store founded by Gerson Fox in 1847 at Hartford, Connecticut. It grew into Connecticut's biggest department store, owned and operated for years by his granddaughter, Beatrice Fox Auerbach, with sales of more than $60 million. She sold it to the May Company in 1965 for 720,000 shares of stock, then worth more than $40 million.[7]

W. & J. Sloane, the famous home-furnishings firm, started in New York in 1843. Mark Cross began as a harness store in Boston in 1845 and later moved to New York. Cartier, Inc., the jewelry firm, was founded in Paris in 1847. The Joseph Horne Co. of Pittsburgh began in 1849. Famous Barr of St. Louis also began in 1849, and what became Scruggs-Vandervoort-Barney, Inc., started there in 1850.

At this time a French silk-stocking manufacturer, dissatisfied with the turn of politics in his country and hearing of gold in California, sold his business and sailed for San Francisco with a shipload of merchandise. He was Félix Verdier, who arrived in May 1850 and set up a waterfront store which he called the City of Paris, after his ship and also the big French store of that name, giving it the motto of the French capital, *"Fluctuat nec mergitur*—It floats, and never sinks." The gold-mad Californians bought his merchandise as fast as he could unload it. The establishment grew into a great and distinctive store guided for generations by the Verdier family.

Eben Jordan, a ribbon clerk from Maine, started Jordan Marsh in Boston in 1851. It is now the biggest of the 149 units of the Allied Stores Corporation, the second-largest department-store chain. Under Thomas M. Macioce, this chain had sales of about $1.5 billion in 1972. Carson, Pirie Scott Co., the great Chicago store, was founded by Scotch-Irish immigrants at La Salle, Illinois, in 1854. The store had sales of $289,912,000 in 1972. Mandel Bros., Inc., was started in Chicago a year later in 1855.

Younker's, the biggest store in Iowa, was founded by three Polish immigrants, Lipman, Samuel and Marcus Younker, at Keokuk in 1856 and later moved to Des Moines. It has nineteen branches and sales of more than $86,000,000 a year.[8] Meier & Frank of Portland, Oregon's largest department store, traces its history to 1857. Julius L. Meier, of the firm, served as Governor of Oregon and organized its state police. Goldwaters, Inc., was founded at Phoenix in 1860. The Higbee Co. began the same year in Cleveland. The Daniels & Fisher Stores Co. started in Denver in 1864.

As communities gained in population, many of the stores established by peddlers grew into great specialty shops and, in some cases, famous department stores with buildings like palaces. A specialty shop is a store that, regardless of size, limits its merchandise to certain specialties and appeals to its customer on the basis of fashion or price rather than completeness of stocks. The limitation may simply be the broad classification of "soft goods." It may be as limited as clothing and accessories for brides, expectant mothers or even tall girls.

A department store is a large store, organized by departments, selling under one management a wide variety of merchandise, including at least ready-to-wear, dry goods and home furnishings. The U.S. Census Bureau considers only stores of this type with sales of $100,000 or more as department stores.

It is difficult to determine at what date many stores met these qualifications, and the "first" department store is a matter of controversy. Macy's, Wanamaker's and A. T. Stewart's all have their partisans. Joseph Kane, the author of *Famous First Facts,* thinks the distinction belongs to Zion's Co-operative Mercantile Institution founded in Salt Lake City in 1868 by Brigham Young, the Mormon leader. This had sales of $43,914,000 and earned $1,616,000 in 1972. The Mormon Church has a third interest in the store.[9]

In any case, America's leading merchant in the middle of the nineteenth century was Alexander Turney Stewart, a self-made millionaire. Born at Lisburn, near Belfast, Ireland, and educated at Trinity College, Dublin, he emigrated at twenty to New York. Two years later, in 1823, he opened the biggest store in the world at Broadway and Tenth Street. He was a single-price pioneer, hired handsome clerks to charm his women customers and sold quality merchandise, much of it from Europe. "I got it at Stewart's" was a phrase denoting value and satisfaction. Mrs. Abraham Lincoln redecorated the White House with goods from his store.

Stewart sent shiploads of food to famine-stricken Ireland and generously aided sufferers in the Franco-Prussian War as well as the American Civil War. He was appointed Secretary of the Treasury by President Grant but was kept from office by a law forbidding importers to hold the post. He died in 1876. In a bizarre crime, his body was stolen and recovered, to be buried in the Episcopal Cathedral he donated to Garden City, Long Island, a community that he founded as a model city.

A Philadelphia merchant named John Wanamaker replaced Stewart in the American scene and in 1896 acquired his New York store. The son of a bricklayer, he became a partner in 1861 of a brother-in-law in the Oak Hall Clothing Bazaar, a Philadelphia men's clothing store. On the latter's death, Wanamaker expanded the business into a department store. He was the first merchant to buy a full-page newspaper advertisement and personally wrote much of his copy, which appeared in national magazines as well as the Philadelphia and New York newspapers.

As early as the Civil War, he had his famous "money back" guarantee in print. He advertised in 1865:

Any article that does not fit well, is not the proper color or quality, does not please the folks at home, or for any reason is not perfectly satisfactory, should be brought back at once, and if it is returned as purchased within ten days, we will refund the money. It is our intention always to give value for value in every sale we make, and those who are not pleased with what they buy do us a positive favor to return the goods and get the money back.[10]

In 1878, he moved his store into a vast unused Philadelphia freight depot, soon made it the first store completely lighted by incandescent lamps and advertised that his ground floor of nearly three acres was "the largest space in the world devoted to retail selling on a single floor." The Wanamaker stores sold nearly everything—for a time even airplanes and Ford automobiles.

Wanamaker, termed "Pious John" by rivals, had other interests, especially Sunday schools, the Young Men's Christian Association and the Republican party. President Harrison appointed him Postmaster General, and possibly the high point of his life was in 1911 when President William Howard Taft dedicated a new Wanamaker store building in Philadelphia.

In 1920, when nearly eighty-two years old, he foresaw a postwar downturn in business. Though prices were at a peak, he ordered storewide 20 percent discount sales. On Saturday, May 8, more than $1 million worth of merchandise was sold, believed to be a world record up to that time. In addition to his advertising contributions, John Wanamaker was a pioneer in employee training and public relations. One of the last lines that he wrote before his death in 1922 was: "You have got to run a store that people will feel at home in!"

The Wanamaker stores had some adverse years during the depression. They again became profitable under John E. Raasch, a notable management consultant. Employee relations were excellent with Local 9 of the Retail Clerks International Association, AFL-CIO, which at times spent union funds to advertise

Wanamaker's. The firm adapted to changing conditions by opening branches in both the Philadelphia and New York areas, but in Manhattan it clung too long to its lower Broadway location and closed the week before Christmas in 1954 as midtown department stores were enjoying a record holiday business.

Mail-order or catalog selling and chain stores became important in the latter half of the nineteenth century. A lowering of postage rates and expansion of postal service, an example of government policy to aid the farmer and end his isolation, made selling by mail possible.

While Benjamin Franklin has been called "the father of the mail-order catalog" on the basis of one he issued in 1744 listing six hundred books,[11] young Montgomery Ward, previously a $23-a-week salesman at Marshall Field's, was the first to make a big thing of the idea. In 1872, he and a friend, George R. Thorne, started business in Chicago with $2,400 in capital. They began in one room with a catalog of one page. "Our business," Ward recalled later, "was looked upon with suspicion by those whom we wished as customers. It was ridiculed by retail merchants, doubted by manufacturers and predicted a short life by all." The results were quite different. In 1972, Montgomery Ward had sales of $2,640,122,000, earnings of $49,469,000 and Booton Herndon recounted its story in *Satisfaction Guaranteed,* a centennial history published by McGraw-Hill.

The firm's hundredth anniversary was marked by a U.S. commemorative postage stamp honoring the mail-order business in general. Robert E. "Tom" Brooker, the chief executive officer largely responsible for Ward's success in recent years and its merger with the Container Corporation of America to form Marcor, Inc., received the thirty-sixth Gantt Medal for "distinguished achievement in management as a service to the community."*

The idea of one merchant or one company operating many stores is an old one. The Fuggers of Augsburg had branches in a score of European cities as early as the fifteenth century. It

* See Chapter XV.

remained for George Huntington Hartford with his Great Atlantic & Pacific Tea Company and Frank W. Woolworth to develop the low-cost merchandising possibilities of chain opera- tion to create chain-store empires.*

Notable successes in the variety and drug chain fields have been attained by S. S. Kresge, S. H. Kress, W. T. Grant, J. G. McCrory, G. C. Murphy, J. J. Newberry, H. L. Green, L. K. Liggett, Charles R. Walgreen and numerous others. There are also highly successful clothing chains like Robert Hall, Bond's, Hughes & Hatcher and the Lerner Stores Corporation.

But to go back to post-Civil War retailing, L. Hart & Son Co., Inc., began in San Diego in 1866. Strawbridge & Clothier was started by Philadelphia Quakers in 1868. Luckey, Platt and Company, biggest store of the Hudson River valley, began in 1869 in Poughkeepsie, New York, and since 1971 has been headed by Arthur Bressman, a former Korvettes vice president. The Herpolsheimer Co. began in Grand Rapids, Michigan, in 1870.

A "Trade Palace" started in 1872 by a former wagon peddler grew into the great L. S. Ayres store in Indianapolis. The Joske Brothers Co. of San Antonio, Texas, was formed in 1872. Forbes and Wallace, Inc., of Springfield, Massachusetts, dates from the next year, as does the Rogers Peet Co., New York and Boston men's clothiers. The Hecht Co., with big stores now in Washington, D.C., and a dozen other cities, also began in 1874. The Fair of Chicago started in 1875. Hochschild, Kohn & Co. of Baltimore began in 1876. Two famous jewelry stores, Lambert Brothers of New York and Linz Brothers of Dallas, started in 1877.

David May in Leadville, Colorado, in 1879 abandoned mining to open a clothing store. He moved it to Denver in 1888. The enterprise, now headed by his grandson, Morton D. May, has grown into the May Department Stores Co. with seventy- two great stores, many of them with branches, located from

* See Chapters XI and XIII.

Hartford to Los Angeles. Besides stores under the May name, the company owns the Famous Barr Co. of St. Louis; Kaufmann's, the big Pittsburgh store; the M. O'Neil Co. of Akron, Ohio; the Hecht Co.; and others. Now the third-largest department store chain, in 1972 it had sales of $1,467,931,000.

Miller & Rhoads of Richmond began as a partnership in 1885. Peck & Peck began as a hosiery firm in 1887. The Bon Marché of Seattle started in 1890. The Halle Bros. Co. began in Cleveland in 1891. Stix, Baer & Fuller started in St. Louis and Abercrombie & Fitch Co. in New York in 1892. The latter sells sporting goods, including pith helmets, scuba suits and rifles for big-game hunting. Bonwit Teller and Henri Bendel, famous New York fashion stores, were born in 1895 and 1896. Two remarkable women, Mildred Custin and Geraldine Stutz, were among the presidents placed in charge of these stores by Genesco, Inc., which owns them. New York's Bergdorf Goodman store was born in 1901 when Herman Bergdorf, an Alsatian tailor, sold first half and then all of his Fifth Avenue business to Edwin Goodman, a designer and tailor from Rochester, New York.* In 1902, Franklin Simon opened his Fifth Avenue specialty shop, the Dayton Co.† began in Minneapolis, Titche-Goettinger Co. got under way in Dallas and A. Schwartz came out of Mexico to start the Popular Dry Goods Co., the big store of El Paso, Texas. Marvin and Obadiah Leonard, two energetic Texas farm boys, started a high-volume low-price food and general-merchandise business in Fort Worth at the end of World War I. It grew to be the city's biggest advertiser. Leonard's clerks some days cash more checks than local banks. In 1925, Bert Gamble and Phil Skogmo opened at St. Cloud, Minnesota, the first of many Gamble Skogmo, Inc., one-stop shopping centers. It acquired Aldens, Inc., in 1964 and the next year had sales of $608,243,214. By 1972 this total had more than doubled.

The depression thirties proved an opportunity for many mer-

* See Chapter XX.
† See Chapter XIV.

chants. In 1932, when Max Hess took charge of Hess Brothers, the Allentown, Pennsylvania, store founded by his father and uncle back in 1897, its sales were around a million dollars. By a series of dramatic innovations, the best known of which is a "Fashion Caravan" of trucks providing traveling fashion shows, he increased sales to more than $67 million a year. The caravan has been the subject of a motion picture. The store has a children's barbershop, which gives the customer a diploma and a lock of his hair with his first haircut.

Gertz of Jamaica, Long Island, expanded from a stationery and phonograph shop to a full department store in the depression. It built a new building and added parking lots, clubs for kids and a Consumer Advisory Board of forty women's club leaders. The store boasts one of the highest sales per square foot of any department store. It was purchased by Allied Stores Corporation in 1941.

The late Fred Harvey, a former basement merchandise manager at Marshall Field's, found an opportunity at the same time in Nashville, Tennessee. In 1943, he took over a moribund department store there with sales of $560,000. He remodeled, introduced night openings and advertised with blimps. In a decade, he raised sales to $11 million and made Harvey's Nashville's leading store.

Discount houses* and shopping centers flowered after World War II but had their beginnings much earlier. Back in the fifteenth century, Nizhni Novgorod (now called Gorki) took a step toward the shopping center when traders at the fair there began to have "permanent buildings and bazaars, often of stone." When automobiles spurred growth of the suburbs and began to clog downtown streets, stores in several cities began to establish outlying branches with parking areas. One of the earliest was the Country Club Plaza of Kansas City, Missouri, developed by the J. C. Nichols real-estate interests in the twenties.

Any wide place in the road with a strip of stores and some

* See Chapter XXV.

parking can call itself a shopping center. But those of importance are groups of retail establishments, planned, developed and managed as units, with off-street parking and ready access by auto or public transportation to at least thirty thousand people.

Three of the oldest are noteworthy because all big centers follow to some degree one of their designs. Northgate in Seattle, built at a cost of $12 million by Allied Stores, was opened in 1950. The Bon Marché, Butler Bros. and other stores pull shoppers back and forth across a pedestrian mall. It has an underground service concourse. The eighty-odd stores are grouped by merchandise and emphasize competition. This design proved so successful that the architect, John Graham, has since designed seventy more mall-type centers, such as Ala Moana in Honolulu; Gulfgate in Houston; the Halifax Shopping Center in Nova Scotia; Bergen Mall in Paramus, New Jersey; Tacoma Mall in Tacoma, Washington. The newer ones are air-conditioned.

Shoppers' World in Framingham, Massachusetts, the first big center in the East, was opened in 1951 and has had a less happy history. A domed Jordan Marsh store dominated a U-shaped building containing some forty stores double-decked around a wide mall or court. There was no separation of service and customer traffic, and many customers did not walk past Jordan Marsh to the other stores. The center went bankrupt in 1954 and was taken over by an insurance company. It has been operated since 1957 by Alstores Realty Corporation, an Allied subsidiary. With more parking space, a large theater and increased population in the area, it is now prospering.[12]

Northland, the third basic type, designed by the Vienna-born Victor Gruen, was completed at a cost of $25 million in 1954 by the J. L. Hudson Company twelve miles northwest of downtown Detroit.* Truck delivery is underground. To reach the Hudson store in the center from the 7,500-car parking areas, a shopper must pass many of eighty smaller shops. Northland has parlayed beauty and efficiency into success.

* See Chapter XIV.

As of 1974, the world's largest enclosed shopping center, boasting two million square feet of retailing space, was spectacular multilevel Woodfield. This is at Schaumburg, Illinois, near O'Hare Airport, northwest of Chicago, on 191 acres owned largely by Bob Atcher, cowboy singer and longtime mayor of the village. It is a joint venture of A. Alfred Taubman and the Homart Development Company, a subsidiary of Sears, Roebuck, which has the most space. Other major stores are Marshall Field, J. C. Penney and Lord & Taylor. There are Waldenbook and also B. Dalton Bookseller shops among the 200 smaller stores. It is a seven-day operation with shoppers driving many miles for the Sunday "champagne brunch" served by Field's Seven Arches restaurant, one of more than thirty eating places in the big development.

Since 1950, shopping centers in the United States have increased from fewer than one hundred to about fifteen thousand, according to the International Council of Shopping Centers. Their effect on downtown shopping has been serious. But downtown is fighting back successfully in many cities.

Shopping developments with nearly all the advantages of a suburban center can be constructed downtown. The great Lloyd Center, only a mile from the heart of Portland, Oregon, is an example. This city within a city is America's largest central downtown shopping center. A big Meier & Frank branch is at the center. J. J. Newberry and F. W. Woolworth are at the ends of pedestrian malls. Stores with complementary merchandise are grouped. Sidewalks and second-floor balconies are covered. Pedestrian malls are fifty feet wide and landscaped with flowers and fountains. Lloyd Center has 1,200,000 square feet of floor space, more than one hundred stores, a medical arts building, an outdoor skating rink, a Sheraton Hotel and parking for nine thousand automobiles.

Rochester, New York, has revitalized its downtown area with a $30-million Midtown Plaza designed by Gruen. A two-level air-conditioned mall that makes shopping pleasant even when icy winds sweep off Lake Ontario connects the big B. Forman and

McCurdy stores and forty shops. The complex includes a nineteen-story office building with a hotel on the top four floors, a post office, a bus station and an $8,500,000 underground garage where closed-circuit television cameras watch cars. The city built the garage, is paying off bonds with parking charges, closed a street bisecting the site and with state aid has built limited-access highways leading to it. All this came about only after the merchants gambled $5 million in quietly buying the land required.

The biggest downtown development as of 1974 was the $100-million seventy-four-floor Water Tower Place complex on North Michigan Avenue in Chicago. It is a joint venture of subsidiaries of Aetna Life & Casualty and Marshall Field. Field's, Lord & Taylor and other stores will occupy a seven-story mall. Overhead will be a new twenty-floor Ritz-Carlton Hotel and forty floors of apartments. It will be part of Chicago's "magnificent mile" on North Michigan.

Shopping centers accounted for about $140 billion in annual trade in the United States and Canada as of the end of 1973. This was 45 percent of total retail trade in the United States and 30.6 percent in Canada, excluding automobiles, gas stations, building materials, hay, grain, fuel and ice. In some states (Arizona, Delaware, Florida, Nevada), shopping-center sales topped 70 percent. Edward J. DeBartolo of Ohio, leading builder of shopping malls say these figures can only go higher.

The shopping-center idea has spread to many lands. Japan has underground shopping centers in Tokyo, Nagoya, and Osaka, the last a development of 4.4 acres two levels below the streets and opened in 1963 at a cost of $88 million. The Osaka municipal government owns 51 percent of the shares. It contains 80 general stores, 55 restaurants and coffee shops, 47 food stores, a barbershop, a travel agency and other service establishments. It adjoins a railroad station and two electric lines. Some 700,000 people shop there daily.[13]

There are shopping centers in England, West Germany, the Netherlands, Australia, Mexico, Argentina, France and Sweden. Topping them all for imagination and flair is the Helicoid, a terraced pyramid of three hundred stores on the huge Tarpeya Rock above Caracas, Venezuela. It is a $40-million project. Access is by a road that spirals for a mile and a quarter to the summit, which in turn features a gigantic aluminum dome covering a two-thousand-seat auditorium. From this point a shopper can view Caracas from an observation deck 492 feet above sea level, a height equivalent to that of a forty-five-story building.[14]

II
The Hudson's Bay Company

Resurgence of the Oldest Retailer

The Hudson's Bay Company is the world's oldest retailer. Founded in 1670, to develop the fur trade of then largely unexplored Canada, it is North America's oldest chartered trading company.[1] For years it issued its own money and maintained forts. Over its stores, ships and trading posts it still flies its own flag, the Company coat of arms on a white background. Its original fur business is the world's biggest, but the company is an increasingly big retailer. Eighty percent of its sales and 70 percent of its earnings come from 250 stores located from Newfoundland to the Yukon and from the Arctic islands to the Niagara Peninsula.

It has undergone more changes in recent years than in the previous centuries of its colorful history. The venerable but lively company celebrated its tercentenary in 1970 by moving its headquarters from London, England, to Winnipeg, and also paying to Queen Elizabeth II, who attended the ceremonies, the rent of two beaver pelts and two elk heads as required by its original charter.

Later that year, George T. Richardson became the company's thirty-second governor, the first Canadian-born man to fill the post, which corresponds to chairman.[2]

The company finally began to pay dividends in Canadian dollars instead of pounds sterling. Stockholders began to be called "shareholders" instead of "proprietors" in the annual reports. These became brighter typographically and financially. For the fiscal year ending January 31, 1973, the company had sales of $672 million, a record, and earnings of $15,700,000. Both retail and wholesale sales were largest in the company's long history.

Donald Scott McGiverin, managing director, retail stores, was named chief executive December 1, 1972 upon the retirement of James R. Murray, managing director since 1959, who had urged the move from England and had taken the company into department stores in eastern Canada by the 1960 acquisition of Henry Morgan & Co., Ltd. A native of Calgary, McGiverin earned a master of business administration degree at Ohio State University and worked twenty-three years for T. Eaton Co., Ltd., Canada's biggest retailer, before joining the Hudson's Bay Company in 1969.

He became its first executive with the title of president. At the same time Hugh W. Sutherland, formerly deputy managing director, became senior vice president; Ronald E. Sheen, formerly a deputy managing director, vice president, merchandising; and Peter W. Wood, formerly treasurer, vice president, finance. These were the company's first vice presidents.

Hudson's Bay has been called "the most rambunctiously modern old-fashioned company in the world." Airplanes and radiotelephones have replaced canoes and dog teams in supplying and communicating with its Arctic stores. It is the most outstanding example of a commercial enterprise successfully adapting to tremendous changes. It might easily have vanished along with the East India Company, the Muscovy Company and the other great companies chartered in the century of the first Queen Elizabeth. Instead, it developed a vitality that enabled it to survive Arctic cold, wars and rivalries of all kinds, to become one of Canada's most fascinating and important enterprises.[3]

Though the term was not applied to the Morgan stores until 1972, the company in 1965 adopted "the Bay" as its name for retail activities and had Lippincott & Marguiles, Ltd., create new letterheads and wrappings. The big and little Hudson's Bay retail stores have been enlarged and expanded to keep pace with Canada's quickening economy. Let a new uranium mine open or a new hydroelectric development start and the company is likely to start an adjoining store.

It is possible to buy a marriage license in the great Hudson's Bay department store in Winnipeg. The company also has big department stores in Vancouver, Calgary, Edmonton, Victoria, Saskatoon, Montreal, Toronto and Ottawa. All carry a complete line of ready-to-wear apparel for men, women and children; house furnishings and floor coverings, appliances, notions, sporting goods, china, furs, diamonds and drugs. In Toronto, the company has sited a new downtown department store at the high traffic junction of two new subway lines and has circled the city with attractive suburban stores in Bramalea and other shopping centers. It has established a new national merchandising office in Toronto.

The company also operates "junior" department stores in small cities or towns, usually built around primary industries and scattered from British Columbia to Newfoundland. In addition, the company sells merchandise at its fur-trading posts, now known as Northern Stores, many of which are north of the Arctic Circle. Many offer a U-Paddle Canoe Rental Service whereby for fifty dollars a week you can rent a canoe at one store and leave it at another.

The wholesale department had record sales of $111,519,000 in 1972. This division supplies its "Best Procurable" Scotch whisky and other company-brand products. The wonderful woolen Hudson's Bay "point" blankets, which have warmed Antarctic explorers and the climbers of Mount Everest, indicate how things have changed. A four-point blanket once meant that it could be exchanged for four first-grade beaver skins. It now means that it fits a double bed. The company gives every woman employee who has worked five years a four-point blanket when she marries. The wholesale department has twenty-nine branches from Halifax to Victoria. It is the largest distributor of tobacco in Canada.

The company owns a 21.2 percent interest in Hudson's Bay Oil and Gas Company Limited, a company organized in 1926 with the Continental Oil Company of Delaware to develop the oil and gas in western Canada. This contributed $2,205,000 in royalties to the Bay in 1972. The oil company has oil and gas rights to more than 12,000,000 acres, of which 4,500,000 are mineral rights of the Bay. In 1951–52, speculators attempted to buy control with a view toward exploiting the oil and possibly liquidating other activities. But the management was alert to the threat and the proprietors cold-shouldered the idea. The agreement with Continental Oil was extended to 1999.

Though now a small part of the volume, Hudson's Bay's fur business is bigger than when it was the company's principal activity. In 1972, it sold furs of its own, mostly from ranch-grown animals, for $6,386,000 and sold on consignment for others pelts from sixty countries for $109,238,000. The company's traders buy furs in Iran and Tibet. Prior to World War II, it sold only its own furs through auctions in London. It now sells also in Montreal and New York. Arthur F. Frayling, who retired as manager of fur sales in 1972, traveled the world for forty-three years building this business.

The story of the fabulous company began with two Indianized Frenchmen, Pierre Esprit Radisson and his brother-in-law, Médart Chouart, Sieur des Groseilliers, of Trois Rivières, Quebec. "A more daring pair of international promoters cannot be found in the history of commerce," wrote one historian. "Glib, plausible, ambitious, supported by unquestionable physical courage, they were completely equipped fortune hunters."

Less than fifty years after Henry Hudson sailed into the bay while seeking the Northwest Passage, Groseilliers and Radisson made their way there overland from the French settlements and returned in 1660 to Quebec with Indians carrying beaver skins worth $300,000. Of this, the French colonial authorities took in taxes and fines for illicit trading all except $20,000. Unable to obtain redress in France, Groseilliers and Radisson turned to England.

They met rebuffs. London was ravaged by plague in 1665 and in 1666 by the Great Fire. There was war with Holland. At last in 1668, they talked Prince Rupert, a cousin of King Charles II, and others into outfitting two ships for Hudson's Bay. One was damaged in a storm and turned back.

The other, the *Nonsuch*, a fifty-ton ketch in which Groseilliers sailed, won through to Hudson's Bay and after 118 days anchored in what was christened Rupert's River. The Hudson's Bay Company still has a fur-trading post at the spot. After a winter of trade with the Indians, the *Nonsuch* returned to England with a fortune in beaver skins, highly valued for men's hats. Thus encouraged, the adventurers and Prince Rupert, their first governor, on May 2, 1670, obtained from King Charles their celebrated charter.

This assured "The Governor and Company of Adventurers of England trading into Hudson's Bay . . . the sole trade and commerce" and absolute control of all lands they should discover through Hudson Strait, which was later interpreted to mean the watershed of Hudson's Bay. This meant 1,486,000 square miles of territory, nearly a sixth of North America. The company was given "the fishing of all sorts of fish . . . and all Mines Royal, as well discovered as not discovered, of gold, silver, gems and precious stones. . . ."

As part of its tercentenary celebration, the Bay had a faithful full-scale replica of the *Nonsuch* built by Alan Hinks at Appledore, in Devon. After being exhibited in England and Canada she was presented to the Manitoba Museum of Man and Nature at Winnipeg.

Obligations of the company included a promise to seek the Northwest Passage. Two of its ships eventually made this voyage and its *Fort James* sailed almost entirely around North America. The company adopted as a coat of arms a design of elks and beaver with the motto "Pro Pelle Cutem," literally "For Pelt, Skin," meaning that a man risks his own skin for the skin of an animal. This summed up accurately the early activities. Ships took out guns, knives, hatchets, glass beads, brass kettles, blankets and other items and brought back furs. Hudson's Bay men early established a reputation for integrity and fair dealing in their trading with the Indians. The company's affairs prospered. In 1684, the company paid its first dividend, 50 percent on the original capital of 10,500 pounds.

French attacks reduced the enterprise to a single trading post toward the end of the seventeenth century. In 1697, the company's ships and the French fought the greatest naval action in Arctic history, with the French victorious. Over in Europe, however, the Duke of Marlborough, for a time governor of the company, led the British to victory in the War of the Spanish Succession. In 1713, the Treaty of Utrecht gave Hudson's Bay back to the British. From 1690 to 1718, the company paid no dividends. General James Wolfe's capture of Quebec in 1759 and the surrender of Montreal the next year ended French authority in Canada, but in 1782, during the American Revolution, Count Jean-François de La Pérouse, the French admiral, led a final raid into the bay, capturing and burning the company's forts.

As trading moved inland, Hudson's Bay men came into conflict with other traders as tough as themselves, who ignored the royal charter. These were Scottish Canadians from Montreal who moved west and in 1784 formed the North West Company. By 1818, it was powerful enough to buy the Pacific Fur Company of John Jacob Astor, which had sent traders into what is now Oregon.

Rivalry reached a bloody peak in 1816. In that year, Northwesters encouraged half-breeds to massacre settlers established in what is now the Winnipeg area by Thomas Douglas, Earl of Selkirk, who controlled the Hudson's Bay Company. Twenty men, including the local governor, were killed. Merger of the companies in 1821 ended the conflict.[4]

From this struggle, Sir George Simpson rose to head Hudson's Bay Company. An illegitimate son, Simpson was born in Ross-shire, Scotland, in 1787. At thirty-three, he was still a clerk in a London office when he was noticed and sent to Canada by Andrew Colvile, a member of the Hudson's Bay Company's governing London committee. Though bland in manner and short in stature, Simpson proved a man of iron will and advanced rapidly. With the companies merged, he eliminated duplicating operations and found new sources of revenue.

One was the shipment of ice from Alaska, then in Russian hands, to what is now San Francisco, thus adding "the first ice-man of the Pacific" to his distinctions. Under Simpson, the company added posts in San Francisco, Honolulu, Okhotsk in Siberia and Fort Yukon in Alaska. Hudson's Bay furs were sold profitably to the Russian American Fur Company and two thousand skins a year were paid for rent of Alaskan territory. When British and Russians fought in the Crimea in the 1850s, the companies preserved neutrality in North America.

Simpson's firm rule was abhorrent to some, but the company prospered. Dividends were paid every year and additional stock was issued in 1825, 1850, 1852, and 1854 to bring the capital of 500,000 pounds. Simpson in 1841 crossed Siberia in a trip around the world, to be knighted by Queen Victoria in recognition of the company's Arctic exploration. Sir George entertained the Prince of Wales on his Canadian tour in 1860 and died of apoplexy a few days later. He was mourned not only by Lady Simpson's four children but by at least seven others from extramarital unions of his early years.

By this time it was obvious that the Canadian West would be opened to settlers and that the Hudson's Bay Company would have to surrender some privileges. Sensing the chance for a bold financial coup, Sir Edward Watkin, a railroad builder, and others in 1863 bought control of the company, paying stockholders three hundred pounds for shares previously valued at less than two hundred pounds. Watkin and his friends named a new London committee and increased the stock to two million pounds, most of which was sold to the public.

In 1867, the Dominion of Canada was proclaimed by authority of the British North America Act, a clause of which provided for admission of the company's territory into the new confederation. The details were worked out in a Deed of Surrender. Under this, the Hudson's Bay Company gave up its governmental powers and most of its vast lands. In exchange, the Canadian government paid the Hudson's Bay Company 300,000 pounds. The company retained five to three thousand acres around each of its 120 posts and, in addition, was allowed to claim one twentieth of the fertile plain area, some seven million acres, for sale to settlers.

Some of the Indians who had depended on the company for food, shelter and government feared the settlers and Dominion authority. Under Louis Riel, a persuasive half-breed, the métis rose in rebellion and for a time held Fort Garry, the forerunner of modern Winnipeg. As troops approached, Riel, a tragic figure, fled to the United States but later returned, led a new uprising, was captured and hanged.

From this turmoil Donald A. Smith, later Baron Strathcona and Mount Royal, emerged as a powerful Hudson's Bay figure. He was born in the Scotch village of Forres, grim scene of Shakespeare's *Macbeth*, and joined the company as a boy apprentice. A man of thirty years' company experience, he dashed six hundred miles by sleigh to prevent serious bloodshed in the rebellion. He also induced the new management of the company to distribute 107,000 pounds to the traders hitherto entitled to share in the company profits.

Lord Strathcona speculated successfully in the building of the Canadian Pacific Railroad and many other ventures and became such a large stockholder in the Hudson's Bay Company that he was made its governor in 1889. He was then sixty-nine years old and divided his energies among many projects. He believed the fur trade doomed and was interested only in sale of the company's seven million acres of land. Oil was undreamed of, but coal was a possibility and mineral rights were reserved as the acreage was sold to settlers.

As the population grew and gold seekers rushed to the Klondike in the late 1890s, the trading posts became stores, but the aged Lord Strathcona was more interested in other matters, including a regiment of Canadian cavalry he dispatched to the Boer War. He let Timothy Eaton and James Simpson launch their great retail enterprises in the cities without challenge. He was still governor of the Hudson's Bay Company when he died at ninety-three on January 21, 1914, leaving an estate of $25 million.

His successors took charge vigorously. With the outbreak of World War I, the Hudson's Bay Company became purchasing agent for the French government on a 2.5 percent commission basis and also undertook to deliver supplies to Russia via the Arctic port of Archangel. A subsidiary shipping company amassed a fleet of 275 vessels. Of these, 110 were lost, principally to submarines.

Five of the company's vessels were frozen in the ice in the winter of 1915–16. An explosion gravely damaged five other vessels. In 1917, the icebreaker *Iceland* blew up wrecking a steamer alongside, damaging three more and setting munitions on shore afire to start a blaze that lasted for days in weather eighteen degrees below zero. To replace cranes destroyed at the time, the company located a floating one, capable of lifting 125 tons, at the Spanish port of Cádiz and one even larger in Holland and towed them to the Arctic port.

Despite mishaps, the company delivered eighteen million tons of cargo. In addition to munitions, this included breadstuffs secured from Algeria, Australia, the Argentine and Canada; sugar from Cuba, Java and Martinique; timber and woodpulp from Canada; coal from England, Canada and the United States; groundnuts, palm kernels and other produce from West Africa and Morocco. During 1918, the company delivered one thousand tons of freight daily in French ports.

One of the most exciting war episodes involved the tug *Vigilant*. Caught in a heavy gale 480 miles out of Queenstown (now Cobh), Ireland, the eighty-six-ton vessel seemed doomed. Her captain and most of the crew abandoned her and were picked up by a passing steamer. The second mate, a fireman and a greaser, however, brought the ship safely to Ireland. The company gave them five thousand pounds as a reward.

The *Nascopie*, an icebreaker named for a tribe of Indians in Labrador and in time of peace the summer supply ship for the company's Arctic posts, made many wartime voyages to Murmansk and Archangel. In June 1917, shortly after sailing from Archangel for Montreal, she was attacked by a large enemy submarine. The *Nascopie* shot back. Her fourth shell was a direct hit. The submarine exploded and disappeared. The captain and crew received the thanks of the Admiralty. With peace the *Nascopie* returned to her supply-ship duties and was the best-known ship of the Arctic until her thirty-five years of service ended in July 1947, when she sank after striking a reef at the entrance to Dorset Harbour in Baffin Island.

In 1920, Sir Robert Kindersley, the twenty-eighth governor of the company, visited Canada for celebration of the 250th anniversary of the company. With its war profits, the company built a new London headquarters, Beaver House, on Great Trinity Lane. This contained the finest facilities for the storage and sale of pelts from all over the world. It also provided a magnificent board room, on the walls of which were hung portraits of Prince Rupert, King James II and other great figures of its long history.

Under the leadership of Charles Vincent Sale, deputy governor from 1916 to 1925 and governor from then until 1931, the company belatedy spent lavishly on new store buildings in Canada. Before amassing a fortune as a trader in Japan, Sale had married a Canadian girl and was interested in the Dominion. He created the company's Canadian Committee for on-the-spot direction. He was the first to interest the company in fur farming and also the first to throw open the company's archives to historians.

There had been some building earlier. In Edmonton, a store building completed in 1905 had been one of the first in the area to have elevators. These and also mirrors were a source of wonder to the Indians. On seeing his reflection for the first time, a chief once said, "Now I can see into the Spirit World."

Employing some of the experts who had built Harrod's great store in London, the Hudson's Bay Company in the twenties erected new store buildings in Winnipeg, Vancouver and several other cities. These were no sooner completed than the depression struck. The company began to lose money in all departments and was soon in arrears on dividends on preferred stock issued in 1912 and later. Even in the land department, sales failed to cover salaries and taxes. The London Committee resigned and a committee of stockholders chose a new governor in 1931.

Major and later Sir Patrick Ashley Cooper, who had been born in Aberdeen, Scotland, in 1887 and had studied law there and in Cambridge, was their choice. He had also seen army service in World War I. He at once made a tour of the company's properties and, something that no previous governor had done, began to make annual visits to Canada. "On arriving in Canada on my first visit," he reported later, "I was dismayed at what I found—a very extravagant administration and, worse still, a disheartened staff." In Philip Alfred Chester, an astute former accountant, Major Cooper found the executive to lead the company's rehabilitation. Born in Long Eaton, Derbyshire, in 1896, Chester had run away from home to serve with the King's Rifle Corps in World War I. He then earned his articles as an accountant and joined this department of the Hudson's Bay Company in London in 1923. He was transferred to Winnipeg the next year and became chief accountant in 1925. He was promoted to general manager in 1930.

At the 1932 annual meeting, Major Cooper read a letter from a Canadian farmer setting forth the plight of many of the company's customers. "I got your letter about what I owe," wrote the man. "Now be pachant. I ain't forgot you. Please wait. When I have the money I will pay you. If this was the Judgement Day and you was no more prepared to meet your maker than I am to meet your account you sure would go to hell. Trusting you will do this."

Major Cooper was convinced that much of the company's trouble stemmed from the remote control that the London Committee had attempted to exercise over its operations. He turned to the Canadian Committee, which had been given real power only in 1930, and it began to function as a frequently meeting board of directors. Drastic economies were instituted to meet the depression. Many positions were abolished. New executives took charge in all departments. The organization was strengthened by new attention to the selection, training and welfare of the company's employees.

No employer looks after his workers with greater care than the Hudson's Bay Company expends on its fur-trade post managers and their families. All the resources of science are employed to mitigate the hardships of the Arctic. Each manager and his family have a completely furnished rent-free six-room home specially designed for the climate. The company looks after the household needs, supplying and replacing some twenty-seven different items as required. There are books for adults and children, also toys and textbooks for the latter.

"A striking feature of life in the far north," noted the company's 285th Annual Report in 1954, "is the very close cooperation, both official and personal, which exists between representatives of the Federal and Provincial Governments, the Royal Canadian Mounted Police, the Missions, and the Company's personnel." Each fur-trade post usually consists of a store, warehouse and the residence of the manager, all immaculate white buildings with red roofs. Electric power for these, and sometimes for neighboring missions and police stations, is generated by a company-developed gasoline-powered unit. There are stoves that operate on electricity as well as on wood or coal.

Many of the posts have radiotelephone facilities. During World War II these became weather-observation posts and in many cases sent out hourly observations for the guidance of airplane pilots.

But the company's greatest rejuvenation has come in its retail-stores department. One of the new executives employed in the 1931 search for fresh talent was Frank F. Martin, a New Englander who for some years had done an outstanding job as controller of the Wm. Taylor Son & Co. department store in Cleveland, Ohio. As a boy in Lynn, Massachusetts, Martin had worked briefly for the famous Lydia Pinkham patent-medicine company and also in General Electric's personnel department. During World War I, he served with the Quartermaster Department in Washington. He joined the Hudson's Bay Company as controller of its Vancouver store. He later became assistant general manager and in 1935 was promoted to general manager of the department.

Merchandise lines were expanded and improved. The company became the exclusive Canadian outlet for products developed by the Associated Merchandising Corporation buying organization. Executive salaries were increased. Prior to 1931, no Hudson's Bay buyer earned as much as $15,000 a year. Systematic training and profit-sharing programs were introduced.

In addition to the usual employee benefits of discounts and vacations, the company pays its employees interest on their savings. At sixty-five, those employed for twenty years are eligible for pensions. Cash awards and extra holidays with pay are given veterans. An employee with fifteen years' service can be discharged only with the approval of the president.

All these measures, along with Canada's improved economy, made the retail-stores department profitable. In 1936, the company resumed payments of dividends on its preferred stock and retired all of this stock by 1945. Dividends were resumed on the common stock in 1938 and since then have been paid continuously.

Many executives have spent all of their business careers with the company. Vice President Sutherland, a chartered accountant, has been with the company since graduation from the University of Manitoba and Vice President Director Sheen since graduation from the University of Toronto.

Sir Patrick Ashley Cooper, who had been a director of the Bank of England, retired as governor of the Bay in 1952 and died at sea in 1961 while returning to England from South Africa. His successor was William Johnston Keswick, previously managing director of Jardine, Matheson, Ltd., Far Eastern Trading Company. He had flown out of Singapore on the last airplane before occupation by the Japanese and had helped Field Marshal Bernard Montgomery plan the Normandy invasion.

Upon retirement in 1965, he was succeeded by Viscount Amory, previously British High Commissioner to Canada. Born

Derick Heathcoat Amory on December 26, 1899, and educated at Eton and Oxford, he had won distinction in business, politics and military service. He was a director of his family's firm of John Heathcoat & Co., textile manufacturers, and Imperial Chemical Industries. He had been a member of Parliament and had held several British Cabinet posts, including Minister of Agriculture, Fisheries and Food and Chancellor of the Exchequer. He was an officer in the Territorial Army for twenty years, broke a leg in a parachute jump and was captured by the Germans at Arnhem, the Netherlands, in World War II. He served the company until 1970.

The Bay's capital spending, mainly for stores, averaged $14 million a year in 1967–71, rose to $27 million in 1972 and about $45 million in 1973. To finance future expansion issuance was authorized of $100 million in debentures convertible into the Bay's shares of the Hudson Bay Oil & Gas Co.

Acquisition of a 35 percent interest in Siebens Oil and Gas Ltd., principally in exchange for the Bay's mineral rights on 4.5 million acres in western Canada, was approved. A stock purchase plan for regular employees was inaugurated with the company paying 10 percent.

Mrs. Josette Leman, a Montreal travel consultant, in 1973 became the first women director in the company's long history. Fifty-six percent of the 17,000 employees were then women. There were 258 women executives, 23 more than the year before, and they comprised about 17 percent of the executives, a percent which President McGiverin hoped would increase.

III

Brooks Brothers

America's Oldest Men's Apparel Store

What do these illustrious people have in common: Abraham Lincoln, Theodore Roosevelt, Franklin D. Roosevelt, John Foster Dulles, Charles Lindbergh, Gene Tunney, the Duchess of Windsor and Marlene Dietrich? All have been customers of Brooks Brothers, the New York firm whose existence since 1818 gives it the distinction of being America's oldest men's clothing store.

Ulysses S. Grant, Theodore Roosevelt and Woodrow Wilson were all clad in Brooks Brothers suits when they took their oaths of office as Presidents of the United States. At the Yalta Conference, President Franklin D. Roosevelt wore a Navy cape made by Brooks, immortalized in a statue of him in London's Grosvenor Square. President Lincoln was wearing a Prince Albert coat, a waistcoat and trousers from Brooks Brothers when he was assassinated.

Other famous customers included Herbert Hoover, Charles Evans Hughes, Adlai Stevenson and Dean Acheson. In fact, this predilection of diplomats set for the store led Charles Lindbergh to it. When the airman landed in Paris without luggage after his historic flight alone across the Atlantic Ocean, Ambassador Myron T. Herrick lent him a Brooks Brothers suit. Lindbergh liked it and became a staunch customer.

To wear clothing made by Brooks Brothers is the equivalent of membership in a club. Identification as a Brooks Brothers customer is usually inescapable. A novelist has only to write that one of his characters is wearing a shirt, suit or coat made by Brooks Brothers and the reader knows instantly what type of person is being described.

Such a person is an executive or would-be executive, presumably well born and well schooled and well behaved. In his appearance, he follows the advice of Lord Chesterfield to "take great care to be dressed like the reasonable people of our own age, in the place where you are; whose dress is never spoken of one way or another." Such a man always wears the right clothes to the right place at the right time.

The quiet conservatism that characterizes clothing made by Brooks Brothers is one of the factors that have made the concern such an American institution. In a nation dedicated to speed, change and flamboyance, Brooks Brothers has endured under the founder's original policies of good taste, fine-quality merchandise and expert workmanship. Its advertising features understatement rather than strident superlatives and comparisons.

Some old-line customers feared this might end when Brooks Brothers was purchased in 1946 by Julius Garfinckel & Co., the Washington specialty store. But the new management of the corporation—called Garfinckel, Brooks Brothers, Miller & Rhoads, Inc.—attempted few changes. When it removed the button behind the collar of a button-down shirt and eliminated shirttails that reached all the way to the knee, certain customers complained. The long shirttail was at once restored and those who want it can have a button sewn behind the collar and a buttonhole added.

The store's dignity and graciousness were maintained. The new owners merely introduced more efficiency in the production of Brooks' fine merchandise and brought it to the attention of more people. John C. Wood, who had just taken off a lieutenant colonel's uniform, was installed as president. A native of Newark, a 1922 graduate of Dartmouth and a former corporate-merger specialist at the old New York Trust Company, prior to Army service he had been a vice president for ten years at B. Altman & Co., a New York store also known for its taste.

When Wood took over the presidency, Brooks' volume had declined to about $4,750,000. Twenty-one years later, when he moved up to the chairman's post after having served as Brooks' president for a longer period than any other man, its sales reached the $30-million level.[1] By 1972, volume of the Brooks' stores amounted to more than 25 percent of the $211 million registered by the parent company—with a profit margin of more than 5 percent that ranks at the top of the industry.

At the time when Wood became chairman in 1967, Russell Hatch Tucker—a great-grandson of Edward Payson Hatch, a former president of Lord & Taylor and a veteran Brooks Brothers employee—was elected president. Wood became honorary chairman before his death in 1969, while Tucker took command of the store.

"We have no ground rules," he has said about Brooks' expansion plans. "If anything looks good, we look into it. We do it by brainstorming cities that look right to us—and then finding the right location."

Brooks Brothers has never been averse to changes of the right sort in clothing and has pioneered dozens of innovations that rival clothiers have adopted. These include the button-down shirt (still called by Brooks the polo model), the foulard tie, the four-button suit, the rounded collar, the Shetland sweater and the polo coat. Its famous No. 1 sack suit, three-buttoned and single-breasted with natural shoulders and straight hang, has been for about five decades the "uniform" that stamps a man as being correctly dressed.

Brooks was also the first in modern times to sponsor linen crash, shantung silk, cotton cord and other cooler summer suits for men, jackets with odd trousers, and many styles in boys' clothing. It has introduced such items as the Norfolk jacket, the Tattersall vest and the deerstalker cap, and was in great measure responsible for the once overwhelming vogue of the box-cloth spat. More recently it launched new man-made materials and was the first in the world to offer shirts made of Dacron-and-cotton oxford cloth, called Brooksweave, and Dacron-and-cotton broadcloth, copyrighted as Brookscloth.

Possibly the most important feature of the Brooks Brothers tradition is the personal service given to regular customers. Salesmen refer to these people as "see-you" customers. Because of a policy of "open book" selling—whereby one clerk may serve all the needs of a customer regardless of where in the store the merchandise is selected—strong relationships are established. These customers are frequently reluctant to be served by any other than their favorite salesman, who remembers their apparel preferences and tastes, and they wait until his return if he is ill or on vacation. "Mr. So-and-So wants to see you," goes the word. Some customers never bother to learn their own measurements but rely wholly on the little black book of their favorite salesman.

So unswerving is their loyalty to the store and these "see-you" customers that salesmen have been known to serve four or five generations from one family. One salesman, the late Frederick Webb, served five generations of Morgans, calling them by their first names. It is doubtful if any store in the world can equal such continuous patronage as that given Brooks Brothers by the late John R. Voorhis, onetime Grand Sachem of Tammany Hall and a man noted for his immaculate dress. When he was ten, his mother bought him his first long pants at Brooks Brothers, and until his death at 102 he never bought a suit elsewhere.

Other long-term customers include notables in every walk of life—Presidents, bankers, diplomats, prizefighters, military officers, Hollywood stars and European royalty. Eighteen hundred elite European customers order by mail when necessary and embassies abroad keep extra Brooks Brothers suits on hand in case of emergencies.

John Stahl, a former California postal clerk known as "Old Iron Legs" because he walked thirteen thousand miles *after* retiring, once landed in Madrid with his clothes shabby and unpressed. He appealed to the American embassy there and was loaned a custom-made Brooks suit that had the name Nicholas Duke Biddle sewn in it. Stahl wore the suit for an audience with Pope Pius XII.

That respect for customer whims pays is shown by the fact that today the firm has thirteen units throughout the United States. In addition to two New York City stores, branches are operated in Chicago, Boston, Pittsburgh, San Francisco, Los Angeles, Atlanta, St. Louis, Washington, Scarsdale, Cincinnati and Houston. Its mail-order business serves customers from coast to coast. Customers in twenty-eight other large cities are also served seven or eight times a year by Brooks "travelers," who, with some six hundred swatches of materials and a variety of samples, set up shop for short periods in leading hotels.

The company has its own clothing and neckwear factory in Long Island City, New York, and has its own shirt plant in Paterson, New Jersey, which supply almost 50 percent of all merchandise sold in its stores. Brooks Brothers is thus its own largest supplier.

Brooks Brothers' history parallels the growth of both New York and the nation. The founder of the business, Henry Sands Brooks, son of a Connecticut physician, opened his shop on the northwest corner of Catherine and Cherry Streets on April 7, 1818. New York, with less than 125,000 inhabitants, was then a seafaring city. Four months after the clothing shop was opened, the *Savannah*, the first American ocean-going steamship, was launched a few blocks away.

Henry Sands Brooks, who was forty-six years old when he opened his shop, was noted for his fine taste in clothes. Prior to that time, he had been a successful provisioner. He was a dapper gentleman who made frequent trips on sailing ships to England, from which he returned with new items for his wardrobe. Each time he sailed some friend would say, "Henry, bring me back a waistcoat like yours," or "Henry, have your London tailor make me a coat like yours."

Just when the idea struck him to pioneer in ready-made

clothing nobody knows, but Brooks was among the first in the world, if not *the* first, to offer such clothing. His sea-captain friends often couldn't wait for something to be made. He also offered tailored clothes "to measure" as did clothiers everywhere, but his shop, offering the dual service, was unique in those days.

The site selected for the shop was in the center of New York's busiest mercantile district and within a block or two of the most fashionable residences. Brooks bought the ground and a frame building for a little over $17,000, and his first bookkeeping entry on opening day is significant.

It wasn't for a sale but rather for a loan of $25 to a friend. Then and there was established the Brooks dictum to make friends of all customers. He also treated seafaring customers to a drink of Medford rum and often wrapped packages in black-silk kerchiefs for which he did not charge.

Henry Sands Brooks guided the first store for fifteen years until his death in 1833. By then he had initiated his two older sons, Henry and Daniel H., into the business, firmly implanting in them this principle: "To make and deal *only* in merchandise of the best quality, to sell it at a fair profit *only* and to deal *only* with people who seek and are capable of appreciating such merchandise." In 1850, the company name was changed from H. & D. H. Brooks & Co. to Brooks Brothers.

By this time, the familiar Golden Fleece trademark of the firm was in use. A sheep suspended in a ribbon, the Golden Fleece had long been a symbol of British woolen merchants. Dating from the fifteenth century, it had been the emblem of the Knights of the Golden Fleece, founded by Philip the Good, Duke of Burgundy. Worn suspended over each knight's heart, it symbolized the Lamb of God.

As New York City grew and moved northward, the firm followed. While the original store was occupied until 1874, a second and larger store was opened in 1858 in new quarters at Broadway and Grand Street. Henry Brooks, the eldest son of the founder, was dead by then and control passed to the four younger brothers, Daniel H., already initiated, and John, Elisha and Edward S. Brooks.

The elaborateness of the new premises is indicated by an entry in Mrs. George Shepard's diary of 1861, now in the Burton Historical Collection of the Detroit Public Library. Mrs. Shepard, a cousin of Ralph Waldo Emerson, was spending the winter with her husband at the Astor House in New York. On December 9, 1861, she wrote:

Fair warm like the spring of the year. . . . Smith came with his carriage we drove to Brooks Brothers Clothing House corner of Broadway & Grand Street where Mr. Shepard changes his Scotch wool Drawers for 2 pair English Merinos we went upstairs and looked over this large establishment where all kinds of Garments for Men were cutting out & making . . . they employ 400 persons cutting and sewing. . . . Columns & pillars bronze colour, with large looking glasses: were well worth seeing.

Mrs. Shepard did not mention the unique pagoda in the store, a structure fifteen feet in diameter by thirty feet in height, which was occupied by the desks of the "measurers" for all clothing made to order. Another feature of the store was an enormous four-dialed globe clock, illuminated from the inside by gaslight.

A store advertisement of the time stated:

Our Custom Department will at all times be found complete in stock and variety of piece goods, imported expressly for our trade, consisting of French, English and German Cloths, Cassimere, Doeskins, rich Velvet, Silk, Satin and every new style of cloths, etc. of the finest quality, which will be made to order in the best manner and most fashionable mode.

During the Civil War, many of the Union Army notables patronized this five-story establishment, then probably the largest of its kind in the world. Generals Grant, Sheridan, Sherman and Hooker, and thousands of the men they led, were outfitted in uniforms made by Brooks Brothers. The contract for these came from Governor E. D. Morgan of New York.

The most illustrious of all Civil War customers was President Lincoln. He bought the overcoat for his second inaugural—its lining was embroidered with an eagle holding in its beak a pennant inscribed "One Country, One Destiny"—and many other articles at the Grand Street store. One of the store clerks still tells of the eerie feeling he had on a Lincoln's Birthday when the first customer was Raymond Massey.

Times were perilous while the Civil War raged, and the Cherry Street store was sacked from top to bottom by a rowdy mob during the Draft Riots of 1863. *Valentine's Manual*, a publication of the time, in its account of the sacking has probably given one of the best descriptions ever made of the character of the Brooks brothers and their associates. The reporter states: "We can find no reason for the looting, for the Messrs. Brooks are fair, upright gentlemen, of mild manners and such simplicity of deportment as to allay and conciliate rather than excite ill feeling in any with whom they come into intercourse."

In 1868, store spokesmen mentioned "having the most fastidious among our regular customers," and said that "the one-price system is always observed." The firm valued its property at $750,000 and stated that "half of the sales of this house are for cash, yet the firm carries from 3,000 to 4,000 accounts which are extended to approved credit."

In 1869, Brooks Brothers became a neighbor of the Singer Company on Union Square and began to use Singer sewing machines. Garments, however, continued to be finished by hand, as they still are today.

The day of the famous blizzard of 1888, March 12, Brooks Brothers had only one customer. What did he buy? A pair of white-flannel trousers.

During migrations farther north, two of Henry Sands Brooks' grandsons entered into a partnership with six of the oldest employees. In 1889, two more grandsons came into the business. The four grandsons and six veteran employees incorporated the business in 1903.

The presidency went to one of the old employees, Francis Guerin Lloyd, who had been senior partner. Frederick Brooks, one of the grandsons of Henry Sands Brooks, became first vice president, and Eugene Mapes, an employee since 1880, became secretary. Lloyd had been with the firm for forty-one years when he became president in 1903. He stayed at the helm until his death in 1920, thus completing fifty-eight years of service to the store.

There were many reasons why the group selected Lloyd for president, but certainly one was his appearance. A goateed man addicted to bow ties, he was as impeccable in dress as any member of the Brooks clan. He had an exceptionally fine color sense, and many of the East Indian and British design blocks still used for printing Brooks' exclusive ties were selected by Lloyd in England.

During his regime, a branch was opened in fashionable Newport, Rhode Island, at 220 Bellevue Avenue. It was more a club than a store, and some of society's most colorful notables dropped in daily. Charley Sands stopped in every morning to buy just one polo shirt and Joe Harrison would flip coins with friends for $50 polo coats. This branch and another resort shop in Palm Beach, Florida, were later closed.

In 1915, Lloyd supervised the move of the firm's executive offices and main store to its present ten-story walnut-paneled building at 346 Madison Avenue. Although the building was modern in every respect, Lloyd persisted in a few antiquated business methods. Since he was able to add up columns of four-digit figures faster than the first adding machines, he saw no reason why everyone else couldn't do the same and the store had none of these machines until after his death.

Lloyd, who had a fine Spencerian style, continued to write the company's direct-mail advertising by hand just as he had in the early years. This was mailed as a personal letter to customers and called their attention to new imports, new styles or new patterns.

Under Lloyd's guidance, the store weathered World War I, outfitting General John J. Pershing and many other officers, some of them the store's own employees.

When the war made it increasingly difficult to import woolens, Frederick Brooks, then chairman of the board, exhibited the same paternalistic attitude toward regular customers that has always characterized the store. Outsiders who had never been in the place before started flocking to Brooks Brothers, particularly on Saturdays, to buy up as many woolen items as their budgets permitted. One Saturday morning in May 1917, Brooks came down to the main floor and, for the first time, saw them.

"Who are all these people?" he wanted to know.

When told who they were and why they were there, he said firmly: "Close the store on Saturdays. We must save this merchandise for our regular customers."

And every Saturday thereafter during the summer of 1917 the store remained closed, the first time in its history for it to have Saturday closings in any month other than August.

After Lloyd died three years later, Eugene Mapes, who had then been with the store for forty-three years, became president. He had started to work for Brooks Brothers at the age of fifteen and progressed to the top through the uniform and livery department. The store's collection of lively buttons, incidentally, dates back to about 1870 and is a museum record of the Goulds, Vanderbilts, Morgans, Rockefellers and other families prominent in American society.

The firm had started wooing college and prep-school trade back around 1900. By the 1920's, to look "Brooksy" was practically a requirement for entering any of the Eastern or Ivy League schools.

F. Scott Fitzgerald, who chronicled American life in this era, alluded to Brooks Brothers so often in his novels that quotations from *This Side of Paradise* helped the firm obtain an injunction against a California company using the Brooks name. Characters also wore Brooks Brothers clothing in novels by Ernest Hemingway, W. Somerset Maugham, and John P. Marquand. Mary McCarthy called a short story about a romance aboard a train "The Man in the Brooks Brothers Shirt."

Mapes increased the store's display advertising and Donald G. Vaughan, advertising manager, wrote most of the copy. It helped increase the sales volume to over $6,500,000 in 1929, a record figure at that time. Vaughan, a slight, bookish man who retired in 1948 and died in 1959, described the Brooks Brothers advertising policy of those days as "no policy at all," adding that the store's real advertising was "done by loving friends."

One of these friends was another literary man, Frederick Lewis Allen, who was editor of *Harper's Magazine*, a Brooks Brothers customer and a Vaughan friend for thirty years. Vaughan translated and adapted Honoré de Balzac's *Art of Tying the Cravat* for the firm in 1921, and the booklet proved as useful to customers as an earlier compilation called *On Going Away*, a handbook for travelers.

Age forced Mapes to resign in 1935 and and the presidency was taken over by Winthrop Holley Brooks, a great-grandson of the founder and a son of Frederick Brooks. Winthrop Brooks had entered the store four years after graduating from Yale in 1915. Although professing to dislike the clothing business—he had been living on a Wyoming ranch his father gave him—he headed the store for eleven years, following a call from his father to join the firm.

Douglas Fairbanks, Sr., and other motion-picture stars had been urging the store management for years to open a branch in or near Hollywood. In 1939, Winthrop Brooks reluctantly consented to opening shops in San Francisco and Los Angeles. There the stars could at least examine samples of clothing and buy furnishings. It was not at all unusual to see the sartorially correct movie stars shopping leisurely there—among them Fred Astaire, Burt Lancaster, Robert Montgomery, Tyrone Power, Chester Morris, Cary Grant and Clark Gable—and the Brooks Brothers clerks were instructed to pay no more attention to them than to less celebrated individuals.

Occasionally a customer recognized one of the movie greats with unmistakable delight. One Christmas, for example, an elderly little woman was buying a cashmere muffler as a present for her husband when she recognized a tall, lanky figure beside her.

"Why, you're Gary Cooper, aren't you?" she said. With characteristic aplomb, Cooper raised his hat, bowed and said, "Howdy, ma'am" and went on with his shopping.

No one could much blame Winthrop Brooks if he found the clothing business a pretty big task when he took over. He had the responsibility of directing the store through World War II and of seeing many of its employees march off to fight, including his own son, Frederick. It was an honor to outfit Generals Jonathan Wainwright and James Doolittle and other illustrious military figures, but the employees experienced real grief when customers like Theodore Roosevelt, Jr., failed to return. Roosevelts from both Oyster Bay and Hyde Park have always been among the favorite Brooks Brothers customers.

Because Brooks Brothers depends so heavily on materials from abroad, especially Great Britain, for its merchandise, World War II was a special hardship. Its volume was down to $4,750,000 and the 1946 sale to Garfinckel followed.

This did not end the Brooks blood in the business. Winthrop Brooks, who died in 1963, had continued as president until 1946 and chairman until 1951. His nephew, Ashbel T. Wall, a fifth-generation representative of the Brooks family, became a vice president under the new management.

While no change was made in the original Brooks policy of quality merchandise for quality customers, there have been some changes made under the Garfinckel ownership. Advertising remains distinctive and underwritten, but the linage in the leading newspapers has been increased considerably. More clothing in a greater variety of styles is being stocked and customers can get what they want when they want it. Special-order clothing, made in the ready-to-wear factories but to specific measurements, is widely available too.

Under Wood's leadership, Brooks Brothers established a "346" department—named after the main store's address—aimed at the younger man who wants the Brooks look and label but cannot afford the prices of its regular merchandise. The "346" merchandise is made by outside contractors to Brooks Brothers designs and specifications, while its other clothing is made in the company's own workrooms. The University Shop was also strengthened to attract more college men to the store.

More emphasis was also placed on the rapidly growing boys' department. A young man of four can be completely outfitted by the store, the idea being that potentially long-time customers ought to be caught early in the Brooks Brothers habit.

Not that all small fry want to be little gentlemen. Abe Burrows, the theater writer and director, once took his young son into the New York store for an outfit. Master Burrows shied away from a suit with coat and trousers that matched until reassured by a diplomatic salesman that such an outfit was really being worn. It was then suggested that some new shirts be purchased to go with the suit.

"I want the kind with writin'," announced young Burrows.

"You mean shirts with your monogram?" asked the clerk.

"I mean with writin'—like the Dodgers and Giants," was the answer.

Store executives sometimes growl about women invading a store run for men. Still, it is quite a tribute when some of the nation's best-dressed and most glamorous women adopt a men's store for their very own. The Duchess of Windsor, Marlene Dietrich, Elizabeth Taylor, Katharine Hepburn and Audrey Hepburn are among the women who have insisted upon wearing Brooks dressing gowns, slacks, pajamas, sweaters and shirts. In fact, it was the pink shirt that Brooks Brothers first made at the turn of the century to inspire color consciousness in men that caused the first big invasion of the store by women, when they finally "discovered" it in 1949 and 1950. Women bought thousands of these shirts at eight dollars each.

The little-boy look, popular with women since 1953, has caused Brooks Brothers to "allow" women to buy Bermuda shorts and English raincoats originally designed for boys. But Brooks Brothers has no intention of sacrificing its men's business or changing the character of its merchandise to cater to women.

"If colors or styles change, and if, for example, women's sweaters become longer or shorter, we will be out of the women's business," says Vice President Wall. "Women's styles just aren't our dish of tea. We believe in the maxim 'Shoemaker, stick to your last.' "

The Brooks management takes pride in the store's old-time employees. Twenty-five years of service makes an employee eligible for membership in the Quarter Century Club, an organization that meets once each year in September. The club has more than 150 members, well over 10 percent of all employees. Many of these have worked for the firm much longer than twenty-five years. The record for continuous service, however, is held by the late Horatio Kiernan, who served the firm sixty-seven years.

Many of the Brooks Brothers employees speak foreign languages. When the United Nations sent a letter to the store in 1954 asking how many languages were spoken, in case some of the foreign delegates wanted to shop there, the personnel department counted up and returned a letter enumerating twenty-five.

Ancedotes about Brooks Brothers are legion. One of these concerns the wife of an elderly Boston Brooks customer who announced that he intended to do away with himself. "I'm seventy-two years old," he complained. "And I'm no use to you or anybody else. I'm going out and drown myself." He took a coat from a clothes rack and started for the door. His wife, weary of the oft-repeated threat, looked up briefly from her knitting. "No need to wear your new Brooks coat," she told him calmly. "Not if you're going to drown yourself. Leave it for John. He's being proposed for membership in the Somerset Club this week."

Brooks Brothers has become such an institution in New York City that when its lower Manhattan store was robbed of 1,250 suits and sport jackets in 1964, newspapers covered the story with both seriousness about the $200,000 loss and humor about the style-conscious thieves in their three-button suits. Said one clerk at the time, "We could have saved 20 percent if they had stolen it during our sale two weeks ago."[2]

Russell Tucker, the president of Brooks Brothers, wears clothes that are very much in the store's tradition: three-button natural-shoulder suits, button-down shirts and narrow ties. Like most Brooks men he rarely volunteers information, but he always answers questions fully.

"We have no limits on the number of stores we'll open," he says. "But when we plan a new store, it's much more than just that. We must enlarge our manufacturing facilities for ties, clothing and shirts too."[3]

Despite Brooks' reputation for traditional merchandise, the stores, under Tucker's leadership, have taken a position with fashion-oriented merchandise for their customers. "We have to recognize the changing scene or we're going to get left behind the barn door," Tucker believes. "But we do it our way."

Thus when the knit boom burst in tailored clothing, Brooks Brothers offered Brooks-Knit, a French-made polyester-and-wool knit for suits. Later as stretch wovens came on the suit and sport-coat market, it presented Brooks-Ease, a Swedish-made stretch worsted.

Early in 1966, the quiet sales floors and offices of Brooks Brothers reverberated when a bid for control of its parent company was made by Genesco, Inc., one of the nation's largest manufacturers and retailers of apparel and footwear. After making two acquisition offers to the management of Garfinckel since 1961, Genesco took its case directly to the stockholders with a tender offer to buy more than 50 percent of the common stock for cash.

When the tender offer expired in April 1966, Genesco had obtained only about 10 percent of the Garfinckel shares. As a result, the management remained in control and there wasn't even the hint of a change in the modus operandi and merchandising practices of Brooks Brothers.

Brooks thus intends to continue to stress its century-and-a-half old traditions of taste, quality and workmanship. There's no doubt, moreover, that its customers like it that way.

IV
Tiffany's

The Most Famous Jewelry Store

A spirited struggle developed in 1955 for control of Tiffany & Company, the New York jewelry firm founded in 1837 and owned by the Tiffany and Moore families. Sales and earnings were low. The latter failed to cover a modest $1 annual dividend on the company's 132,451 shares in 1953 and barely did so in 1954. There was an air of somnolent splendor about the Fifth Avenue store. Promotion in the usual sense was nonexistent and there were no relations with the press. To obtain information for a magazine article and the initial version of this chapter, the senior author of this book had to buy a few shares and question the management at two annual meetings.[1]

But the company had a surplus of $4,544,395, its stock was selling at less than half the book value, and it was the most famous jewelry store in the world.

Several entrepreneurs began to buy Tiffany stock and in a few months it soared from $19 to more than $70 a share on the over-the-counter market. Irving Maidman, a New York builder and real-estate man, amassed 33,000 shares and Arde Bulova 12,000 shares. Bulova wanted to sell watches to Tiffany and Maidman hoped to build a skyscraper above the store. At that point Walter Hoving, president of the Hoving Corporation, which then owned the adjoining Bonwit Teller fashion-apparel store on Fifth Avenue, entered the contest.

Promising to maintain the store's standards, Hoving asked the Tiffany heirs to sell their stock to him and not to Bulova, who acquired Maidman's shares as the struggle continued. They began to do so but the contest was close. Hoving chartered a small plane and flew in bad weather to Portsmouth, New Hampshire, to plead with Mrs. Ralph Laighton, a ninety-two-year-old stockholder. On a brown-paper grocery bag, she wrote an order transferring her 1,000 shares to him.[2] A smaller block of stock purchased in Boston gave the Hoving Corporation 51 percent. In all, he bought 68,000 necessary shares for $3,825,000, an average of $56.25 a share. He became board chairman, a post vacant since 1946.

Vice President William T. Lusk, a great-grandson of the founder and a member of the firm since graduation from Yale in 1925, became the fifth president of Tiffany's on October 20, 1955, succeeding President Louis de Bebian Moore. Henry B. Platt, a great-great-grandson of the founder, became vice president.

Chairman Hoving became chief executive officer. In the next decade he had Tiffany in the news more than in all its previous history. He began with a store-wide sale, the first in a century. Markdowns of 50 percent cleared white elephants. He threw out a line of china stocked for years because he felt the designs were dull. He eliminated leather and antique silver items. He demanded "esthetic excitement" in merchandise.

Hoving purchased the business of French-born Jean Schlumberger, proprietor of a small shop on East Sixty-third Street, who began to design some of Tiffany's fine jewelry. Hoving put Van Day Truex, formerly president of the Parsons School of Design, in charge of china and silver design. Hoving brought Gene Moore—not related to Tiffany's other Moores—from Bonwit Teller to dress Tiffany's windows. During a water shortage, Moore substituted gin for water in a fountain display and the news went around the world.

Hoving added a publicity director and instead of avoiding publicity the store began to seek it. Letitia Baldrige, a tall graduate of Vassar, was the first.[3] She helped Tiffany stage a great benefit ball at Newport, Rhode Island, and held the post until she became social secretary to a Tiffany customer, Mrs. John F. Kennedy, in the White House.

Tiffany's opened one Sunday in 1960 to allow the filming of Audrey Hepburn in a scene for the movie version of Truman Capote's *Breakfast at Tiffany's*. The sequence was short but favorable. Miss Hepburn, as the heroine, Holly Golightly, explained that her remedy for worry is "to get into a taxi and go to Tiffany's. It calms me down right away, the quietness and the proud look of it; nothing very bad could happen to you there. . . ."

With the backing of some associates, Hoving in 1961 bought control of Tiffany's from W. Maxey Jarman's General Shoe Company (later called Genesco, Inc.), which in 1956 had increased its holdings of Hoving Corporation stock to 65 percent.[4] Additional stock was authorized and some of it was distributed in stock dividends.

Back in the 1830s, Alexis de Tocqueville in his *Democracy in America* predicted that a decline in taste is inevitable in a democracy. Hoving bought a page in the November 16, 1962, *Life* to say that Tiffany's was dedicated to refuting the prediction. Inspired by his experience with his own children, Tom and Petie, he dashed off a book, *Tiffany's Table Manners for Teen-Agers*. This was published by Ives Washburn and launched with a press breakfast.

Promotion was stepped up. Advertising in *Vogue, Harper's Bazaar* and *Town & Country* was increased and the regular daily space at the top of page 3 in the *New York Times* continued. Employment of attractive actresses and socialites as extra Christmas help produced newspaper photographs and headlines.

Hoving opened a Tiffany branch in San Francisco in 1963, at 223 Post Street, opposite Gump's and Shreve's. The branch increased the number of Tiffany's San Francisco charge accounts from four hundred to more than eight thousand. Branches followed at Houston the same year, in Beverly Hills in 1964 and Chicago in 1966. A branch first located in downtown

Houston was moved in 1970 to Houston Galleria, a regional shopping center. In 1969, another was opened in a shopping center in Atlanta. American Express and BankAmericards began to be honored. Tiffany's leaped the Pacific in 1972 to start a jewelry department in the venerable Mitsukoshi department store in Tokyo and stock it with diamonds and jewelry.

The Tiffany management's time-honored ban on the sale of cultured pearls was lifted by Hoving soon after he took charge. Natural and cultured pearls are the same except that the irritant which puts the oyster to work is man-inserted in the latter. Early cultured pearls were crude and irregular, but the patient Japanese have so perfected the process that any difference now in attractiveness is likely to be in favor of the cultured.

At Idar-Oberstein, Germany, center of the European gem trade, Henry B. Platt in 1968 bought some extremely attractive transparent deep-blue stones—a variety of zoisite discovered only a few months earlier near Mount Kilimanjaro in Tanzania. He named it tanzanite. The stones have since become world famous.

Tiffany does a substantial business in trophies and awards. It designed the Vince Lombardi Super Bowl Trophy, a simple silver football on a pedestal. Replicas of the ornate Woodlawn Vase, made by Tiffany in 1860, go annually to the owner of the horse winning the Preakness Stakes. Countless dog-show, polo and yachting trophies have come from the Tiffany workrooms.

In 1963, Hoving put the firm itself into the trophy field with the Tiffany Design Award. This is a six-pound cube of solid silver given every two years or so for outstanding industrial design and to business executives who encourage it. The first went to Frederick R. Kappel of A.T.&T. Thomas J. Watson Jr., of I.B.M. received one for "trying to make machines glisten like jewels." They went also to Dr. Frank Stanton of C.B.S. and J. Irwin Miller of the Cummins Engine Company.

At the same time Hoving denounced design that he did not like. When the *Wall Street Journal* reported approvingly in 1971 of a San Francisco tattooist selling his art "as permanent body jewelry," Hoving purchased an advertisement in the same newspaper to say: "We take exception to the . . . article on July 6th which says that tattooing on female posteriors or any other part of the anatomy is 'tasteful.' We think it is the absolute height of bad taste."

Criticism of a 1972 modernistic Christmas tree of the First National City Bank as "polluting the esthetic atmosphere of Park Avenue by lighting that is loud and vulgar" via another *Wall Street Journal* advertisement attracted even more attention. Respondents to "The Inquiring Fotographer" of the *New York Daily News* backed Hoving 4 to 2.

It all added up to success for Tiffany's. In his first decade, Hoving increased the company's sales volume 170 percent (the New York store alone gained 140 percent), and the company's profits increased over 900 percent.[5] For the fiscal year ending January 31, 1966, there were earnings of $1,500,989 on sales of $19,437,032. Sales soared past $28,000,000 in fiscal 1969 and 1970. As a result of what Hoving called "America's first man-made recession," they dropped to $23 million in 1971 but started upward again and were a record $28,487,963 in 1972.

Tiffany's is neither the largest nor the oldest jewelry company in America. Volume honors go to the Dallas-based Zale Corp., founded by Morris Zale in 1924, whose 920 jewelry stores and departments had sales of more than $250 million in 1972. The 385-unit Gordon Jewelry Corp. chain of Houston had sales of $122 million. On the longevity side, Bixler's of Easton, Pennsylvania, dates from 1785. The Shreve, Crump & Low Co. of Boston began in 1800. Galt & Bro. of Washington, D.C., whose widowed owner married President Woodrow Wilson, dates from 1802. Black, Starr & Frost of White Plains has a history extending back to 1810. C. D. Peacock started in Chicago, the year Tiffany's opened in New York. It is now a unit of Dayton's and Hudson's.

To appreciate these firms, it is necessary only to review the difficulties of the business. Jewelry is a romantic luxury. Many persons live and die without buying or wearing a ring. Some religious denominations regard such display as sinful. Jewelry sales are the first to drop when general business declines and are among the first to be taxed when governments need extra revenues. The levy has been as high as 100 percent in Great Britain.

Selling fine jewelry demands not only probity but experience, technical knowledge and taste. It is difficult to find individuals with all these qualities. The jeweler selling precious stones competes not only with department stores and mail-order houses selling them but with countless outlets offering synthetic and imitation stones in costume jewelry.

While the Jewelry Industry Council has achieved some success in promoting jeweled gifts for anniversaries and birthdays, the business continues to be largely seasonal. Twenty to twenty-five percent of the year's volume comes in December and about eight percent in the graduation and wedding month of June. Expenses continue all year. If the inventory is too low, impulse sales will be lost. If it is too high, some may go out of style, and costs of safeguarding it mount.

Tiffany's serenely survives such difficulties. If a fine stone doesn't immediately find a purchaser, the firm will keep it until somebody with the proper discernment comes along. It thus held for several years a fine emerald from the belt buckle of Sultan Abdul-Hamid of Turkey.

"Tiffany's isn't just a place of business," the head of a neighboring store once remarked. "It's part showplace, part museum, part institution and part legend." No other store has so much impressed itself on the business world, and the greatest accolade that any company can earn is to be called the Tiffany of its industry.

The store's reputation for integrity and fair dealing extends far beyond Fifth Avenue. Poor pensioners have been customers. There was the farm girl who turned up an unusual stone while helping her father chop cotton at Searcy, Arkansas. She cherished it until she grew up and, in 1946, mailed it to Tiffany's.

The stone proved to be a 27.2-carat diamond, the third largest found in North America.

Man or nature somehow had moved the single stone to Searcy from a little-worked diamond mine 140 miles to the southwest. Tiffany's bought the stone. It is displayed in the store near the celebrated Tiffany Diamond.

This is a 128.51-carat yellow gem as big as a bird's egg, the largest and finest canary-colored diamond in the world. It was purchased by Tiffany's soon after it was found as a 287-carat rough in a DeBeers mine at Kimberly, South Africa, in 1878. It is a showpiece, but on November 17, 1972, was offered for sale at $5 million in a limited edition of one for one day only to satirize the current craze for limited editions. No buyer appeared but the advertisement was the talk of New York.

The name of the store also was given to the Tiffany Queen Pearl, an 83-grain pink freshwater pearl found only seventeen miles away at Notch Brook, New Jersey. Tiffany's paid the carpenter who found it $2,500 cash and $250 in trade. It was sold to the Empress Eugénie, then to a German industrialist and later to the King of Saxony.

Tiffany's has enriched the vocabulary of the jewelers' world with its creation of the Tiffany catch and the Tiffany setting. The first is a device for the safe locking of a brooch. The latter is the almost universally used six-prong setting for engagement rings created many years ago by the firm. It holds and protects a stone and makes it appear a little larger.

At the Fifth Avenue edifice, you can usually find a $250,000 diamond necklace. However, if you are not in a hurry, the sky is the limit. The store's Christmas catalog offers diamond solitaires as high as $259,000. But there are many items under $100 and a few as low as $10, such as silver thimbles, baby spoons and key rings.

A lost-and-found service goes with Tiffany key rings and chains. A tag asks finders to return them to the firm, which forwards them to the registered owners. Oldsmobile gave Tiffany key rings to the buyers of five thousand Regency models built in celebration of its seventy-fifth anniversary. Each piece of Tiffany jewelry bears a number as well as the Tiffany mark. This has made possible the remarkable return of some items. A man's ring lost off Florida was found fourteen years later by a skin diver in Bermuda waters and returned to the owner in Cuernavaca, Mexico.

Fine stationery is on the first floor of the Fifth Avenue store. Farnham Lefferts, who became the sixth president of Tiffany's in 1967, advanced via this department. He joined the firm in 1948 after Navy service and graduation from Williams College. On the upper floors are wedding gifts, where five generations of brides have registered their silver, china and glassware. They cherish even the boxes in which they arrive. The firm's artisans fashion its fine jewelry and set its gems in the building. Its silversmiths create Tiffany silverware at a factory in Newark, New Jersey.

Kings and nobility are few these days, but Tiffany has a file of all the peerages and almanacs of blue blood. Its craftsmen can turn out articles authentically marked with any current or past coat of arms, but the firm will not knowingly make such items for persons not entitled to display the arms.

The famous firm is named for Charles Lewis Tiffany, who was born February 15, 1812, at Killingly, Connecticut. At fifteen, he ran a general store started by his father, a small cotton manufacturer. In September of the depression year of 1837, when Charles was twenty-five, he borrowed $1,000 from his father and went to New York. He went into partnership with a schoolmate, John B. Young, who had preceded him by six months and had been working in a stationery store. They rented half of a lower floor of a dwelling on lower Broadway. A dressmaker had the other half. From the beginning they stocked unusual items: Chinese goods, Japanese papier-mâché and terra-cotta ware, umbrellas, walking sticks, cabinets, fans, fine stationery, pottery and all manner of novel bric-a-brac.[6]

Young Tiffany had no special training for the jewelry business but brought to it qualities valuable in any business. These included New England integrity, energy and courtesy, love for the genuine and scorn for the spurious, a belief that bills should be paid and debts collected promptly, and a flair for publicity and faith in continual advertising, a talent for recruiting loyal and expert employees and treating them well.

Receipts for the first three days totaled only $4.98. But on Christmas Eve the sales reached $236 and on the last day of the year $675. In 1839, burglars carried away $4,000 worth of merchandise, virtually the whole stock, but the fledgling establishment continued to grow.

Tiffany further united the business by marrying Young's sister in 1841. This was an eventful year. Young made the first of many trips to Europe to buy French and Dresden porcelain, cutlery and clocks and Parisian jewelry. A third partner, J. L. Ellis, joined the firm and the store expanded into adjoining quarters.

Until 1848, Tiffany jewelry was of the sort that is not now allowed in the store. In that year the partners decided to go into precious gems and to manufacture as well as sell gold jewelry. This was a year of revolution in Europe. Prices of diamonds declined 50 percent in Paris, and Tiffany, Young and Ellis, bought all that they could, including a necklace once owned by Marie Antoinette. They opened a Paris branch for both buying and selling.

When gold from California began to arrive in New York the next year, Tiffany and his partners had merchandise for the newly rich. In 1850, when P. T. Barnum brought Jenny Lind to America, she visited Tiffany's and ordered a silver tankard as a gift for the captain of the vessel that brought her over. Barnum was so impressed with the tankard that when his famous midgets, General Tom Thumb and Lavinia Warren, were married, he gave them a silver chariot from Tiffany's almost big enough to carry the tiny couple.

Tiffany's early introduced the sterling silver standard from England and advertised "every silver article we sell is guaranteed

English sterling (925/000)." In 1851, the firm also advertised that "every article is marked in plain figures, upon which there will not be the slightest variation." The one-price system was then far from general.

The short-lived Atlantic cable of 1858 gave the firm an opportunity for a publicity stunt. The store bought cable fragments and fashioned them into paper weights and cane and umbrella handles. A jeweled inkstand for President Lincoln and a fabulous sword for General Grant were among the Civil War products made by Tiffany's. The hilt of the latter was encrusted with precious stones. But the firm's factory soon was converted to the actual making of military supplies. This set a pattern for World War I, when Tiffany's made surgical instruments, and World War II, when precision airplane-engine parts were made.

Tiffany & Company, the present firm, was incorporated in 1868 coincident with the merger of the partnership, from which Ellis and Young had retired, with John C. Moore's Silverware Company, which had been supplying its American-made silverware. Tiffany was the first president. Members of the Tiffany and Moore families have been officers ever since.

The founder's son, Louis Comfort Tiffany, was a vice president of the store but spent most of his long life in art. He developed a remarkable iridescent glass, Tiffany Favrile, used for vases and bowls sold in the store and also for stained-glass windows. He redecorated the White House for President Chester A. Arthur, putting in some glass screens, and supplied a $100,000 curtain made of small crystals for the National Theater in Mexico City.[7]

Tiffany's won medals at expositions and opened an office in London. When the French Republic sold the French crown jewels, Tiffany's was the largest purchaser, buying a third of them. The store also bought heavily at the sale of diamonds of Prince Esterházy of Hungary. A Tiffany-made silver centerpiece, reproducing the Statue of Liberty, was presented by New Yorkers to Frédéric Auguste Bartholdi, the French sculptor, on completion of this famous symbol of freedom. Mrs. Finley J. Shephard, daughter of Jay Gould, also had Tiffany's make a five-pound sterling-silver copy of the statue's torch for New York University academic processions.

After three locations on lower Broadway, the store moved in 1870 to Union Square and in 1905 to Fifth Avenue and Thirty-seventh Street. This was near the first Waldorf-Astoria Hotel, where John W. "Bet-a-Million" Gates and some other Tiffany customers resided. There the firm erected its own seven-story building, modeled by McKim, Mead & White after the Palazzo Grimani in Venice.

A remarkable feature of this building was the fact that for twenty-nine years it bore no sign of any kind. It was not until 1935 that a modest "Tiffany & Co." went up over the doors. Five years later, the store moved to its present site at Fifth Avenue and Fifty-seventh Street. In this move, an old whistle that had long sent Tiffany craftsmen to lunch was discarded, but taken along was the old Tiffany clock, supported by a carved wood figure of Atlas, which dates from 1853.

Tiffany sales soared from $7 million in 1914 to $17,700,000 in 1919, a record that stood until Hoving's figures for 1966. Tiffany lost money through the depression, with sales dropping to $8,352,977 in 1930, $5,358,899 in 1931 and $2,941,305 in 1932. In addition to the general decline in business, Tiffany faced increasingly aggressive competition in its neighborhood from Cartier, Van Cleef and Arpels and especially Harry Winston, who imported the Jonker, Vargas and other spectacular diamonds. Out in Texas, oilmen began to buy diamonds in Dallas from Marcus Baerwald and Neiman-Marcus.

But Tiffany had cash reserves to maintain its unbroken dividend record and found $2,484,079.09 with which to pay for the new building. World War II closed the Paris and London branches and they were not reopened. Earnings were $1,068,134 in 1946 but droppd to minuscule amounts a few years later and the Hoving take-over ensued.

Other men outside the Tiffany and Moore families have also figured in the history of the firm. One of these was Charles Cook, a Tiffany man for fifty-nine years. He was president from the death at ninety-four in 1902 of the first Tiffany, who left an estate of $35 million, to the accession of John Chandler Moore in 1907.

Of greater renown was Dr. George Frederick Kunz, dean of the world's gem experts. As a New York boy of ten, he began to collect colored stones from excavations. He sold a tourmaline to Charles Lewis Tiffany, who like other leading jewelers until then had been interested only in diamonds, emeralds, rubies, sapphires and pearls. Educated at Cooper Union, Kunz went to work at twenty-three in 1879 as Tiffany's gem expert and continued there until his death fifty-three years later. In a score of books and countless lectures, he championed the beauty of gemstones. One of his chance remarks about their abrasive qualities led an admirer, Dr. Edward G. Acheson, to invent the valuable abrasive carborundum.

Dr. Kunz was the confidant of the elder J. P. Morgan and sold him collection after collection of rare gems. The greatest of these is at the American Museum of Natural History.

Dr. Kunz named a newly discovered pink beryl gem morganite in honor of Tiffany's great customer and also dedicated his book *The Curious Lore of Precious Stones* to him. In this work, the gem expert reviewed all of history's superstitions about jewels. These he did not accept, but wrote: "Nevertheless, the possession of a necklace or a ring adorned with brilliant diamonds, fair pearls, warm, glowing rubies, or celestial-hued sapphires, will today make a woman's heart beat faster and bring a blush of pleasure to her cheek."

A rare milky-blue Brazilian diamond, which Dr. Kunz noticed glowing in his wife's ring when she hung a gown in a dark closet, he named tiffanyite in honor of the store's founder. This gem has a phosphorescent inclusion. In addition to receiving decorations from France, Norway, Japan and other nations, Kunz was honored by one of his admirers' giving the name kunzite to a lilac-colored variety of spodumene discovered in California that the expert identified.

Tiffany employees are a devoted group. Fifty-six of the slightly more than seven hundred store and factory employees belong to the firm's Twenty-five Year Club; twelve have been employed for more than fifty years. The late George F. Heydt, who began as secretary to the founder and rose to advertising manager, served the firm sixty-eight years before retiring. William Tants and William J. Fielding also have had long records.

But Tiffany has had some crime, and job applicants are now asked to take a polygraph, or lie detector, test. An employee embezzled $10,000 long ago by payroll padding. From an inside caged-off enclosure on the repair and manufacturing floor, three pear-shaped diamonds, weighing twelve carats each and valued at $80,000, later disappeared and were never located. These stones were cut from the famed Excelsior Diamond, once the largest in the world.

More recently a Tiffany man was victimized by one of the oldest swindles in the confidence man's book. An attractive blonde entered the store and said her fiancé had asked her to select some rings. She chose two, a solitaire and a diamond wedding band, valued at $6,300, then told the clerk she would like her mother's approval before buying. She demurely asked the clerk to deliver the rings at her Riverside Drive apartment.

When the clerk arrived, she took the kid-covered box and walked through a door, calling, "Mother, the Tiffany man is here with the rings." When she failed to reappear after fifteen minutes, the clerk became alarmed. He knocked on the door, got no answer and turned the knob. The door was another exit into the hall. Tiffany's never saw the blonde or the rings again.

Two men with sledgehammers drove up to the Fifth Avenue store on a summer Sunday morning in 1958, smashed a display window of supposedly shatterproof glass and made off with diamond jewelry worth $163,000. The biggest loss of all came in 1966 at the Chicago branch. Four gunmen captured employees as they arrived one Saturday morning and forced the manager to deactivate alarms and open the vault. Jewelry worth $800,000 was stolen. Security has since been redoubled at all Tiffany units.

Most retailers study their customers and try in every possible way to give them what they want. Tiffany's doesn't. At Tiffany's, customers can have only what Tiffany's thinks they should have.[8] Through the years, a great many wealthy, powerful and beautiful people have accepted this idea with little complaint.

The formidable Mrs. Cornelius Vanderbilt was a Tiffany customer. The late Payne Whitney spent a million dollars at the store in a single year. Jewels were a sizable part of his estate, the largest ever probated in America. Charles M. Schwab once strolled into the store, wrote a check for $91,000 and walked out with a sixty-carat diamond pendant for his wife.

Shirley Booth, the actress, and perhaps half a million other women have been given Tiffany wedding rings that sell for $18 to $450 and higher. Tom Girdler, the industrialist, had Tiffany's make him a solid-gold miniature of an airplane that one of his firms produced. William C. Durant, the founder of General Motors, regularly ordered golden small-scale duplicates of his cars.

When friends of the late Al Smith wanted to honor his completion of the Empire State Building, they could think of nothing more appropriate than a fourteen-carat Tiffany model of the skyscraper. Smith later gave it to Pope Pius XI. James W. Gerard, former ambassador to Germany, had Tiffany bind for presentation to President Wilson a historic letter written to him in Kaiser Wilhelm's own hand. The late Crosby Gaige, when running a Broadway theater, had Tiffany's make permanent sterling silver tickets for dramatic critics, each engraved with the recipient's name and the location of his opening-night seats.

When Mrs. Stuyvesant Fish, the famous New York and Newport hostess, coughed in the night air, her husband considerately asked, "Can I get you something for your throat, my dear?"

"Yes, you can," she replied. "That diamond necklace I saw today at Tiffany's."

Eartha Kitt entertained Broadway audiences with a song demanding that somebody trim her Christmas tree "with ornaments from Tiffany."

Presidents from Abraham Lincoln to Richard Nixon have ordered from Tiffany's many carefully chosen gifts for heads of state and other foreign dignitaries. President Lyndon B. Johnson, for example, gave Pope Paul VI a small silver globe from Tiffany's, and during his administration friends of the White House gave it an $80,000 Tiffany set of china of a wildflower design created by Van Day Truex and approved by Mrs. Johnson.

The pearl necklace and earrings worn by Mrs. Lincoln in her best-known photograph came from Tiffany's. Despite the rigors of the Civil War, she and the President spent $2,600 in the store in two years. When President Grover Cleveland married his ward, Frances Folsom, in the White House, Tiffany produced the invitations.

President Franklin D. Roosevelt was a lifelong customer. The last entry in the diary that he began while a Harvard student reads: "Still awful cold. Got E.R.'s ring at Tiffany's after much inspection and deliberation." The date was October 7, 1904. The diary is displayed at the F.D.R. Museum in Hyde Park.

As a paperweight souvenir for aides who helped him during the Cuban missile crisis, President John F. Kennedy wanted Tiffany to make a lucite calendar showing October 1962 and mount it on a silver base. Miss Baldrige, formerly of Tiffany's and then in the White House, relayed this request to Chairman Hoving. He objected to the lucite and proposed a silver calendar plaque on a wooden base. JFK ordered the lucite but capitulated when it struck Miss Baldrige as hardly a precious item.

"Order the Tiffany silver ones," he telephoned. "You and Hoving won."

In 1955, President Eisenhower appeared at Hoving's office with a sketch that he had made of a medallion he wanted to give his wife after forty years of marriage. Hoving and Lusk said they would be happy to make it.

"As President of the United States don't I get a discount?" asked Ike.

Hoving glanced at a picture on the wall of Mary Todd Lincoln wearing her Tiffany jewelry and asked Lusk to reply. "Well," said the great-grandson of Charles Lewis Tiffany, "we didn't give any discount to Lincoln."

Nor did they to Eisenhower.

V

The Singer Company

Worldwide Pioneer of Installment Selling

Penniless and beset by lawsuits, a forty-year-old sewing-machine inventor named Isaac Merrit Singer turned for help in 1851 to a New York attorney named Edward Clark and they became partners. From this modest beginning grew the Singer Company, America's first multinational corporation with operations now in more than two hundred countries. From these it had in 1972 sales of $2,217,500,000 and earnings of $87,500,000, both figures the highest in its long history.

One third of the business was in home sewing machines. A million were sold in the United States and another million abroad. Singer has been the only American maker of these for years. Manufactured in sixty models, they are sold around the world, mostly direct to user, through 4,000 retail outlets, 1,300 of them in the United States and Canada. The busiest is in New York's Rockefeller Plaza, a few yards from Singer corporate headquarters. The second in sales is one in Honolulu's Ala Moana Shopping Center. There are also 1,200 franchised Singer dealers in the two nations. Sewing machines and related items, plus other home products, and homes themselves—for Singer is in the medium-priced housing business—accounted for half of the huge volume.

Thanks to the successful diversification program pushed by Donald P. Kircher, who became president and chief executive officer in 1958, Singer in 1972 also had an equal amount of business from information systems, industrial products, aerospace and marine systems and education and training products as compared to consumer products. The company is the foremost maker of aircraft and spacecraft simulators. The famous Link trainer is now a Singer product. There were Singer instruments in the Apollo lunar modules.

A revolutionary new electronic cash register, the Modular Data Transaction System, or MDTS for short, was an important new development. This is a computer terminal doing everything that a mechanical cash register can do only faster and also, if desired, transmitting sales and inventory data instantly to a central office miles away. Singer makes the whole package: the terminal, the software and a small computer that can handle the input from as many as 180 terminals.

MDTS was first developed for the Singer stores, where it speeded up the reporting of sales and saved thousands of dollars a year in auditing and bookkeeping expenses. The system was then offered to others, with President Kircher explaining it in a 1970 address to the National Retail Merchants Association. Strawbridge & Clothier bought systems for its Clover store at Cherry Hill, New Jersey. F.A.O. Schwarz, the famous New York toy firm, equipped sixteen stores with them. The big break came when Sears, Roebuck and Co., for which Singer had long made portable power tools, placed an order that eventually was for more than 30,000 systems. J. C. Penney followed with an initial order of 10,000 units.

By the fall of 1973, despite competition from National Cash Register and others, 85,000 Singer MDTS had been sold for $277 million and 23,000 of them installed. Singer and Hitachi, Ltd., undertook a joint venture to market the system in Japan. Accords negotiated with Soviet Russia and Poland in 1973 projected eventual manufacture of MDTS in these countries.

From sewing machines, fabrics and notions, Singer has expanded into vacuum cleaners, furniture and heating and air-conditioning equipment for the home. Education and training services include filmstrips, multimedia programmed learning devices that allow a teacher to analyze responses from as many as 240 students at once and a new automobile-driving simulator system. Singer has learning centers for small children at Cherry Hill; Port Washington, Long Island; Columbia, Maryland; and elsewhere.

Singer had an affirmative action program for the employment and advancement of women and minority groups before the Department of Labor began to require this of government contractors. A third of Singer's employees are women. Minority employment by Singer in the United States increased from 6.7 percent in 1966 to more than 11 percent in 1972.

One of Singer's women, Janet L. Norman, who might be mistaken for a fashion model, is known in the company as "mother" of the MDTS. (Samuel B. Harvey is called the "father," though he insists that many others contributed importantly.) Miss Norman is vice president of communications for the business machines division. She and four other women managers were pictured in the 1971 annual report. The others were Carol Tutundgy, investor relations; Leslie Unger, employment opportunity; Joy Levien, senior attorney; and Jessie Hutton, director of sewing education.

In addition to making sewing machines of a mechanical excellence that is the standard of the world, Singer has facilitated their sale by everywhere pioneering installment selling, a development that has affected the economy of mankind almost as much as the sewing machine itself. Singer is the foremost exponent of manufacturer-to-consumer selling, and its family sewing machine is the most widely used product in the world. The company has paid dividends since incorporation in 1863.

While in jail, Mahatma Gandhi learned to sew on a Singer sewing machine. "It is," he said, "one of the few useful things ever invented." Singer is better known and occupies bigger buildings than the United States government in parts of India. A native-language letter, for example, was delivered addressed: "Exalted Holiness of the Consul General of the United States of America by the backside of the Singer Sewing Machine Company, Calcutta."[1]

The company prints directions for using machines in fifty-four languages. South Pacific islanders rate a sewing machine high among the necessities of life. First comes food, then shelter and next the sewing machine. The only reason shelter comes ahead of the Singer machine is to protect it from the rain.

It might be an exaggeration to say that Japanese dress was Westernized to provide a market for Singer machines, but the company had a great deal to do with the process. With the encouragement of Marquis Shigenobu Okuma, one of the last elder statesmen, Singer opened the first sewing school in Japan. Its graduates taught the nation. When Japanese Army Sergeant Shoichi Yokoi, a onetime tailor, returned to Nagoya a hero in 1972 after hiding on Guam for twenty-eight years since World War II, the local Singer shop gave him a new machine.

Singer machines are popular throughout Europe. A shop in Norway is above the Arctic Circle. Africa had them before Stanley went searching for Livingstone, and there is a Singer-equipped shirt factory in the heart of the Congo. In the Americas, Singer centers marked with the big red "S" extend from Anchorage, Alaska, to Magallanes, Chile.

Singer executives describe the workings of the organization in a modest sentence. "All we do," they explain, "is make a machine, take it out and sell it, collect the money and then send it back to make another machine."

As most sewing machines are sold on the installment plan, this may require two or three years. Singer machines are made in dollar, sterling, franc and lira nations and sold not only in those currencies but also elsewhere for pesos, pesetas, yen, kroner, rupees, guilders and other moneys. Singer probably does business in more currencies than any other company.

Isaac Merrit Singer, for whom the company is named, was a restless Yankee machinist. When thirty-nine years old, he borrowed forty dollars and made his first sewing machine in Boston in 1850. When completed, it would not work. He was about to give up when he recalled a neglected thread adjustment. He returned to the shop after midnight, made the change and the machine functioned. It was the first device with which it was possible to sew continuously. He was granted patents and began to make machines, first in Boston and then in New York.

As a relic in the Smithsonian Institution shows, the Singer machine was the first practical sewing machine and the first to resemble modern models. It was far from being the first sewing machine. As early as 1790, Thomas Saint, "cabinetmaker of Greenhill Rents, Parish of St. Sepulchre," obtained an English patent on a forgotten machine for chain-stitching leather. The first sewing machine of any success was made by Barthélemy Thimonnier, a French tailor, and patented in 1830. Eighty of his machines, which employed a single thread to make a chain stitch, were put to work making French army uniforms only to be smashed by a mob of jealous tailors. Walter Hunt, an American Quaker genius who invented the safety pin, made a machine in 1834 but abandoned it when his daughter told him it would throw seamstresses out of work. In 1843, Dr. Frank Goulding, a Presbyterian clergyman of Macon, Georgia, made a machine. Neither he nor Hunt patented their devices.

Elias Howe, Jr., a Cambridge, Massachusetts, machinist with more forethought, in 1846 won the recognition of history with a patent on a sewing machine employing an eye-pointed needle with a shuttle. When Singer and two other makers appeared with their improved machines, Howe sued them. After a few lawsuits, in one of which Rufus Choate, the greatest attorney of the day, represented Howe, it was apparent that the new machines could not be made without the needle-and-shuttle idea. At the same time, it was obvious that Howe's machine, which sewed only straight seams a few inches at a time, could be marketed only with the new improvements.

Soon each of four manufacturers was suing all of the others. Each maker also denounced his rivals in scathing newspaper advertisements, and what the public called "the sewing machine war" was under way.

Singer turned to the New York law firm of Jordan & Clark. As Ambrose Jordan, the senior partner of the firm, was the state attorney general, Singer saw Jordan's junior partner and son-in-law, Edward Clark. For a third interest he agreed to fight the legal battles. The man who had advanced the original forty dollars fell ill a little later and for six thousand dollars sold his third to Clark and Singer. The two became equal partners in I. M. Singer and Company in 1851. Singer remained in charge of manufacturing, while Clark took charge of finances and sales as well as legal matters.

Two more different men than Clark and Singer would be difficult to imagine. Born of poor German immigrant parents, Singer had little education and left his Oswego, New York, home when twelve years old. He grew up to be a truculent man of lusty appetites. He was without success a farmer, a machinist, an actor in a Shakespearean troupe and an inventor of machines for excavating rock and carving wood. He employed the vertical action and horizontal work platform of the latter device in his sewing machine.

By contrast, Clark, a man of the same age, was a well-educated, quiet-spoken lawyer from upstate New York. He was a graduate of Williams College, where a building was later named for him. His father was a pottery manufacturer, and Clark grew up with some knowledge of business.

He and other lawyers ended "the sewing machine war" by organizing the Sewing Machine Combination, America's first patent pool. Manufacture was licensed at fifteen dollars a machine. Because of the greater importance of their patents, the Howe and Singer interests received five dollars each and the others less. Twenty-four companies were licensed and machine making greatly increased. Though he made few machines himself, Howe received at least $1,185,000 in royalties before his death in 1867. The Combination continued until 1877, when the last of the patents involved expired.

The earliest sewing machines were heavy devices for tailors and harnessmakers, but by 1856 the leading companies were making lighter models for home use. A machine enabled a housewife to do in one hour what took ten to fourteen hours by hand. The great obstacle was the fact that the average family income was less than $500 a year and the price of a sewing machine was $125 or more. Edward Clark attacked this problem with a trade-in allowance for old machines, the barter of machines for advertising, discounts to schools and, most important, installment selling.

Installment sales kept the Singer business going when the panic of 1857 struck the next summer with the failure of many banks, railroads and insurance companies. Only five dollars was needed now to place a new Singer sewing machine in a home. The remainder was amortized in small monthly payments. If the purchaser failed to make payments, the machine was repossessed.

Installment selling became a bulwark of Singer sales in the United States and soon was instituted in Great Britain and many overseas countries under the original term of "hire purchase." Nearly all machine purchasers everywhere were found to be honest. All Singer records in Manila, for example, were destroyed during World War II but with peace fifty thousand persons owing money on machines voluntarily paid up their accounts. A small army of collector-agents long collected the installments but most payments are now made by mail.

Clark managed so well that Singer was happy to leave everything to his partner or others while he pursued pleasures he could not afford in his youth. After incorporation of the business as the Singer Manufacturing Company in 1863, the inventor spent nearly all of his time in Europe. He was completing a great house, called the Wigwam, at Paignton, England, when he died there in 1875, leaving $13 million, mostly in Singer stock, to a numerous progeny.[2] Clark, who then became president of the company, left an even larger estate when he died in 1882 at Cooperstown, the beautiful upstate New York community to which his family was devoted. The Civil War, meanwhile, demonstrated the advantages to the Singer Company of foreign trade when the dollar was depreciated temporarily, and of integration. With the establishment of its own cabinet factory in 1867, Singer became virtually a maker-to-user manufacturer and has remained so. Starting from pig iron, rough forgings or wire, Singer makes its machines in four thousand varieties and its own needles in ten thousand sizes. It makes its own electric motors.

Some extraordinary salesmen introduced Singer machines to the world. It was a difficult business at first. James Bolton, an early agent in New Haven, recalled in his memoirs that as he started for his post Isaac Singer slapped him on the shoulder and said, "Jim, we'll send you all the machines you want but not one cent of money." Singer men had to be mechanics, collection agents, sewing teachers and versatile adventurers. They traveled mostly in well-marked buggies but also by dugout canoe and every other form of conveyance.

Some Singer machines moved abroad early. One took a grand prize at a world's fair in Paris in 1855. They were advertised the next year in Rio de Janeiro. Despite great growth in domestic business, the company by 1861 was selling more sewing machines abroad than in the United States.

The manufacture of Singer machines overseas began in 1867 in Glasgow, Scotland. Fifteen years later, Clark's successor as head of the company, George Ross McKenzie, who left Scotland as a barefoot immigrant boy, returned there and built the biggest of all Singer plants at nearby Clydebank. It is so important in the community that a Singer machine is now part of the burgh's coat of arms. Assembly of Singer machines began in Montreal, Canada, in 1873, the same year that the big Elizabeth, New Jersey, plant was completed and United States manufacturing shifted there from New York.

When Singer salesmen found people lacking coordination to operate the usual treadle machine, they were sold hand machines. When one African tribe, believing that "good iron makes good noise," demanded noisy machines, a Singer man obligingly loosened up his machines until they achieved the required clatter. Agents even sold them to customers who thought the machine a piece of witchcraft.

As the native Japanese kimono was sewn with a few long

stitches that allowed it to be taken apart for washing and drying, the first Singer machines introduced there were adjusted to make such stitches. The company then taught thousands of Japanese how to make westernized garments by machine. In later years, sewing lessons were radiobroadcast.

One of the most amazing Singer pioneers was George Neidlinger, first employed as a factory water boy in New York. At twenty-two, he went to Hamburg as a European agent. Against heavy competition, including that of machines sold under imitation Singer labels, he introduced the Singer products into Germany, Denmark, Sweden, Norway, the Balkans and eventually into Russia, where he had 250,000 tents for the Czar's army made on Singer machines.

Singer sales organizations employ where possible the citizens of the countries in which they function. "A Frenchman," a Singer executive once remarked, "knows better than anybody else how to sell a sewing machine to another Frenchman." Natives head the Singer organizations in every European country. The Australian and South African Singer organizations are 100 percent national.

Singer has had only four presidents since the retirement in 1889 of George Ross McKenzie. These have been Commodore Frederick G. Bourne, Sir Douglas Alexander, Milton C. Lightner and Donald P. Kircher, all of them world-traveling forceful executives.

Under Commodore Bourne (the title was from the New York Yacht Club), Singer made its first electrically powered machines, separated the family and factory business in the United States and began to organize overseas subsidiaries. Sales of machines passed the million-a-year mark.[3]

Sir Douglas, a Canadian, rose from a clerical job to head the company for forty-four years. These saw erection of the Singer Building in New York, the tallest in the world for some years, and world-wide expansion. This included construction of a great Singer plant at Podolsk, near Moscow, and the opening of Singer shops across Russia to Vladivostok. In recognition of his and the company's services in World War I, he was made a baronet by King George V.

World War I saw the end of the vast Russian development. All of the Singer property, representing an investment estimated at $115 million, was seized by the Soviet government. Years later Singer received more than $2 million in damages. After World War II, Russians also stripped the machinery from a Singer plant in Wittenberg, Germany, and took it to Podolsk.

Singer suffered other serious World War II losses while winning acclaim with record production of intricate fire controls, airplane parts and other military items. Thirty-nine Singer workers were killed in the vicinity when the great Clydebank Singer plant was blitzed by high explosives and incendiary bombs. The fire burned for days. Bombs hit two hundred other Singer shops in Great Britain and many on the Continent. Some Singer workers were killed in the French factory at Bonnières, which was both bombed and sabotaged. Singer men also died in the Far East while several executives suffered in Santo Tomás in the Philippines and other concentration camps.

Two Singer men, one Japanese and one American, helped effect the surrender of the Korean port of Inchon in 1945. The American, George Jones, who had traveled for Singer in the Orient, served with Army Intelligence and was with the fleet that steamed in to accept the surrender. Because of his knowledge of English, one Tani, who had been a Singer agent in Seoul under the Japanese, headed the Korean party that came out in a small boat.

"Why, it's our Mr. Jones!" shouted Tani as he saw the American.

Singer machines are found in all sorts of places. Nearly every ship carries at least one. They are used in prisons, leper colonies and mental institutions, where the satisfaction of creating something is an important factor in rehabilitation. The Wright brothers stitched the wings of the first airplane on a Singer, preserved in Dayton, Ohio. Admiral Richard Byrd took six Singer sewing machines with him to the Antarctic.

Both the gowns and shoes of Queen Elizabeth of England are made on Singer machines and Westminster Abbey has one for repair of the ceremonial robes of the British royal family. The Empress of Ethiopia visited the Singer shop in Addis Ababa and enrolled two of her ladies-in-waiting for a sewing course.

Long before the basic sewing-machine patents expired, the Singer management shifted emphasis to quality, service and advertising. As maker of the first article sold all over the world, Singer pioneered the use of trademarks. Singer machines were marked with the name from the first, and the bases of many spelled "Singer" in metal. By 1870, the company had an oval trademark. It included a large "S," crossed needles and a shuttle.

About this time, the famous red "S" with a woman at a sewing machine also began to be used. Since then it has become the world's best-known trademark. The woman has been drawn in appropriate costume as the native of many lands. Her machine is always up-to-date and every few years the woman herself is given a new hairstyle and has her skirt lengthened or shortened to keep her modern.

There had been surreptitious counterfeiting of Singer trademarks earlier, but with expiration of the last basic patent in 1877, imitators came into the open. Besides imitating the Singer design, they called their machines Singers and imitated the Singer trademarks. Singer filed suits.

The hardest fought of these was one against Frank T. June, head of the June Manufacturing Company of Chicago, and George P. Bent, a Chicago and Kansas City sewing-machine dealer. Stationery of the June firm described it as "manufacturers of the new and greatly improved Singer Sewing Machine." Metal stands of its machines embodied the word Singer and a mono-gram, "S. M. Co.," which was explained as standing for Standard Machine Co., an earlier name of the June enterprise. Bent sold the June-made machine as an "Improved Singer," "June Singer," "New York Singer" and "Philadelphia Singer," though he had offices neither in New York nor Philadelphia.

The litigation lasted nineteen years. The defendants contended that the name "Singer" had entered the public domain along with the Singer patents just as in the case of the harmonica, the mackintosh coat and linoleum, all names of once patent-protected articles that had become generic. Singer attorneys put forth the trademarks, introduced the full line of Singer machines and argued that the name meant "the source of manufacture" rather than a type.

In a decision by Justice Edward D. White, the Supreme Court ruled finally against June and Bent, saying each manufacturer should indicate who made his machine and "unmistakably" inform the public. Justice White termed June's imitation of the Singer marks "an injury to private rights and a deceit upon the public." The deceptive practices of the defendants were "perpetually enjoined."

Since then Singer has consistently succeeded in protecting its famous trademarks against efforts at imitation in many lands.

Milton Lightner became head of the Singer empire on the death of Sir Douglas in 1949, after twenty-two years as vice president and earlier service as legal counsel. He rehabilitated the war-damaged European properties and built new plants in Anderson, South Carolina; Campinas, Brazil; Karachi, Pakistan; Penrith, Australia; Taytay, the Philippines; Querétaro, Mexico; and Maltepe, Turkey. He met German and Italian competition with a slant-needle zigzag machine. In the face of a flood of Japanese machines encouraged by the U.S. occupation authorities, he preserved part of Singer's market there by buying a half interest in the Pine factory in Japan. He replaced the single sheet of figures given by Sir Douglas to stockholders with a conventional annual report. He chose as his assistant and successor another lawyer, Donald Peter Kircher, a native of St. Paul, Minnesota, who had been a twice-wounded, eight-times-decorated tank captain in the U.S. Third Army.

Under Kircher, who became president at forty-two in 1958, executive offices were moved uptown in New York from the Singer Building, later sold for $8 million, to the Radio Corporation of America Building in Rockefeller Center. They were adorned with new abstract art. Into Kircher's office went James Brooks' "Sarpolo," catalogued as creating "an atmosphere of suspension and potential action." This came fast.

Kircher launched a worldwide planned internal and external diversification, which dwarfed the company's previous success and doubled sales and earnings. He met Japanese competition with low-priced machines from Singer plants in Italy and Scotland. Medium-priced machine production was concentrated in Scotland and that of higher-priced models in the United States and West Germany.

In outside diversification, Fridén Inc., an important maker of office equipment, was purchased for stock then worth $175 million. The company gained high technology in various areas with the acquisition of General Precision Equipment, Inc., in 1968. Additionally, companies manufacturing air-conditioning and heating equipment were acquired, along with home-building operations. The word "manufacturing" was dropped from the company name and its stock was listed on the New York Stock Exchange. Mandatory retirement for executives at age sixty-five was instituted.

With few exceptions, everything was successful. An office copier supposed to compete with Xerox didn't. The company lost several millions in the Thurso Pulp & Paper Company in Canada, and its interest in the enterprise was sold in 1964. Selling by catalog proved unproductive in the United States but successful in Europe, and Singer paid $14 million for control of Friedrich Schwab & Co., the third-largest mail-order house in Germany. In the "culture boom" even the abstract art in the executive offices increased in value.[4]

In a few years Singer changed from one of the most secretive companies to one of the most candid. Quarterly reports are longer than the annual ones under Sir Douglas. Full-color annual reports, which have received awards from *Financial World* and others, break down sales and earnings by geographical regions and product divisions. Annual meetings are held in other cities as well as New York. Stockholders receive after-meeting reports.

Group vice presidents as of 1973 were Alexander H. Dunbar, industrial consumer products; Dr. Donal B. Duncan, information systems; Edwin J. Graf, products; Charles F. McDevitt, home furnishings and climate control; William F. Schmied, aerospace and marine systems.

Senior vice president was Donald G. Robbins, Jr. Vice presidents included Richard O. Baily, Vernon L. Brown, Jr., William J. Brown, Edward W. Cattan, Edmund H. Damon, Colin C. Gabriel, John A. Gearhart, James F. Healey, Edward J. Keehn, Robert N. Lesnick, Richard D. McDonough, Daryl D. Milius, George R. Potter, Andrew J. Reinhart, O. Glenn Saxon, John N. Sprague, and Elliott E. Vose.

VI

Filene's

The World's Largest Specialty Store

Boston has been famous for its stores for generations. More than one hopeful retailer opening far from New England has paid tribute to this reputation by calling his establishment the Boston Store. Milwaukee's Boston Store grew into a great institution, and in Rochester, New York, a Boston Store prospered as the Sibley, Lindsay & Curr Co.

In Boston itself, the biggest store in volume long has been the Jordan Marsh Company. Eben Jordan, one of its founders, gave Boston an opera house. Its magnitude is epitomized by its boast "New England's Greatest Store." It is a complete department store, headed in 1973 by Robert Hoey, and is the biggest unit of the Allied Stores Corporation. Other notable Boston stores, some of them more than a century old, include Gilchrist Co., R. H. Stearns Co., the Shreve, Crump & Low Co. jewelry store and Goodspeed's bookshop.

It is Filene's, short for the William Filene's Sons Company, however, that is the Boston store most often in the headlines.[1] This is the world's largest specialty store. Its main building, a city block in width, stands at Washington and Summer Streets and the spot is brass plaqued as "the hub of the universe," a variation of Oliver Wendell Holmes' phrase about the Boston State House. With access to two subways, high fashion upstairs and low prices downstairs in a unique basement, its dollar sales volume per square foot, more than $1,000 a year in some departments, is one of the highest in the world.

Its total sales were about $165 million in 1972, and *Women's Wear Daily* estimated them even higher.[2]

Filene's contributions to retailing include important advances in employee selection and training, sustained showmanship and community service, and merchandising innovations that have been adopted widely. Cycle billing, which changed a frantic end-of-the-month operation to an orderly procedure, was born at Filene's. The need of the store for a simple identification device for charge customers spurred invention of the Charga-Plate, and Filene's was the first to use it.

Branch-store operation was pioneered by Filene's and, because many branches were in college towns, led the store to develop first college and then high-school student advisory fashion boards. When students became more interested in blue jeans than fashion, Filene's also was the first to discontinue the fashion boards.

William Filene was born in 1830 in the Polish city of Poznan (Posen) when it was within the borders of Prussia, where his name was sometimes spelled Filehne. There his father sold ribbons, profitably enough to send William and another son to Berlin to study law. The latter died there and William, discouraged, abandoned the law. It was 1848, a year of revolt in Europe that brought a bloody uprising in Posen. Instead of returning home, William renounced the religion of his Jewish fathers and emigrated to England and then to the United States.

At eighteen, he went to work as a tailor in Boston. Three years later, in 1851, he opened a tiny shop, stocking some dry goods, on Washington Street. This lasted only a short time and 1856 found him with a small store on Essex Street in nearby Salem. There in 1856, he married Clara Ballin, an immigrant from Bavaria. To them were born four sons and a daughter.

Of these, only the second son, Edward Albert, born in 1860 in Salem and named for the Prince of Wales, who had just visited America, and the youngest son, Abraham Lincoln, born April 5, 1865, in Boston, figure in the history of Filene's. The latter shortened his name to A. Lincoln Filene and eventually legally dropped the first name.

During the Civil War, William Filene left retailing for an unsuccessful venture in New York, moving there in 1863 and losing his money in wholesale dry goods by 1870. He then moved his family back to Lynn, Massachusetts. Despite the business troubles that culminated in the panic of 1873, he launched two small stores at Lynn, one at Salem and one at Bath, Maine.

The older boys had a year at the Handels Institut, a famous boys' school in Segnitz, Bavaria, their mother's birthplace, before the collapse of the New York venture. They continued their education in the Lynn High School. After classes, they ran errands, washed floors and cleaned the windows of their father's Lynn stores, one of which was devoted to women's wear and the other to men's and boys' clothing.

These prospered and college was planned for Edward. But he had no sooner passed the Harvard University entrance examinations in 1879 than the father fell ill. Since Rudolph, the eldest son, had no aptitude for or interest in the work, Edward had to abandon his college plans and at nineteen go to work full time. He cherished his Harvard entrance certificate, No. 276, all of his life, however, and became a benefactor of the Harvard Business School. Young Lincoln soon followed his brother into the stores. It was William Filene's hope that each of his sons would take over one of the stores, and the one in Bath, Maine, eventually was given to Bertram Filene, the brother born between Edward and Lincoln.

In 1881, the father and sons opened a store at 10 Winter Street in Boston and soon afterward sold the Lynn and Salem properties. The Boston store was only twenty-four feet square but was described as "one of the most modern of the day with its genuine white marble floor and most artistic windows." Bearded William Filene respectfully advertised that "purchasers can save a large percentage on esmeralda and embroidered sleeves from 25 cents to $3 a pair . . . dress trimmings in the latest patterns . . . lisle thread and silk gloves and mitts . . . and cotton stockings." A glove shop was added the next year, also on Winter Street.

With the sons gradually relieving their ailing father of responsibilities, the business grew. The brothers came in on Sunday to clean the store. Father and sons did all of the buying and employees were few enough for all to discuss their plans every Friday evening at William Filene's home. In 1890, much larger quarters were leased in a five-story-and-basement building at 445-447 Washington Street, and the business was moved there. The space was the largest in Boston at that time devoted exclusively to women's wear and accessories.

The father, who suffered from a heart ailment, turned the management over to Edward and Lincoln in 1891 and they inherited the store at his death in 1901. The company was organized briefly as William Filene, Sons and Company and then as William Filene's Sons Company. Edward proved a wizard at merchandising, and Lincoln a genius at managing a store staff. They owned equal shares of the business, took turns using the title of general manager and became one of the most famous brother teams in retailing.

They were among the first to recognize the value of good employee relations and systematic employee training. They went on record against absentee ownership and nepotism. As Edward remained a bachelor and Lincoln, who married in 1895, fathered only daughters, this action, of course, was no personal hardship but it helped establish a remarkable spirit among the workers.

"If we were to create contentment in front of the counter," explained Lincoln Filene, "we had first to create contentment behind it. Many employees learn their manner of serving the public from the manner in which they are served by their managers."

Without offending its carriage trade in piece goods, the store stocked machine-made dresses and lingerie as they became available. Its sales passed the half-million-dollar mark in 1900. The next year the store trebled its space by moving to the buildings numbered 453 to 463 on Washington Street. In 1902, sales exceeded a million dollars for the first time, with a volume of $1,165,183. The next year the previous quarters were leased again and designated as a "Baby-to-Miss" annex. In 1904, the intervening structure, Oliver Ditson's music shop, was occupied and the two Filene stores became one. But more space was needed.

The architect Daniel Burnham, remembered for saying "make no little plans," was commissioned to design a store to include eight floors above ground level and a basement, subbasement and cellar beneath it. The space would enable the store to enter the men's wear field. Plans provided for underground access to the new Boston subway to permit customers to arrive in comfort regardless of the weather.

When the new building was completed, so great was the interest that 235,000 persons visited it when it opened, decorated with American Beauty roses, on September 3, 1912. Within a week, 715,000 persons went through the doors. So well planned and constructed was the building that, with only slight changes, it is still in service more than sixty years later.

To obtain the well-known Hart Schaffner & Marx line of clothing for its men's department, Filene's bought two Boston stores of the Continental Clothing House. One was resold and the other, a nearby structure, was absorbed into Filene's when the store spread over the entire block. A public-address system and air conditioning were added later, with the Filene basement becoming the first large-scale application of air conditioning in retailing.

Outlying branches began to be established immediately after World War I. Taxation rather than traffic was the initial impetus. Many localities undertook to collect a year's taxes from any store that presented a fashion show or showed merchandise there. The early branches at Providence, Rhode Island, Falmouth, Massachusetts, and Portland, Maine, did not survive. Those remaining at Wellesley, Belmont, Burlington and Hyannis proved very profitable small specialty-shop branches. Much larger Filene high-fashion branches have been opened at South

Shore Shopping Plaza, Braintree; Natick Mall in Natick; North Shore Shopping Center, Peabody; Chestnut Hill on Route 9; and in Worcester, Massachusetts, with all except the last designed by Raymond Loewy-William Snaith, Inc.

As the store became a great business, sales leaped from $4,810,899 in 1912 to $8,466,467 in 1913. With completion of the new building the Filenes pioneered a four-pyramid organization for their business, modeled somewhat on the branches of the national government. Under the top authority, originally the two Filene brothers, were four executives. One headed merchandising, another supervised advertising and publicity, another managed the store's services and the fourth was the controller, in charge of accounts and money. These divisions successfully checked and balanced each other, and this form of organization was adopted by many big stores as a result of its use at Filene's. [3]

"I always believed that the store would grow if it had the right people," said Lincoln Filene, "and that if it didn't have the right people, it wouldn't grow." Booklets outlining opportunities in retailing and containing an application blank for employment at Filene's were distributed to graduating high-school and college students in the area.

Promising young men and women were hired and systematically trained, long before such personnel methods were general. Among those employed in the work were the late Professor Frank Parsons of Boston University, "the father of vocational guidance"; Robert G. Valentine, one of the first industrial counselors; and Frank B. Gilbreth, the noted motion-study specialist and exponent of scientific management. In recognition of his own contributions to vocational training, Lincoln Filene, whose formal education stopped with high school, was awarded an honorary master of arts degree by Dartmouth College and elected to honorary membership in Phi Beta Kappa by the parent William and Mary College chapter.

Filene training ranges from instruction in how a waitress shall place silver in the store restaurant to courses in the Harvard

Graduate School. Job specifications are printed. Workers are told how to perform their duties, how these fit into the store operations, why they are important. Workers are encouraged to make suggestions. An employee suggestion system, something that many businesses discovered only in World War II, was in effect as early as 1899 and $25,000 was once distributed in a single contest.

Humorous drawings by Francis Dahl, a famous Boston newspaper cartoonist, enlivened Filene's instructions to salespeople. These are taught not that the customer is always right but that she is a guest and must be treated with consideration and tact.

In line with their oft-expressed belief that it is possible to attain more by cooperation than by conflict, the Filenes encouraged formation in 1898 of a remarkable employee organization called the Filene Cooperative Association. The complaint of a cashier whose pay had been docked for a shortage was responsible for the start of a liberal system of settling employee grievances through this organization.

"If I'm short in my accounts," said the girl, "it's supposed that I've stolen the money. If I happen to be over, it's a 'clerical error,' and you pocket the money. It isn't fair."

Three arbiters decided for the girl. As a consequence an elected Board of Arbitration was made part of the Filene Cooperative Association. It was given power to settle, without interference from management, any matter regarded as an injustice to an employee, or group of employees, resulting from a store rule, a discharge or a question of wages. The rules were drawn by the great Louis D. Brandeis, an attorney for Filene's who later became a justice of the United States Supreme Court. Because they gave the employees on the board greater power over management than was later possessed by any labor union, some business leaders predicted dire consequences.

These did not develop, nor did the leaders of the F.C.A. evince any ambition to assume responsibilities of the management. This was a sad disappointment for Edward Filene. He had hoped that the organization might be the means eventually of turning over ownership of the store, in whole or in part, to its employees. The workers proved more interested in immediate problems of hours, wages and various disputes, and the management met them more than halfway.

The store was one of the first to establish a minimum wage for women and girls. In 1913, the store inaugurated Saturday closing during the summer months, the first in Boston to do so. In 1924, winter vacations were instituted in addition to the usual summer holiday.

In its thirty years of existence, the Board of Arbitration handled nearly a thousand disputes. In 308 cases studied by Russell Sage Foundation investigators, the board ruled for employees in 55 percent of its decisions, for management in 42 percent, while 3 percent were compromises.[4]

With passage of the Wagner Act in 1935, the Filene Cooperative Association became the Independent Union of Retail Store Employees and conventional bargaining replaced the Board of Arbitration. But relations between Filene's and its four to five thousand workers continued smooth. For its personnel who served in World War II, the store made up any difference between the service pay and regular earnings and sent checks to families each month. The store became the first in Boston to establish a year-round forty-hour five-day workweek. Filene's and the union shared the expense of a job-evaluation study. Filene workers have group insurance, their own newspaper, the *Echo,* restaurants and cafeterias, a clinic with two doctors and three nurses in attendance during working hours.

The Filene employees' credit union, which has loaned $15 million for the purchase of homes, payment of doctors' bills and similar purposes, is the prototype of credit unions throughout the country. While on a trip around the world, Edward Filene in 1907 found credit unions functioning successfully in Bombay, India. As a result, an informal loan fund that the store maintained to keep its employees out of the hands of loan sharks eventually was changed into a credit union operated by employees with their own money.

So enthusiastic was Edward Filene about the economic value of credit unions that he employed Roy Frederick Bergengren, a lawyer who had been an outstanding finance commissioner for Lynn, to lead a national credit-union movement. A Credit Union National Extension Bureau was formed and later reorganized as the Credit Union National Association. State and then national legislation was obtained authorizing credit unions. There are now thousands of credit unions lending millions of dollars to workers. Filene and Bergengren quarreled over the tactics to be pursued and the views of the latter prevailed, but the "shopkeeper from Boston," as Edward Filene often called himself, is entitled to a sizable share of credit for the success of the credit unions. This was acknowledged when the Credit Union National Association's headquarters building at Madison, Wisconsin, was dedicated by President Truman as Filene House and in 1960 when a monument on Boston Common recognized Edward Filene's role in the movement.

It was also from his fertile brain that came the store's unique contribution to retailing. This is the world-famous Automatic Bargain Basement started in 1909. There was nothing remarkable about a basement store. Many firms had one, often as an outlet for the mistakes of buyers on the upper floors. But a basement in which prices were plainly marked and automatically reduced by a definite percent on a definite day, if the goods remained unsold, was unique in 1909 and after more than sixty years still is unique.[5]

Under the Filene system, basement goods are automatically reduced 25 percent after twelve selling days, another 25 percent if still unsold at the end of eighteen selling days, a third 25 percent if remaining after twenty-four selling days. If still on hand after thirty days, items are given away to organized Boston charities.

The business world predicted failure for the scheme, but by faithfully adhering to these rules, candid advertising and paying cash for distress stocks, the Automatic Basement became a spectacular success after losing millions during its first three years. In the depression, earnings of the basement were great enough to keep the store profitable when every upstairs floor was operating at a loss. When President Roosevelt closed all banks in 1933, the entire Filene payroll was met from the basement cash sales. Two Crown Russian sable coats from Bergdorf Goodman previously priced at $19,900 and $19,000, respectively, were offered at $10,000 in 1973. Sometimes diamond jewelry is sold.

Buyers for the basement, which has a staff separate from the rest of the store, scour the world for bargains. As the Germans approached Paris in 1940, buyers for Filene's basement picked up four hundred of the latest dresses by Schiaparelli, Lelong, Chanel and other famous couturiers and shipped them out through Spain. A week after Paris fell, the basement announced a sale of the dresses, normally priced at several hundred dollars, for $11 to $49 each. Fifteen thousand women were on hand when the doors opened. Within sixty seconds, every dress was off the racks. Fifteen minutes later all had been sold.

Another wartime coup was the Austin Reed of London haberdashery from the liner *Queen Mary*. Buyers laid out the inventory in the liner's swimming pool and acquired it for Filene's basement. Included were cashmere sweaters, pajamas and ties of the highest quality. Among the ties were 412 of an identical design, yellow, royal purple and red stripes against a dark-blue background, made for the *Queen Mary*. These were marked at one dollar and, along with everything else, sold out in two and a half hours. For years afterward, strangers wearing the ties would greet each other as fellow members of Filene's *Queen Mary* club.

As many as 150,000 bargain hunters have swarmed through the basement in an eight-and-a-half-hour day. This mark was hit during a 1947 sale of $1,400,000 worth of smoke-damaged luxury goods from Neiman-Marcus, the famous Dallas store. An imported $190 black lace brassiere then went for $8.95. In 1965, this renowned store's $410,000 stock of slightly smoke-damaged fur coats was sold in a few hours. Included were a $1,500 polar-bear rug and a $17,000 Russian sable.

Probably the biggest crowd of expectant mothers ever assembled in Boston showed up for the sale of two thousand baby carriages. Mourning handkerchiefs from Ireland were once sold at three cents each. At the end of one Folies-Bergère season, a Paris buyer sent to Filene's a lot of hip-length silk stockings made specially for the chorus. They went fast at fifty-nine cents a pair.

Charity gets less than 1 percent of the basement merchandise, but the basement has had some long-remembered mistakes. One involved two thousand woolen overcoats bought to sell at $12. The sample was all right but when the whole lot arrived the coats literally stank. They still stank at $9 and $6 but most moved at $3. Another involved a whole carload of fifty-cent "hard" collars, some 1,100,000 in number, from Van Heusen. These were seconds and Filene's offered them at 25 cents each. That day neighboring stores offered first-quality Van Heusen collars at fifteen cents each. In addition, the lot contained many size 18 and 13 collars which even the Salvation Army refused as they had no necks that big or small. Filene's finally made a bonfire of the remaining collars.

The Automatic Basement has had famous customers and noted help. John Roosevelt began his business career in the basement at $18.50 a week while his father was President. The youth's job was to keep the bins filled. He worked faithfully and modestly but attracted so much attention that he had to be hidden in the stockrooms. Failing to find him, one portly lady unrolled and gave the manager a big scroll bearing an ode starting, "Oh thou youth of sterling character."

Show-business notables regularly visit the basement. One of the principal ballerinas of Britain's Royal Ballet buys formal dresses there. Joe E. Brown boasted in the Hollywood Brown Derby of shirts from Filene's basement. The famous Joseph Kennedy family of Boston like the place. The population of remote Pitcairn Island, descendants of the *Bounty* mutineers, once bought shoes in the basement by sending a sailor there with pencil tracings of all the feet in the colony.

Why haven't other stores been able to establish similar operations? Attempts have been made in Boston, Philadelphia and a few other cities but without success. The principal reason seems to be that there is only a limited amount of worthwhile distress merchandise and the fame of Filene's is likely to give it first call.

While the basement was winning its fame, Filene's upstairs had the benefit of some of the most notable talents in retailing. One was Louis E. Kirstein of Rochester, New York. He was induced to leave the Stein-Bloch Company, a men's clothing manufacturer there, and join Filene's in 1911 as a vice president when the store entered the men's-wear field. He later was given charge of all upstairs merchandising and publicity as well. He made great contributions to the store for thirty-one years until his death in 1942.

This colorful and forceful figure's aphorisms on management are still quoted. Some of the best known are:

> The expense rate cannot be lowered by worrying about it.
> Overnight we have all become accountants rather than merchants.
> Retailing needs less figuring; more fingering.
> One thing wrong with business is that business men do not attend to it.
> We need more individuality and less foolish straining to be all things to all men.
> No industry can rise higher than the caliber of men in it.
> Advertising pays when it is believed.

Expenditures for advertising, he believed, should be increased and not curtailed when business became sluggish. He argued that it was a waste to use huge newspaper space at Christmastime, when without persuasion customers were struggling to get into the store.

A major contribution to merchandising initiated by Lincoln Filene enabled the company to exchange information hitherto regarded as confidential with important stores in other cities.

After some preliminary discussion, he invited the principals of eighteen stores to lunch on September 6, 1916, at the Aldine Club in New York. Stores represented included L. S. Ayres & Company of Indianapolis,[6] the Dayton Company of Minneapolis, the Emporium of San Francisco, B. Forman Company of Rochester, Joseph Horne Company of Pittsburgh, the J. L. Hudson Company of Detroit, F. & R. Lazarus & Company of Columbus, the Rike-Kumler Company of Dayton and the William Taylor Son & Company of Cleveland.

Lincoln Filene suggested that an organization be formed for the scientific study of the problems of merchandising and store operation. He contended that this would enable all to operate more efficiently, cut expenses and reduce distribution costs. Two months later the Retail Research Association was organized and opened a modest office in New York with Alvin E. Dodd, previously secretary of the Society for Vocational Education, as director. When he joined the U.S. Chamber of Commerce five years later, he was succeeded by Dr. Paul H. Nystrom, Columbia University professor of marketing.

One of the first projects of the Association was the working out of a uniform system of records so figures of the cooperating stores could be compared. Some of these later were telegraphed to permit the prompt detection of any new trend. Detailed studies also have been made of every store activity, and members often have helped each other on special problems without going through the Association office. Of the many reports supplied its members, the most important are the annual and semiannual general manager's reports. These are as large as an atlas and present a complete picture of every department.

As an outgrowth of this activity, the same stores beginning in 1918 formed a twin organization, the Associated Merchandising Corporation for cooperation in buying, recruiting of executives, training of employees, improvement of advertising and other matters. In 1920 a committee chaired by Vice President Kirstein of Filene's toured Europe and opened A.M.C. buying offices in London, Paris, Brussels, Berlin and Milan, the last later removed to Florence. Buying offices subsequently were opened in the Orient—Hong Kong, Tokyo, Bombay—as well as in Munich, Copenhagen, Barcelona and Dublin. At the same time, A.M.C. began to buy in the American markets for important foreign stores as well as for its members. Firms thus represented included Harrods Ltd., of London, John Orr and Garlicks of South Africa; the Hudson's Bay Company of Canada; and the Panama Railroad Co., which operates stores in the Canal Zone.

As A.M.C. buying became a multimillion-dollar activity, more famous stores joined. Bullock's of Los Angeles became a member in 1919; Strawbridge & Clothier of Philadelphia, in 1921; Abraham & Straus of Brooklyn, in 1923; Hutzler Brothers Company of Baltimore, in 1925; the H. C. Capwell Company, Oakland, California, in 1927 and others later.

Lincoln Filene served as president and chairman of the executive committee of the R.R.A. from its organization until 1943 and of the A.M.C. from 1921 until that date, when he retired with a notable collection of gavels as souvenirs of his long service. As of 1973, A.M.C. represented thirty U.S. department stores with total sales of more than $4 billion. It is headed by Steven L. Osterweis, formerly head of Gimbels Pittsburgh. He is a graduate of the Harvard Business School.

At Filene's, top management, meanwhile, went through a grave crisis. On March 1, 1913, in a reorganization after completion of the new building, control was vested in six executives, the Filene brothers and the heads of the four pyramids in the store's organization chart. Each brother had 26 percent of the stock. Each of the other four had 12 percent. These were Vice President Kirstein, merchandising; John R. Simpson, publicity; Thomas K. Cory, the store manager; and Edward J. Frost, the controller. The Filenes pledged that they or their heirs by the same date in 1928 would transfer 4 percent of their holdings to the others· and yield them control of the store. These six men and five other employees composed the company's board of directors.[7]

All went smoothly for a time but tension and antipathy developed between Edward A. Filene, who under the reorganization had the title of president of the company, and Vice President Kirstein. Both were intense, ambitious, driving personalities. As both were merchandising men, collision possibly was inevitable. Kirstein was a big kindly bear of a man. "Little Eddie," as some old employees termed him, was a small, dapper fashion plate with a close-cropped bristling mustache. They differed more in ideas.

Kirstein was a man of family, interested in the Boy Scouts, headed the Boston Jewish charities for a time and was a conventional and understandable executive.[8] Sigmund Freud would have been greatly interested in Edward A. Filene. From a shy youth who suffered from eczema, he grew into an aggressive, complicated, tactless, restless, brilliant and dictatorial man.[9] In his thirties, he became engaged to a young woman but, as he explained later, the engagement came to an end one evening on a streetcar when he neglected her to conclude a business deal with a man he had been seeking who chanced to be on the car. He had little use for conventional charities. With no family interests, he flung himself intensely into all manner of causes. He was the leading spirit in the Boston Chamber of Commerce, the U.S. Chamber of Commerce and finally the International Chamber of Commerce.

He made an annual trip to Europe at first to buy merchandise but soon to visit leaders of all sorts and pursue his causes. Outbreak of World War I found him in Paris helping Ambassador Myron Herrick care for stranded Americans. During the war, Filene was a dollar-a-year organizer of procurement. After the war, he resumed his European trips, even studying retail stores in Soviet Russia. With writers as notable as Lincoln Steffens polishing his sentences, he spoke in favor of the League of Nations, the Dawes Plan, daylight-saving time, sickness insurance that evolved into the Blue Cross plan, tourist rates on steamships and low-cost housing.

Invention also interested him. A footstool that he designed came to nothing but, with Thomas J. Watson of International

Business Machines, he worked out the Filene-Finlay simultaneous translator for the meetings of the International Chamber of Commerce. With this, earphone-equipped listeners hear in their own tongues addresses as they are made. Produced by I.B.M., the equipment later was adopted for the Nuremberg war-crimes trials and sessions of the United Nations. All of these interests, of course, took Edward A. Filene away from Boston for long periods, and responsibility fell increasingly on his associates.

The cleavage with Vice President Kirstein became evident in 1918 when Vice President Simpson enlisted for war service and resigned. His associates could not agree on a successor. His stock was purchased and placed in trust and his duties were assumed by Vice President Kirstein. In 1925, Vice President Cory died. With Edward A. Filene dissenting, the directors allowed Cory's stock to be purchased and divided by Vice Presidents Kirstein and Frost and the latter assumed the late executive's duties.

Events came to a head in 1928. A further reorganization of the store's financial structure that year and a compromise division between Edward A. Filene and the others of what had been Simpson's share of the business left the original 100 units of common stock divided this way: Edward A. Filene 30; Lincoln Filene 24; Frost 19.5; Kirstein 19.5 and the last three together 7. In that year, it was proposed that the store join Abraham & Straus of Brooklyn and F. & R. Lazarus & Co. of Columbus, Ohio, with whose principals the Filene executives had worked successfully for a decade in the Associated Merchandising Corporation, in formation of a holding company to be known as Federated Department Stores, Inc. One aim was the stabilizing of earnings through a geographical distribution of risk. Edward A. Filene opposed the idea. All his associates favored it.

Weary of the quarreling and fearful of the future of the store, Lincoln Filene then voted his stock with the others and deposed his brother as head of the company, but not without conditions. No loser in a store struggle was ever treated more generously. The elder brother was to continue to have the title of president for life, occupy the president's office and draw a salary of $100,-

000 a year, the same as the younger brother, Frost and Kirstein (all these salaries came down in the depression). He could make suggestions to the operating committee of the store but was not to interfere in its management. He could not start a business in competition with Filene's but he was free to do anything else he liked.

For the next nine years, the man derided by some "as a cross between a pack peddler and the prophet Isaiah" did exactly this. He spoke and traveled more than ever. He offered but never awarded a $25,000 prize for an essay on world peace. He became a well-known figure of the New Deal, serving as Massachusetts administrator for the National Recovery Administration and campaigning for President Roosevelt. The night before the 1936 national election, the President, Senator Robert F. Wagner, Democratic National Chairman James A. Farley and Edward A. Filene spoke over the combined National Broadcasting Company and Columbia Broadcasting System networks. The next day his candidate swept every state except Maine and Vermont. It was the happiest day of Edward A. Filene's restless, lonely and ambitious life.

Death in the form of pneumonia overtook him less than a year later on September 25, 1937, in Paris. In accordance with his wishes, his ashes were returned to Boston and cast into the Charles River Basin, which his apartment at 12 Otis Place overlooked. His will left the bulk of his $2 million estate to two foundations which he had started and to which he had given larger sums earlier. These were the Twentieth Century Fund, Inc., and an organization that was renamed the Edward A. Filene Good Will Fund, Inc., and later liquidated.

One of the obligations of the latter was to advance $1 million to the Consumer Distribution Corporation, founded earlier to start cooperative department stores as part of the donor's hope of finding ways to cut distribution costs. It was not until 1948 that the first cooperative department store, backed by $550,000 of Filene's money, was opened in Shirlington, Virginia, a suburb of Washington, D.C. Five years later its assets were sold for $260,-

000. A similar experiment failed, not necessarily because of the form of operation, in Providence, Rhode Island.

The Twentieth Century Fund proved more fortunate. Since 1919 when E. A. Filene founded it with $5 million in securities, by grants to others and through its own operations, the Fund has conducted economic research on timely subjects of public importance and disseminated the results by pamphlets, books, motion pictures, radio and, in recent years, television. Though expenditures have been more than $1,500,000 a year, the Twentieth Century Fund has been so well managed that the endowment in 1973 had increased to more than $32 million.

In large part this was due to the dividends of Filene's and Federated Department Stores, Inc., of which Filene's became a unit by a share-for-share exchange of common stock in 1929. Net sales of Filene's for the fiscal year ending January 31, 1929, were $34,173,186. Sales reached $47,422,264 the next year as the depression hit the nation. "The honeymoon is over," Vice President Kirstein then told the store staff. "Now the labor pains begin."

Thanks to the remarkable basement, Filene's sales during the depression were never less than the $30,620,089, the figure for the fiscal year ending January 31, 1934. On this figure there was a profit of 3.35 percent, though only 1.90 percent had been earned on sales of $32,593,795 the previous year. Filene's sales reached $52,320,951 during World War II and a few years afterward passed $70 million. They have since doubled.

Lincoln Filene, a serene and courtly gentleman, died at ninety-two on August 27, 1957, at his summer home in Marstons Mills, Massachusetts, after outliving all of the men he and his brother had picked in 1913 as their possible successors. After his brother's departure, he became president of the firm, relinquished the title for a time to Vice President Frost, who died in 1944, and again resumed it. Vice President Kirstein died in 1942. His successor in charge of publicity, Vice President William McLeod, died in 1946. A new generation of executives came from the store's training system.

Chief of these was Harold Daniel Hodgkinson, a six-foot-three executive of boundless energy. He was born May 8, 1890, in Wallingford, Connecticut, where his father, Samuel Hodgkinson, was a small silverware manufacturer, and attended Yale. There he studied engineering and earned his first money by breaking in pipes for his less robust classmates at ten cents a pipe. Work as a campus correspondent for the Associated Press shifted his interest to journalism, but the AP had no job for him when he received a degree in 1912 from Yale's Sheffield Scientific School.

"Why don't you try Filene's in Boston?" suggested the New Haven correspondent of the news service. "They are expanding and I hear it's a good place for college men."

Hodgkinson obediently went to Filene's and was hired by Ernest Martin Hopkins, a personnel man who later became president of Dartmouth College. Hodgkinson first addressed envelopes and then sorted overshoes in a subbasement. Meanwhile, he studied at the Harvard Graduate School, a bit of application that later gave him the distinction of being the first Yale man ever to become a governor of the Harvard Club of Boston. He married Laura White Cabot, descendant of two old New England families.

After Navy service in World War I, he became copywriter, advertising manager, buyer and merchandiser and then, in 1931, manager of the Automatic Basement. Hodgkinson traveled widely for the basement, buying linen in Ireland, rugs in Africa and even the wardrobes of movie stars in Hollywood. In 1942, he became top executive for the whole store as vice president and general manager and two years later chairman and chief executive officer.

The store was rebuilt and remodeled at a cost of $5 million. Its showmanship continued. Some World War II war-bond promotions earned congratulatory advertisements from the rival Jordan Marsh. Ackley Slee, an assistant store superintendent at Filene's, single-handedly sold $4,824,525 in bonds to lead individual sales in the Seventh War Loan. A Liberty Ship was named the *Edward A. Filene.* The day the atom bomb was announced, the store assembled, with the aid of Harvard scientists, a window display explaining fission of the uranium atom.

A series of postwar promotions, many of them planned by a notable woman executive, Harriet Wilinsky, fashion director and later sales manager, attracted wide attention. She flew to France on the first postwar Boston-to-Paris plane and conducted a fashion show there for French war brides awaiting passage to the United States. After showing clothes suitable for various sections of America, she answered questions like "How do I get along with an American mother-in-law?" and "Is it true that American men go out at night without their wives?" Back in Paris later, she was hostess at a party at which French friends of Bostonians heard recordings of messages from them and posed for movies which she took back to Boston. Goods from Ireland, Italy and other foreign lands were the subject of promotions. The maiden voyage of the American Export liner *Constitution* featured a Filene fashion show, and the French Line's *Ile de France* made a special stop in Boston for a Filene event.

A promotion of New England products, called the New England Revelation, was staged with a special New Haven train carrying designers, manufacturers and editors from New York to Boston. A fashion show was presented en route to the tune of a specially composed musical number entitled "New England— It's Grand."

A cartoon-illustrated 1947 advertisement in the *New York Times,* headed "One doesn't wear Jones Beach fashions on Cape Cod," urged vacationing New Yorkers to take empty suitcases to New England and let Filene's outfit them. This drew business and a favorable reaction for Filene's. "You are helping all New England," wrote a hosiery-mill president.

All innovations of Filene's have not, of course, proved successful. Those which failed to justify expectations have been abandoned, usually without delay. In an effort to reduce and equate distribution costs among different classes of customers, the store during World War I undertook to collect a fee of fifty cents a month from customers who maintained charge accounts. It also began to collect a ten-cent fee for each parcel delivered. Both ideas were abandoned when customers complained and rival stores continued to provide the services without special charges.

In 1929, Filene's acquired R. H. White's, an important Boston store dating from 1859. It was the first store to have an electric stairway and to use pneumatic cash tubes. The purchase was made with the idea of shifting some nonfashion departments out of Filene's and operating the stores as complementary institutions. This goal was not realized, and in 1944 White's was sold to the City Stores Company. A ten-year experiment in discount selling in a warehouse at Needham, Massachusetts, was concluded in 1966 as not consistent with Filene's merchandising.

Few civic enterprises are launched in Boston without somebody from the store having a part. "I always tell people," Lincoln Filene once remarked, "that just making money out of a city and its inhabitants isn't the only thing to do."

A Lincoln Filene Professorship of Retailing in the Harvard Graduate School of Business Administration was established with $300,000 given by Federated Department Stores, Inc., and the Lincoln and Therese Filene Foundation. Coincident with Lincoln Filene's eighty-fifth birthday, Professor Malcolm P. McNair was chosen as the first to fill the chair.

In 1954, seventeen years after his death, Edward S. Filene was elected to the Retailing Hall of Fame at the Chicago Merchandise Mart, and Hodgkinson helped Ralph Lowell, a Boston banker, secure the license and more than half the funds for the building of WHBH, Channel 2, an $800,000 educational television station, one of the first, as a memorial to the Filene brothers. The Ford Foundation joined the Twentieth Century Fund and other Filene foundations in paying for the transmitter at Blue Hill adjoining the Harvard Observatory. It is operated by the Lowell Institute Cooperative Broadcasting Council.

After fourteen years as chief executive, Hodgkinson was succeeded in 1958 by Maurice Lazarus, son of Fred Lazarus, Jr., and previously executive vice president of Foley's, Federated's

Houston store. Harold Krensky, previously at Bloomingdale's, became president in 1963. Maurice Lazarus went to Federated Department Stores in 1964 as vice chairman, Hodgkinson became chairman of the executive committee and Krensky took over as chairman and chief executive officer.

He returned to Federated eventually, becoming president, and was succeeded in 1968 by Richard G. Shapiro, a former Lord & Taylor executive, who headed Filene's until becoming president of Gimbel Brothers, Inc., in 1973 at $185,000 a year.

At that time, Weston P. Figgins, a New Englander who had been chairman of Bullock's of Los Angeles, became chairman and chief executive, while Joseph E. Brooks, who had been president of Rike's, Dayton, became president at Filene's. At the same time, Ralph B. Pendery, who had been president, became a Federated corporate vice president at Cincinnati.

In the retail world, a man trained at Filene's has something of the prestige of a hotel man who worked for E. M. Statler or a surgeon who interned at the Mayo Clinic. At least sixty great stores, at one time nine in New York alone, have been headed by alumni of Filene's.

Graduates of Filene's also have won fame in other fields. Donald David was dean of the Graduate School of Business Administration at Harvard University and vice chairman of the Ford Foundation. Paul Mazur became a partner of Lehman Brothers. Muriel Cox became director of the Chamberlain School of Retailing. Owen Stoner became president of Prince Matchabelli, Inc., and Glenn Frank later was president of the University of Wisconsin. Robert L. Moore helped start the Sheraton Hotel chain. And Charles Merz became editor of the *New York Times*.

VII

F. & R. Lazarus & Company

Ohio's Famous Department-Store Dynasty

A shopper is like a baby who wants milk. When he cries for milk, he doesn't want a meal ticket. He doesn't want an argument or an excuse. He wants warm milk that is right for him—and he wants it at once.

Providing this sort of service is all there is to success in retailing, often remarked Fred Lazarus, Jr., the most famous member of the Ohio family that built the extraordinary Lazarus and Shillito department-store businesses in Columbus and Cincinnati. From 1946 to 1966, he was chief executive officer of Federated Department Stores, Inc., of which these stores are model units.

When Mr. Fred, as the cocky, 5-foot-5½-inch gentleman was called to distinguish him from his numerous relatives in retailing, became head of Federated, the group consisted of five stores, only one with branches, and sales totaled $200,900,942. When, at eighty-one, he yielded the executive title to his Dartmouth-educated fifty-two-year-old son Ralph, Federated had sales of $1,330,736,617 for the year ending January 29, 1966.

As of 1973, when Mr. Fred died at eighty-eight, Federated had fourteen department-store divisions operating ninety-three headquarters and branch stores from Massachusetts to California.

In addition, Federated's I. Magnin division had twenty-one high-fashion specialty stores along the West Coast and a new store on Michigan Avenue in Chicago. Three specialized discount divisions in Ohio, Florida and California were operating sixteen units and planning further expansion. Ralphs, a Los Angeles-based supermarket group acquired by Federated in

1968, had sixty-seven stores in southern California and, during 1972, established a beachhead in northern California with seven stores in the San Francisco area.

These 205 diversified retail stores totaled nearly 32 million square feet of store space and had about $2.6 billion in sales and more than $108 million in earnings in fiscal 1973. Federated is the nation's biggest department-store chain and the ninth-biggest retailer. It was listed by *Dun's Review* in 1971 as one of the nation's ten best-managed corporations. Its common is the department-store stock most widely held by mutual funds.[1]

All of this growth reflects Mr. Fred's restless ideas. These also have found expression in the Ohio State Council of Retail Merchants, formed in 1922 at his suggestion, and the American Retail Federation, similarly organized in 1935 to speak for retail groups in Washington. For his ideas, he received the gold medal of the National Retail Merchants Association, a Tobé award and other honors. One of his ideas affected everybody in the country.

This was the date of Thanksgiving, which traditionally starts the Christmas shopping season. In 1939, when the depression still lingered, the last Thursday of November, on which the holiday was then observed, fell on the last day of the month. At a dinner in Cincinnati on June 14, Mr. Fred remarked to George V. Sheridan, executive director of the Ohio State Council of Retail Merchants, that there would be six more days of Christmas business if Thanksgiving could be advanced a week.

Next day Sheridan visited a library and found no legal bar to changing the date; in fact, it had been observed on many different dates. The late William F. Wiley, publisher of the *Cincinnati Enquirer,* endorsed the idea. Sheridan and Ed Martin, secretary of the Ohio Newspaper Association, took the proposal to Washington and through Lowell Mellett presented it to the White House, where President Roosevelt gave it a warm welcome. He promised to proclaim the earlier date and to give Lazarus and Wiley advance notice.

"But he forgot that part," Mr. Fred recalled later. "The

announcement came just as I was sitting down to the first company dinner of the bride of my son Ralph. She had broken her back over it but I spent the evening on the long-distance telephone talking to retailers. Wiley did the same with publishers. But it was too late. Everybody knows about the big squabble that broke out and continued for three years. We hadn't thought of the long-planned football schedules, school holidays, almanacs and calendars, railroad timetables and other things. Even my brothers who were interested in Ohio State's football team were annoyed."

Eventually nearly everybody conceded the value of the change and Congress on December 29, 1941, legalized the fourth Thursday in November as Thanksgiving. This can fall no later than November 28, and may be as early as November 22. Manufacturers, shoppers and store workers as well as retailers benefit.[2]

Some less spectacular ideas of Mr. Fred were conversion of store buyers into department managers, making them responsible for operating costs, including selling, warehousing and delivery, as well as the selection and sale of merchandise; the display of merchandise by "size selection"; the use of perimeter stock rooms adjacent to selling departments; and the adaptation to a store of the latest industrial materials-handling techniques and devices.

But Mr. Fred's favorite idea was that a store's success is almost in direct ratio to its hippodrome qualities and that older customers as well as children like to shop in a lively, animated atmosphere. In the tradition of Mr. Fred, Federated enlivened a 1973 meeting of security analysts in Cincinnati with a fashion show demonstrating merchandising know-how.

"A good store is like a big circus," he explained. "You can have one ring, or five or twenty. That is why a department store has it all over others in attracting people to come in and look around." He also believed a store should be exciting to those who run it. "Retailing is our life," he once said. "We enjoy its excitements. It is a life in itself full of challenge."

Showmanship combined with sound merchandising helped Lazarus become Ohio's largest department store. In 1912, it had its first million-dollar sales year; in 1962 it enjoyed its first million-dollar sales day. By 1973, million-dollar days were commonplace and annual sales volume was around $200 million.

The attractions have changed over the years, but the Lazarus stores retain an air of excitement. A live alligator, brought back from Florida by an uncle of Fred, Jr., was a basement attraction at the Lazarus store until the reptile died after eighteen years of exhibition. For years the store had a raucous whistle that tooted a weather forecast daily. One toot meant "fair," two "rain," three "unsettled." Santa Claus early became a Lazarus property, with the store bringing the old gentleman into town with a parade. When an early automobile crashed into a show window, up went a sign reading "Everything Comes to Lazarus." Each year the store entertains customers over eighty years old at a tea party. The store auditorium is in use for hobby shows, club meetings and similar gatherings, and a blimp was once employed to announce a change in store hours.

Dramatic exploits also turned Shillito's in Cincinnati from a moribund fifth-place store doing a $4-million business when the Lazarus family bought it in 1928 to the biggest department store in a tristate (Ohio, Kentucky, Indiana) market with annual sales of more than $135 million. Cincinnatians still talk of the service of Shillito's in the record 1937 Ohio flood. Food, blankets, gasoline and other merchandise, as well as drinking water, went from the store to refugees, and its staff fumigated, sorted and distributed thousands of garments donated for flood sufferers.

Telephone for the time in Cincinnati and you will be connected with a Shillito number, where will be, along with the time, an announcement of a sale or a suggestion that you support the local opera or some other civic enterprise. Shillito's sponsors community forums at which high-school students, their parents and authorities from many disciplines discuss such subjects as the use and abuse of drugs. The store gives space to a Craft

Shop of the Handicapped, profits of which go to the local blind or crippled.

Behind the dramatics are generations of solid merchandising. The original Lazarus store was opened as a tiny men's clothing store in Columbus in 1851 by Fred, Jr.'s, side-whiskered grandfather, Simon Lazarus, an immigrant from Prussia. He also served as the first rabbi of Temple Israel, the oldest Jewish congregation in Columbus and one in which his descendants are still active.

Simon Lazarus started with $3,000. His store on South High Street was twenty by fifty feet. There was one clerk. The founder had four daughters and two sons, Fred and Ralph, the great-uncle of a later Ralph. When not in school, they helped in the store, sometimes breaking ice in the Scioto River for water to mop the floor.

The first of many expansions came in the 1860s when an adjoining boot-and-shoe store was purchased for $3,500. In 1870, the Lazarus store, then one of sixteen local retail clothiers, became the first Columbus store to operate a delivery wagon. In 1877, the founder died and his sons took charge.

Store advertising then emphasized "One Lowest Price" or "Strictly One-Price Store" and "Every Article Marked in Plain Figures." In 1887, the store added men's, women's and children's shoes. In 1888, on the occasion of the state fair and the centennial celebration of the state's first permanent settlement, all the employees, led by Fred and Ralph Lazarus and a brass band, went to the fair.

Ralph Lazarus wrote most of the store advertising in the nineties. "He would just sit down," a veteran employee once recalled, "and write on a piece of wrapping paper." The store at this period consisted of eleven ground-floor rooms with connecting doors. "Uncle Ralph" Lazarus, as he was known, had an office in an elevated cubbyhole. This was equipped with a system of mirrors so arranged that by their reflection he could see every part of the store. In another expansion the space between the store and the southwest corner of Town and High

Streets was acquired and a clock tower, a landmark for many years, was constructed.

Merchandising at the turn of the century involved presents and premiums. A baseball and bat usually went with a boy's suit. A man received a pair of suspenders with each suit. A purchaser of a pair of shoes expected a strip of tickets entitling him to free shines. Complaints were loud when the practice was stopped in 1903.

All Lazarus employees, called associates then as now, wore nickel lapel buttons bearing their number. These buttons were required to be polished and in evidence at all times. Even floor-walkers wore large badges saying "Lazarus Floor Walker."

In 1903, Ralph Lazarus died. He never married. The business continued under his brother Fred, with the latter's four sons, Simon, Fred, Jr., Robert and Jeffrey, all assuming store responsibilities as they grew up.

Nearly all of the founder Simon's sons, grandsons and great-grandsons have gone into the business. They all have been competent and successful merchants, but the most kinetic and peripatetic of them was Fred Lazarus, Jr. A childhood illness left him with a hand tremor, but this did not deter him from starting in the store at age ten as a collar salesman on Saturdays.

Until he and his brothers began to take charge, the Lazarus store was little more than a men's clothing shop. Simon, the eldest, had a flair for employee relations and headed the store for thirty years. The younger brothers, Robert and Jeffrey, became notable merchandise and sales-promotion executives and then respectively chief executive officers of the stores in Columbus and Cincinnati. To Fred, Jr., was left finance and the freedom to consider bold innovations.

He cut short his education in his freshman year at Ohio State, where he was a straight-"A" student, to take the place of his dying uncle in the store, and soon induced his family to construct a new building and expand into the department-store field. He supervised the building of a five-story structure that is part of the present Lazarus store and once termed its opening in 1909 the happiest day of his business career. He was then twenty-four years old. After that, he supervised so many expansions that he could talk to architects and engineers in their own language.

Though Lazarus sales mounted to $4 million a year during World War I, its business still was exceeded by one Columbus store and equaled by another in 1920. That summer, Fred, Jr., visited New York and became convinced that the war inflation had run its course. Markdowns, greater than the profits of the previous year, were taken, especially on silk shirts, the prime symbol of wartime affluence. The store's 1921 gross of $5,773,000 was the largest in Columbus.

Fred, Jr., early developed a liking for travel, and out of his trips came many ideas. While visiting Europe, he once wandered into the Printemps store in Paris and noticed that all the dresses of one size, regardless of price, were grouped in single alcoves. The simplicity of the idea impressed him and he adopted it at once. Why should stores scatter garments of the same size all over a floor, perhaps even on different floors, simply because they are of a different price or a different brand? After all, the customer had to determine one fact before all else—would the garment fit? With all dresses of one size grouped, customers often buy an item of better quality than they had planned. Size selling is now used widely.

Out of Mr. Fred's interest in construction has come adoption of horizontal warehousing, the practice wherever possible of storing merchandise, except the bulky furniture, on the same floor level that it is sold. It places salespeople close to the stock and enables them to do work in slack hours that might otherwise require a separate staff in a warehouse. Errors in handling are greatly reduced.

One of the Lazarus family's most successful ventures was the purchase for $2 million of the John Shillito store in Cincinnati. Founded in 1830, it had the distinction of being the oldest store west of the Alleghenies. Mrs. Fred Lazarus, Sr., a native of Cincinnati, bought her wedding dress there. It had been the city's biggest store, but after the death in 1925 of Stewart Shillito, a son of the founder, it was not better than fourth. Shillito's was rehabilitated with startling speed under Fred Lazarus, Jr., president for some years, and his brother Jeffrey, who first was general manager and then president.

In the first year of Lazarus management, sales increased to $5.7 million and in 1929 reached $6.5 million. While other large Cincinnati stores lost as much as half of their volume during the depression, Shillito's dropped only to $4.5 million in 1932. For 1935, the volume was $7.3 million, more than it had ever been at the peak of the Shillito family's operation. The building was expanded and air-conditioned and a customers' garage constructed. In 1939, sales passed $10.7 million and Shillito's was definitely the No. 1 store in Cincinnati. At the end of World War II, sales were nearly $30 million and were accounting for a third of the Federal Reserve department-store figures for Cincinnati. Jeffrey Lazarus retired in 1965 after seeing Shillito's sales increase more than twentyfold.

Shillito's and Lazarus did so well downtown that they were slow to open branches. But as of 1973, Shillito's had six of them —four in suburban Cincinnati and two in Kentucky—one in Lexington, and one in Louisville. Fred Lazarus III, a son of Mr. Fred, had then been chairman of Shillito's for seven years. *Women's Wear* then estimated 1972 sales at $137 million.

At the big Columbus store, Robert Lazarus, a gentle, ascetic-appearing Phi Beta Kappa graduate of Ohio State who had been active in countless civic enterprises, became president in 1947 and a director of Federated. He was made chairman in 1959 and became chairman emeritus in 1969. He received the Tobé award, the Oscar of retailing, in 1961. At his death in 1973, at the age of eighty-two, an editorial tribute in the *Columbus Citizen-Journal* said: "The great merchandising complex bearing the Lazarus name is admired throughout the nation. But his interests ranged far beyond the family business empire. It would be difficult to walk more than a few blocks in any direction in downtown Columbus without seeing evidence of his civic leader-

ship and philanthropic activities. Over the 61 years of his . . .
career, his energies and organizational talents often were brought
to bear on projects that have made the Columbus community a
better place for living."

Robert Lazarus was succeeded as president by a nephew,
Charles Y. Lazarus, a Yale graduate and is a son of the late
Simon Lazarus. As of 1973, he was chairman and William P.
Giovanello was president.

Lazarus now operates four full-line branches and a home-
furnishing specialty store in suburban Columbus shopping centers. There are full-line branches at Mansfield, Ohio, seventy
miles to the northeast, and at Lima, Ohio, eighty miles to the
northwest. In 1973, Lazarus expanded two hundred miles west
into Indiana with a branch in the New Castleton Square Mall
in Indianapolis.[3]

Federated Department Stores, Inc., was born on a yacht in
Long Island Sound one weekend in the summer of 1929. The
craft belonged to Simon Frank Rothschild, president of Abraham & Straus, the big Brooklyn store. Guests included Fred
Lazarus, Jr.; Louis Kirstein, general manager of Filene's in
Boston; and Samuel Bloomingdale, head of Bloomingdale's, the
big New York store. They had been associated with the Retail
Research Association and the Associated Merchandising Corporation. They returned from the cruise with the first three
agreeing to a proposal by Paul Mazur, the former Filene man
who had become a partner in the investment-banking firm of
Lehman Brothers, that they share the risks of their businesses
through a holding company to be set up by an exchange of
stock.

The new company was incorporated in November and a
majority of the stock of each company was exchanged. Holders
of each Lazarus share received 19/37 of a Federated share, an
A. & S. share received two thirds of a Federated share and
Filene shares were traded evenly. Lehman Brothers, the investment bankers, were interested, and first Arthur Lehman and
then Mazur served as directors.

Bloomingdale's joined the group the next year on the basis of a share of Bloomingdale stock for three fourths of a Federated share.

Bloomingdale's and Abraham & Straus are curiously entwined in history. Just before the Civil War, the small Bettlebeck & Co. dry-goods store in Newark, New Jersey, employed three clerks. They were Benjamin Altman, Abraham Abraham and Lyman Gustave Bloomingdale. Each founded great stores, the first B. Altman & Co. in New York, the second Abraham & Straus in Brooklyn and the last Bloomingdale Bros., Inc.

The depression struck just as Federated was organized, and it was not until October 31, 1931, that the first dividend was paid. They have continued unbroken since then. Until the end of World War II, Federated continued to be simply a holding company, without authority, headquarters offices or formal work. Between 1933 and 1945, the number of stockholders increased only from 1,173 to 2,861.

A trip of Fred Lazarus, Jr., in 1944 to visit his son Ralph, then an Army Air Force lieutenant at Ellington Field, in Texas, led to Federated's becoming an operating company. Fred, Jr., stopped in Houston, visited the local stores and discovered the largest to be Foley Brothers. This was founded in 1900 by Pat C. and James A. Foley with $2,000 borrowed from an Irish immigrant uncle. Since 1917, it had been owned by the George S. Cohen family.

When Fred, Jr., found Foley's doing only a fourth of the business of Shillito's in a city as big as Cincinnati, he decided that Federated should expand into Houston. At the end of the war, Mr. Fred induced his Federated colleagues to build a store there, a step that required a considerable departure from the original idea of Federated's simply acting as a holding company. He became Federated's president in that same year of 1945, and set up headquarters in Cincinnati in a small office over a bank across from Shillito's. There were two secretaries, a telephone operator, and two men who began doing research on ways in which the stores could better share their most successful techniques. An early improvement was to expand the use of "revolving credit," whereby customers have a monthly credit balance and pay stipulated amounts each month. Today more than 60 percent of Federated's sales are on credit. The office was soon moved to the top of Shillito's garage, where it remains. It became his command post for expansion, at a time when some retailers were retrenching in fear of a postwar depression.

While sites were being purchased for the Houston store, the owners of Foley's decided to sell. After several discussions, one of which lasted eighteen hours, Fred, Jr., worked out a plan that in 1945 gave Federated the Foley business and real estate in exchange for $3,250,000 in securities. As the real estate included a surplus store site, this gave Fred, Jr., the chance to turn real-estate salesman. He sold the extra site, which had been optioned at $1,250,000, to Woolworth's for $3,055,000, a matter of $2,000 a front inch, a record price even for busy Houston.[4]

This profit helped pay for a new $13-million store completed in 1947 and embodying all of the Lazarus ideas of perimeter stock rooms, movable walls, station selling by size and scientific operation. A tunnel under Travis Street connected the six-story-and-basement store with a garage and service building. Packages of shopping customers reached their cars by a system of chutes and conveyor belts. Kenneth Franzheim was the architect and Raymond Loewy designed the interiors, including a luxurious Crystal Room. It was the first entirely new department store built in the country in almost twenty years.[5]

Even before the new store was completed, the new management increased Foley's sales from $6.5 million in the year before it was purchased to $16 million. By 1950, Foley's sales passed $29 million. Max Levine, a Harvard graduate trained at Filene's, Abraham & Straus and Lazarus, first became president and then chairman at Foley's. Sales reached $50 million by 1955. Four additional floors were added to the store, and later branches were opened at Pasadena, Sharpstown, Almeda Mall and Northwest Mall. As of 1973, Milton Berman, formerly of Abraham & Straus, was chairman and chief executive of Foley's. Stewart Orton, formerly of Shillito's and Milwaukee's Boston Store, was president.

With Fred Lazarus, Jr., as president, Federated abruptly changed character. All its stores were enlarged and rehabili- tated. The transformation at Bloomingdale's, under James S. Schoff and J. Edward Davidson, made it one of the most profit- able Federated units. At Federated headquarters, operations, finance, research and acquisitions divisions were set up. Owen C. Frost, son of the Filene executive, headed the last. Research was headed by Myron S. Silbert, coauthor with Paul Mazur of *Principles of Organization Applied to Modern Retailing*. Within a few years, the number of stockholders increased to more than ten thousand; in 1973, shareholders numbered about twenty- eight thousand.

Federated attempted to buy the John Taylor Dry Goods Store in Kansas City but was outbid by Macy's. Halliburton's, an Oklahoma City store, was purchased in 1947 and sold a few years later. In 1948, Federated bought the Milwaukee Boston Store, one of the largest in Wisconsin, along with three branches. Pat Maher, a Lazarus executive who as a boy had been a golf caddie for Mr. Fred, headed the Boston Store until his retire- ment. In 1973, Edward E. Watson was chairman and Orren J. Bradley, a graduate of Foley's executive group, was president.

Sanger Brothers, a pioneer Dallas store, was purchased in 1951. It was founded in 1872 by Isaac, Lehman and Philip Sanger, immigrant brothers from Bavaria who previously had a succession of stores at the railhead of the Houston & Texas Central Railroad as it was built northward from Houston. On the basis of some of their earlier retailing, the store claims to date from 1857 "as an institution." Eli Sanger, a later member of the family, headed the local Civic Music Association and gave it an office in the store. It was the first in the area to hire women as clerks and the first to grow to department-store status. It was long the biggest store in Dallas but, after passing from Sanger ownership, suffered from the competition of Neiman-Marcus in fashion and from Sears, Roebuck in hard lines.

Under Federated, the company expanded spectacularly, acquiring the local A. Harris & Co. and becoming Sanger-Harris, opening additional branches and in 1965 completing the first new downtown Dallas department store in thirty years. With an exterior marked by an arched colonnade and a great mosaic mural, it occupies almost a block at Akard and Pacific, far uptown from the old site. There are eight branches whose total square footage is about twice that of the headquarters store. Chief executives under Federated have been Henry X. Salzberger, from Bloomingdale's; Ray Cummins, from Lazarus; Weston P. Figgins, who earlier had been an executive vice president of Woodward & Lothrop of Washington, D.C.; and, since 1970, Alan B. Gilman, another Lazarus alumnus.

In 1953, the Federated Retirement Income and Thrift Incentive Plan, called RITI for short, was inaugurated. This is an employee retirement benefit program similar to that of Sears, Roebuck. The company makes an annual allocation in cash, which over the years has averaged about 6.5 percent of each employee's earnings. This is used to buy Federated stock at various times during the year for the retirement income part. Employees may invest up to 5 percent of earnings in the thrift incentive part of the plan. The company then makes a second allocation based on the individual employee's own savings. At the close of 1972, the program had more than twenty thousand participants and net assets valued at more than $234 million.

Burdine's of Miami, the biggest department store in Florida, was acquired by Federated in 1956 in an exchange of stock with the heirs of W. M. Burdine, who launched it in 1898. With it were acquired four branches, new and colorful like the main store, in Miami Beach, North Miami, Fort Lauderdale and West Palm Beach. Federated built four more—Dadeland, Hollywood, Pompano Beach, and Westland. Thomas C. Wasmuth, previously executive vice president of Rike's in Dayton, Ohio, is the current chief executive. Burdine's annual sales are estimated at something in excess of $150 million.

In 1959, Federated added Rike's, a store dating from 1853, in a "pooling of interests"; and Goldsmith's in Memphis, Tennessee, dating from 1872 and the largest store in the area, for 200,000 Federated shares. Douglas M. Thomsen, a former senior vice president of Abraham & Straus, became Rike's chief executive in 1972.

Raymond H. Cummins is now chairman and chief executive at Goldsmith's and Edmond D. Cicola is president. Rike's has four branches—three nearby and one thirty miles distant in Springfield, Ohio; Goldsmith's has three branches. All of the branch stores of these two divisions were built after the acquisition by Federated.

In 1964, through another "pooling of interests," Federated acquired Bullock's and I. Magnin* on the West Coast. These are now operated as separate divisions. Bullock's has eleven stores in the sprawling Los Angeles market with an annual sales volume estimated at about $200 million. Early in 1973, Howard Goldfeder became Bullock's chairman and chief executive officer, and Herbert R. Bloch, Jr., formerly executive vice president of Shillito's, was named president.

Under Federated, I. Magnin has maintained its reputation for leadership in high fashion while expanding into affluent new market areas. I. Magnin had twenty-two stores at the beginning of 1973 and its chief executive officer was Ross F. Anderson, a veteran Federated merchant and a director of the parent company.

In 1971, Federated abandoned a venture attempting to bring its major city merchandising know-how to smaller cities primarily in the Southwest. While these stores, known as Fedway, had produced a profit, Federated saw greater opportunities in

* See Chapter XXI.

its metropolitan divisions and sold the Fedway stores to Dillard Department Stores, Inc., for their approximate book value of $6 million.

Abraham & Straus in Brooklyn and Bloomingdale's in Manhattan have added branches and increased sales steadily in the face of competition from all directions. Sales of the great Brooklyn store and its eight branches are reported to have passed $400 million by 1973. It challenges Macy's in the metropolitan area and has met changing conditions by building a downtown garage, updating the parent store and opening branches on Long Island and, most recently, in New Jersey. Walter N. Rothschild, grandson of the founder, died of a heart attack on October 8, 1960, while in White Sulphur Springs, West Virginia, for a meeting of Federated executives. He was succeeded as chairman and chief executive officer by Sidney Solomon and as president by his son, Walter N. Rothschild, Jr.[6] In 1966, Solomon, a graduate of Harvard who began his career at Filene's, received both a Tobé award and the gold medal of the National Retail Merchants Association for distinguished contributions to retailing.[7] The current A. & S. management team consists of Sanford J. Zimmerman, chairman, and Edward Goodman, president. Zimmerman previously headed Famous-Barr, St. Louis.

Bloomingdale's has added branches in Fresh Meadows and New Rochelle, New York; Stamford, Connecticut; Bergen County and Short Hills, New Jersey; and Garden City, Long Island. In 1971 and 1972, Bloomingdale's undertook a new venture with home-furnishings specialty stores in Manhasset and Scarsdale, New York; Jenkintown, Pennsylvania and Chestnut Hill, Massachusetts. This move capitalized on the national fame of Bloomingdale's home-furnishings departments. As of 1973, Bloomingdale's total sales were reported approaching $250 million. Lawrence Lachman is chairman and chief executive officer, and Marvin S. Traub is president.

Federated's central office staff grew with the recruitment of talent from many fields. Some executives moved on to head store divisions. Abe Fortas, long a legal adviser, a month after becoming a Federated vice president was appointed by former President Lyndon B. Johnson to the United States Supreme Court. Directors include Howard W. Johnson of the Massachusetts Institute of Technology; Walter L. Lingle, Jr., retired executive vice president of Procter & Gamble Co.; Dillion Anderson, attorney; General Alfred M. Gruenther, former Supreme Allied Commander in Europe; T. Spencer Shore, chairman of the executive committee of Eagle-Picher Industries, Inc.; William H. Dennler, retired vice chairman of General Electric; and Jerome H. Holland, former U.S. Ambassador to Sweden.

Ralph Lazarus, the second of Fred, Jr.'s, three sons, began his career in the family store in Columbus following his 1935 graduation from Dartmouth College. In 1951, when he was vice president and general merchandise manager of the Columbus store, he was called to Cincinnati to become Federated's executive vice president. He became president in 1957, and ten years later succeeded Fred, Jr., as chairman and chief executive officer.

J. Paul Sticht, previously president of Campbell Soup International, joined Federated as executive vice president and a director in 1960. He was elected president in 1967 and continued in that position until 1972, and later became president of R. J. Reynolds, Inc.

In January 1973, Harold Krensky, who during thirty years with Federated had earned a national reputation as a leader in fashion merchandising, became president at sixty. He had been a chief executive officer of both Filene's and Bloomingdale's, and, by 1971, when he was made a vice chairman, he had supervised all of Federated's department store divisions.

The Lazarus family continues to supply top management personnel to Federated. Maurice Lazarus, a graduate of Harvard with heavy retail experience at Shillito's, Foley's and Filene's, is chairman of the finance committee of Federated's board. A third brother, Fred III, is chairman of Shillito's.

When Harold Krensky was elected president, Ralph Lazarus said that Krensky and he would operate much as Federated's divisions do, "with a two-man team at the top."

"We have three clear assignments," Ralph Lazarus said. "The first, of course, will be to continue improving Federated's day-by-day performance. The second is long-range planning for the corporation. The third is to identify and qualify our successors. We have given ourselves five years to do this, and we believe we have the most able group of young department store executives in the country from which to choose."

VIII
Marshall Field & Company

Elegance for the Middle West

Every great store is a showplace in its community, but Marshall Field's with its elegance and its clocks has achieved and retained an attraction value for visitors to Chicago that probably is unmatched in any other city. Out-of-towners go to Field's before visiting the Art Institute or the great museums. The store's tooled-leather guest book includes the autographs of Presidents Taft and Nixon, Prince Philip of England, Queen Marie of Roumania, Prime Minister Winston Churchill, Eleanor Roosevelt and many others.

It is a sentimental store, where Hughston M. McBain, its sixth president, kept five red roses on his desk in memory of his five illustrious predecessors. It is also a resilient enterprise that survived the Great Chicago Fire and since has surmounted many difficulties. It has trebled its sales in recent decades by divesting itself of wholesale and manufacturing operations and investing in purely retail expansion downtown, in the suburbs and in other cities.[1]

Under Gerald A. Sivage, its eighth president, the company had record sales of $492,794,000 and record earnings of $21,457,000, the latter figure a 12.6 percent gain, for the fiscal year ending January 31, 1973. Contributing to these figures was its ninth outlying Chicago unit, a beautiful three-level store in the Woodfield Mall, the world's largest enclosed shopping center, in suburban Schaumburg, Illinois, to the northwest. It opened in 1971.

Two more new branches were built in 1973. One is in New Century Town, a planned community in Vernon Hills thirty miles north of Chicago, which will have an enclosed-mall shopping facility, Hawthorn Center. The other is in the enclosed Cherry Vale Mall at Rockford, Illinois. Planned for 1974 were a downtown North Michigan Avenue branch in the huge Water Tower Plaza and another enclosed-mall branch in Fox Valley East, a new planned town in Du Page County, thirty-four miles west of the Loop. All these are joint ventures with other companies.

There are older branches in Evanston, Lake Forest, Oakbrook, Oak Park, Old Orchard (Skokie), Park Forest and River Oaks, Illinois, and in the big Mayfair shopping center at Wauwatosa, near Milwaukee. A Field unit is within easy driving distance for anybody in the big Chicago metropolitan area.

The company owns one of the finest stores in the West, Frederick & Nelson of Seattle. This has three attractive suburban branches, Aurora Village, Bellevue Square and South Center.

In 1969, Field's acquired the Crescent, an eighty-year-old downtown Spokane, Washington, department store, along with its Northtown Shopping Center and University City branches, for 600,000 shares of Field common stock. The Crescent is famous in Spokane history for a spectacular display of public-spiritedness in the first year of its existence when it survived unscathed a fire that destroyed all its competitors. Instead of reaping a fortune, Robert B. Paterson and J. M. Comstock, the founders, cut their prices 10 percent to help the devasted city rebuild.[2]

In a move eastward, Field's purchased Halle Brothers of Cleveland by an exchange of stock in 1970. This company then had sales of nearly $70 million a year from five stores in Cleveland and branches in Fairlawn Village, a suburb of Akron; in Canton, Ohio; and two stores in Erie, Pennsylvania. Walter M. Halle, son of the founder, wrote personal letters to all charge customers who spent $1,000 or more a year at Halle's.[3] Paul H. Strohn, a Field veteran of thirty-nine years, was named chief executive of the division in 1973.

When completed in 1907, the huge Chicago Field store at State, Washington, Randolph Streets, and Wabash Avenue was "the largest store in the world." With over 450 departments in seventy-three acres of space on thirteen floors, Field's still is one of the largest stores in the world. Macy's of New York and Hudson's of Detroit boast only a few more square feet. The longest selling aisle in the world is in Field's basement; on the Wabash Avenue side it extends six hundred feet under Washington Boulevard into the Field's Store for Men across the street. Each December Field's displays what is said to be "the largest indoor Christmas tree in the world" and issues handsome toy and fashion catalogs.

Field's boasts more show windows than any other store and each is numbered to enable a shopper to be specific when asking for something displayed. As of 1973, it claimed the largest department-store restaurant operation in the world; the largest retail shoe operation under one roof; the largest china department, the largest year-round toy department, the largest book department in the United States; the largest imports of linen and one of the largest imports of women's fashions. Historically, Field's was the first to establish an underprice basement and to use the basement for selling. It was the first to offer a personal shopping service and was among the first to offer a delivery service.

What the Biltmore Hotel clock is to rendezvousing New Yorkers, the two Field clocks are to Chicagoans. Visible for blocks, they have marked the State and Washington and State and Randolph corners since the turn of the century. Each is twelve feet six inches high, has minute hands more than two feet long, and weighs seven and three-quarter tons. One was shown on a 1945 *Saturday Evening Post* cover. Executive Vice President Joseph A. Burnham has the original in his office.

The store traces its history to 1852, when a young Quaker

named Potter Palmer, later famous for hotels and his social-leader wife, arrived in Chicago from Lockport, New York, where he had operated a small dry-goods store. He started a modest store in Chicago on Lake Street. Palmer was a student of *Godey's Lady's Book* and saw the importance of the ladies as customers. Everything about his establishment was calculated to please them. There was a tempting array of stylish shawls, laces and cloaks. There were price tags on them. Above all, there was acceptance, even cordial acceptance, of the fact that women sometimes change their minds.

Four years later, Marshall Field, a twenty-one-year-old Presbyterian youth, also arrived in Chicago, from Pittsfield, Massachusetts. One of nine children, he had started life as a farm boy but had become a $4-a-week clerk in the store of Henry G. "Deacon" Davis at Pittsfield. There for nearly five years the shy, conscientious youth put in ten hours a day, six days a week. He swept the floor, dusted the counters and shelves, arranged the goods and waited on the shrewd New England customers. Women liked him. He was polite and painstaking, with a good memory for names and faces—bolstered by a little book in which he made notes about the customers.

In Chicago, through the help of his brother Joseph, Marshall found a job with Cooley, Wadsworth and Company, the largest dry-goods firm in the city. He saved half of his $400-a-year salary by sleeping in the store and buying nothing for himself except some overalls. Hard-working and single-minded, he rose to a junior partnership and finally to a full partnership with Cooley and Farwell. The firm of Farwell, Field and Company— the first in which Marshall Field's name appeared as a partner —was formed in 1864, when Cooley stepped out. The next step came next year, when Peter Palmer decided to retire from his store. He sold an interest to Field and one to Levi Leiter, Field's junior partner, and the firm of Field, Palmer and Leiter was launched.

Their first advertisement made it clear that they were "Sucessors to P. Palmer." The pioneer merchandising ideas that had made Palmer's so popular formed a solid foundation for the company and for Field's own farsighted convictions about successful storekeeping. "The best way to show a lady that the merchandise she purchased is worth the dollar she paid for it," said Field, "is to give her the dollar in return." He laid down as one of the company's rules: "What we write and what we say about our merchandise or service must be strictly, scrupulously, unfailingly the truth." Low prices, Field believed, could not do the trick alone. Nor could goods of the highest quality. There must be the personal touch—that atmosphere of honest, pleasant service that makes customers feel they are *special* customers and brings them back faithfully, year after year.

It worked then, as it does today. The ladies liked the courteous attention. They liked the three female clerks who were hired to make them feel more at ease when buying the elaborate lingerie of the period. They appreciated the distinction lent to the store's front entrance by the two men hired to sweep the street three times a day. They loved the goods-on-approval policy. Through the years some of them, of course, have taken advantage of it. There was the society woman who returned a cape the day after a ball, maintaining that she had not worn it. It was such an expensive cape that the matter was brought to the attention of Field himself. He took her word for it—and found, after she had left with her refund, a lace handkerchief tucked into one of the folds of the cape. His comment was characteristic: "If she said she didn't wear it, she didn't wear it! But I guess we'd better send her handkerchief back to her."

Business was so good that by 1868 Field and Leiter decided to take Palmer up on his offer to rent them his palatial marble store building on State Street. The $50,000-a-year rental was breathtaking. So was the grand opening, which a Chicago newspaper described as "A Dazzling Assemblage of Wealth, Beauty and Fashion." The main attraction was the first floor, the retail floor, with its walnut counters, frescoed walls, and—lit by splendid gas fixtures—its rich display of silks and satins, sable-trimmed cloaks, black and white astrakhans, Persian cashmere and point-lace shawls.

While the wholesale trade was important, Field noted that the retail floor drew the ecstatic "ohs" and "ahs" from the ladies who swarmed into the store. He was there to greet them, unobtrusively polite, his youthful shyness ripened now into dignity. A quiet-mannered, handsome man, he made his presence felt among customers and clerks alike.

Striding through the store one day, Field encountered one of his assistants arguing with a woman customer.

"What are you doing here?" demanded Field.

"I am settling a complaint," the man explained.

"No, you're not," said Field. "Give the lady what she wants."

This was done and the phrase became a motto for the store and, years later, the title of a book on its history.[4]

Representatives of Field and Leiter ranged far afield, visiting the fashion centers of Europe and buying high-quality mill products on the spot in England. "In 1871," recalled Prince Philip of England when visiting Chicago long afterward, "Marshall Field sent his brother Joseph to Manchester to open the first buying office abroad for any American retail store—and it's been going strong ever since."[5] Congress made Chicago a federal port of entry, and the first direct Field and Leiter importation triumphantly arrived that year. But before it could be displayed, disaster struck the whole city.

News of the fire sweeping Chicago roused both partners out of their beds. Field organized a brigade to hang wet blankets in the store windows while Leiter supervised the job of moving the most valuable merchandise to safety—to the lake front first, later to Leiter's home and a nearby schoolhouse. Luckily, somebody thought to hurry to the basement and fire up the furnace so the steam elevators would run, thus speeding the removal of goods from the store. For it was doomed, in spite of all the partners and their faithful employees could do. By morning nothing was left but smoking ruins and twisted steel. A notice was posted on a pole stuck in the rubble: "Cash Boys &

Work Girls will be Paid what is due them Monday 9 A.M. Oct. 16th at 60 Calumet Ave. Field, Leiter & Co."

In two days Field found a new site—a brick barn at State and Twentieth Streets that had been built by the Chicago City Railway Company for its horses. Here the merchandise salvaged from the fire was arranged on pine counters hastily set up in the horse stalls. New orders arrived from New York in such quantity that bobtail horsecars were needed to help haul the goods from the railroad depot. In Field's opinion, speed was vital. The big store that opened first after the fire would not only make money but would be doing an important service for Chicagoans. All but $750,000 of the firm's $2,500,000 loss was covered by insurance. Less than two weeks after the catastrophe the partners announced their new location, adding, "We sincerely thank our friends for their many kind expressions of sympathy and hope soon to renew our former pleasant business relations."

In the spring Field and Leiter moved to Market and Madison Streets. It soon became clear that the ladies did not care to travel so far west to shop. State Street, rebuilt after the fire, was again Chicago's logical shopping center, and back to State Street Field and Leiter moved their store. Business continued to be excellent. Even the panic of 1873 failed to hurt the firm. Soon they were expanding their delivery system, which had hardly existed except when an errand boy occasionally carried packages to waiting carriages. Now, for two dollars a week, boys were hired specifically to make deliveries to residences within a few miles of the store. At first the youngsters went on foot, later on the street cars. As the store and the city grew, the delivery boys were replaced by horse-drawn delivery carts. When an epidemic of distemper hit Chicago horses, the store used oxen for deliveries.

Today Field's corps of deliverymen, more than four hundred strong and making about twenty-five thousand deliveries a day from store-owned trucks painted a special green, are trained to be goodwill ambassadors. A Field deliveryman wouldn't think of barging right up a customer's steps with a Christmas sled or bicycle. He reconnoiters first, empty-handed. If the coast is clear he goes back to his truck for the gift; often he is requested to leave it with a neighbor. He knows which of the customers on his route have a new baby that may wake up screaming if he leans on the doorbell at nap time. He is a regular Boy Scout when it comes to good deeds. Maybe he'll be called upon to climb up a house and open the window for a customer who has forgotten her key, or pack down snow in a driveway with his big truck tires to clear the way for the owner's car. Field's deliverymen are proud of their ten-million-mile no-accident record. Some of them have been on the same route for forty years.

In 1877, fire once more ravaged the Field and Leiter store on State Street. The Italian-style building the Singer sewing machine people had put up for Field was destroyed, and with it $750,000 worth of merchandise covered by insurance. Again the partners moved, to a vacant hall on the lake front. An offer from the Singer people to sell Field what was left of the store, plus the corner lot, was declined. Singer put up a new building and offered to rent it to Field; this too was declined and James Bolton, the Singer agent in Chicago, leased the structure to Carson, Pirie and Company. But Field changed his mind and wound up paying the Singer company $700,000 for it and giving Carson, Pirie $100,000 to relinquish its lease.

Field and Leiter took possession of their new store in 1879. There was a uniformed official greeter at the entrance. Clerks no longer shouted, "Cash! Come Cash!" The cash boys, scrubbed and brushed until they shone, now had numbers. Tense in their tight-fitting uniforms, they waited on a bench for their numbers to flash on a nearby board. There were still only two elevators, but they were fancy ones, and a splendid staircase led to the second floor. An impressive stock of carpets and upholstery occupied the entire third floor, while on the fifth three hundred women worked at making dresses.

Field and Leiter parted in 1881. Leiter, never an easy man to get along with, did not share Field's enthusiasm for the retail end of the business. Field proposed a figure at which either of the partners might buy or sell the business. He named $2.5 million, low for a business with sales of more than $24 million the previous year. Leiter made up his mind to buy, only to discover what Field had already made sure of—that none of the key executives would stay with Leiter in case Field left. Leiter was cornered, and he knew it. "You win, Marshall," he said. "I'll sell."

At forty-seven, Marshall Field was one of the richest men in America. The country boy had made good in the style that Horatio Alger was popularizing. Spare and erect in carriage, with cold blue-gray eyes, prematurely gray hair and ruddy complexion, he was a dignified, aloof figure who wore white gloves even in summer. Although he and his ailing wife lived with their two children in a mansion on Prairie Avenue, Field never cared for lavish ostentation. His tastes were simple, his friends few, his life—outside of the store—lonely and pathetically lacking in satisfactions that his wealth should have brought him. His wife, Nannie, spent more and more of her time abroad, trying to regain her health; she died in France in 1896.

The standards for even the humblest of Field's employees were high. Wages and praise were scant, but the prestige of working for Field's made up for these lacks. Field's had "tone," a quality that was recognized even in shoplifting circles. One shoplifter, an old-timer who was nabbed repeatedly by the store detectives, was asked why she didn't sometimes work the other side of the street. She explained why. "I'm no jitney thief boosting cheap stuff," she said. "I work your store because you got all the best stuff in the city!"

Though Field's usual attitude toward his employees was one of awe-inspiring reserve, he could be surprisingly indulgent. Once two clerks playing with a heavy basket on wheels managed to send it down the aisle just in time to knock Field down. The clerks were struck dumb with horror. But Field's only comment was, "Boys, don't forget to be gentlemen." Again, when he happened on four clerks who had organized an impromptu quartet during working hours, he remarked, "Sing it again, boys, but this time just a little softer." It was his custom to arrive every morning at nine o'clock. He rode only part of the way in his carriage; the last few blocks he covered on foot. No morning passed without his making a tour of the store, during which his sharp eye noted mistakes and commendable performances alike. After conferences with his department managers he repaired to the wholesale store, where a similar routine was repeated. This system enabled Field to spot talented executive material among his employees.

The career of John G. Shedd is a case in point. As a clerk in the women's neckwear section, Shedd attracted Field's attention and approval through a method he worked out for keeping track of sales by sizes so that the store's buyers would have an accurate basis for their purchases. The method, when tried out, was a success, and Shedd advanced rapidly.

A man who worked his way up from office boy at Field's was Harry Gordon Selfridge, who later became a merchant prince in his own right in London. Selfridge, known as "Mile-a-Minute Harry," was a fountain of imaginative ideas. As general manager of the retail store, he hired a window-display genius named Arthur Frazer away from a store in Creston, Iowa, and Field's show windows became famous. Selfridge lit up the merchandise displays with more and more electric globes. He tripled the number of telephones, and today the store handles more than a million customer calls a year. He ripped out counters and piled up piece goods on tables in the middle of the first floor so that customers could paw through them. At his urging Field increased the newspaper advertising budget, but advertising in Sunday newspapers was forbidden. Selfridge himself wrote a good share of the advertising copy; it was exuberant and eye-catching but also completely honest. Basement merchandise was described as "trustworthy" and "less expensive but reliable," out of deference to the store's more conservative partners, who shuddered at such words as "cheap" or "lower priced." Field's sold in the basement as early as 1868, but it was Selfridge who made it a bargain center. Eventually the basement, which grew to be the largest single salesroom in the world, was known as the "Budget Floor."

It was Selfridge, too, who persuaded Field to open a tearoom on the third floor, arguing that many women cut short their shopping to go home or elsewhere for lunch. Customers were quick to appreciate this new convenience. In a year the tearoom was serving as many as fifteen hundred each day. Today Field's entire seventh floor is devoted to five restaurants—the Walnut Room, the Narcissus Room, the English Room, a cafeteria called the Crystal Buffet and the Veranda ($1.50 in advance, limited menu, no tipping). Field's menus still include such specialties as the chicken pot pie featured on the opening day, back in 1890.

Selfridge took advantage of the Chicago World's Fair of 1893 to lure the Infanta Eulalia of Spain and other visitors from all over the world into Field's. At this time an admirer wrote a poem in honor of Field's, calling it "Cathedral of All the Stores." A Wabash Avenue addition to the store was completed that year. Later a new twelve-story building was erected north of the original store and spread over the remainder of the block to Randolph Street.

In 1904, Selfridge left Field's to run another store briefly in Chicago and to make and lose two fortunes in London before his death there in 1947. An earlier alumnus of Field's, a $23.08-a-fortnight salesman named Montgomery Ward, by this time had founded the great mail-order house bearing his name. More recently, the late Fred Harvey, once a Field's basement merchandiser, built the biggest store in Nashville, Tennessee, while the late Hector Escobosa and Egil E. Krogh, executives of a Field's subsidiary, became respectively president of I. Magnin & Co. in California and Sibley, Lindsay & Curr in Rochester, New York. The influence of Field's has been felt throughout retailing.

Marshall Field, the founder, outlived most of his early associates. Golf was his only recreation. On New Year's Day of

1906, he played in the snow, using red balls, with his nephew, Stanley Field; an employee, James Simpson; and Robert Todd Lincoln, the Pullman executive who was the surviving son of the Civil War President. The seventy-year-old merchant caught cold but insisted on making a trip to New York as planned. He developed pneumonia and died there on January 16, leaving an estate of $120 million. His last months had been brightened by a second marriage and shadowed by the mysterious fatal shooting of his son, Marshall Field II, officially termed an accident but later believed suicide. The merchant's funeral was attended by three thousand store employees. One of these, Pierre Funck, a veteran of forty-three years who had been left a pension, was so affected that he made a daily pilgrimage to the Field grave and soon died himself, apparently of grief.

The store remained as Marshall Field's monument. His grandson and great-grandson of the same name served on its board of directors as did his nephew, Stanley Field, until his death in 1964, but no member of the family has ever run it and the estate's interest has shrunk through the years. Executors of the estate of the fourth Marshall Field, who died September 18, 1965, sold 126,000 of his 177,000 shares at $51.50 a share in 1966 on the Midwest Stock Exchange for a total of $6,498,000.[6]

John Shedd, stepping into Field's shoes as president, took over by tearing down the original store and building a new one. The thirty-five acres of selling space in the main store were divided into more than 150 retail sections; a fabulous dome of multicolored Favrile glass, the biggest glass mosaic in existence, was designed by Louis Comfort Tiffany for the light well; a Belgian sculptor was commissioned to develop the central theme of the opening, the contribution of merchants to civilization. A few years later Field's leased the one remaining corner of the square block, that at Randolph and Wabash, and constructed there a twelve-story building to match the rest. And in 1914 the firm, spreading across the street, put up a twenty-one-story structure to house its famous Store for Men.

Two extraordinary doormen, first Eddie Anderson and then

Charles Pritzlaff, the latter a former coachman, greeted Field's carriage-trade customers by name at the Washington Street entrance for years. Charley in particular made a point of jotting down names and other pertinent details in a notebook. Among the famous names in Charley's book were those of Mrs. Potter Palmer, Grover Cleveland and Theodore Roosevelt, Prince Henry of Prussia, Mrs. William McKinley, who came to Field's for her inaugural gown, and Isadora Duncan, at that time an unknown dancer.

Out of the services of these doormen developed Field's personal shopping service and the personal information service desk on the third floor, where courteous experts answer questions about Field's and Chicago, translate for those speaking foreign tongues, find hotel rooms, arrange sight-seeing tours or just take messages.

The shopping service started one morning when the doorman found a note on the Washington Street door, placed there before opening time and ordering a pair of baby shoes and a spool of thread. A LaSalle Street broker had thought up this effortless method of carrying out the shopping errands assigned to him by his wife. The doorman took care of the order himself, and when the broker's coach turned up again in the afternoon the package was ready and waiting. Evidently the broker spread the glad tidings among the other husbands, because from then on similar notes appeared with increasing frequency.[7]

The personal shopping service, with a staff of twenty-five shoppers, averages more than two thousand purchases a day for customers with problems. Often they are complicated problems. There was the Milwaukee woman, for instance, who was going to spend Christmas in Europe and thought it would be nice to take a present for each member of her husband's family. The list of relatives turned out to be forty-seven names long and time was alarmingly short. Then the woman thought of Field's. She turned the list over to the personal shopping service, with a description of each of the forty-seven relatives, and when she boarded her ship in New York there were the forty-seven gifts, each labeled and ready for presentation.

All executives have made a great point of public service at Field's. During World War I the store was the headquarters for Red Cross and Liberty Loan drives; and when the steamer *Eastland* capsized in the Chicago River in 1915 with a toll of 812 lives, the survivors were supplied with clothes and other necessities by Field's, and the store's employees worked all night making stretchers to carry the victims on Field trucks to a temporary morgue.

When Shedd retired in 1923, his place was taken by James Simpson, who had started out as an office boy at Field's. In an effort to pump new life into the wholesale part of the business, Simpson built the huge $28-million Merchandise Mart. It was the largest commercial building in the world. Half the space was to be occupied by Field's wholesale and manufacturing divisions, and the rest was to be leased out to jobbers' representatives and manufacturers' agents. But depression was gripping the entire country, there was a dearth of tenants for the Mart and the wholesale division kept on sinking. Even the retail store, for the only time in its history, lost money in 1932.

A. T. Stewart, John Wanamaker and Macy's years earlier had built up big manufacturing and wholesale operations only to abandon or reduce them. "Manufacturing is quite another business," explained Wanamaker once, "and a man had better attend to the business he knows." But because Field's wholesale trade had once been highly profitable, Simpson, by then the principal stockholder, and others clung to it.

His successor, John McKinlay, who rose from cashboy to president of the store, struggled with the growing losses. Simpson, who was board chairman, could help but little. Chicago banks had given him the even greater task of salvaging something from the wreckage of the Samuel Insull utility empire. Year after year, retail earnings were almost wiped out by wholesale losses.

In 1935, James O. McKinsey, a management consultant,

was called in by the directors. Once professor of accounting and marketing at the University of Chicago and a founder of the management-consulting firm bearing his name, he had improved the workings of several companies. Pointing out that the whole-sale division had lost $12 million in five years, he recommended that the losing operations be lopped off. He was put in as chair-man, the first time an outsider had such a job at Field's. McKin-lay resigned.

In what came to be called "McKinsey's purge," domestic jobbing and eight hundred wholesale employees were dropped. Manufacturing operations were streamlined. But McKinsey was unfamiliar with retailing and Field traditions. When cotton and wool went down instead of up after he had made heavy pur-chases for the manufacturing division, he found himself in hot water with the directors. He died in 1937, a victim of worry and work as well as pneumonia. While it took more than a decade, virtually all of his recommendations were carried out, and employees who once derided McKinsey came to speak of him with respect. Frederick D. Corley, the president, became executive officer and continued in charge until retirement in 1943.

Hughston M. McBain, once an office boy for John Shedd and a Field's man since 1922, then became president. He was only forty but had had experience in every part of the business. At the same time, James L. Palmer, a native of Maine and a graduate of Brown University, became first vice president and second in command. Palmer had come to Field's in 1937 from the University of Chicago, where he was professor of marketing. He also had been an adviser to Sears, Roebuck and Co. and a number of other firms. The two worked as a team to regain Field's profits and prestige.[8]

One step was the opening of the "28 Shop," so called because of the 28 Washington Street address, the old carriage entrance of the store. It is reached by a private elevator, and there are facilities for serving lunch or tea. Here, in a luxurious setting of carpeting, hand-woven draperies and subtle lights, today's equivalent of the carriage trade views and buys clothes ranging from simple daytime clothes and accessories to fabulous imports.

McBain and Palmer redecorated notable old departments, such as the Store for Men and the book department. Built by Marcella Hahner and Rose Oller Harbaugh, the latter division pioneered book fairs and autographing parties in the department stores and has assured the success of many a book. Though its volume is not as great as that of the Doubleday or Brentano stores, its sales often have run more than a million dollars a year and it vies with Macy's for the honor of being the biggest in the department-store world.

McBain and Palmer modernized employee training. The store's girl elevator operators, who once included Dorothy Lamour, later of the movies, were sent to charm school, beginning in 1947. Instruction manuals, little changed since the days of the founder and John Shedd, were revised. A film on employee courtesy, titled *By Jupiter*, proved so successful that prints were sold to other stores.

Public relations also received attention. A research firm was employed to determine what the customers thought of the store. Advertising and promotion were expanded. In local newspapers, a new "newspaper within a newspaper," called *Pace*, proved an effective vehicle for institutional advertising. In 1952, Field's centennial was publicized nationally. A matchbook promoting the 28 Shop received a 1953 award as the most distinguished example of that form of advertising in the department-store field.

The innovations combined to achieve an operation more profitable than many larger companies in the department-store field and enabled the store to solve long-standing financial problems. Rent was eliminated by the purchase of the store site from the Field estate. Half of the preferred stock was retired. Finally in 1946, the Merchandise Mart, a white elephant for most of its existence, was sold to Joseph P. Kennedy for $18 million. It was a good deal for both parties. The loss that Field's took materially cut the taxes that otherwise would have been paid in that prosperous year. In 1949, McBain and Palmer became respectively chairman and president. In 1953, Fieldcrest Mills, the last of the firm's textile-manufacturing interests, was sold and McBain that year received the Tobé award.

These transactions made available millions of dollars for expansion. Field's established suburban branches at Lake Forest and Evanston in 1928 and another at Oak Park in 1929. These were modernized and enlarged following World War II. More branches were built beginning in 1954.

Chairman McBain retired in 1958 and was succeeded as chief executive officer by President Palmer. On reaching retirement age in 1964, Palmer was succeeded by Executive Vice President Sivage, general manager of the Chicago stores and a Field man since 1931. David W. Davidson succeeded him and Harry D. Perkins succeeded Davidson as senior vice president. As of 1973, the company had around fifteen thousand full-time employees and approximately eighteen thousand stockholders.

One of the most important ventures in the history of Field's was the purchase for about $6 million of Frederick & Nelson, Seattle's largest department store. This was founded in 1890 by Donald E. Frederick, son of a Georgia farmer, and Nels Nelson, a Swedish immigrant. The store prospered during the gold rush to Alaska and a new store modeled somewhat on Field's was built in 1918. Nels Nelson died at sea and by 1929 Frederick, then seventy, was ready to retire.

An admirer of Field's, which he often visited with his daughter, Frederick called at President Simpson's office. Finding him absent, the Seattle merchant picked up an envelope and wrote on the flap: "I will sell my business to Marshall Field & Company and to them only." The purchase was concluded on July 25, 1929. The staff was almost undisturbed, with only Treasurer Thomas Lewis going out from Chicago.

William H. St. Clair, a Frederick & Nelson man, became president, and was succeeded by Charles C. Bunker and then William S. Street, a native Californian who for some years was general manager at Field's. He retired in 1962 and was succeeded by Cornelius J. Byrne. Sales, which had been $12 million in

1929 and dropped to half that in the depression, rose to more than $30 million after World War II. Five additional floors were added to the main store at a cost of $6,250,000, increasing the space 50 percent. Later, an adjoining parking garage costing $3,250,000 was constructed. John Graham & Co., Seattle, were architects for the main store addition and also the branches in Bellevue Square and Aurora Village.

Frederick & Nelson's follows Field's customer-pleasing policies. Mrs. Kathryn Kavanaugh of Seattle, for example, made a trip to Eire and photographed her relatives and Irish scenes in color. On her return, she took the films to Frederick & Nelson to be developed. Somebody lost them. To keep her good will, the store had her list and describe the pictures, then commissioned Joseph Hollander, London photographer for the Fairchild News Service, to retrace Mrs. Kavanaugh's journey and duplicate her pictures.

IX

Brentano's

"Booksellers to the World"

Brentano's, Inc., is one of the oldest and most respected names in bookselling. With 31,000 square feet of selling space and 250,000 volumes, its Fifth Avenue headquarters is New York City's largest bookstore. In the United States the only larger bookstores are the Cokesbury store in Dallas, 66,000 square feet, and Kroch's & Brentano's in Chicago, a former affiliate, with 40,000 square feet. There is a Brentano's in Paris, no longer part of the firm, and a score of branches stretching from Boston to San Francisco, and including the Pentagon in the District of Columbia, which are owned by the firm.

The Crowell-Collier Publishing Company (now legally called Macmillan, Inc.) in 1962 paid "less than a million in cash" for Brentano's in the course of an acquisition program that added the Macmillan Company, Berlitz Schools of Languages, G. Schirmer, Inc., Gump's, the San Francisco jewelry store, and other firms to the publishing empire. As Brentano's then had sales of less than $4 million, some Crowell-Collier stockholders were critical of the purchase at their next meeting.[1]

But under Robert G. Luckie, Jr. the urbane current president; Leonard Schwartz, who headed the operation for the first seven years of the new ownership; and some executives in between, Brentano's has enjoyed a remarkable revival and expansion as an autonomous subsidiary of its big parent. Sales soared past $15 million and with the renewed interest in books and more branch stores seem destined to go higher.

The Fifth Avenue store, which had been shrunk for economy

under the previous ownership, was expanded upward, downward and laterally and now has entrances also on both West Forty-seventh and West Forty-eighth Streets. It and all of its branches became specialty stores of the arts, selling original graphics, museum sculpture replicas, jewelry, unique handcrafted objects from around the world and adult games as well as books. Among the first booksellers to recognize that the market for books was no longer limited to an economic elite, Brentano's has steadily expanded its paperback book department; today its stores stock more paperback titles than most paperback specialty stores.

In 1965, Brentano's embarked on a major expansion program, opening a new store in Hartford, Connecticut, and another in Boston's Prudential Plaza, as well as doubling the size of its Fifth Avenue store and of suburban stores in Short Hills and Paramus, New Jersey. A two-level store was opened in New York's Greenwich Village, not far from where the company was founded in 1853 as a hotel newsstand. The main Washington store was moved to larger quarters in the National Press Building, tripling in size with the move. In 1969, Brentano's replaced its long-time department in the City of Paris department store in San Francisco with a full Brentano's store on Sutter Street.

All the progress was not smooth. Computerization of the firm's 145,000 accounts, 30,000 of them active, proved a serious problem. It was solved eventually by doing away with personal accounts and asking these customers to use credit cards. American Express, Diner's Club, BankAmericard and all major cards were accepted. Company accounts were continued. From this situation, Luckie emerged as general manager in 1969 and president in 1970. The son of a Navy captain, he had been a Brentano customer in Washington as a boy and had become a Crowell-Collier Macmillan executive by way of the Harvard Business School and Standard Oil of New Jersey.

There are now twenty-two stores in the Brentano's group, three of them opened since the fall of 1970 under the direction of President Luckie. Brentano's stores are grouped in the New York and Washington, D.C., areas and in Boston, Hartford and

San Francisco. New stores were opened in Beverly Hills, San Rafael, Woodland Hills, and Costa Mesa, California; Chevy Chase, Maryland; Queens Center and Massapequa, Long Island; and Atlanta, Georgia.

While firmly maintaining its reputation as a leading retailer of books—it sold more than sixty thousand hardcover copies of Richard Bach's *Jonathan Livingston Seagull,* a Macmillan title —Brentano's in recent years has added sophisticated new lines of merchandise not generally available. In the process, it has initiated some trends and given strong impetus to others. It was the first major retailer to revive kite flying when, in 1969, it opened departments devoted to unusual kites from around the world. It was the first major retailer to establish a "Mysterum" devoted to books and objects relating to the occult. In 1971, before American Indian jewelry and crafts were considered elegant, Brentano's opened American Indian shops in a number of its stores.

The firm owes its success to a combination of nostalgic friendliness, reminiscent of the tiny bookshop, and shrewd operation. New books cost less in quantity, the difference between 40 and 45 percent or more, a margin that may mean profit or loss to a store. Hardheaded Brentano buyers order the quantity their intuition tells them is the optimum. By correctly estimated original orders, Brentano's usually enjoys maximum discounts. At the same time, clerks and branch managers know the tastes of many customers so well that books are sent them unordered and returns are few. Unlike the majority of booksellers, many Brentano's stores are managed by women and its hardcover book buyer and vice president is a woman, Mrs. Lillian Friedman.

Celebrities have always been among Brentano's shoppers and visitors, from the day Admiral George Dewey, the hero of Manila, caused a near-riot at the New York store in 1901, through the crush in both the Fifth Avenue and San Francisco stores in 1970, when the late Maurice Chevalier held autographing sessions. The Fifth Avenue store has been patronized by the former King of Greece and the late Duke of Windsor and shoppers have found themselves browsing with Mrs. Aristotle Onassis.

The Beverly-Wilshire store, opened in 1972, counts Cary Grant, Irving Stone, Irving Wallace and Tom Smothers among its customers.

Every President since Theodore Roosevelt has been a customer of Brentano's F Street store and other branches in the Washington area. When Eisenhower's Cabinet wanted to give him a lasting gift, they came to Brentano's and selected a large assortment of Skira art books and had the store bind them in leather.

Through the years, Brentano's has managed to create about itself a blend of the romance and knowledge that its customers seek in the books it sells. It has maintained this despite fire, flood, book clubs, bankruptcy and inroads on the time of the human race by motion pictures, automobiles, radio and television.

The business was founded by an immigrant news vendor shrewd enough to supply sporting news ahead of his competitors. Young and ambitious August Brentano was newly arrived from Austria in 1853 when he set up a newsstand in front of the New York Hotel. Newspapers at that time usually were peddled from door to door, but the hotelkeeper allowed Brentano his space because he was handicapped by a withered arm.

Observing that the hotel guests were betting on the great English horse races, Brentano ordered newspapers from England and met the clipper ships bringing them to dockside. The Atlantic cable was still in the future and Brentano's newspapers made him first with the racing news. He prospered and moved his stand to a hallway of the old Revere House, at Broadway and Houston Street. Above the table, which offered books as well as papers, he had an imposing sign reading "Brentano's Literary Emporium."

The John Heenan–Tom Sayers prizefight in England, in which an American and an Englishman fought a bloody thirty-seven-round draw for the heavyweight championship in 1860, aroused so much interest that young Brentano sold bundles of papers at a dollar apiece, and became rich enough to open a real emporium. His store was a basement at first; seven years later it took up half the building at 708 Broadway.

Brentano's, because it catered to a cosmopolitan patronage and offered foreign books and periodicals, became a rendezvous for the fashionable hotel guests from across the street, and for the carriage trade from all over the city. By 1870, when August moved his store to 33 Union Square, next door to the Goelet mansion and just down the block from Tiffany's, Brentano's was already one of New York's landmarks. Sightseers came to gape at the browsers, who included Ralph Waldo Emerson, James Russell Lowell, Lillian Russell, John Drew, U. S. Grant and other important customers.

August created a successful business. His nephew, Arthur, who started in the store in 1873 and sold books from the floor for seventy-one years, made Brentano's an institution. He was fifteen years old at the time he first set foot in the store. A cholera epidemic in Cincinnati had killed his father, a sister and brother. His mother moved with the remaining six children to Evansville, Indiana, where she had two brothers, and soon thereafter Arthur was sent to his uncle in New York to earn his fortune.

His first job was a paper route for the store, from Broadway to the East River. Later, because he did so well at it, he was rewarded with a route that reached to Central Park. He delivered papers morning and evening; during the day he sorted books and also delivered them, becoming so familiar with the stock that he was consulted by the customers in preference to the senior salesmen.

A few years after Arthur's arrival at the store, his younger brothers, Simon and August Brentano, came from Evansville and were taken into the business. The store was open seven days a week, 9 A.M. to 8 P.M. All worked hard. In 1882, the three brothers bought out their uncle. August, Sr., by then an elderly man, wanted to retire and make a tour of the world. After extensive farewells, he got as far as Montreal, when nostalgia brought him back to the Union Square store. Until his death in 1886, he remained there, working at the cashier's desk.

Meanwhile, in 1884 Brentano's opened a Washington branch; and in 1887 Arthur went to Paris to open another branch. Three years later, in Paris, he married a California girl, Maria Louise Sepulveda Lan Franco. His best man was Robert W. Chambers, the novelist, and another friend at the ceremony was Whitelaw Reid, publisher of the New York *Tribune* and United States ambassador to the Court of St. James's.

Financial difficulties afflicted Brentano's after the great business depression of 1893. Another disaster occurred in 1898. The Union Square establishment and all its stock were destroyed by a fire that started in the house next door, and the store had to be rebuilt. To straighten out their finances at this crisis, Simon Brentano sued his two brothers for dissolution of the partnership, and in 1899 the firm was reorganized. Simon became president. Charles E. Butler, president of the American Booksellers Association, who represented the publishers' interests in working out credit, became secretary; and Clive Mecklim, a veteran employee, was made treasurer.

Arthur, who hated office work, fled from financial statements and wanted to stay with his books, was named vice president. Arthur had never attended high school, a fact that embarrassed him all his life. "I don't know a scrap of Latin or Greek," he once admitted, "and for more than sixty years I have been in perpetual fear of being exposed." He learned French and German fluently, however, and through the books he handled gave himself a remarkable education. His courtly manners, his impeccable appearance—he always wore a navy-blue suit, starched collar, dark tie and pince-nez—and his considerable knowledge made him a great favorite with the customers; indeed, in the store he became the good friend of many eminent men and women in art, politics and society.

He inaugurated the old and rare books department, which became his special pride. As well as collecting fine old books of great value, the store was also offering a service at that time unique among bookstores—scouring the market to locate any publication requested, no matter when and where published, including privately printed pamphlets, books and periodicals in foreign languages, first editions, out-of-print and other rare items. This service brought Brentano's orders from all over the world and gave it international importance in the book world.

Arthur Brentano once listed the two things that he liked most about his business: "Getting a nice library . . . good, solid, useable, permanent books," and "Making a good sale—getting those good, solid, useable, permanent books into the hands of an appreciative buyer." Arthur's idea of hospitality—that each customer should be greeted at the door and made welcome—was followed as long as he was alive.

A reporter for *Publishers Weekly*, who interviewed this gentleman when he was eighty, remarked that Arthur Brentano was always at the door. For years the reporter had been visiting the store and talking to him without realizing it. "Brentano," he wrote, "had been as gracious, as friendly, as urbane, as kindly, as communicative when I bought nothing as if I were negotiating for the four Shakespeare folios."

Salesclerks hired by Arthur Brentano were carefully selected and instructed by him to maintain the store's tradition of boundless erudition and limitless, unhurried service. Laurence Gomme, long head of the old and rare books department, recalled that when he arrived from England in 1907 and applied for a job, Arthur subjected him to a lengthy test of his knowledge, manners and grooming, then hired him at $12 a week. It was considered a rare privilege to work for Brentano's.

In 1907, Brentano's, keeping up with the fashionable trend, moved again, this time to Twenty-seventh Street and Fifth Avenue. In this new headquarters, a great deal of literary history was made. "I can remember the wonderful store they had down there," recalled Bennett Cerf, the publisher, years later in the *Saturday Review*.[2] "There were originals of all the magazine covers in the side-street windows and the huge pile of periodicals from all over the world in the basement! Theodore Roosevelt came in one day and ordered the pigskin library that he took with him to Africa. The store had an indescribable glamour; the staff harbored some rare and congenial personalities." Mayor William Jay Gaynor of New York, Andrew Carnegie, J. P. Morgan, Henry Clay Frick, George Ade, Oliver Herford and other celebrities of the period congregated at the Twenty-seventh Street store. There an autographing party for Gertrude Stein was mobbed by her readers and nonreaders. The firm discontinued the sale of sheet music, newspapers and theater tickets, but there were more books and magazines. Displays of art work for the covers of these by Charles Dana Gibson, James Montgomery Flagg, Maxfield Parrish and others attracted a daily crowd.

When Simon Brentano died in 1914, Arthur became president. The sons of these brothers—Lowell and Arthur Brentano, Jr.— joined the business. Since the elder Brentano continued to avoid administrative details and devoted himself to rare books, his son worked at retailing, store management and the development of branches. It was a period of expansion for the firm. Additional New York branches were established, and stores followed in Pittsburgh, Cleveland and Philadelphia.

An author and playwright himself, Lowell Brentano in 1918 took charge of the firm's publishing department after his graduation from Harvard, where he attained Phi Beta Kappa despite a serious congenital hearing defect. This part of the business previously had been directed by Volney Streamer and Temple Scott. From 1879 to 1881, Brentano's published a magazine of field and water sports; from 1881 to 1882 it issued a chess monthly. In place of catalogs, announcements and a monthly bulletin previously supplied to its customers, the store in 1907 started *Book Chat*, advertised as "a periodical which should be chained to the desk of every man in search of literary information." The subscription was first twenty-five cents, then a dollar a year. *Book Chat* offered news about books and authors, notes written by prominent authors, answers to queries, scholarly information about old and rare books and manuscripts offered for sale at Brentano's; and, of course, announcements of the new books—including those in Spanish, Italian, German and French —which Brentano's stocked. South American literature and foreign Christmas cards also were advertised.

At the same time Brentano's published noteworthy books. It was the first to print the plays of George Bernard Shaw in America, and the letters in the company's files attest to the fact that even then Shaw was a vigorous and unorthodox correspondent. Other Brentano authors included George Moore, Margaret Sanger, whose books on birth control were the subject of violent controversy, David Loth, Robert Briffault, Eugène Brieux and Channing Pollock.

The Brentano family once went to meet the unpredictable Shaw when he landed in New York. An elaborate program was planned but the great dramatist remained only a few hours and sailed home the next day. Later in London, Arthur Brentano one day rushed in to his daughter, Rowena, and said, "Come, Lambie, it's time for lunch with Mr. Shaw." Rowena replied, "Papa, I'd rather stay here and knit if I may."

All Brentano departments were profitable as the main store moved northward again in 1926 to its present location. The new store, a journalist noted, had the "same admirable features" as the old with "The varied and enormous stock, the easily accessible galleries, comprehensive foreign department administered by clerks who understand the languages of the literature to which they are accredited, and the fascinating display of periodicals on the tables of the basement." The Bible was stocked in several versions and a dozen languages. There were thousands of technical books.

Books of its own authors sold well and those by Sinclair Lewis, F. Scott Fitzgerald and Anita Loos went by thousands to the customers. American tourists going to Europe read books from Brentano's in New York on the way over and from Brentano's store in Paris on the way back. In 1928, Arthur Brentano, Jr., told the convention of the American Booksellers'

Association that the store had delivered as many as twenty thousand books to one liner. The firm's sales were more than $3 million a year.

The stock-market crashed the next year, and the book business was hit hard. With a huge inventory of expensive books, several new branches and a big new main store, Brentano's was in serious financial trouble. Because it was one of the largest retail outlets for books in the world, publishers could not afford to see it go out of business. A publishers' committee took over the management.

Salaries were cut drastically, in some cases to as low as $7 and $12 a week, but employees continued loyally at their jobs. The American rights to the plays of George Bernard Shaw were sold to Dodd, Mead & Company. The remainder of the Brentano book-publishing department went to Coward–McCann. At this point, Lowell Brentano left the firm, except for an interest in the Paris branch, and devoted himself successfully to his own writing. He lived until 1950, turning out plays, novels, motion-picture scenarios, anthologies and a final book, *Ways to Better Hearing*, inspired by his own lifelong struggle against deafness.

As the depression deepened, the business shrank further. All outlets except the main store in New York and the branches in Washington, Chicago and Paris were discontinued. But even these economies were not enough. After the "bank holiday" in 1933, Brentano's was bankrupt. The Irving Trust Company was named receiver.

A savior appeared in the person of a wealthy Brentano customer, Stanton Griffis, a partner in the investment banking firm of Hemphill Noyes & Co. and a man of many interests. He was chairman of the executive committee of Paramount Pictures and the Lee Tire & Rubber Co., and a director of Madison Square Garden. He had backed some Katharine Cornell stage productions and reorganized many corporations. He heard of the plight of Brentano's in the course of a bridge game on his yacht and promised to help. "I thought it would be amusing," he explained later, "to see what a hard-headed businessman could do in such a situation with a famous name like Brentano's as an asset."

On June 4, 1933, Griffis paid $150,000, only $72,000 of it in cash, for nearly all of the firm's assets. It had grossed $1,500,000 the previous year, listed assets at $745,983 and liabilities at $511,445. Three-year notes were signed for the remainder and book publishers assured Griffis liberal credit. He was joined in the purchase by Adolph Kroch, a leading Chicago bookseller, who acquired a 20 percent interest. After three years, Kroch was given the Chicago branch and bought out in New York. Merged later in larger quarters on South Wabash Street, Kroch's & Brentano's advertises as "the world's largest bookstore."[3]

Griffis became chairman of the board of Brentano's Inc., as the new firm was titled. The courtly Arthur Brentano continued as president until his death in 1944 and his son, Arthur, Jr., remained as vice president and general manager. Some of Griffis' bookish Wall Street friends, Amos Tuck French, Winky Thomas and Bruce Ryan among them, came to work in the store for a time but Griffis himself remained so much in the background that fifteen years later a noted Broadway columnist breathlessly printed, "Has Stanton Griffis purchased the Brentano bookstores?"

While Griffis had counseled his friend Arthur Brentano, Sr., against expanding earlier, when the financier took charge he believed on the basis of business trends that a chain of bookstores could be run something like the A & P or even Woolworth's, and that bookselling could profit from an application of large-scale merchandising. This reasoning seemed valid for a time. Under his regime, the business quickly began to improve. Thousands bought *Anthony Adverse* and *Gone with the Wind,* the heavyweight historical romances that were the best sellers of the depression. "Best sellers are the vitamins of the book business," explained Joseph Margolies, formerly Washington manager who then became vice president and chief buyer. "They bring in the customers who buy not only the best seller but a classic like *David Copperfield* for a niece or nephew."

Griffis amazed his publisher creditors by paying their notes after only six months, giving them a 35 percent return on their claims against the old company. The firm earned profits in 1937, operated at a deficit of $16,918 in 1938 and from the next year onward had profits through World War II.

A branch was reopened in Philadelphia. More branches were opened in the Washington area, including one on the concourse of the Pentagon Building. Under the management of Mrs. Virginia Ward, it soon numbered the highest military brass as customers. A leased department established in the City of Paris store in San Francisco became the largest bookstore west of Denver. Lillian Friedman, now a vice president, was promoted from there to be chief buyer for the firm. Several other branches were opened, including one at Waikiki Beach, Hawaii, to which Horace Hutchins was dispatched as manager after a hilarious hula-hula party.

World War II caused a boom in the book business. With gasoline rationed and television still in the future, many people read books to forget their worries. Brentano's sold twenty-eight thousand copies of Kathleen Winsor's *Forever Amber*. More bought books to help them qualify for commissions or to obtain jobs in war industry. Soaring taxes created a demand for the works of J. K. Lasser, Brentano's own tax adviser. Hundreds of copies of Professor Henry DeWolf Smyth's *Atomic Energy for Military Purposes* were sold. Governments bought books in quantity for instructional and propaganda purposes.

At the request of the Free French government, Brentano's returned profitably to publishing during the struggle. With French publishing plants in the hands of the enemy and the sale of their books banned in occupied countries, Brentano's produced paperback editions in French of the works of such writers as André Maurois, Pierre Lazareff and André Girard. These were shipped by the thousands to North Africa, the French colonies and via the underground into occupied France.

The Brentano branch in Paris, at 37 Avenue de l'Opéra and extending through to Rue des Petits Champs, felt the tramp of Nazi soldiery. As the Wehrmacht marched into the city in June

1940, the store executives, who were British subjects, fled by motorcycle and bicycle to the coast. The French employees remained until the Nazis took over. But first an official of a German library walked in and placed an order for six thousand books, including 349 assorted titles in Everyman's Library, a variety of art books, the unexpurgated *Lady Chatterley's Lover* and some expensive erotica. He paid 755,000 francs for his order and sent trucks to carry the books away.

After that the Nazis confiscated without payment all leather goods, stationery, fountain pens, guidebooks, dictionaries, encyclopedias, maps and atlases, and converted the premises into the official film and camera supply center for the Wehrmacht in Paris. The firm name on the windows was covered over with black paint; the fixtures and remaining stock were moved to the rear of the store and to the basement. In a period of almost five years, the converted photo shop, which was also a place where German soldiers could have their pictures taken or developed, made a profit of a million francs ($20,000). Deposited in a Paris agency and left behind when the Nazis departed hurriedly, that money was turned over to Brentano's by the French government after the liberation.

When Arthur Brentano, Jr., who became president of the firm at his father's death, reached Paris on March 15, 1945, he found that, along with hundreds of pictures of German soldiers, in the cluttered-up basement and rear of the store approximately a third of the previous stock remained—about twelve thousand books. The concierge and his wife, who lived on the premises all through the occupation, and the office secretary were also waiting for him. While they were all digging through the debris to clean up and refurbish the place, a truck arrived with a shipment of five hundred books; these had been ordered from London early in 1940, had been stored in a Paris warehouse during the German occupation and were now being delivered per order.

To determine prices in the new inflated currency, Brentano simply marked up each item 500 percent of its prewar price. That was in line with the inflated prices existing in other Parisian bookstores and also permitted the firm to buy books in France, where they were expensive, to restock the depleted shelves.

By great effort and much slashing of red tape, he managed to reopen the store on April 19, giving it the distinction of being the first American retail establishment in the city to resume business. The first customer on the day of reopening was an American sergeant who bought two Penguin books—*Walden* and *City of Beautiful Nonsense.* This Parisian shop, which since its beginning in the eighties has been a favorite meeting place for Americans traveling abroad, began to do a thriving business with European customers, too, filling the great demand for American technical books useful in rebuilding war-devastated areas.

Sales volume of Brentano's passed $4 million in the years following the war, but profits dropped and some branches failed to develop enough volume to sustain themselves. Beginning in 1948, the firm operated at a loss for three years. By this time the versatile Stanton Griffis was far away. During the war, he had embraced a chance to make history as well as sell books about it. He headed government missions to England, Finland, Spain, Portugal and Sweden, in the last stopping the export of vital ball bearings to Germany. He served as Red Cross Commissioner in the Pacific. He then became successively ambassador to Poland, Egypt, Argentina and Spain.

He wrote of Brentano's and bookselling as well as diplomacy, in an autobiographical volume, *Lying in State,* published on his return from Spain in 1952.[4] Among difficulties besetting a bookseller, he listed: the book clubs, which sell some current books at lower prices than the wholesaler can buy them; and the department-store "loss leader," a method of attracting customers into the store by selling items such as books below cost. These practices, Griffis charged, have been promoted by publishers. "In no other industry," he said, "does the manufacturer go to such lengths and use such vicious means to destroy his outlets." In the old days, he related, bright young intellectuals found the satisfaction of working in a bookstore to be payment enough, and so they worked for very little. At present, the unions "tell us what we should pay everyone in the business from the shipping clerk to the buyer." Years earlier, incidentally, Arthur Brentano and some other booksellers had protested against the book clubs by refusing to sell the early selections of the Literary Guild. The gesture was abandoned when it was found that its only effect was to deprive the stores of more sales. Brentano's now accepts book clubs as a fact of life and recognize that they give great exposure to books.

His investment in Brentano's, Griffis said, had brought him fun rather than cash. "I would spend sleepless nights of horror if I heard that any customer of Brentano's felt that we had made a profit on his purchase," he wrote. "We are in trade only for dignity, atmosphere and service." And to make this point even more emphatic, he added, "I am happy to have had the experience of high hopes and failure in the retail bookselling business."

But even as the diplomat wrote, his son, Nixon Griffis, was making the century-old enterprise again a profitable one. Like his father, Nixon was a graduate of Cornell University, where he studied astronomy and became a boxing champion. After Army service and work at Hemphill Noyes, he joined Brentano's in 1947 as secretary of the firm. In 1949, he became president and the next year, on the retirement of Arthur Brentano, Jr., became chairman of the board as well. Young Griffis was then thirty-two. Leonard Schwartz, who had been with the firm since 1937 except for war service, became vice president.

The changes involved both expenditures and economies. The Paris branch was modernized. At a cost of $100,000, the main New York store was refurbished and rearranged. The Waikiki Beach branch was sold and Horace Hutchins returned to take charge in Philadelphia. Several branches were closed. Machine bookkeeping replaced a hand ledger system with a reduction in cost and a gain in efficiency. Modern window displays were introduced.

Branches established for a time on the *Independence* and *Con-*

stitution, new liners of the American Export Line sailing to the Mediterranean, proved reasonably profitable and tremendously successful from a Brentano's morale point of view. The floating branches and libraries were managed each cruise by a manager or employee who had done an outstanding job in New York or Washington. Many cruise passengers, however, felt that their passage should include free library service, as it did on many liners, and the free voyages to Naples, Capri, Sorrento, Genoa and the Riviera came to an end.

Efforts were made to find merchandise that could be sold along with the books, magazines and stationery that are the backbone of the business. Sophisticated greeting cards by artists like Rosalind Welcher proved successful. So did games like Scrabble, which Brentano's discovered early; many purchasers were found for a $15 toy planetarium, though 16-millimeter films, rare postage stamps and seashells did not work out. In the latter case, however, timing was the critical factor. In the winter of 1969, an Art in Nature Boutique comprising shells, butterflies and minerals was a resounding success. Reproductions of museum sculpture were also very successful. Prior to their presentation by Brentano's, these museum replicas, in most cases, had been available only in those museums owning the Aphrodites, Han Dynasty horses and Egyptian Sacred Cats. This effort was pioneered by Leonard Schwartz.

In 1953, Brentano's centennial year, which passed without any special celebration, it all added up to give the venerable enterprise a modest profit on sales of $2,823,326. This was roughly a million dollars more than the volume from many more outlets a decade earlier. The unique commerce between Brentano's far-flung customers and its erudite employees continued.

Customers of Brentano's include the famous, the learned and the eccentric. Most notable of all, perhaps, was twenty-three-year-old Dorothy Arnold, daughter of a millionaire. On December 12, 1910, she bought a novel from Ernest Dell, a salesman in the New York Brentano store. She then stepped out into the Fifth Avenue traffic and was never heard from again. Her family exhausted its fortune seeking her and the case remains New York's leading unsolved mystery.

Many of Brentano's customers have been the subject of books. Others have chosen to launch their own books at the store. During a one-month period, Brentano's was host, at a series of after-hours parties, to a crush of Beautiful People toasting Gloria Vanderbilt on the publication of her book on collage, to a mixed bag of celebrities congratulating David Frost for his book *The Americans* and to a crowd that included such legendary personalities as Jack Dempsey and Joan Crawford there to mark the publication of the late Maurice Chevalier's autobiography. It was at the last of these that Hermione Gingold looked at the still bouncy and youthful eighty-two-year-old Frenchman, flipped her fur boa and said, "It does give one hope."

To customers from Allahabad to Zomba, Brentano's importance rests not only on the forty thousand titles it keeps in stock and on its long-standing ability to obtain others, but also on the fact that the United States for years after World War II was the only country where so many books were freely obtainable. Brentano's, as the best-known American bookseller, became a kind of literary United Nations.

The Brazilian government, for example, ordered $8,000 worth of books to be sent to its embassies all over the world. One of the books listed in the order was out of print, and Brazil wanted a thousand copies. So Macmillan, the publisher, printed a special edition at Brentano's request.

Unless asked to do so, Brentano's does not attempt to guide or improve a customer's taste. An order for "60 feet of white books" to fit the decorative scheme of a customer's new apartment was filled without comment largely with volumes from Italy, where publishers favor such bindings. Attempts of pressure groups to censor or prevent the sale of books usually are ignored by Brentano's, though titles likely to incite any important segment to riot are not displayed prominently.

Early in his career as a bookseller, Stanton Griffis refused to stock *The Truman Merry-Go-Round* by Robert Allen and William V. Shannon because it was critical of Griffis as an ambassador. Drew Pearson reported the fact and the book received more notice than it would have otherwise. Since then the policy has been: "Brentano's believes that the condemnation of any given book should be determined by the courts and the publishers themselves, and not by the booksellers." Friends of Senator Joseph McCarthy were ignored when they attempted to stop Brentano's selling copies of a Senate report on his financial affairs; so were his foes when they protested display of an admiring biography of him.

When the store gave a window to *The Frenchman* by Philippe Halsman, a French committee protested that the book was in bad taste and would give Americans "the wrong impression of Frenchmen." The author-photographer solved this problem by obtaining a letter from the French ambassador certifying that he found "the book delightful, in excellent taste, and fine for promoting good relations between the two countries." In the next printing, Simon and Schuster left out one of the more sexy photographs in the volume to be on the safe side.

While selling more copies of Rachel Carson's masterpiece *The Sea Around Us* than were initially printed, as well as hundreds of volumes of T. S. Eliot's plays, Brentano's also sold nine thousand copies of Dr. Alfred C. Kinsey's *Sexual Behavior in the Human Male*. Its female sequel, skimmed by countless magazine articles, was much less popular. Mention of this subject at Brentano's recalls two women customers. One with an accent asked a salesman to direct her to "Sex." He took her to the clerk in charge of the store's array of Havelock Ellis and similar volumes. Everybody was embarrassed. She wanted the store across the street, Saks Fifth Avenue. At another time, a woman shopper stopped a Brentano employee and asked, "Do you have *Fun in Bed?*" As he was the store detective and unfamiliar with the writings of Frank Scully, he politely replied, "I manage to get along."

Sometimes the courtesy of the Washington staff costs it a sale. One day the embassy of a new country telephoned frantically for a book on etiquette to be delivered within a matter of minutes. The distance was too great for this and the clerk asked discreetly what was the problem.

"Somebody left cards for the ambassador with **P.P.C.** written in the corner," said a desperate diplomatic voice.

"Oh," explained the all-knowing clerk, "that just stands for *pour prendre congé,* French for good-by."

"Thanks," gasped the relieved diplomat, "never mind the book."

While firm figures on retail book groups are elusive, trade sources believe Brentano's volume is ahead of that of the more numerous Doubleday stores but is probably less than that of the 120 Dayton-Hudson bookstores. Headed by Bruce G. Allbright, Jr., this has the Pickwick Bookshops in California and B. Dalton, Bookseller, stores in thirty-three states. The biggest book operation is the 300-unit Walden Book Company, since 1969 a subsidiary of Broadway-Hale.[5] It is named for Henry David Thoreau's Walden Pond, near which Lawrence W. Hoyt, the founder, grew up. Originally consisting of only leased departments, Walden stores now stretch from New England to Honolulu and have sales of $50 million a year. A new entry of a big book publisher in the retail field is that of McGraw-Hill, headed by Leonard Schwartz, the former president of Brentano's. It has stores in the McGraw-Hill Building in New York, in Princeton, New Jersey, and an unusual one in the Smithsonian Institution. Others are planned.[6]

X

R. H. Macy & Co., Inc.

The Straus Family and the World's Largest Store

Macy's, the world's largest store, in Manhattan's Herald Square, and the branch stores in its New York division rang up $4 million in sales one Saturday during the 1971 Christmas season, undoubtedly the highest day's volume in a metropolitan area by a department-store group up until that time. The store was in business eighty-six years before its first $1-million day in 1944, but only thirteen more years were required to reach a $2-million day, eight additional years to achieve a $3-million day and just six years to hit the new mark.

Since 1944, moreover, R. H. Macy & Co., Inc., the company that owns the New York store, has expanded from an organization of seven stores to a nationwide chain of sixty-eight in six regional divisions. In its fiscal year ended July 1972, Macy's became a billion-dollar corporation, compared with $542 million just ten years earlier. And during the same period, its earnings almost tripled to a record $27,952,000 from $9,793,000. During the next fiscal year, the company rang up sales of $1,133,479,000 and profits of $31,900,000.

This gigantic expansion of Macy's over the last three decades was led during most of these years by Jack I. Straus, whose family supplied chief executives of the company for four generations and who retired as chairman of the board in 1968. Other strong businessmen—like Donald B. Smiley, chairman and executive officer, and Herbert L. Seegal, president—have also helped push Macy's into its present position of retailing leadership. But perhaps the single most important fact in this success story is the remarkable relationship of Macy's and New York.

Macy's is the store that Manhattan built. To New York alone belong its polyglot, tolerant crowds, its competitive nervousness, its din, its reflex response to the customer. New Yorkers are always mildly surprised to learn that their city holds more Italians than Rome, more Jews than Tel Aviv, more Poles than Warsaw. Through the years, though, millions of these shoppers have become convinced that no matter what they want, they can usually find it at Macy's.

Macy's is fabulous the way New York is fabulous. When an Oriental camel driver invited to America by President Lyndon B. Johnson showed up at the store, someone was available to talk to him in his native Urdu—one of the forty-two languages spoken by over a thousand bilingual Macy employees. Tourists visit Macy's just as they do the Empire State Building and the Statue of Liberty. Babies have been born on the premises and a young lady named Ann Macy Hettrich is growing up with a middle name to remind her of where she came into the world.

"The World's Largest Store" has been a Macy slogan since the store moved to Herald Square at Thirty-fourth Street in 1902. This boast was challenged by big John Wanamaker, Marshall Field and J. L. Hudson store buildings erected in later years, but Macy's put on additions in 1924, 1928 and 1931 to bring its space up to 2,157,330 square feet. Today no one questions the fact that one Macy's flagship store has higher sales each year than any other.

Every solvent American pays his income tax on the pay-as-you-go plan devised by Beardsley Ruml, long treasurer and later chairman of Macy's. James P. Mitchell, who learned about labor as Macy's director of personnel and industrial relations, was appointed Secretary of Labor by President Eisenhower.

The impact of Macy's is everywhere. "Macy's basement" has passed into the language for any mob scene; "Macy's window" is well understood as the ultimate in public exposure. Traffic engineers say there is statistical truth as well as poetry in these popular expressions. With as many as 165,000 on a typical day and 300,000 daily during the Christmas season, the human population per square yard in this huge store occupying a full city block has rivaled a throng of Hindu worshipers along the Ganges, and Macy's windows look out on the intersection of more transportation facilities than any other store enjoys.

Macy's shoppers have been able to buy anything from an iguana to a painting by Joan Miró, from a set of Tom Swift books to fresh beluga caviar. Some nine hundred private-label items are on sale at prices 10 to 15 percent below comparable nationally advertised brands.

Macy's security force of young men and women chosen for their resemblance to customers is deputized by the New York City police force. It zealously protects their anonymity, even from its own sales staff. They patrol a different beat every day and are not ever permitted to eat in the company lunchroom. Four Doberman pinschers help watchmen guard the Macy treasure house at night.[1]

Macy's bigness creates a number of small problems as tragicomic as the inability of the fat woman in the circus to tie her own shoelaces. Macy executives have had to use all their wit to cope with the unnaturally large size of the operation. Here is how some problems have been solved over the years:

Problem: How to keep 25,000 charge purchases a day moving smoothly to the basement for delivery or shipment.

Solution: Once a day, a clerk slips a numbered block of wood down each of the nine main tubes and times their appearance on the conveyor belt in the basement. If they don't show up promptly or if a telltale thud is detected, he calls for a professional akin to a chimney sweep who dons protective clothing and slides through the chute to the site of the trouble like a youngster going down the enclosed spiral slide of the fun house at Coney Island.

Problem: How to get over a million dollars in small cash to the bank every day.

Solution: An honest and infallible robot sorts, counts and wraps the change in an elaborately guarded cashier's room mined with secret alarm devices.

Problem: How to maintain the personal touch with hundreds of thousands of customers.

Solution: Customer letters are answered in the same style in which they are written. If Macy's receives a poem, it sends a poem back. Equally adaptable are the complaint adjusters. A woman who bet she could duplicate a $369 antique lamp for practically nothing if she had a picture of it was supplied a photograph. When a newlywed couple didn't get their bedroom set, Macy's sent a bed by special truck to the rescue. In fact, this particular emergency is so painful that the complaint department keeps a special bed in readiness for victims of mis-delivered furniture. When the right bed is retrieved, the emergency bed is returned and sterilized for the next time.

Macy's 168 selling departments in Herald Square carry more than 400,000 items, half of which didn't exist about a decade ago, and customers simply take it for granted that Macy's has everything. A battery of correspondents cope with letters like the one from the woman who wanted a sort of love seat "something in which two could snuggle and have the luxurious feeling of being crowded yet not uncomfortable . . . strong and tasteful," or the one from the man who wanted a dead horse for eel bait. The late President W. V. S. Tubman of Liberia completely furnished his executive mansion from Macy's. Sailors of the U.S.S. *Argonne* once sent the store their 104-page Christmas list, an $8,730 order.

Personal shoppers assist customers looking for a pony, a prefabricated house, an antique chess set or a left-handed pair of scissors. When Macy's advertised Bob Froman's *One Million Islands for Sale,* salesgirls had to explain they were selling a book about islands, not the islands themselves.

The fifteen stores in the New York division of Macy's—the largest division in the company and responsible for almost half of its sales—boast more than 50,000,000 sales transactions annually, including over 20,000,000 charges to customers' accounts. It has 1,500,000 charge accounts outstanding and issues more than 200,000 new account cards a year. Other merchants throughout the world marvel at Macy's variety, value and depth of stock.

To live up to its title as the biggest retail competitor, Macy's has become one of New York's biggest retail customers. Dozens of comparison shoppers disguised as typical customers spent hundred of thousands of dollars a year in competing stores. If any identical item is sold for less, the Macy price comes down immediately. Competitive price reductions are posted on a big blackboard and in ordinary times there are hundreds every week. In a battle such as the one following release of many items from fair-trade pricing in 1951, prices may tumble several times a day or as fast as Macy shoppers can phone from their posts in other stores. During that field day for consumers, aspirin tablets, for instance, fell to four cents a hundred. Macy's may buy up the entire stock of a competitor running a limited-quantity loss-leader sale, but store policy forbids a wounded merchandise buyer from withdrawing a competitive item from the fray.

Macy's Bureau of Standards, the arbiter of the store's conscience, is unique in all retailing. Under laboratory conditions, thousands of products are annually put through tests of fire, water, high pressure and simulated wear. A flunking mark means that the product—even a private-label item—cannot be sold at Macy's.

Among the 37,000 Macy employees throughout the country are stylists, carpenters, nurses, chemists, researchers, traffic engineers and tax advisers. These specialists take their place beside the 16,000 salespeople on the firing line who serve 30,000,000 customers a year.

This, then, is Macy's. How did it become the biggest store in the lushest and toughest retail market in the world? Perhaps the best answer is simply the continuity with which the store has maintained three basic policies for over a century: (1) selling at fixed prices, (2) selling for less, and (3) advertising vigorously.[2]

Macy's did not invent any of these policies, although all of them were radical when they were adopted. What its founder did was to stick with them as articles of faith through thick and thin, and pass them on to successors who stuck to them too. The result of this persistence was not only a fabulously profitable business but also a development of a new way of retailing, the department store, which was very soon to have many followers.

No such institution existed in 1858 when Rowland Hussey Macy scraped together the resources to start a small fancy dry-goods store with an eleven-foot front on Sixth Avenue, now officially the Avenue of the Americas, near Fourteenth Street. Nor did Rowland Macy himself, all of thirty-six years old, seem likely to create such an institution. A Nantucketer, he had spent what should have been his high-school years on a four-year whaling trip around the world aboard the *Emily Morgan.*

In 1844, he had started a little thread and needle shop on Hanover Street in Boston. It promptly failed and so did another store in Boston. He made a profitable trading venture in Marysville, California, during the gold-rush days. Then he had another store in Haverhill, Massachusetts, which also did not prosper. Yet through all these ups and downs, Macy was developing the philosophy of retailing that later made his big New York store a revolutionary influence.[3]

What is known of Rowland Macy hardly adds up to the stereotype of a merchant prince. A stocky, bearded veteran of hard times, he was frugal (he refused to shade the lamps in the store because he was paying for the light) and his temper was hot (he once broke all the umbrellas in stock because a customer complained of a weak handle). He was known to flirt with the girls on buying trips to Europe, lunch alone at Delmonico's, play billiards and get religion all over again at a Moody and Sankey revival meeting.

A surviving advertisement for the "Haverill Cheap Store" might spell Macy's to any modern New Yorker. Headed by the Macy rooster, the very style of the ad is a radical departure from the tombstone formality of trade notices in 1852. It reads, in part:

Macy! ! !

Haverhlil Cheap Store!

Ever Onward! !   Ever Upward! !

English, French and American

DRY GOODS

1. We buy exclusively FOR CASH!!!
2. We sell exclusively FOR CASH!!!
3. We have but one price, and that is named first! No deviation except for imperfection!

These are the three great principles upon which we base our business. Buying *exclusively* for cash, we keep our stock in constant motion and are having new goods from New York, Philadelphia and Boston *every day*. It also enables us to procure many of our goods under the market price, and our customers have the advantage of these bargains for this reason, viz: selling exclusively for cash, we have no bad debts on our books, consequently our good customers do not have to pay them in the shape of extra profits.

By adopting one price and never deviating, a child can trade with us as cheap as the shrewdest buyer in the country.

Possibly because of these principles, the Haverhill Cheap Store failed. In spite of its failure, Macy carried them to his New York store. There obscure changes in distribution were unwittingly creating more favorable conditions for them.

Preindustrial retail channels were already cracking under the rising volume and diversity of goods pouring from factories— much of it merchandise that formerly had never been sold because it was made and consumed at home. The peddler and the general storekeeper could no longer supply the more sophisticated wants of the growing number of city wage earners. As more everyday necessities had to be bought, shopping became a recurrent chore for customers and they were ready to have it made easier. One store for everything with standard prices and selling methods could draw patrons from a widening urban area.

Rowland Macy's bid for this dynamic market was unpretentious. On October 28, 1858, he offered ribbons, laces, embroideries, artificial flowers, feathers, handkerchiefs, cambric flouncings, hosiery and gloves on two long counters at 204–206 Sixth Avenue. His first-day sales were $11.06. A specialized shop confined to "fancy goods," an offshoot of the general dry-goods store, it had the luck to occupy a central crossroads of the growing city. But possibly the most important influence on its spectacular future was Macy himself.

The significant aspect of the character of Rowland Macy is that he was brought up a Quaker. In all his retailing ventures, he adhered, as a matter of religious principle, to the one-price policy originated by George Fox in 1653. Many other merchants in the New World as well as in Europe had recognized the good business sense of the Quakers, but few merchants before the Civil War could resist the temptation to deviate from it. Implicit in the Quaker thinking were further Macy policies of "true value"—policies that were later to flower in the Bureau of Standards and the fight to sell for less in spite of restricting laws.

Macy had furthermore experienced the seamy side of the credit system, which was the biggest hazard in retailing in his time. Some say that his credit was so badly dented by his previous business failures that a cash policy was sheer necessity. Nevertheless, his early misfortunes with credit convinced him of the competitive advantage of dealing in cash. This was a saving grace during the period of rapid changes and alarms in which he lived.

There was also a bit of P. T. Barnum in this Nantucket Quaker. He wrote much of that modern-sounding advertising at Haverhill, and the promotional flavor in New York was a reflection of his own personality. By temperament he was fitted to reach out to the new middle-class customers and draw them to his store with informally written messages quoting actual prices to prove his claim of bargains. He was one of the first to use typographic devices to gain attention and spent a healthy 3 percent of sales on advertising at a time when well-established competitors were spending only 1 percent.

But the most dramatic part of the rise of Rowland Macy was the way in which he turned to good account the restlessness and impatience that had early marked him a ne'er-do-well by New England standards of storekeeping. As a young man he had gone whaling, enjoyed gold hunting in California and disappeared from sight on several occasions to engage in nonretailing ventures. Settled down in the New York store, he was to express his need for adventurous fields by taking on new items of merchandise.

In his first year in business, he took a flier in gloves and hosiery for men, the nucleus of a men's furnishing business. He tried a small stock of towels and sheets and found himself in home furnishings. In 1860 he added a miscellany of "French and German fancy goods," including pocketbooks, tea sets, photograph frames, games, dolls and toys. Four years later came costume jewelry; in 1868, clocks and silver; and in 1869, baby carriages and kitchen utensils.

By 1872 he was scandalizing more conservative competitors by selling books, rocking chairs, garden tools and fancy groceries for picnics. If books for children, why not books for adults? If books, why not stationery and magazines? Soon came velocipedes, bathing suits, barometers and even a short-lived experiment with potted plants. Every year saw wider assortments of each line. It is no accident that he was in Paris hunting for new lines when he died in 1877, leaving an estate of $300,000 to $500,000.

At the time of Rowland Macy's death, there was no doubt that his store was a department store. Among the characteristics of such a store, Macy's filled the bill in these respects:

1. Its volume was large. From $90,000 during the first thirteen months, sales rose to $1,612,788 by 1876.

2. It sold a wide diversity of merchandise in a variety of departments, including white goods, linens, curtains, laces and embroideries, corsets, ladies' underclothing, small wares and notions, ribbons, silverware, hosiery and furnishings, ladies' ties, furs and parasols, fancy goods, jewelry, toiletries, boys' and youths' clothing, home furnishings, toys and dolls, books, stationery, albums, worsteds and worsted embroidery, china, glass and crockery, soda fountain preparations and candy, kid gloves, millinery, flowers and feathers, ladies' and children's shoes, cloaks and suits, black dress goods and silks.

3. It was organized by departments, each with its own buyer completely responsible for selection of merchandise, amount of stock and profits. Meanwhile, bookkeeping, cash handling, marking and personnel were centralized.

4. It was directed to the woman customer.

5. It was drawing customers from faraway Brooklyn and enticing others by mail order.

6. It offered delivery service, planned the first store lunchroom in America and opened a writing room with daily papers. Macy's liberal attitude toward the customer and a concern for making shopping convenient presaged further developments in the direction of the "free" services.

The department store Rowland Macy left behind him was already committed to most of the policies for which Macy's has an international reputation today. In addition to competitive low fixed prices and aggressive advertising, he left a lasting aversion to extravagant quarters. Quaker and Nantucket simplicity ruled against the marble palaces competing storekeepers were building. Macy's at Fourteenth Street expanded into a labyrinth of nearby buildings that were not primarily designed for retailing. The big store on Thirty-fourth Street is efficient and spacious but seems designed to give the shopper the impression that overhead is not adding unnecessarily to prices.

Macy was the first great merchant to employ a woman to run what has since aptly been called a "woman's business." In 1860 he engaged Margaret Getchell, a pretty and bright schoolteacher from Nantucket and a distant relative, to preside over his cash drawer. She rose to bookkeeper and in 1866 became the store's first general superintendent. Macy not only relied on her aptitude for figures to keep his books but also generously attributed a large part of his success to her accounting and administrative talent.

Macy even became involved with her social life. When he learned that she had lost her heart to a good-looking young salesman she had seen visiting the store, he connived to bring them together at parties. The upshot was that Abiel T. LaForge took a job in the store to be near its cashier, married her and wound up as a partner in the business. Appropriately enough, the LaForges lived over the store and Margaret continued to lend a hand when she could spare time from her growing family. Abiel LaForge's pride in Margaret's ability and his respect for her opinion was all that a career wife could wish. "She is the Superintendent, having full charge of the entire business," he boasted in a letter to his sister. "As we sell a million dollars' worth of goods a year and have nearly 200 employees, her position is a very responsible one."[4]

Finally, Macy planned for his own succession so well that his store survived the biggest hazard of a one-man business. Realizing that his son, Rowland, Jr., was unfit for business, Macy shifted increasing responsibility to two junior partners, LaForge and Robert Macy Valentine, the son of his youngest sister. They bought out his estate at his death, but the well-loved LaForge succumbed to tuberculosis. Valentine survived LaForge just long enough to buy out his share and bring in a Macy relative and employee, Charles B. Webster.

Webster had neither extensive funds nor retail experience, but he solved the first problem by marrying Valentine's widow and the second by bringing in a brother-in-law, Jerome B. Wheeler. But when Webster proceeded to interest himself in a lady employee whom he insisted on promoting to positions for which she was unqualified, Wheeler objected to this breach of store discipline. Webster, in turn, objected to Wheeler's growing interests outside of the store. Thanks to its solid foundation, however, Macy's continued for the next ten years to grow with the times although it did not break any new retailing ground.

When Webster finally bought out Wheeler in 1887, he was able to turn for new blood to a great merchant family named Straus, which has had a unique association with Macy's that remains unbroken to the present day. Lazarus Straus, the head of this remarkable line, was a well-to-do cultured Jewish grain merchant of liberal principles who left his farmlands in Bavaria following the uprisings of 1848. Two years later, his wife—who was also his cousin—and four children followed him to the United States. Unlike most immigrants, he by-passed the melting-pot cities to start a modest little store in Talbotton, Georgia.

During the Civil War, the Strauses were Confederate sympathizers—one of them, in fact, attempted unsuccessfully to bring arms to the blockaded Southern states. Following the war, they moved north to Philadelphia and then to New York to form the wholesale chinaware importing firm of L. Straus & Sons.

The family association with Macy's began in 1874, when L. Straus & Sons established leased departments to sell china, glassware and silver. At that time Macy's was the largest New York customer of the Straus concern and the arrangement was a logical one.

Under the Strauses, Macy's china and crockery departments grew until 1888, when they accounted for nearly 18 percent of the company's sales and returned the highest profit in the store. It was the first to feature bargain sales and public exhibitions. To the china department, too, goes the credit for introducing Macy's famous odd price policy—$3.98 instead of $4.00—to make the customer feel she is getting a bargain.

Webster offered the Strauses a partnership in 1888 and joined with them in 1893 in acquiring a half interest in the Brooklyn store thereafter called Abraham & Straus, an interest that they later sold. Webster finally disposed of his remaining half interest in Macy's to the Strauses.

Isidor Straus, the oldest son of Lazarus Straus, was a typical patriarch: confident, dignified and reliable. He watched the store's finances and developed the operating system required to keep a growing business under control. His hobby was foreign exchange and his idea of recreation was advising his friend President Grover Cleveland on currency reforms.

In his autobiography, Isidor Straus analyzed his own personality when he said: "Possibly at times I was subject to an acute sensitiveness and caused, I confess, many nervous anxieties. To take things calmly, always to be optimistic and not forbode troubles, which in many cases I admit prove imaginary, is a happy faculty, but I am not ready to say, likely to lead to success."

His younger brother Nathan, on the other hand, was enthusiastic, gregarious and popular. He endeared himself to employees by wandering around the store whistling "There'll be a Hot Time in the Old Town Tonight" and by thinking up most of the stunts and promotions which kept Macy's name before the public. A natty dresser, he loved horses and amused himself with Tammany politics and spectacular philanthropies like the Free Milk Fund. Nathan was so visible, in fact, that most New Yorkers thought he ran the store single-handedly.

Under this well-balanced team, Macy's sales inched upward from about $5 million in 1888 to $10.8 million in 1902, the year of the move uptown. There were no radical departures from previous policies, but assortments and lines grew steadily as the middle classes filled their gaudy parlors with the first luxuriant fruits of mechanization. Selections from the long lists of products the Strauses added every year afford a provocative backward glimpse into the days of bloomer girls and bicycles built for two: 1889, Oriental rugs, engraved stationery, buggy whips; 1890, brass beds, rowing machines; 1891, bicycles; 1892, diamonds, Tokay wines; 1893, oil paintings, fancy groceries; 1895, amateur photographers' supplies, sleighs; 1897, firearms; 1898, wallpaper, pianos, talking machines; 1899, cocktail shakers.

Progress was slow because Macy's was not the only big store in New York. During this period, many other stores were vying for the privilege of supplying almost all of the customers' wants. While none of them equaled Macy's assortments and few even tried to compete with Macy's low cash prices, their success proved that many customers were still willing to pay for additional convenience and service.

Macy's competed on service as well as it could. Like other stores, it adopted the "satisfaction guaranteed or your money back" principle, as a steadily rising rate of returns testified. At the close of the century the store was teaching purchasers of bicycles how to ride, installing ovens and ranges and packing the provisions the wealthy bought for their yacht trips. In order to dramatize a delivery service that required hundreds of horses to serve customers lured into Macy's from New Jersey and Long Island, Macy's imported two Mercedes horseless carriages, which attracted a great deal of attention but did little to lighten the delivery burden.

It became increasingly clear that a great store could no longer make do with the makeshift quarters that were now spread on both sides of Sixth Avenue—to the confusion of shoppers and to the point of at least one merchant who encouraged the public to think that he was part of Macy's. Furthermore, trade was on its historic march uptown and Macy's would have to downgrade its merchandise or upgrade its address. Isidor's sons, who were already in the business, campaigned successfully for a new building uptown.

The choice of Macy's present location on Thirty-fourth Street and Broadway, a crossroads that has gained the importance over the years, was at the time a radical leapfrog over the competition in the movement of New York retailing. It was particularly alarming to Henry Siegel, a Chicago merchant who had just pushed the center of shopping gravity northward by building Siegel Cooper New York on Eighteenth Street. Through agents, Siegel bought up a little over a thousand square feet of the strategic Thirty-fourth Street and Broadway corner, paying $375,000 for it. Then he offered it to the Strauses for only $250,000 if they would sell him the unexpired lease on their old Fourteenth Street store and with it, of course, the custom of shoppers used to the location.

The Strauses refused to pay tribute. They instructed their architects to build around the little corner—which is still not occupied by Macy's—and used the $250,000 they had earmarked for its acquisition to acquire land to the west, on which a twenty-story building was erected in 1924. The new land was first used to house the store's generating plant, which had been planned for the north side of Thirty-fifth Street on the site of two famous brothels, the Pekin and the Tivoli.

Over a half century of hard usage and architectural progress has not made the store the Strauses built in 1902 obsolete. It was the first to install a vacuum-cleaner system for removing stale air, pneumatic tubes for transporting cash and escalators with flat steps instead of inclined ones with cleats against which riders had to brace their feet.

The new building put Macy's in a position to compete on service instead of price. Still the Strauses sought new ways to dramatize Macy's low cash prices. To dramatize the advantages of cash, Macy's adopted the "6% cash policy," which soon became more than an idle slogan.

Macy's virtually guaranteed to sell merchandise offered in charge-account stores at 6 percent off. Socks that sold for $1 in other stores became 94 cents at Macy counters in a clever adaption of the store's traditional odd pricing policy to accentuate the new policy. New York's bargain-hungry crowds took Macy's at its word, calling lapses of the price challenge to the attention of the management in such numbers that it became necessary to hire a small army of clerks to verify the claims. From this beginning was born the comparison-shopping department.

With the opening of the new store, Macy's launched its own answer to the inconvenience of carrying cash. Customers who traded regularly at Macy's could deposit their money with the store and draw against it as they made purchases. To the surprise of competing merchants, the Deposit Account system worked. Thousands of housewives transferred their secret savings out of the grocery budget into Macy's Bank, since the store was destined to get the money in the end anyway. This system remained in effect until 1960, when the number of such purchasers became such a preponderance of Macy's customers that a conventional charge-account arrangement was adopted and the slogan "No one is in debt to Macy's" had to be dropped.

The store's fight against fixed prices began early in the century when an association of book publishers sought to maintain retail prices and contended that Macy's underselling process lowered the value of their copyright. Macy lawyers charged that the book publishers were a trust under the Sherman Anti-Trust Act and sued for damages. Meanwhile, secret agents ranged the country to buy up popular titles and in one case, at least, secured copies from the author, who told the publisher he was buying the copies for his own use.

In 1913, after nine actions in Federal and state courts, the Supreme Court of the United States vindicated the Macy contention. A photograph of the $140,000 damage check the publishers paid to Macy's is still one of the store's prized exhibits. A similar protracted dispute with the Victor Talking Machine Company ended its attempt to control prices by licensing instead of selling its Victrolas.

But price-fixing measures gradually were enacted by more and more legislative bodies and Macy's had no choice but to obey them. It increased its emphasis, however, on items manufactured to its specifications and sold under its own brands. Some of these date from the days of Rowland Macy, who had the store make its own cigars. Housewives began to be encouraged to buy Supre-Macy towels, Lily White canned goods and Red Star articles of many kinds.

Macy's New York advertising and public-relations department, now headed by Harold F. Haener, has always attracted many men and women of talent. Kenneth Collins, who first advertised the Macy Bureau of Standards, moved on to a series of executive posts. William H. Howard became executive vice president of the big store and later joined Young & Rubican. And in 1948, a Macy Christmas advertisement, headlined "Oh Darling—You Shouldn't Have!" and written by Barbara Collyer, was chosen by Julian Watkins as one of the hundred greatest advertisements.

Best remembered of all is Bernice Fitz-Gibbon, a forceful former teacher of English from Wisconsin. For Macy's, she coined "It's Smart to Be Thrifty," a slogan that was even painted on the store roof for the benefit of air travelers and was later expanded to "It's Smart to Be Thrifty, It's Smart to Be Sure."

A widely publicized "feud" between Macy's and Gimbels, its Herald Square neighbor—similar to the one that Fred Allen and Jack Benny used to engage in—has drawn great consumer interest and generated additional sales for both stores. The two stores occasionally vary the battle with friendly gestures. In 1946, they buried the hatchet long enough to adopt a uniform outdoor decorating scheme for Christmas. Seven years later, Gimbels called attention to Macy's flower show with an advertisement that trumpeted, "Does Gimbels Tell Macy's? No, Gimbels Tells the World!" Macy's responded politely with a thank-you: "Nobody but nobody said it more prettily than Gimbels." In 1955, each of the retail giants temporarily posted signs on their Manhattan buildings directing shoppers to the other's store.

Macy's started its Thanksgiving Day parade in 1924 and it has been an annual event ever since, with the exception of two war years, heralding the arrival of Santa Claus in New York. The parade is a two-mile panoply of celebrities, bands, majorettes and six-story balloons. Over a million people crowd the line of march to get a glimpse of the fabulous characters and some 67,000,000 more watch the parade on national television. It has even inspired a popular motion picture, *Miracle on Thirty-fourth. Street*, which was later made into a television program and a Broadway musical, *Here's Love*.

During the early part of the twentieth century, Macy's growth paralleled that of New York City. Sales climbed steadily to

$17.3 million at the outbreak of World War I. Inflation, as well as a war-detonated explosion in consumer expenditures, pushed Macy's sales to $35 million by 1919, the year the store was incorporated.

In the speculative years following World War I, the Strauses expanded by buying a controlling interest in Toledo's LaSalle's in 1923 and Atlanta's then ailing Davison's four years later. In 1929 they bought Bamberger's, a Newark store founded in 1892 and notable for its pioneer radio broadcasting. In 1945, they bought O'Connor Moffat & Co. of San Francisco and in 1947, the John Taylor Dry Goods Store in Kansas City, both of whose names were later changed to Macy's.

Macy's Parkchester store in the Bronx was one of the first department-store experiments in decentralizing to follow its customers to the suburbs. Although a branch store in Syracuse that carried only best-selling items failed in 1940, Macy's New York has since opened branches in White Plains, New Rochelle, Jamaica, Elmhurst, Flatbush, Kings Plaza, Staten Island, Roosevelt Field, Huntington, Bay Shore, Smith Haven, Colonie and New Haven. And its big Elmhurst, Queens, unit—a 300,000-square-foot store-in-the-round surrounded by twin parking helixes and catering to an audience of over 600,000 people within three miles—is one of the most novel approaches to store construction in history.

In 1922, Macy stock was offered to the public, but the Straus family still retains a substantial stock interest in the company. Allocation of the leadership within the family seems to have followed the law of primogeniture. Isidor, the eldest son of Lazarus, was the head of Macy's until he refused to enter a lifeboat of the sinking *Titanic* ahead of women and children in 1912. A bronze plaque in the store pays tribute to the memory of him and his wife, who died at the same time.

His sons, "Mr. Jesse" and "Mr. Percy," had already taken over running the store. Their younger brother Herbert and the two sons of Nathan Straus, while contributing in other ways, never overcame the head start of the legendary pair. Whenever the slightest disagreement arose in public, Jesse and Percy would retire behind locked doors until one of them could emerge with the traditional pronouncement "My brother and I have decided."

A disagreement between Isidor's sons and Nathan Straus led to a friendly sale of the latter's interests to his nephews Jesse, Percy and Herbert. For a time Jesse held the top post at the store and then the leadership descended to his eldest son, Jack.

Jack Straus, who was president and chairman of Macy's for a total of twenty-eight years and is now chairman of the executive committee, is not the only Straus at the store these days. His only son, Kenneth, a World War II infantry veteran and a well-known fire buff, is senior vice president for domestic and international corporate buying. And his cousin Edward, son of Herbert, is president of the two Macy shopping-center subsidiaries—Garden State Plaza Corporation and South Shore Mall.

Jack Isidor Straus was only two years old when he performed his first official act for the store. That's when he held a silver trowel in his hands at the laying of the cornerstone at Macy's Thirty-fourth Street store.[5]

A tall, slim, quiet man whose accomplishments as an amateur jazz pianist have won him wide admiration among his friends as well as from his teachers, Eddy Duchin and Teddy Wilson, Straus was imbued with retailing principles and philosophy from the days of his youth when he sat around the breakfast table listening to his father and uncles discussing merchandising.

"The image of Macy's," he says, "has been built on providing a wide assortment and many services to our customers. We intend to continue offering a variety of merchandise and whatever services are necessary in order to maintain this traditional retailer image. The bull's eye of our target is on the middle income group."

Straus joined the famed Macy executive training squad after his graduation from Harvard and worked in such jobs as a main-floor stocking salesman and a clerk in the handbag counter before moving into management positions. His father taught him that merchandising is the most important aspect of department-store retailing, a lesson he has never forgotten. Veteran employees still call him "Mr. Jack," following the old Macy tradition of referring to members of the Straus family in this manner.

As soon as people he meets at parties or other social occasions learn of his affiliation with Macy's, they usually take the opportunity to voice whatever complaint they may have about the store, no matter how minor. Straus was finally forced to get an unlisted telephone number because of the many calls he received at all hours from people who wanted to talk directly to the top man about their problem.

At the time of his retirement, Straus completed forty-seven years of service to Macy's. During this period, the company grew at the fastest pace in its history and became firmly established as one of the world's great merchandising institutions.

Don Smiley, who has been chief executive officer of the corporation since 1971, is a lawyer who is married to a lawyer and has two lawyer daughters who are also married to lawyers. But his father was a retailer in Davenport, Iowa, and Smiley has been a member of the Macy's organization since 1945.

A firm believer in teamwork within a big company like Macy's, Smiley rose initially through its legal ranks and became secretary and general attorney in 1953. Three years later, he became vice president and treasurer and has continued to oversee the Macy's financial and administrative organization as he moved up through senior executive posts to become chairman and chief executive officer.

"Retailing is a complicated people business," he believes. "In a big company such as ours, we can afford to have people operate segments of it with full responsibility for profits. This gives them the opportunity of functioning as though they were small businessmen within the framework of a large company. And the benefits to the company are the multiple results that come from these separate efforts.

Herb Seegal was elected president of Macy's in 1972, following a year-long period in which he served as one of the two vice chairmen—along with David L. Yunich—and a member of the three-man corporate executive office that ran the business after the retirement of Ernest L. Molloy as president. That spot was left open for a while until the board of directors named Seegal to the company's top merchandising job, one of the most prestigious in the entire field of retailing.

Mr. Seegal, like the others at the top of Macy's, is a veteran retailer. He garnered his extensive merchandising experience at Filene's and R. H. White's in Boston and Thalheimer's in Richmond. He joined Macy's in 1953, was named president of the Bamberger's New Jersey division in 1962 and appointed chief executive officer of the twelve-unit group—the corporation's most profitable division—three years later.

The heads of the Macy divisions, key factors in the company's progress, are K. Wade Bennett of Macy's New York, Mark S. Handler of Bamberger's New Jersey, Edward S. Finkelstein of Macy's California, Herbert Friedman of Davison's, Harold S. Olsen of Macy's Missouri-Kansas and John G. Griffin of LaSalle's.

One tangible symbol of Macy's unwavering faith in the future survival is its five-pointed Red Star trademark used on everything from delivery trucks to letterheads and derived from a lucky star that Captain Rowland H. Macy once saw at sea to guide him to land. Since 1918 it has also been adopted as the symbol of the Red Army. Because of that, many have urged Macy's to stop using it as a label and a cable address. But Macy's feels that this is not at all necessary, since the store had the mark first and intends to have it last.

XI

The Food Giants

The A & P, Safeway and Their Rivals

The supermarket, the ingenious retailing innovation that changed the food-buying habits of tens of millions of American shoppers, was developed in its present form by an employee of an Illinois food chain who couldn't sell the idea to his bosses.

The innovator was Michael Cullen, a man who foresaw in the late 1920s that grocery stores, usually clerk-served and occupying less than 2,000 square feet apiece, could not fulfill the requirements of the populace in a changing society. Anticipating the further growth of the automobile industry, he recognized that most of the grocery stores were scattered throughout heavily populated urban areas and relied entirely on foot traffic or on-street parking facilities.

Cullen's idea was to develop self-service stores on a cash-and-carry basis, 5,000 or 6,000 square feet in area with an equal amount of surrounding parking space and located outside the high-rent district. Loss-leader and low-markup merchandise would be flanked by high-profit items, mass displays of groceries would be featured in aisles that contained few fixtures and newspaper advertising on a major scale would boost traffic and promote volume by making customers aware of what these stores offered.

Self-service food selling per se was not Cullen's invention. The Piggly Wiggly stores, started in 1916 by Clarence Saunders of Memphis, Tennessee, used self-selection, turnstiles and check-out counters as principal features. Drive-in markets for quick service developed in southern California in the 1920s. What

Cullen did was to take these ideas, add his own concepts about grocery selling and fuse them into a large, integrated market— a supermarket. He called himself "The world's most daring price wrecker."

When his employer, the Kroger Company, wouldn't buy this idea, Cullen quit his job and opened what is generally accepted to be the first supermarket, King Kullen's, in an abandoned garage in Jamaica, Queens, New York, on August 30, 1930. The extent of this revolution in marketing during the depression can be seen in Cullen's immediate success. Two years later, the King Kullen Grocery Company, Inc., was operating eight markets with grocery sales of $6 million annually and total sales of almost $9 million. When Cullen died in 1936, he was running fifteen large units.

The news of King Kullen's operating technique quickly spread throughout the country. Although there had been chain stores in other merchandising categories before this—some of them dating back centuries—here was the first effective application of the supermarket-chain principle. Soon a few other small and large food chains and independents, like the Big Bear group of "cheapies," began to open supermarkets and these were followed by the entire industry.

In 1972, 75 percent, or $71,589,850,000 worth, of the total grocery store volume of $95,020,000,000 was done in supermarkets. This compares with 59 percent, or $33,560,000,000 worth, of the overall grocery volume of $57,079,186,000 a decade earlier.[1] More people are now exposed to supermarkets than they are to schools, churches, or most other influences outside the home. There are currently more than 42,000 supers in the United States, of which some 30,000 are operated by chains.

This growth in supermarket volume, moreover, has occurred despite the proliferation of so-called superettes and the continuing presence of small stores. The supers, with sizes of about 23,000 square feet, do the overwhelming bulk of the nation's grocery business in a relatively small number of stores. Only

19 percent of the 205,800 grocery stores can be defined as supermarkets, but their influence is so great that their marketing trends have an impact on the entire nation. Late-night hours of operation, for example, which extended in some cases to twenty-four-hour-a-day service, have recently become a widespread phenomenon on the American scene. The spread of supermarket merchandise to nonfood items is another factor in modern retailing.

When it comes to supermarkets, though, there is one company which not only has more supermarkets than any other but whose name is also known everywhere as the symbol of a food chain. That name, of course, is the A & P.

The A & P, as shoppers know the Great Atlantic & Pacific Tea Company, Inc., is just about the world's largest food retailer and one of the greatest exponents of chain-store operation. In its fiscal year ended February 26, 1972, its sales amounted to $5,508 million, making it one of the biggest retailing organizations in the nation.

Earnings slumped badly that year, however, to $14,619,000 from $50,129,000 in the previous fiscal period. In fiscal 1973, moreover, the A & P showed a loss for the first time since it became publicly owned in 1958[2] and reported a deficit of $51,277,000 on sales of $6,368,876,000. But the company returned to profitability with earnings of $2.4 million on sales of $1.64 billion for the quarter ending May 26, 1973. The A & P is such a part of Americana that when Gulf & Western Industries attempted to buy 3,750,000 shares of common at $20 a share early in 1973, it made headlines throughout the country. But the A & P management fought back successfully.

What is the A & P? To Americans who visit them at the rate of about twenty million a week, it is four thousand unpretentious stores, approximately 80 percent of them supermarkets and most of them early American in design, so devoid of frills that they are simply machines for selling food. Though the stores are few in the West and are not to be found at all in fifteen states, into their cash registers go more than six cents of every dollar of retail food sales in the country.

The A & P is also the largest food-processing plant in the country, at Horseheads, New York, and a cheese warehouse at Plymouth, Wisconsin. It is twenty-two bakeries turning out bread and cakes, six coffee-roasting plants, fresh-milk plants in Pennsylvania, Wisconsin, Louisiana and North Carolina, evaporated milk plants in Pennsylvania and Wisconsin, a delicatessen plant in New Jersey, fish plants in Massachusetts and Maryland, a buying organization in South America, two laundries for washing uniforms and a print shop just for the printing of its private labels. Around three hundred of these labels are registered with the United States Patent Office.

The A & P is also research that developed the big-breasted "chicken of tomorrow" and is continually working to improve its turkey and hog quality. It is a meat-purchasing empire that buys around 2.5 billion pounds a year, and processes produce in eight plants. It is the biggest user of eggs, 215 million dozen a year, both for sale and as ingredients in its bakery products.

The A & P is 140,000 employees, from clerks throughout the company's thirty-two decentralized divisions who mark cans and packages in stores to traveling auditors who report to headquarters in New York's Graybar Building, where statisticians analyze and chart the figures. It is also a computerized network linking these divisions from coast to coast and tying in an increasingly automated warehouse distribution system.

The huge organization was started by George Huntington Hartford, a shrewd, solemn, full-bearded Yankee from Augusta, Maine, who in 1859, when he was twenty-six, was employed by George F. Gilman in a New York hide and leather importing business.

Tea then retailed in New York at a dollar a pound. Hartford convinced Gilman that this could be reduced to thirty cents by eliminating middlemen. Gilman abandoned hides and leather and the two formed the Great American Tea Company, a partnership that promised "to do away with various profits and brokerages, cartages, storages, cooperage and waste, with the exception of a small commission paid for purchasing to our correspondents in Japan and China, one cartage, and a small profit to ourselves which, on our large sales, will amply repay us."

Initially they sold tea on the docks of New York directly to consumers. Their first shop at 31 Vesey Street in New York resembled something from the Arabian Nights. A gigantic capital "T," blazing with gaslights, illuminated the store's vermilion-and-gold front. Strings of red, white and blue globes festooned the windows. Inside the store, tea bins were painted red and gold, the cashiers' cages were built in the shape of Chinese pagodas and a green parrot stood on a stand in the center of the main floor. A band played on Saturdays, often far into the night.

To advertise the store, eight dapple-gray horses pulled a tremendous red wagon through the city streets. A prize of $20,000 was offered to anyone who could guess the combined weight of team and wagon. All kinds of premiums were given away—dishpans, china, crockery and colored pictures of babies. "This is the day they give babies away" was one of the song slogans used to attract customers.

New Yorkers swarmed to the store. Hartford and Gilman gradually added spices, coffee, soap, flavoring extracts, condensed milk, baking powder and other staples. Wherever possible they applied the same middleman-eliminating purchasing they inaugurated with tea.

They added more stores. There were five by 1865 and eleven in 1869 when the partners adopted the more grandiloquent name of the Great Atlantic & Pacific Tea Company. Hartford envisioned a chain of stores that would reach from coast to coast, as the Union Pacific Railroad linked the two seaboards. The older name was preserved until 1964 in a subsidiary that operated tea and coffee truck routes in forty-nine cities.

By 1876, there were sixty-seven A & P stores, all with the familiar red-and-gold façade, all conventional grocery stores with charge accounts and delivery service. They were operating as far south as Baltimore, as far north as Boston and as far west as St. Paul. A comic advertising card a little later listed twenty-five stores in New York and five in Brooklyn.

Gilman retired in 1878 to a life of luxury in Bridgeport, Connecticut, and left his partner, Hartford, to run the stores. Hartford was soon joined by two of his five children. These were his sons, George Ludlum Hartford and John Augustine Hartford. A third son, Edward, became an inventor and did not enter the business, and there were two daughters.

George, the eldest, born November 7, 1864, and named for his father, started to work in 1880 as an office boy to fire the boiler. After two weeks, he took the place of a cashier who quit, strangely enough because he thought the business might fail. There were then 110 stores and George counted and banked the cash from all of them. This came in by express, sometimes as much as $55,000 a day.

Keeping tabs on the money aroused his interest in economy. Hearing that baking powder was only alum and sodium bicarbonate, George set a chemist mixing the ingredients behind a screen in the Vesey Street store. This brought down the price of baking powder and was the start of the company's own manufacturing operations.

John Hartford, eight years younger than his brother, went to work cleaning inkwells and sweeping floors in the Vesey Street store in 1888, when he was all of sixteen years old and fresh out of high school. His salary was five dollars a week, and his mother, as frugal as his father, charged him a dollar for board and made him bank another dollar. When he received a two-dollar raise, his mother increased his board bill. Soon he was clerking and also buying and handing out premiums, then an important lure.

In the panic of 1907, John's gift for strategy was credited with saving the business. He was sent to withdraw the company funds from a bank on which there was a run. Finding many depositors already in line, he asked the first, a little man who had been there all night, how much money he had in the bank.

"Four hundred and forty-seven dollars and ninety cents," he replied. "All I have in the world."

"I'll give you $450 for your place," John said. "Get back in line and maybe you'll get your deposit, too."

As it turned out, John Hartford salvaged thousands of dollars for the A & P and the little man who had been at the head of the line also collected his deposit in full, becoming probably the only one actually to double his money in a panic that caused even J. P. Morgan some trouble.

At this time, A & P headquarters were moved to Jersey City, New Jersey, not far from Orange, where the Hartford brothers grew up and their father was mayor for twelve years without salary.

Cash and carry, one of the biggest innovations in A & P history, was introduced in 1912 by John Hartford. At this time there were four hundred stores, but charge-account paper work, thousands of delivery horses and wagons and premiums limited profits. The success of a New Jersey grocer named Henry Cole with some cash stores caused John Hartford to think along this line. He proposed to his father and brother that they open "economy" stores to be staffed by one man, to be run without charge orders or premiums and to sell at low profit aimed at large volume. They thought it a crackpot idea.

He persisted, however, until he persuaded them to let him open just one to prove his point. They invested $3,000, and for a real test John opened his store on West Side Avenue in Jersey City, around the corner from the company's biggest money-making store. The economy store didn't even have a name but the customers rushed in when they saw its bargains. In six months the regular A & P store was out of business, and the economy store was in to stay.[3]

For the next two years John opened economy stores at the rate of one every three days. By the end of 1915, there were one thousand A & P stores and each establishment was laid out exactly alike so customers could find things in the same location in any store. John often remarked he could go blindfolded into any store and find a can of pork and beans.

The company borrowed $5 million to finance the new stores and the sales volume more than doubled to $75 million in 1916. The father then turned the business over to George and John to run as a trust for themselves, their two sisters—Mrs. William B. Reilly and Mrs. A. G. Hoffman—their brother and, as they died, their heirs. The most famous of these heirs is Huntington Hartford, the well-known art connoisseur and patron of the arts. In 1917, the founder died at eighty-four. The trust, incidentally, was not dissolved until after George L. Hartford died in 1957.

"Our one desire," the sons wrote later in an instruction book for store managers, "is to perpetuate A & P as a great public service, to have it stand forever as a monument to the integrity, perseverance and human understanding of the man who founded it, George Huntington Hartford." When the Chicago Merchandise Mart years later established its Hall of Fame of Retailing, the father of the A & P was among the first four elected, along with Marshall Field, Frank W. Woolworth and John Wanamaker.

Under the sons, the A & P became an even bigger integrated business empire. Among the new subsidiaries organized were the Quaker Maid Company (later named the Ann Page division), processing and packing more than forty products, many bearing the Ann Page label; the White House Milk Company, with milk-processing plants in Wisconsin; and the Nakat Packing Corporation, America's largest canner of Alaskan salmon and operator of an Alaskan fishing fleet. Meanwhile, the American Coffee Corporation hired thirty coffee-purchasing agents in Colombia and Brazil, and the company's agents attended tea auctions in India and Ceylon. Cigarettes later became an important profit item for the stores.

Departments for the sale of meat, now the most important single line in A & P volume, were added in 1925. That year also saw the company expand into Canada, buy group insurance for its employees and decentralize its operations into geographical divisions and unit offices.

John Hartford was the merchandising genius of the A & P, while his brother George looked after the financial end. But both realized the importance of decentralization in a business as large as theirs and had each division run virtually like an independent corporation.

Each division was given a president, treasurer, director of sales, director of purchases and director of operations. Each unit had a similar group of specialists. Except in finances, each unit and store manager was free to run his business as he wished within overall company policy. New York continued to keep directly in touch with stores and units through traveling auditors, who inspected stores and their records and were responsible directly to headquarters.

Sales passed the billion-dollar mark for the first time in the fiscal year ending February 28, 1930. The number of red-fronted stores the next year reached a total of 15,709, the record number in the company's history. Sales then topped $1 billion and earnings were more than $30,700,000.

In the next quarter of a century or so, the A & P abandoned almost three-quarters of the stores it owned in 1930, but its total volume during this period increased more than fourfold. The average A & P store also boosted its annual sales from about $68,000 to approximately $1,167,000.

During the 1930s, the A & P was big but not beloved. Because of its bigness and success, it was one of the most unpopular of companies. In part, this was the result of the temper of the times. In part, it was due to disregard for public opinion on the part of the management. Like all mass buyers, the A & P drove hard bargains with its suppliers through allowances and discounts which then were legal. Competitors who were hurt by this, middlemen who were by-passed and others complained to the government. Bills having the principal aim of hampering or destroying the A & P were introduced in Congress and in state legislatures.

While most chains had expanded, the A & P's growth had been the most phenomenal. At the same time, the A & P had done nothing to explain itself to the communities in which it operated. While the "A & P Gypsies" were on the radio and the company's advertising appropriation had been increased from $2 million to $6 million, this still amounted to less than $8 a week per store.

Expansion had been so rapid that all sorts of men were A & P managers. "We went so fast," John Hartford once explained, "that hobos hopping off freight trains got hired as managers." While instructions from headquarters insisted that the stores give sixteen ounces to a pound and mark and sell goods at correct prices, there were complaints of short change, short weight and "selling the broom." In the last instance, a broom was leaned against the checkout stand and its price added to each check as if the patron had purchased it. If this was noticed, the checker would simply apologize. It was an accusation made against every chain food store.

The company left its gathering troubles to its lawyers. They succeeded in having an early North Carolina tax against chain stores declared unconstitutional in 1928, but several setbacks followed. One came in 1931 when the United States Supreme Court, in upholding an Indiana chain-store tax, ruled that chain stores could lawfully be taxed differently from independent stores. Another came in 1936 when John Hartford sat in a Washington, D.C., courtroom and saw A & P store managers convicted of short-weighing chickens in forty-eight out of fifty cases.

A stickler for complete honesty with customers, he spent the next six weeks personally signing forty-six thousand letters to A & P employees warning against any recurrence of this practice. In a case of a different sort, he heard of a New York City manager helping a butler cheat the woman for whom he worked. John Hartford required complete restitution and sent an apology and his personal check to the customer, who had not known that she was being cheated.

Regarding his employees, Mr. Hartford—a slim, gray-haired, impeccably dressed executive—once said that "no man can be asked to do better than his best. If he does his best, he will do a little better than he thinks he can and usually a little better than others think he can."

He thought constantly of his customers too. John Hartford's merchandising philosophy was summarized with these words: "We would rather sell 200 pounds of butter at a penny a pound profit than 100 pounds at 2 cents a pound profit."

Under his leadership, customers were encouraged to write their complaints to headquarters. John Hartford personally investigated many of these. A letter from a mother about the hours her son worked in an A & P store in Virginia, for example, led to the discharge of a store manager. Stores were forbidden to sell anything below cost. While the A & P continued its lone-wolf policy of not joining trade associations, it began to make contributions to some and eventually became a member of various state chain-store councils and other trade groups.

Although the A & P was not the first food chain to take up the supermarket idea in the early 1930s, it eventually became the leading proponent of this method of distribution. The company was also a pioneer in the self-service sale of cellophane-wrapped meat and was an early user of packaged produce.

An important development in the company's promotion program was the conversion in 1937 of a giveaway "menu sheet" to a full-fledged women's service magazine. In a contest, two customers received $1,000 each for naming it *Woman's Day*. While other retailers had attempted and abandoned magazines, *Woman's Day* was a success from the start. It expanded from the thirty-two pages of the initial issue to as much as two hundred pages. The bulk of the advertising was naturally from A & P suppliers, but makers of sewing machines and similar items also advertised.

Woman's Day was sold by the company in 1957 to Fawcett

Publications, Inc., which had printed it for the A & P. It is now sold in other stores as well as the A & P.

Also in 1958, a year after the death of George Hartford and seven years after John Hartford died, the A & P corporate organization was simplified. The New York A & P, which had been owned by the trust established by the founder, was merged into the Maryland A & P, the holding company for all A & P companies and subsidiaries. This recapitalization extended voting rights for the first time in 1959 to the general public, which previously had had access only to nonvoting common and preferred stock. Nevertheless the John A. Hartford Foundation still owns the controlling interest in the company with 35 percent of the A & P stock.

After World War II ended, the A & P was slow to take on two of the merchandising ideas that advanced throughout the supermarket field. The first was the increased use of supermarket space to sell nonfood items.

From small areas in the back of supermarkets, high-profit departments selling health and beauty aids, baby needs, housewares, toys and apparel spread throughout the store. Rack jobbers, or merchandisers, emerged whose sole function was to develop and run these nonfood departments in food stores. While many of these items are sold at A & P stores, the company has not developed them to the extent of some other food chains, which used their nonfood departments as the nucleus of their emerging discount-store divisions.

The other major postwar development at supermarkets was the use of trading stamps. Though trading stamps have had their ups and downs in the past as chains have taken them on or dropped them because of varying and changing estimations of their overall value, they have frequently served as important traffic builders for food stores. Sperry & Hutchinson, the Green Stamp pioneers, is an example of the many stamp companies that have evolved; in 1972 its revenues from trading stamps and other promotional services were $363,395,000 out of total revenues of $592,433,000.

After most of their competitors had acted, the A & P brought in Plaid Stamps, owned by the E. F. MacDonald Company, to about half of its stores in 1961 (although for a short period beginning in 1912 it had offered Green Stamps). The New York City stores, for instance, first started giving out Plaid Stamps in 1965. But by 1972, the A & P dropped stamps completely—resulting in a mob scene at a Manhattan redemption center for Plaid Stamps because thousands of A & P customers mistakenly believed that their stamps would not be redeemed afterwards—when the chain converted all its stores to the WEO discounting program.

WEO food discounting may very well be the most controversial and potentially the most far-reaching program ever adopted by the A & P. For when the A & P took on this idea of operating without frills, many other chains were already on the food-discount bandwagon. The company had initially experimented with this concept in 1969 and 1970, when it built A & P Discount Food Stores and then converted about 500 stores to A & P A-Marts, but it was in May 1970 that the first actual WEO opened in Pennsauken, New Jersey, operating (according to trade estimates) at a gross margin of around 12 to 14 percent in contrast to the conventional supermarket margin averaging 21 percent. Sales climbed so dramatically that a decision was made in January 1972 to convert the entire chain —regardless of where the stores were located—to the discount method of distribution as soon as possible.[4]

At that time, the initials stood for a Warehouse Economy Outlet, but the name has since been changed to Where Economy Originates. For the chain, moreover, it was virtually a return to the days of 1859 when George Hartford sold cut-price tea and 1912 when Mr. John opened the first no-nonsense, cash-and-carry stores featuring low prices and high volume. By the fall of 1972, all of the A & P stores became WEOs and a national supermarket price war got underway that did not end until 1973 after total food-industry profits declined by about 50 percent. Even so, bids from outsiders continued to be made, as they had been throughout the last decade, for the Hartford Foundation's controlling stock in the A & P.

The senior executive of "the Tea Company," as its old-time employees call it, is William J. Kane, chairman and chief executive officer. Mr. Kane began his career with the company in 1931 as a part-time clerk in his home city of Philadelphia while attending St. Joseph's College there. He rose steadily through the ranks of A & P's units and divisions before being named a vice president in 1964. Four years later he was elected to the presidency and moved up to his present position in 1971.

Robert F. Longacre, the No. 2 man in the hierarchy, also started as a store clerk in Philadelphia. In 1950, two years after joining the A & P, he became a store manager, a post that led to further advancement all the way up the line. Mr. Longacre was appointed president of the A & P's western region in 1969 and president of the company two years later.

Other key executives at the New York headquarters are William Corbus and Edward LaPage, vice chairmen; William I. Walsh, executive vice president; and Harry C. Gillespie, vice president and treasurer. The top men in the field are Noble F. Whittaker, president of the Eastern region; J. Albert Ziegler, president of the Western region; James S. Kroth, president of the central region; and Percy A. Smith, president of the Southern region.

The A & P is one company that has kept out of the real-estate business. George Hartford's short-term lease with many options helped it meet the 1929 crash without entangling real-estate commitments. But the concern has long since abandoned the short-term lease in favor of contracts averaging twelve years with five-year renewal options in order to move into new shopping centers as its competitors have done.

Though temptations have been great, the company keeps only a few weeks' inventory in its supply lines and has avoided speculation in commodities. "If we are in the grocery business," John Hartford often said, "let's stay there. If we want to speculate, let's sell out and go on the stock exchange."

A remarkable feature of A & P operation is its accounting system, one of the best in the world. Every item stocked is numbered and recorded. Costs are calculated to tenths and hundredths of a cent. Even electric-light bills are figured to the last cent. Percentage profits are worked out regularly. A division vice president knows exactly how much stock each of his stores has on hand and what their percentage of profit and wastage is. Store returns are analyzed and compared. Economies in one store are immediately passed on to others.

Since the company's further decentralization into thirty-two operating divisions went into effect in 1969, weekly sales and profit figures are sent directly to headquarters. Sales are received at the Graybar Building by Monday morning, while profits of each division are computed by Thursday.

If clerks use large paper bags when small ones would do, the accountants can detect it in the added costs. The A & P attempts to sell 100 percent of everything it buys. Shipments are planned to prevent spoilage and loss. Handling is swift and painstaking. In the stores, every empty carton is salvaged and wooden boxes are also saved for reuse or return.

A & P managers and executives are remarkable for their alertness and loyalty. Their achievements in emergencies have been notable. When the Kaw River in 1951 flooded the company's warehouse in Kansas City, Kansas, food trucked overnight from Chicago and St. Louis enabled the sixty A & P stores in the area to stay open and feed the flood refugees. Its people also provided safe drinking water and other help to 1972 flood victims in Pennsylvania and New York. To attract and keep the type of men it likes, the A & P has a national personnel department, training courses of many kinds and employee benefits as generous as any in the retail food field. These include wages that are among the highest in the industry, Christmas food baskets, hospitalization, group insurance and a noncontributory pension plan.

Some former A & P men have established businesses of their own and many hold important posts with other chains. Lansing

P. Shield, who rose from clerk to general auditor with A & P, became president of the Grand Union chain. Roger M. Laverty rose to be president and general manager of the big Fitzsimmons supermarket chain in California. Sherwin Harris became president of the Mary Lee Candy Company of Cleveland. W. A. Coleman headed the Humpty-Dumpty chain in Oklahoma.

All look back at their A & P experience with nostalgic pride. As one says: "The most profitable thing I ever did was work for them, not in money but in education."

Now running neck and neck with the A & P for the title of the nation's largest supermarket chain is Safeway Stores, Inc., with headquarters across the continent in Oakland, California. With 2,291 food stores and forty-five Super S discount stores throughout the U.S. and overseas, Safeway had sales in 1972 of $6,057,633,000 and earnings of $91,056,000. Like its archrival, it accounted for about 6 percent of food sales in the country.

Safeway had its start in 1915 when Marion Barton Skaggs bought an 18-by-32-foot grocery store in American Falls, Idaho, for $1,088 from his Baptist minister father, whose business credo was "He who serves best, profits most." At the age of twenty-seven, Skaggs already had experience in food retailing, but this was his first opportunity to put his own theories into practice. His philosophy was simply stated: "Distribution without waste."

Right from the start, Skaggs did away with the cracker-barrel, pot-bellied stove approach. He built wall-hugging shelves, kept his aisles clear and refused to stack merchandise too high for easy reach. All sales were cash and carry. The company quickly prospered and became the Skaggs United Stores.

In 1926, the 428 Skaggs stores were merged into Safeway. Safeway had come into existence earlier that year when the name was adopted by the Sam Seelig Company, a firm with stores in California and Hawaii, following a contest to choose a new name. By the end of the year, the consolidated companies had 766 stores, $30 million in sales and $800,000 in earnings.

It was 1931 when Safeway reached its peak in number of

store units. From this level of 3,527 stores, the total declined as small stores were closed with the growth of larger supermarkets in conveniently located suburban areas.

Safeway's volume topped $1 billion in 1947, $2 billion in 1957, $3 billion in 1966 and $4 billion in 1969. Most of the company's stores are in the fast-growing Western states, a factor largely responsible for its extraordinary increases in sales. With about 100,000 employees, stores ranging in size to 37,000 square feet and average sales per store at $4,400,000, Safeway is undoubtedly one of the retailing giants today.

Three men have been the key figures in the development of the modern Safeway: Robert A. Magowan, Quentin Reynolds and William S. Mitchell. Mr. Magowan, a former Macy's executive and son-in-law of Charles A. Merrill—the Merrill of the Merrill Lynch, Pierce, Fenner & Smith brokerage firm, which helped incorporate Safeway when it merged with Skaggs—joined the company in 1955 and moved it into new market areas and product categories.

After having served as both chairman and president of the big supermarket chain, Mr. Magowan is chairman of the executive committee. His description of Safeway's goals is made in the briefest terms: "Serving customers better, of course, is the key to success. But part of the challenge is in finding ways to do it."

Quentin Reynolds is chairman and chief executive officer of Safeway, after having spent his entire career with the company. Elected president in 1966, chief executive in 1969 and chairman in 1971, Mr. Reynolds is an articulate believer in the values of consumerism for business corporations as well as for the average shopper.

Thus when Safeway moved into food discounting as a corporate program, Mr. Reynolds did not make a big issue of it. "Discounting is just a return to the basics of supermarketing —high-volume, low-cost distribution," he says. "But the consumer likes the word."

The third member of Safeway's top management triumvirate

is William S. Mitchell, a certified public accountant who was appointed president in 1971. Mr. Mitchell follows in the pattern of thousands of supermarket executives throughout the country who work hard to keep their stores supplied with goods, equipped with attractive fixtures and geared to meet the needs of their customers. "We have always worked long hours in the grocery business," he points out.

The development of the A & P and Safeway is paralleled by the rise of many other giant food chains managed by other capable executives. A roster of these names includes such big organizations as Kroger, Food Fair, Acme, Jewel, Lucky, National Tea, Winn-Dixie and Grand Union, as well as such regional chains as Waldbaums, Bohack and Pathmark.

All these supermarket chains have long since passed through the pine-table and warehouse phase in which they relied on price appeal alone. They have also upgraded their merchandise and added new lines.

The food giants today are at the stage where—despite the self-selection features of their stores—a number of services are constantly being added to attract and hold more customers. This appears to be an important thrust of supermarket merchandising in the decade of the 1970s—one that is receiving more and more attention from merchandisers everywhere who are seeking to capture a greater portion of the fickle consumer's food dollar.

XII
Rich's

"The Store That Married a City"

Rich's Inc. of Atlanta for many years has been the biggest department store, both in sales volume and physical size, south of New York and east of the Mississippi River. It sells everything imaginable for the adornment of a person or the furnishing of a home. Its main store is actually four stores in two buildings, each occupying two city blocks.

One building houses a fashion store for women and children and a store for men. Connected with this building by a four-story glass-enclosed Kubla Khan-like bridge over Forsyth Street is a huge store for homes, and beneath both is a budget store. Each of the four stores has its own restaurants, entrances, restrooms, and escalators, or elevators. Adjacent to the store for homes is Rich's six-level self-park garage, enlarged to handle 1,250 cars at a time and 6,500 a day.

"Do you go by Rich's?" a woman once asked an Atlanta bus driver. He thought for a moment of the ramification of the store's twenty-nine acres of floor space.

"Madam," he replied, "I go by Rich's, under Rich's, through Rich's and around Rich's."

In addition to this huge and unique construction, Rich's as of 1974 had eight branches circling Atlanta, each occupying 85,000 to 329,000 square feet of ground, and five Richway Discount Stores. For fiscal 1973, it had profits of $11,398,000 on record sales of $260,670,000—a volume that was in the neighborhood of $150 for every resident of metropolitan Atlanta, representing a very high per capita figure.

More than twenty million people visit Rich's each year. This is more than the combined population of Alabama, Georgia and Florida. An average day brings crowds of 50,000 to 75,000 and the busiest days 85,000, or the population of a city the size of Augusta, Georgia. Such a crowd spent $2,900,000 the day after Thanksgiving in 1972.

Despite an eight-week strike over promotion of black employees, sales for the half year ending August 4, 1973, were $123,128,000, 12.5 percent more than the 1972 period. Earnings were $3,934,000, an increase of 19.3 percent. As part of the settlement Rich's established an employee relations committee with blacks represented. Independently of the agreement Jesse Hill, Jr., the first black Georgia University Regent, was named a director of Rich's.

Headed during the years of its greatest growth by an engineer, a rarity in retailing, Rich's has made notable advances in stock control and the mechanics of storekeeping. At the same time, in the tradition of the Rich family, it has achieved even greater advances in human relations with its employees, customers and the community. The store is married to Atlanta.[1]

The business was founded by Morris Rich, one of four brothers who as youths emigrated to the United States from Kaschau (Košice), then in Hungary and now in Czechoslovakia, just before and during the Civil War. In America all of the brothers speedily became clerks, peddlers and store owners. Only twenty years old but with six years of work as a clerk and peddler behind him, Morris rode a bay horse from Albany, Georgia, to Atlanta, where his brother William in 1865 had started a wholesale-retail dry-goods business. From William, who soon moved his own business to Nashville, Tennessee, Morris borrowed $500 and established a tiny dry-goods store on Whitehall Street. It opened on May 28, 1867. His brothers Emanuel and Daniel joined him as partners a few years later.

His first move to make his store attractive was a simple one. Whitehall Street, then little more than a country lane, was always ankle-deep in dust or mud. Young Rich laid down a row of planks that permitted ladies to alight from their carriages and enter the store without spotting their high button shoes or ruffled skirts. Inside, a salesman rushed forward to take the shopper's parasol or umbrella. This was in the tradition of Southern hospitality and customers liked it.

In a day of haggling, he began with fixed prices. This did not deter him from granting liberal credit or from trading calico and candles for sorghum, cotton and shelled corn. Another early-adopted policy was that of permitting customers to return goods without question. It is now publicized as "You make your own adjustment at Rich's."

This is interpreted so liberally that several million dollars' worth of goods, $32 million in 1971, for example, are returned each year. The store that year had a 15.3 percent return rate as compared to a 9.7 percent AMC store average. Adjustments are made in the departments involved and it is not necessary for customers to seek out a bureau of adjustment or complaint department.

An analysis of a year's returns once revealed that the store had refunded the price of an unused pair of women's button shoes thirty years old, an unworn man's shirt ten years old and a dead canary. Also included was a suit inaccurately altered by the wife of the sad but resigned gentleman who returned it, who explained that his wife had not liked the work of the alterations tailor and had sought to improve upon it.

In addition, some fifteen customers presented goods for credit or exchange that were not even bought at Rich's. In such cases Rich's customarily points out that the store does not carry these lines. Invariably the customers brightly reply, "But I never shop anywhere but here." Facing such a delicate impasse, Rich's clerks accept even these items and requested adjustments are made.

There also was a lady who dropped in to explain that the wedding cake she had ordered had been yellow inside, not white as specified, a fact that caused her some sorrow, even though the cake had been excellent, the wedding party had eaten of it heartily and the bridesmaids had taken away the traditional slices to put beneath their pillows. The lady received another cake, white inside, and went away unaware that she had made history by becoming the first person ever to eat her cake and have it too.

With men like Lucian W. York, David H. Strauss and members of the Rich family as executives, the store grew steadily through the years. York was a colorful figure who rose from bundle wrapper to general manager. As a boy, he had been ticket taker in an Atlanta theater and all his life collected autographs of stage folk who became his friends. Any parade of minstrels or show people was likely to turn into Rich's and wind up in York's office. Long before a cow named Elsie became an attraction, York filled Rich's with living Georgia animals, including possums and goats, to advertise a harvest sale. For another occasion, the store became a Chinese palace. He inaugurated an annual sale on the anniversary of the invention of Eli Whitney's cotton gin and on this day for years Rich's sold more cotton goods than any other store.

Emanuel Rich died in 1897 and Daniel Rich in 1920. The founder, Morris Rich, lived until 1928 but some years previously yielded his responsibilities to his nephew, Walter Henry Rich, a shy and kindly man who visited each department of the store daily for forty-five years and was one of Atlanta's best-loved citizens.

In 1901, the partnership was converted into a corporation with the number of stockholders gradually increasing to more than three thousand. In 1907, construction of a new building on Whitehall Street made Rich's the largest store in Atlanta. An expanded mail-order trade and an economy basement opened in 1910 increased volume. But Rich's was placed on the defensive in 1918, when its carriage-trade rival, the Chamberlin-Johnson-DuBose Co., moved into a new building.

Rich's answered the challenge with a still bigger building, completed in 1924 a few blocks west at Broad and Alabama Streets. Other important stores moved from Whitehall Street at this time but instead of following Rich's to the west moved north to create a new shopping center along historic Peachtree Street. There were many who said that Rich's new location was a mistake.

With greater space, larger stocks, more help and increased expense, the store did only a tenth more business and was left with a burdensome inventory. At this time, York, the general manager, died of a heart attack. As a final ominous note, Macy's was buying the rival Davison-Paxon store and Sears, Roebuck and Co. was building a $3-million branch in Atlanta.

In this crisis, Walter Rich turned for help to Frank H. Neely, a mechanical engineer without retail experience but who at forty already had a remarkable background.

Neely was born in Augusta, Georgia, into a family which for generations had run largely to preachers, like his grandfather, and teachers, like his father. Neely was not quite five years old when his school-superintendent father died, leaving nine children, of whom the future engineer was the youngest. He had a rough time of it, being farmed out to various relatives, who were chagrined because the young orphan had no liking for school. He was generally regarded as a sweet but backward child by all except a doting sister at Cedartown, Georgia, who kept urging him into regular school attendance. The arrival of some new farm machinery at a nearby farm brought the boy, along with others, to view it. Fascinated, he went home and said, "I am going to Georgia Tech to be an engineer."

A relative in Atlanta took him in and sent him to summer school to cram for entrance examinations. With no Latin to trouble him, young Neely sailed right through and at sixteen was entered as a freshman at the Georgia Institute of Technology. He graduated at twenty with highest honors and the mathematics medal.

Neely was one of the first Southern graduates to be hired by the Westinghouse Electric Company. The starting wage was forty dollars a month. After three successful years in its Pittsburgh shops, he acted contrary to the flow of Southern technical graduates and came home, setting himself up in a small office as consultant on scientific management.

About the same time he married his childhood sweetheart, Rae Schlesinger, and she began to apply the sort of scientific management that an intelligent and doting wife can provide. She kept him on an even keel and directed his enormous store of energy and ability. Once she insisted he spend the rent money to pay his membership fee in the American Society of Mechanical Engineers and attend its annual meeting. His articles were published in the association's journal. One of them, explaining a system he had worked out to increase candy production by a new conveyor-belt arrangement for wrappers, attracted the admiring attention of the late Frederick W. Taylor and Henry Laurence Gantt, who pioneered scientific management in American industry. The three became friends, and Gantt was a frequent guest in the Neely home until his death. Neely developed a passion for Gantt's charts and invented many of his own, applying them to the reorganization of the Fulton Bag and Cotton Mills, which had seven large plants in the South. He had been in charge of these for a decade when Walter Rich offered him the job of general manager.

"I've never worked a day in a store," Neely objected. "I'm too old to learn a new business. Besides, you can't pay me enough." Thinking to end the matter, he asked for a salary roughly equivalent to that then paid the President of the United States.

"When can you come to work?" countered Rich. Thus Rich's in 1924 gained the distinction of becoming the first department store ever to be run by a mechanical engineer. Neely's impact was felt almost immediately. For that year, the store had net sales of $5,450,000. They were more than a million dollars greater the next year.

One of Neely's first moves was to eliminate time clocks and have workers simply sign in for a record of being at work. He urged executives to worry less about this sort of thing and to spend more time training and encouraging their employees.

"Habits of industry," he quoted Gantt, "are far more valuable than any kind of knowledge or skill, for with such habits as a basis, the problem of acquiring the knowledge and skill is much simplified. . . . The general policy of the past has been to drive; but the era of force must give way to that of knowledge, and the policy of the future will be to teach and to lead, to the advantage of all concerned. . . ."[2]

Looking about for executive help, Neely found in the store a young man, a graduate of the University of Pennsylvania's Wharton School of Commerce, who had worked at Bamberger's in Newark. He was Richard H. Rich, a grandson of the founder. A son of a daughter of Morris Rich, he had adopted his mother's surname legally after a family discussion at the suggestion of his uncle, Walter Rich, to insure preservation of the name into the third generation. Born and bred in the department-store brier patch, so to speak, he demonstrated intelligence and ambition.

About this time an eager young man from Georgia Tech presented himself at Neely's office. The young man was writing a thesis on department stores and was interested in whether a store in Rich's location could succeed. This caused Neely—also a seeker in the same market—to quiver in his chair and to peer intently at the young face before him, seeking some hint of leg pulling. There was none, and Neely went on to sweat out the study, leaning on it as a sort of augury. When thesis writer Ben Gordon graduated with an A-plus on a thesis that proved that management could make Rich's location more desirable than any other, Neely hired him in a hurry.

Following the death of Walter Rich in 1947, Neely became president and two years later chairman of the board of directors. At this time, Dick Rich became president and Gordon executive vice president and general manager. They continued as a three-man executive team until Gordon left in 1955 to become president of City Stores Company. He later was a vice president of Allied Stores.

He was succeeded by Harold Brockey, who had moved from Chatham, New Jersey, to Atlanta in 1950 to become general merchandise manager of the store for homes. He was elected a vice president in 1954 and senior vice president and general merchandise manager for the entire store in 1955. He was named executive vice president in 1958 and became Rich's fifth president in 1961. At that time, Neely became chairman of the executive committee and Dick Rich, an impeccably tailored gentleman who likes to drive open cars, was named its third board chairman and chief executive officer. In 1972 Brockey became chairman and chief executive and Rich chairman of the executive committee after the retirement of Neely.

Joel Goldberg, a graduate of Darthmouth and Filene's, rose from dress buyer to senior vice president in nineteen years with Rich's and was named sixth president in 1972. His wife is the former Carol E. Brockwey. They met when she was a member of Rich's College Board and he was a dress buyer.

To meet the challenge of Macy's mass buying, Rich's joined the Associated Merchandising Corporation. This linked the store's buying with more than a score of big stores in other cities but kept the Rich slogan: "Atlanta-born, Atlanta-owned, Atlanta-managed."

Rich's refers to itself as a Southern institution and manages to create in its customers a feeling that they are privileged, dues-paying members. For many years a large share of its advertising has been institutional, identifying the store with the history of the state, its historical figures, colleges, artists, singers, musicians, the PTA, motherhood and so on. The advertising runs not only in Atlanta newspapers but in many others across the state.

When the Winecoff Hotel fire took 121 lives in Atlanta one weekend in 1946, the copy about a Georgia industry that had been prepared for the store's Monday-morning institutional advertisement struck Neely as inappropriate. He undertook to write something else.

After watching him crumple and throw away several drafts, Mrs. Neely, who is the author of a book of poetry, made a suggestion.

"Why not," she said, "just print the Twenty-third Psalm?"

This was done with the comforting phrases set within a black border. Only "Rich's, Inc.," in small italic type in a lower corner identified it with the store. When Atlantans recall the fire, they also recall this advertisement.

One of the stories told in the trade relates that an Atlanta competitor, attending a retail convention in New York, was asked the secret of Rich's success. "All they do," he said, with a wry face, "is stand on the corner and wave that blankety-blank Confederate flag."

But there is more to it than that. Bernard F. Gimbel, merchant prince in New York, spent some days in Atlanta as the guest of Robert W. Woodruff, head of the Coca-Cola Company. Gimbel cased the town thoroughly. A small dinner in Gimbel's honor was attended by Dick Rich, who suffered through seven courses with courage comparable to that of the Spartan youth whose vitals were being gnawed by a fox. The report was around that Gimbel would there announce that he was moving into Atlanta. After dinner, in an off-the-record talk, Gimbel praised Rich's highly and restored Dick Rich to a normal blood pressure by saying, "We don't care to come into Atlanta and buck competition as efficient and thorough as Rich's."

Rich's stumbles, of course, at times. A branch opened in Knoxville, Tennessee, in 1955, with radioactive atoms cutting the ribbons, for example, proved a disappointment and was sold in 1961. Branches in shopping centers around Atlanta, however, have added importantly to sales and earnings. These begin with the Lenox and Belvedere Centers in 1959. A Cobb County Center store was added in 1963. North DeKalb County and Greenbrier Center stores followed in 1965. South DeKalb, Perimeter and Cumberland Mall stores have been built since then, and seven Richway discount stores, two of them in Charlotte, North Carolina. The store operates the largest private automatic branch telephone exchange in the South. This system includes 1,115 internal stations and 120 outside lines. It is the approximate size of the central exchange for a town the size of Hawkinsville, Georgia (population 3,500). At peak periods, seventeen operators handle a switchboard system that receives between twelve thousand and fifteen thousand calls a day.

Rich's painstakingly identifies the store with the life of the city and state, for richer, for poorer, in sickness and in health. In the twenties cotton plunged. Rich's offered to take up to five thousand bales from Georgia farmers at a price well above the market, and did take what came in—a few hundred bales.

In 1930, Walter Rich picked up his morning paper and read that the city council had failed to find the money to meet the teachers' payroll. He telephoned the mayor and suggested that the administration issue scrip to the teachers, which Rich's would cash at full value with no obligation that they spend any of it with them. The city accepted with an alacrity exceeded only by the joyous educators'. Rich's paid out $645,000 to teachers and held the scrip on faith until the city repaid it. The teachers and their families naturally think of Rich's as being more than just a commercial institution.

The Sunday before Labor Day in 1945, Dick Rich had the store's safe opened to provide nearby Fort McPherson with money to pay off a large detachment of troops who had arrived on Saturday afternoon to be discharged on Sunday morning. The fort's funds were in vaults time-locked until Tuesday.

Long before Britain's Sir William Beveridge was advancing his idea of service that commentators described as "from the cradle to the grave," Rich's had it in effect. When the youngsters are old enough to be brought along on shopping tours, Rich's has a nursery—soundproofed, air-conditioned and decorated— waiting for them, with a registered nurse and staff. Germicidal lamps, which glare witheringly at all germs, are a part of the equipment.

Since 1947, when the store was eighty, Rich's has had an annual party for customers that age and over. There are prizes for the oldest man and woman, the couple who traveled farthest, those who have lived in Atlanta longest, and the guest with the most descendants. One had 147!

The Rich Foundation gave radio station WABE-FM to the

Atlanta public-school system. The schools use it daily for instruction, musical programs, lectures and announcements for which it is not possible to assemble the entire student body or class groups. The store provides four trips to Washington for the annual 4-H Club Leadership Conference. A savings bond is awarded to the best English student in each Atlanta public school. The Agnes Scott Freshman Award to the top freshman is also contributed by Rich's.

Rich's gave a building to Young Harris College, in north Georgia, and set up a foundation, through which a $250,000 building was erected at Emory University for a school of business administration, $100,000 was given to Georgia Baptist Hospital and many other gifts were made. These have included an industrial engineering laboratory and an electronic computer center for Georgia Tech, and a wing at St. Joseph's Infirmary.[3]

Rich's provides headquarters for two hundred garden clubs of Greater Atlanta and their twelve thousand members. The traffic to Rich's is heavy. Fashion shows (many of them benefits) and lectures on homemaking, beauty and interior decorating lure adults. Yearly supershows called Fashionatas are staged at the Atlanta Memorial Arts Center for the benefit of the Atlanta Arts Alliance. They are produced by Sol Kent, fashion director.

A shopping service does more than remind citizens of anniversaries, birthdays and special dates. The young ladies on the staff assist with weddings, help plan entertainments and offer suggestions on how to dress and how to decorate tables, rooms or lawns for these occasions. Each year hundreds of weddings in Georgia are planned by Rich's, down to the wedding cake out of the store's fine bakery.[4]

The store does not neglect its eleven thousand employees. As much attention and research are lavished on them as on customers. A forty-hour week was in force at Rich's long before federal laws required it. So was the five-day workweek. In fact, Rich's was the first Southern department store to institute them. There has long been a clinic, primarily for employees, where a registered nurse and staff furnish medical attention in the event of injury or illness, as well as advice on matters of family health. Executives are supposed to visit the clinic at least once a week for a rubdown and sun-lamp treatment. All employees for years have been protected by a hospitalization and sick-benefits plan. Profit sharing, a credit union, four employee cafeterias and a Christmas-bonus plan that includes every regular employee are a part of the program.

New sales employees receive three days' instruction before meeting the public. All are coached on their appearance, manners and attitude. The store has a Management Orientation Program, known as MOP for short, in which young men and women train for management jobs.

As of 1972, Rich's had 546 employees with twenty years of service, 67 with more than thirty years and fourteen with more than forty years. As the anniversaries of these employees roll around, they receive gift certificates. A pension plan provides benefits for those who have given years of loyal service.

The late Walter Rich wanted a store without any fear or awareness of big brass, and the store has none. "We can't expect our employees to be friendly to customers unless we lead a friendly existence ourselves," says Neely. The result of an absence of the big-brass atmosphere is a feeling, on the part of the employees of the store, of "belonging" and of pride in their job and work.

Perhaps the greatest tribute to Rich's was expressed in an address by Preston S. Arkwright, a president of the Georgia Power Company. After recalling that of twenty-three dry-goods stores in Atlanta in 1867, only Rich's survives, he said, "In all Atlanta, there is not a single human being who speaks ill of Rich's."

XIII

F. W. Woolworth Co.

"World's Greatest Variety Chain"

Americans could be sure of three things about Woolworth stores during the life of the founder, Frank Winfield Woolworth, and for long after his death. They were modest, red-fronted downtown structures. They had the whole corporate name across the front. They carried no items priced higher than ten cents, or fifteen cents in the West. And because the founder was from upstate New York and began his retailing career there, the annual meeting of company stockholders was always held in the pleasant but remote community of Watertown, New York. All these are now nostalgic memories.

In 1973, stockholders met in Minneapolis to hear Chairman Lester A. Burcham report that company's 4,779 stores and other units had record sales of $3,148,108,000 in the previous year, a gain of 12.7 percent, and earnings of $79,165,000. Since going to San Francisco in 1966, Woolworth has rotated its annual meeting from one regional headquarters city to another to permit officers and directors to meet more stockholders.

The dime price level was fractured as early as 1932 and rose steadily in the fifties and sixties. To serve an affluent America and to maintain its leading position in the fast-growing mass-distribution field (as Chairman Burcham prefers to refer to the so-called variety-store industry), some very large Woolworth stores now stock as many as forty thousand items, a few as costly as television sets and diamonds.[1] Newer Woolworth stores are big and more likely to be in a suburban shopping center than downtown. They are likely to be of a color other than red. The company's department stores, launched in 1962 with one on the edge of Columbus, Ohio, and nearly all in or adjoining shopping centers, are called Woolco. It owns the Harvest House Cafeterias, and its Kinney Shoe Corporation factories and stores continue under that name. Richman Brothers men's and boys' apparel stores became a subsidiary in 1969.

Frank W. Woolworth is in the Retailing Hall of Fame in Chicago, and the distinctions of the company bearing his name are many. It has paid uninterrupted dividends since incorporation. It trains its own executives and all promotions are from within the organization. The more than 1,900 Woolworth stores of the United States company serve all fifty states and Puerto Rico and the Virgin Islands. Its downtown store in Denver which was expanded in 1963 to 174,000 square feet overall, is claimed to be the largest variety store in the world. The British Woolworth Company, in which the parent company as of 1972 owned a 52.7 percent interest, has nearly 1,100 stores. The British company had profits of $55,698,000 on sales of $940,244,000 in 1972. There also are Woolworth stores in Canada, Mexico, the West Indies, Northern Ireland, the Republic of Ireland, West Germany and Spain.

More than a million Americans a day eat at Woolworth lunch counters or in Woolworth restaurants, some of which are handsomely furnished candlelit places of considerable charm. The company is the world's largest commercial purveyor of foods prepared and served on the premises on a nonfranchised basis. In this field it competes successfully not only with its variety-chain rivals but with thousands of drugstores and restaurants. As of 1972, W. A. Getzelmann, vice president of restaurant operations, was buying annually food to prepare 19,475,000 hamburgers, 6,100,000 turkey dinners, 6,900,000 slices of apple pie and 130,000,000 cups of coffee.

Woolworth's is also the leading retailer of items such as greeting cards and dolls, as well as pocketbooks, phonograph records and pets of all kinds. It is an important seller of candy, Christmas ornaments, brassieres, girdles, panties, hair nets and growing house plants. It is geared to take quick advantage of sudden fads. When the hula-hoop mania hit the country in 1958, Woolworth sold four million in five months. There was similar success later with records of the Beatles and the more recent fads.

It all grew from modest beginnings. Frank Winfield Woolworth was born April 13, 1852, on a farm in the town of Rodman, Jefferson County, New York. The family was of English descent and the name was an Americanization of a British place name, Woley or Wolley; the Colonial progenitor, Richard, a weaver, was known both as Wooley and Woolworth. Frank, his younger brother, Charles Sumner, and their parents later moved to another farm near Great Bend in the same county.[2]

One of his teachers, Emma Penniman Otis, remembered Frank as a tall, thin, somewhat frail but nimble-witted and persistent boy. "Frankie was a bright pupil," she recalled long afterward, "and never gave me the least trouble. He was inclined to be sober-minded, not at all prankish, and always had his lessons." His schooling ended at sixteen and he worked five years on the farm. He had no aptitude for farming and hated it.

In the depression year of 1873, he escaped by becoming a clerk, at first unpaid, in the Augsbury & Moore dry-goods store in nearby Watertown. On his initial day, he appeared in a flannel shirt and was sent home to put on a white one and a collar and tie. He developed a flair for dressing the windows and, after an interlude with another store, advanced to $10 a week. He then married a neighbor, Canadian-born Jennie Creighton, a seamstress.

The store, which had become Moore and Smith, with Perry R. Smith buying out Augsbury, offered a table of five-cent items in 1878. They sold so well during the county fair that young Woolworth became convinced that a store devoted to nothing else would prosper. With $300 credit from Moore and Smith and some money borrowed from relatives, he opened "The Great Five Cent Store" in Utica, New York, on February 22, 1879. The location was poor and it was a failure.

Undaunted, he opened another in Lancaster, Pennsylvania, on June 21, 1879, just ten days after closing in Utica. It was a success and doubly so after he added a counter of ten-cent merchandise. Enlarged and remodeled several times, this is the oldest Woolworth store. The 1969 annual meeting of stockholders was held in Lancaster to mark the store's ninetieth anniversary. Stores at Harrisburg and New York were not successful but one at Scranton, Pennsylvania, opened in 1880 with Charles Sumner Woolworth as manager, was and the chain was launched.

Frank Woolworth liked the red color of the A & P stores and from the first painted his stores the same hue. The gold lettering was his own idea. He opened more stores and took in as partners or managers his cousin, Seymour Knox, and other relatives; also Watertown friends and men encountered by chance, such as Harry Albright, the postman who delivered mail to the store in Lancaster. Meanwhile his brother, Sumner, bought Frank Woolworth's interest in the Scranton store and together with Fred Kirby, a friend from Watertown, began two separate chains. While they minded the stores, Woolworth searched for merchandise in New York and Europe.

By 1895, there were twenty-eight stores and sales were more than a million dollars a year. Five years later, there were fifty-nine stores and sales of more than five million. The chain became a New York corporation, F. W. Woolworth & Company, on February 16, 1905, with Woolworth as president. Carson C. Peck and C. P. Case were vice presidents. The fifty thousand shares of $100 preferred stock were offered at par to store managers and other employees. It carried 7 percent interest payable quarterly. The fifty thousand shares of common stock went to Woolworth and a few New York and Chicago executives. A regional organization was set up in 1908. The British company was started in 1909 with two stores in Liverpool.

Woolworth in 1912 took the lead in merging his and five other five-and-ten chains to form the F. W. Woolworth Co. Included were the stores of S. H. Knox and Co., headed by his cousin Seymour Knox, the stores of his brother, Charles Sumner, those of Fred M. Kirby and Earl Charlton; also the stores of W. H. Moore, his old employer in Watertown, and for sentimental reasons the place was made the headquarters of the new company.[3] Through Goldman, Sachs & Company, $6 million of $15 million par preferred stock and $7 million of $50 million par common stock were sold to the public. They were offered at $101.50 and $55 respectively but soared to $109 and $80.75 the same day on the New York Stock Exchange. The new company had 611 stores. Frank Woolworth had slightly more than half the stock. He became president and the other four founders were made vice presidents. The company had profits of $5,414,-798 on sales of $60,557,767 its first year.

The famous Woolworth Building was completed the next year. Designed by Cass Gilbert and constructed by Thompson-Starrett, this 792-foot edifice wrested skyline honors from both the Metropolitan Tower and the Singer Building, previously claimants of being the "tallest in the world." Woolworth's own office was an array of marble and Napoleonic relics on the twenty-fourth floor. He had personally paid the $13,500,000 construction costs of the building. President Woodrow Wilson, recently inaugurated, pressed a telegraph key to light the building for the first time. His old friends from Watertown were present and it was perhaps the happiest evening of Frank Woolworth's life. The executive offices of the chain are still in the building.

Because of his age and illnesses, Woolworth turned direction of the company over to Vice President Peck but resumed it when Peck died of diabetes in 1915. Woolworth died himself in New York on April 8, 1919, five days short of his sixty-seventh birthday. There were then 1,081 Woolworth stores with annual sales of $119 million. He left an estate, largely in company stock, of more than $27 million to his widow, who died May 21, 1924, and four daughters or their children. One granddaughter was a wistful and beautiful girl named Barbara Hutton, who wrote poetry and married seven glamorous men.[4]

Long after selling all her Woolworth stock, she was still known as a Woolworth heiress.

Buying and selling for cash, buying direct from manufacturers, minimum selling costs, including low wages for sales help (though no lower than many other stores at the time), open displays on the counters and selling for low prices were part of the founder's formula for giving the customer more for his money.

He was generous with his executives and associates, treating many of them like the sons he never had. "At least a hundred men—buyers, heads of departments, managers"—according to his biographer, John K. Winkler,[5] became millionaires through their association with him. These included all who took part in the 1912 merger; C. P. Case, the early vice president; and Hubert Templeton Parsons, who rose from bookkeeper to general manager and became president on the death of the founder.

Stores were opened in Cuba in 1924 and in Germany in 1927. In 1931, the 1,081 Woolworth stores had sales of $282 million. Parsons retired in 1932 and was succeeded for three years by Byron D. Miller, who had been a builder of the British company. Charles W. Deyo, who had started as a stockman in an S. H. Knox store, became president in 1935 and later chairman of the board.

Deyo raised store price levels to twenty cents and then more to continue paying higher wages to store personnel when NRA was ruled unconstitutional in 1935. He was so successful generally that the directors waived the compulsory retirement to have him lead the company through World War II. He was succeeded in 1946 by Alfred L. Cornwell, who had started as a "learner" in Worcester, Massachusetts, and in 1954 by James T. Leftwich, who had started as a bookkeeper.

Profits continued, especially in the British company, and sales rose, but the years after World War II presented many problems to the Woolworth organization. Population shifts made many downtown stores with long leases unprofitable.

All these problems began to be attacked. The company was among the first of all variety chains to move into the suburbs and in adopting self-service. President Leftwich launched an expansion and modernization program. To finance it, $75 million was borrowed from the Equitable Life Insurance Company and $35 million more from various pension funds. A Finance and Policy Committee, which included Leftwich and three directors, Allan P. Kirby, Seymour H. Knox and Fremont C. Peck, all sons of figures in early Woolworth history, spurred innovations.

They were stepped up further under Chairman Robert C. Kirkwood, who retired in 1969 at sixty-five.[6]

Lester A. Burcham, who has been chairman and chief executive officer since January 1, 1970, has spent his entire business career with the company, beginning as a "learner" in the Woolworth store of his home town, Lancaster, Ohio. The first store he managed was in Bellefontaine, Ohio, and he managed three stores in Cleveland when he went to executive positions in the Cleveland and Philadelphia regional offices. In January 1963, he became executive vice president, after being appointed vice president in 1958.

Other top executives as of 1973 include John S. Roberts, president; Ernest L. G. Medcalf, board chairman of the British company; Harold J. McPhail, president and managing director of the Canadian company; W. Robert Harris, executive vice president; Henry R. Wilson, executive vice president international. Other vice presidents include Edward F. Gibbons, finance; Robert W. Young, personnel; Keith L. Sumner, store development; Hubert P. Smith, public affairs; John W. Lynn, merchandising; Willard A. Getzelmann, restaurant operations; Harry E. Moedinger, sales promotion; David E. Chenault, expense and security; John L. Sullivan, operations; Clayton H. Van Buren, treasurer. Urbain Van Laecken is a vice president in charge of the Woolco Department Stores; James B. Stuart is president of Kinney Shoe and Donald J. Gerstenberger is president of Richman Brothers.

Regional vice presidents are William G. Baker, Jr., Northeastern; Walter C. Pierce, Mid-Atlantic; Edmund H. Burke, Southeastern; John T. Arnold, North Central; C. Walton Backhaus, Midwestern; Rolland C. Ladd, South Central and Ernest W. Kauffman, Pacific.

Hundreds of old Woolworth stores have been closed, expanded or moved to better locations. Bigger and bigger stores have been opened, a great many in suburban shopping centers. One was opened in the Orange Mall, in Orange, California, in 1972. Self-service has become the rule rather than the exception. Clerks are in the aisles with the customers in newer Woolworth stores. Recruitment and training of employees has been made systematic and professional.

From a notorious nonadvertiser, the company has become an important user of newspaper space, often full pages in color, and of television and radio time. Its first network show was a Sunday-evening Woolworth musical hour over CBS in 1955. Local managers are encouraged to take part in community activities, and some have won awards for such service.

But the greatest changes have been in the merchandise. Few retail companies have ever upgraded entire lines of merchandise so dramatically. There is now a wealth of fashionable wearing apparel as well as better-grade household appliances and other items. A customer may buy a Java temple bird, an air conditioner or sporting goods.

A chain of competitive mass-merchandising Woolco Department Stores was started in 1962. At the start of 1973, there were 239 of these stores in the United States and Canada and an additional five in England, with more scheduled to open at the rate of approximately forty to fifty each year. Various forms of credit are offered in Woolco Department Stores.

On the social-responsibility front, Woolworth's has one of the most systematic and effective affirmative action programs for the recruiting, training and employment of blacks, Puerto Ricans and other minority groups. An assistant vice president for administrative services, Aubrey C. Lewis, a black former F.B.I. agent and Notre Dame football star, is responsible for much of the program.[7]

"Our management training program provides the opportunity for earning while learning," explains President Roberts. "Mr. Lewis annually visits some thirty black colleges alone to get this point across in our search for young men and women to fill future managerial and executive ranks.

"Interested college students are enrolled in the training program on a part-time basis while still in school. Upon graduation—Woolworth accepts a junior college degree as graduate status—the student continues his training as a full-time assistant store manager. During the period in which he is a student trainee the person receives salary rates comparable to those of full-time trainees."

Woolworth's has undertaken to have a black-staffed store in Harlem, in a building and on land sold to a black community group and leased back from them with the income going to self-help projects in the community. The company is one of the largest customers of such black-owned cosmetic firms as the Cannolene Company of Atlanta and Johnson Products and Supreme Products of Chicago. It also buys whiskbrooms from Friendly Leader Manufacturers of North Carolina and household items from Young Men on the Move of Detroit. President Roberts was a guest when Young Men celebrated its first million dollars in sales.[8]

XIV
Dayton's and Hudson's

The Giants of Minneapolis and Detroit

A young merchant named Joseph Lothian Hudson was one of hundreds of retailers to whom the panic of 1873 was a cruel blow. He was then twenty-seven years old and, in partnership with his father, was running a small men's clothing store in the lumber town of Ionia, Michigan. Soon after the failure of the Jay Cooke banking house in New York, the sawmills stopped in Ionia and Hudson's customers could not pay their bills.

The father died that year, partly from worry, but young Hudson struggled on until 1876. He went bankrupt, losing a flour mill and some timberland as well as the store that year to pay his creditors sixty cents on the dollar. He then started all over as an employee in another store.

Twelve years later, by remarkable enterprise, he owned a bigger store in Detroit. Even more remarkable, he looked up all the creditors whose claims had been erased by the bankruptcy proceedings and paid them in full with compound interest. Such action is rare. In 1888 it astounded the business world. The amazed creditors showered him with gifts and praise.

"We sent today by American Express two cases containing a clock and mantel ornament which we ask you to accept as indication in some small degree our sincere respect and esteem," wrote David T. Leahy of E. H. Van Ingen & Co., New York. "Especially we have wished to make known to you our appreciation of your high sense of commercial honor as shown by your payment—in a quiet and unostentatious way—of principal and interest of debts forgiven to you by your creditors many years ago and indeed almost forgotten by them. Your failure was an honest one that left no stain upon your reputation. You could have found plenty of plausible reasons for not paying when you became able to. You chose the high and manly course. . . . Our best wishes for a merry Christmas and a happy and prosperous New Year."[1]

In 1902, another remarkable retailing institution was founded in the Midwest when George Draper Dayton, a New York-born banker from Worthington, Minnesota, headed an investment company that built a six-story building on Nicollet Avenue and Seventh Street in Minneapolis. Dayton, a member of the family for whom Dayton, Ohio, was named, purchased the property on which stood the shell of a burned-out church, constructed the new building and waited for tenants to arrive.

The wait was long indeed because none of the Minneapolis companies or professional men wanted to move that far "uptown" from what was then the business center of the city. So to protect his investment, Dayton bought the Goodfellow Dry Goods Company and installed it in three floors of the building. The name of that firm was later changed to the Dayton Company, the Nicollet and Seventh corner later became the center of Minneapolis (and naturally a most valuable piece of property) and the store later became one of the best-known retailers in the nation.

In 1969, Hudson's and Dayton's, each of which had by that time become the dominant stores in their area and the backbone of individual retail empires, merged to form the Dayton Hudson Corporation. One of the largest retailing groups in the nation, Dayton Hudson had record sales in 1972 of $1,297,386,000 and profits of $28,195,000.

Dayton Hudson Corporation is a national diversified retailer with 269 individual units, including 82 franchised stores, and eight shopping centers. The chain includes 49 discount stores, 34 jewelry stores, 120 bookstores, nine electronic equipment stores and 2 catalog showroom companies, in addition to such leading department store groups as Diamond's in Phoenix,

Arizona, Lipman's in Portland, Oregon, and John A. Brown in Oklahoma City, Oklahoma. But the bulk of its sales comes from the heart of its operations which consists of two department stores in Detroit and Minneapolis—Hudson's and Dayton's.

Hudson's downtown store alone has forty-nine acres of floor space, and its twenty-five stories make it the tallest department store in the world. Its four basement levels also make it one of the deepest. In space under one roof, it is second only to Macy's Thirty-fourth Street. When Ford, Chrysler and General Motors work overtime, Hudson's downtown volume, about 30 percent of its overall total, sometimes exceeds that of Macy's Thirty-fourth Street.[2]

Hudson's and Macy's, incidentally, have the largest switchboards among retail customers of the telephone company. Hudson's leads on trunk lines and Macy's is ahead on extensions. Only the Pentagon, Metropolitan Life, Union Carbide and a few others have bigger boards.

Hudson's closest retail competitor in Michigan is its own Budget Stores. The two-level operation in the downtown store boasts one of the largest budget volumes in the world. Additionally, Hudson's has seven branch stores in Michigan and Toledo, Ohio, and a separate branch budget store.

One reason for Hudson's success is the completeness of its assortment of merchandise. In an institutional advertisement, it once boasted of carrying 553,921 items "A to Z—from antimacassars to zippers, aspirin to zwieback. An African mask to Zuercher cheese." Detroit's biggest bookstore, biggest drugstore and biggest toy store are all Hudson departments. Even a tiny department for dog owners offers canine candy, deodorants, dog books, leashes trimmed in gold, traveling boxes and supersonic whistles.

The drug departments, which employ thirty-six registered pharmacists, offer fifty thousand items. To serve Detroit's polyglot population, clerks speak fourteen languages and Hudson's stock includes ancient and exotic remedies as well as the sulfas and antibiotics. On the shelves are camomile flowers from Hungary, agar-agar from Japan, orrisroot from Spain and oils from everywhere, including Turkish rose oil that sells for $16 for a few drops or $720 a pound. In addition, the store sells commodes, wheelchairs, canes, crutches, backrests, bed trays, sun and heat lamps, surgical garments, hearing aids and almost any sickroom article.

There is heavy emphasis on related selling. Hudson's is the No. 1 outlet for Simmons mattresses. But along with a mattress, Hudson's likes to sell everything related to it, such as bedroom furniture, bedding, pajamas, nightgowns, bedroom slippers and even an alarm clock. Hudson's encourages home building with a planning center and often sells every item that goes into the home when it is built. At least half of all Wayne County brides are registered with Hudson's Bridal Registry, and Xerox copies of their wishes and purchases for them go daily to all branches to avoid duplication of gifts. Numerous weddings are outfitted even to flowers and tickets for a honeymoon trip. There are whole floors for boys and girls and there is also a barbershop for children, where they can ride a tiger or car while having their hair cut.

Also a factor in Hudson's success is the care with which it recruits, trains and keeps happy its sixteen thousand employees. The store has pioneered in the development of buying and inventory controls and the use of business machines. It lures a hundred thousand customers a day with promotions throughout the year, including a Thanksgiving Day Santa Claus parade that is several years older than Macy's. It has a liberal returned-goods policy.

Most important of all in the growth of the big store has been a continuity of able, civic-minded management. When J. L. Hudson, the founder, died unmarried in 1912, he left the store to his four nephews. Richard H. Webber, who had been his uncle's companion since the Ionia days and who had risen to vice president in the store, then became president. He later became chairman and honorary chairman of the board, serving more than sixty-five years in all. His younger twin brothers, Joseph L.

and James B. Webber, became directors of merchandise and vice presidents. The youngest of the four, Oscar Webber, a Phi Beta Kappa graduate of the University of Michigan, began in the store as cashboy and advanced to president and chairman.

Six-foot Joseph L. Hudson, Jr., who at twenty-nine succeeded Oscar Webber as president in 1961, is a retailer by both inheritance and training. His grandfather, William H. Hudson, was a brother of the store founder who worked with him in Ionia. The young store head was born July 4, 1931, in Buffalo, New York, where his father, Joseph L. Hudson, was treasurer of the Adam, Meldrum and Anderson department store, which absorbed an early Hudson men's store there.[3]

He first worked for the Detroit store as a stockboy and receiving dock hand during summers while attending Yale, where he earned a letter as goalie on the hockey team and graduated in 1953. He then joined the store as an executive trainee, after which he gained experience in the employment office, toy department and the downtown basement, now called the Budget Store. He served two years in Germany as an Army artillery lieutenant and on his return in 1956 became assistant to the general manager and a director. And four years later took over the reins as head of the store. In 1972, he became chairman of Hudson's, and Edwin G. Roberts, a veteran retailer, was appointed president.

Joseph Lothian Hudson, the founder of Hudson's, was born on October 17, 1846, in Newcastle-upon-Tyne, England, where his father, Richard Hudson, ran a small tea and coffee business. In 1853, the father migrated to Canada and found a job with the Grand Trunk Railroad at Hamilton, Ontario. Two years later the family followed. At thirteen, Joseph got his first job, as a telegraph messenger. He also worked as a grocery boy-of-all-work for five dollars a month in Hamilton. In 1860, the family moved to Grand Rapids, Michigan, where the father had another railroad job. Young Joseph worked on a fruit farm and managed to finish eight years of school. In 1861, the family moved again, to Pontiac, Michigan.

There Joseph Hudson, now fifteen, met and went to work for Christopher R. Mabley, who was then running a small men's clothing store with sales of about $25,000 a year. The first month he paid young Hudson $4; this was doubled the next month and the youth showed such an aptitude for the business that, after five years, he was drawing $500 a year and board. The Mabley store volume rose to $100,000.

One of Mabley's many ventures was a store in Ionia, Michigan, operated in partnership with Hudson's father. In 1865, the elder Hudson bought out Mabley's interest and induced his nineteen-year-old son to take over the management. It had attained a volume of $40,000 a year when the panic of 1873 struck.

With this store bankrupt, young Hudson again became an employee of Mabley, this time as manager of his Detroit store while he went abroad for a vacation. Hudson did so well that he was rehired at $50 a week and given 10 percent of the profits, which amounted to $2,500 at the end of six months. Mabley then gave him a quarter interest and a guarantee of $7,500 a year for three years.

At the end of this time in 1881, Hudson went into business for himself. The first venture was in Toledo, Ohio, but within the year he opened a men's and boys' clothing business in Detroit on the ground floor of the old Detroit Opera House on the Campus Martius, not far from the present store site. Within a few years Hudson was prosperous enough to pay his old Ionia debts. He also opened branch stores in St. Paul, St. Louis, Grand Rapids, Cleveland, Sandusky and Buffalo. By 1891 he had eight stores doing a total volume of more than $2 million a year and was the largest individual buyer and retailer of men's clothing in the country.[4]

Business troubles following the depression of 1893 caused the sale or liquidation of all the stores except the main one in Detroit. This was Hudson's favorite enterprise. In 1884, he formed a partnership with Campbell Symington and took over space in another building to sell furniture, rugs and carpets, draperies and curtains. There was expansion in 1887, and in 1891 he moved into a new eight-story building at Farmer and Gratiot Streets and added more departments.

"He'll never make a go of it!" said Hudson's friends. The location was considered too far uptown and the fact that a Presbyterian church had occupied the site previously was deemed an ill omen for a commercial enterprise. But the store was successful. In 1895, it was incorporated as the J. L. Hudson Company.

In 1905, he shortened store hours with the comment, "It has been shown we can produce with the same labor in eight hours what we used to produce in twelve." An addition was made to the Farmer Street building in 1907, and in 1911 a ten-story building was constructed on much of the Woodward Avenue side of the block. Though all of this frontage was not obtained until 1923, the store began to take on its present appearance.

As his nephews assumed responsibilities in the store, Hudson gave more time to other activities. One was helping a niece's husband, Roscoe B. Jackson, and his partners, Howard E. Coffin and Roy D. Chapin, launch the Hudson Motor Car Company. Incorporated on February 24, 1909, the company was named for Hudson, who supplied most of the capital and became chairman of the board. The firm started with $15,000 in cash; models, patterns and dies were valued at $25,000; and subscriptions later paid in cash aggregating $58,990. It proved incredibly successful. On the next July 3, the first Hudson car, an efficient four-cylinder twenty-horsepower model priced at $900, rolled forth. Within a year, four thousand had been sold. There was a profit of $587,355 the next year. This increased to $822,000 in 1912, the year of Hudson's death, and subsequently earnings were as much as $21 million in a single year. The company merged with Nash-Kelvinator in 1954 to create American Motors, Inc. Hudson also had another connection with the automobile industry. A daughter of his sister, Mrs. William Clay, married Edsel Ford.

Hudson was perhaps the foremost philanthropist of Detroit and gave not only of his money but of his energy and personal direction. He was a humanitarian of rare quality, not only in the sense that he aided hospitals, orphan asylums, churches, scientific research, Y.M.C.A. work and innumerable charities, but also in going out of his way to aid unfortunates.

A murderer who had served out his sentence came to Hudson with an idea with which to rehabilitate himself. Hudson said, "Your idea needs publicity. We'll go over to the newspaper editor and talk to him about it." Afterward, the editor asked Hudson why he walked over to the newspaper office with the felon, when he could just as well have called up or sent a note. Hudson answered: "I wanted to help the man regain his self-respect. I wanted to show that I was willing to walk with him and be seen with him publicly."

The store had sales of nearly $3.5 million a year when the founder died in 1912 on a vacation trip to England. In the ensuing years, the spectacular growth of Detroit and the enterprise of the publicity-shy Webber brothers (they were never interviewed and posed for few group pictures) multiplied this volume many times. While the average department store turned its stock four times a year, Hudson's made it seven times. Sales grew from $4 million in 1913 to almost $66 million in 1929. When the depression hit Detroit hard,[5] Hudson's sales slipped to $31.5 million in 1933. Volume then surged ahead again, passing $170 million with the opening of the first Hudson's branch store and increasing steadily since 1955, despite some dips in Detroit's economy.

Physical expansion continued at the store. Air conditioning was installed gradually and a regular cycle of interior modernization was adopted by the store's architectural staff, with increasing emphasis on open displays and greater facilities for self-selection. In 1945, the old Sallan Building at the corner of Woodward and Gratiot was demolished to make way for a twelve-story addition. Completion of this building made the Hudson store a full block square. In 1946, two additional stories were added to the Grand River end of the building, and the mezzanine floors in both the Woodward and Farmer buildings were enlarged.

All of this gave the 2,100,000-square-foot store a ground area of 320 by 220 feet and a building containing 51 elevators, 17 more for freight and two escalator systems. The building also contains five restaurants and an employees' cafeteria. There are 705 fitting rooms, believed the most in any store, scattered over 10 floors. There is a store hospital, considered one of the finest industrial hospitals, with four doctors, four nurses, a laboratory technician and six visiting nurses who make regular calls on employees who are ill. The hospital even includes a silence room where employees may relax during their rest periods.

Suburban shopping centers came under consideration as Detroit began to share the traffic congestion which its products have created. The Webbers decided to build three centers, to be known respectively as Northland, Eastland and Westland after a survey by the Detroit *News* revealed that 50 percent of the city's suburban residents did not come downtown to shop. A subsidiary company was organized, and the first of the centers, Northland, twelve miles to the northwest, was completed in 1954 at a cost of $25 million.

Northland has 108 stores, shops and restaurants, including the nation's largest branch store—the 601,000-square-foot Hudson's. Designed by the Vienna-born Victor Gruen, the center combines beauty and efficiency. All truck delivery is underground. Colonnades, malls, covered walkways, modern art and flowers make the center attractive. Harold Gluckman and Alfonse Rapaczak of Hudson's display department painted a mural 500 feet long for the branch. Fountains, statuary and art objects by Gwen Lux, Lily Saarinen, Marshall Fredericks, Richard Hall Jennings and others adorn the malls. Miss Lux's "Totem Pole," a dramatic abstraction, is a favorite meeting place for shoppers.

Eastland Center, east of the city, was completed in 1957, with the Hudson branch there surrounded by seventy-four smaller stores and shops. Westland, a glass-enclosed mall-type center, was completed in 1965 at a cost of $10 million. It houses a Hudson branch and fifty other stores twenty miles west of downtown Detroit. More Hudson branches have been opened at key suburban locations around the Detroit area.

Hudson's boasts the largest flag in the world and also the tallest flagpole in Detroit. The monster flag, 104 by 235 feet, is too big for any pole but hangs on the Woodward Avenue side of the store at least every Flag Day. Each star is 5½ feet high and each stripe eight feet wide. In a long-remembered public-relations project, Hudson's designed flags for each of Michigan's eighty-three counties and presented them at county-seat ceremonies.

Probably no event of the holiday season except Christmas itself is more keenly anticipated by Michigan youngsters than Hudson's annual Thanksgiving Day parade. Some 300,000 people watch it. Over twenty-five floats, a thousand marchers and more than a dozen bands take part in the huge spectacle, which has wound its way down Woodward Avenue every year since 1920 with the exception of a brief lapse during World War II. It is so much a Detroit tradition that it is considered to be the official start of the holiday season.

Christmas at Hudson's means a Santa Claus, awe-inspiring on a big golden throne amid true North Pole surroundings. It also means ingenious animated windows and the building decked inside and out with trees, lights and decorations of a hundred different kinds. The Hudson Carolers, an employee singing group, appears daily during December on the selling floors, and ends the season with a Christmas Eve television show.

Art and music have always had a prominent place in Hudson's activities. Schoolchildren have been entertained at symphony concerts and store musical organizations have made tours. Since the early years of radio, a daily hour of music has been sponsored by WWJ, Detroit's oldest station. The store's art department is the largest in any department store. For a "Michigan on Canvas" art project, Hudson's in 1946 employed ten leading artists at a cost of $75,000 to paint, without restrictions, scenes about the state. The artists were Arnold Blanch, Aaron Bohrod, Adolf Dehn, John DeMartelly, David Fredenthal, Joe Jones, Doris Lee, Carlos Lopez, Ogden Pleissner and Zoltan Sepeshy. The ninety-six canvases they produced, depicting automobile manufacture, lake freighting, mining, agriculture and similar subjects, were exhibited in thirty showings and won Hudson's notice in *Life*[6] and many other publications. They are now displayed at Greenfield Village, Michigan.

The store's fame rests also on the loyalty and service of its employees. When John Thomas Williams, a Hudson doorman, died in 1961, a *Detroit Free Press* editorial saluted his "scrupulous alertness, tireless politeness and genuine friendliness to every customer."[7] This spirit extends to the handling of telephone and mail orders, and the faithfulness of its deliverymen. Some of this is the reaction of well-trained and loyal employees. Mostly, though, it is the result of planning, for Hudson's has a plan for nearly every contingency. For example, parcel-post shipments are speeded up by recording their addresses by Dictaphone. Or, if it begins to rain, the main-floor superintendent notifies the switchboard and the operators call several departments and tell appointed salesgirls that "It's raining." By the time the first wet customers come in, extra umbrellas have been set out and there is extra help in the raincoat department.

Hudson's has 500 delivery trucks, painted a distinctive green. Large trucks shuttle goods from the Woodward Avenue store to the delivery center a quarter of a mile away to three substations. Others fan out daily from these substations for points as far away as forty-five miles. The 280 men who man these trucks drive 4,500,000 miles a year, deliver 8,000,000 packages and are among Hudson's best salesmen.

Hudson drivers have started countless cars on cold mornings for ladies in distress and pulled cars out of mud with their trucks. They regularly find and return lost dogs and children. They've started the fire on a cold morning when Grandmother was home alone, then stopped to check it later. They've been slugged and robbed. They've hidden their day's receipts from would-be robbers. One had his face pushed through the glass of his truck by a bandit.

A driver named Joe Krul had the most unusual adventure. It was just another busy pre-Christmas Saturday when he started on his delivery route. Before completing his second stop, things happened. He heard a plane's engines close above him, then the thunder of a tremendous crash just one street away. While his assistant ran to pull the fire alarm, Joe dashed to the scene. A DC-3 cargo plane lay with its shattered nose buried in a home, a mass of smoke and flames. Women were yelling, "Save her!"

Joe looked up and saw a woman on the second floor of the shattered house, just staring, in shock. "The house was tilted over, so I ran up the side to the porch, grabbing onto the bricks that were shoved out," said Joe. He kicked the door in, dragged the woman out and passed her down to waiting men. Then he leaped free of the collapsing porch. Wringing wet, dirty with smoke, his knees shaking, Joe called the store and headed home to change uniforms. Then he went back to work delivering his packages.

Just as Hudson's emerged as a colossus as a result of the infusion of talent in each generation of management, so has Dayton's established itself as permanent in its market under the leadership of the sons and grandsons of George Dayton. The store at that "uptown" corner of Nicollet and Seventh moved along quietly—although it demonstrated its promotional flair as early as 1909 by displaying a full-sized replica of one of Glenn Curtiss's early flying machines—until 1917, when a fire destroyed its shoe department and speeded up plans for the twelve-story building that now stands on the same site.

The two sons of George Dayton followed him into the top posts at Dayton's, with D. Draper Dayton serving as general manager from 1906 to 1923 and G. Nelson Dayton moving into that position in 1923. Nelson was named president in 1938 upon the death of his father and remained head of the store until he died in 1950.

It was in the decade of the fifties that the third generation of Daytons, all of whom began as stockroom clerks, came to power in the store and built it into the powerful force in Upper Midwest retailing that it is today, with a trading area stretching from western Wisconsin to eastern Montana. The five sons of G. Nelson Dayton—Donald, Bruce, Wallace, Kenneth and Douglas —and their cousin George, the son of D. Draper Dayton, gave the Dayton stores their present personality of quality, fashion and showmanship.

"We merchandise to dominance," says Kenneth Dayton. "As the dominant store in the area, we have to appeal to the whole pie. And so we'll have everything from the $8.95 dress in our downtown store to a Ben Zuckerman suit."[8]

Dayton's 1,300,000-square-foot flagship store in downtown Minneapolis has been augmented by five branches, including some in company-owned shopping centers. The branch-building program, which got underway in 1954, has resulted in large units now operating in the Minnesota cities of Rochester, Brooklyn Center, Edina, Roseville—and Minneapolis' twin city of St. Paul.

One of the features that has long attracted crowds to Dayton's downtown store is its eighth-floor, 12,000-square-foot public-events auditorium, the largest in the country. Dozens of cultural and promotional exhibitions have been held there over the years, from circuses to rock concerts to Hawaiian villages. For two Christmas seasons, Dayton's built a $250,000 re-creation of Charles Dickens' London with two-story buildings and animated figures that each year drew more than half a million people to the store.

Dayton's special events calendar is filled day after day with activities designed to attract residents of the Minneapolis area to the store. Fashion shows, investment seminars, classes of all kinds, designer presentations and autographing parties are just a few of the events regularly run in Dayton's downtown store and branches. When the nation was talking about Twiggy, or Carnaby Street, or Simon and Garfunkel or Bill Blass, Dayton's was among the first American stores to present them to the public.

Bruce Dayton is chairman of Dayton Hudson and Kenneth Dayton is president. Joe Hudson also serves as vice chairman of the parent corporation as well as president of Hudson's, and William Andres is executive vice president, retail operations, for Dayton Hudson. Carl Erickson is chairman of Dayton's and senior vice president of Dayton Hudson, while Roy Eberhard is president of Dayton's. Donald, Douglas and Wallace Dayton are all members of the corporation's board of directors.

The Dayton brothers confessed in their early years at the company that their long-range goal was a retailing organization doing a half a billion dollars in sales annually. Now that they have passed the billion-dollar mark, their goals have increased considerably, although they are making no further predictions. But with Hudson's and Dayton's as their base, they are moving ahead in size and scope while continuing to maintain the rigorous business principles with which their progenitors began these retailing giants of Detroit and Minneapolis.

XV
Sears, Roebuck and Co.

The World's Biggest Retailer

The new steel, glass, aluminum, granite and concrete Sears Tower housing the headquarters of Sears, Roebuck and Co. is the world's tallest building. In office space it is second only to the Pentagon. Its construction cost more than $150 million. Started under former Chairman Gordon M. Metcalf and completed under Chairman Arthur M. Wood, who became chief executive officer in 1973, the stepped modular structure soars 1,454 feet above Wacker Drive in downtown Chicago.

Its height compares with 1,350 feet for the World Trade Center and 1,250 feet for the Empire State Building in New York, the previous upward-thrust champions, and with the 1,136 feet of the Standard Oil of Indiana Building in Chicago. The Eiffel Tower in Paris is 984 feet; the Gateway Arch in St. Louis, 630 feet; the San Jacinto Monument in Texas, 570 feet; and the Washington Monument, only 555 feet.

Sears towers similarly over rival retailers. It had net sales of $10,991 million—almost $11 billion—for the year ending January 31, 1973. This was about 1 percent of the gross national product and a new record for the eighteenth consecutive year. The earnings of more than $600 million were a record for the twelfth year in a row. No other retailer has had such sales. Since moving ahead of the A & P in 1964, Sears has been the world's biggest retailer. Its common stock continues to be the most popular retail investment of mutual funds.[1]

With $410 million spent locally and nationally on advertising in 1971, Sears has become America's biggest local advertiser though still second to Procter & Gamble in national outlay. Long the biggest user of newspaper advertising space, Sears was big enough in television in 1972 to be named that medium's Advertiser of the Year. One third of all American families shop at Sears at least once a year. Every fourth one has a charge account.

Why has Sears been so extraordinarily successful? There have been two alliterative answers, one was "Bargains, brains and ballyhoo."[2] Austin T. Cushman, a former chairman, said: "Men, merchandise, methods and money—and men come first." Most Sears employees are well chosen and trained. Their salaries and benefits are considerably above average. They are loyal and competitive. If bandits rob a Sears store, employees may chase and capture them. That happened to two gunmen who held up a Sears mall store at Troy, Michigan, soon after it opened in 1965.[3] Many Sears executives have played football. They tackle their tasks as they once did runners on autumn afternoons. Stock-exchange quotations on Sears stock and that of its rivals, J. C. Penney and Marcor, the parent of Montgomery Ward, are posted three times a day in the Chicago headquarters.

As of 1972, the fifty-five-year-old Sears Profit Sharing Fund, in which 224,142 employees then participated, was the biggest owner of Sears stock, 30,735,000 shares—20 percent of those outstanding. The fund's assets at the end of 1972 totaled $4.2 billion. No other retailer has anything approaching this figure. Attitude studies by outsiders of Sears employees on an anonymous basis show that 95 percent of them would rather work for Sears than for any other company.[4]

Sears began as a mail-order seller of watches and later general merchandise to farmers. Eugene Talmadge, several times governor of Georgia, won votes by assuring rural audiences: "Your only friends are Jesus Christ, Sears, Roebuck and Gene Talmadge." Calvin Coolidge, known for his thrift, was a customer.[5] Lyndon B. Johnson, as a young man, wed Lady Bird Taylor with a $2.50 ring hastily obtained by his best man from a Sears store in San Antonio.

Today the company sells nearly everything to everybody, and credit sales accounted for 52.3 percent of its record 1972 volume.[6] In a reversal of the situation that still prevailed in the late twenties, about 22 percent of its huge volume comes from its famous catalogs and about 78 percent from its stores. Since one was opened at Anchorage, Alaska, in 1966, these are in every state, as well as in Puerto Rico, Mexico, Central and South America, Spain, in Canada through Simpsons-Sears, Ltd., and in Belgium through Galeries Anspach. Seibu International began to handle Sears catalog sales in Japan in 1973, relaying orders from Tokyo via the Intelsat Communications satellite over the Pacific to the Sears merchandise center in Los Angeles. The Japanese pay 1,000 yen (about $3.80) for the catalogs.

Between thirty and forty new stores are opened annually in the United States, increasingly in covered-mall suburban shopping centers. These permit all-weather shopping and attract crowds on rainy days. To correlate its business with the elements, Sears maintains its own three-man weather bureau. Through a subsidiary, Homart Development Co., it develops and operates shopping centers as owner or partner in joint ventures. Sears and Marshall Field are the big stores in the Woodfield Mall center at Schaumburg, Illinois, and several other attractive centers in the Chicago area.

There are only two levels of authority between the store manager and Chicago headquarters. Reporting to headquarters are five territorial vice presidents. Under them are forty-seven group managers in metropolitan areas and thirteen zone managers in less populous areas. "Every territory, group, zone, and store operates as a profit center," Chairman Wood has pointed out. "All levels of our management work against a profit-and-loss system that enables us to compare each unit with his neighbor or counterpart."

To speed communication between these levels and to provide instant inventory information, Sears is replacing conventional cash registers with Singer's new computer terminal registers. Eventually the system will utilize 30,000 to 40,000 such devices, more than 640 minicomputers and thirty-three large IBM main computers. Sears is also interested in automatic ticket readers, marking machines and other electronic devices. As of 1973, Sears had twenty-two regional computer centers and a central data-processing operation in Chicago. The success of the electronic register at Sears, incidentally, came a few years after a similar effort by General Electric for J. C. Penney came to nothing.

James W. Button, senior vice president for merchandising and former president of Simpsons-Sears, holds the No. 3 post in the Sears hierarchy. He directs thirty-eight buying divisions in Chicago and fourteen in New York. These buy centrally from some twenty thousand suppliers.

Many of the more than 140,000 items now sold by Sears have been planned by the company and made to its specifications by a supplier it may finance if necessary. More than 90 percent of the merchandise sold carries Sears' own labels.

No other company is as close to the heart of suburban and rural America. No company has been more astute in forecasting future social trends and adapting its operations to capitalize on them. No company has had to overcome more bitter prejudices in attaining success. No retail operation has about it a greater wealth of humor, lore and legend.

Sears men give the principal credit for Sears stature to three remarkable executives, General Robert E. Wood, Julius Rosenwald and the founder, Richard Warren Sears. The last was born December 7, 1863, at Stewartville, Minnesota. His father was a farmer-blacksmith who lost all his money in a stock farm and died when Richard was fourteen. To help support his mother and three sisters, the boy learned telegraphy and went to work for the Minneapolis and St. Louis Railroad.

The turning point in his life came in 1886 when he was twenty-three and earning $6 a week as agent for the railroad at its North Redwood station. This served Redwood Falls, Minnesota, a county-seat town, two miles to the south. In an effort to increase its small freight business there, the line allowed its agent special rates and he dabbled in selling coal and lumber and also in buying and shipping meat and fruit.

Opportunity knocked when a local jeweler refused to accept a C.O.D. express shipment of watches. It was then a common practice for wholesalers to send unordered goods to retailers and when the "mistake" was discovered to offer it at half price. But the Redwood Falls jeweler would have none of these watches. So Sears opened up the box, made a deal with the shipper to buy them at $12 each, and began to sell the flashy gold-filled timepieces himself.

While similar watches retailed for $25, Sears priced most of his for $14. He sold watches to his neighbors. He sold watches to the train crews. Finally, he sent sample watches to his brother agents up and down the railroad and they began to sell for him. In six months, he made about $5,000 and left the railroad to start the R. W. Sears Watch Company, first in Minneapolis and then in Chicago, where Montgomery Ward had been in the mail-order business since 1872. The railroad later gave the green frame depot building in which Sears started business to the Redwood County Historical Society. Fire destroyed it in 1961.

While the watches that Sears sold were attractive and low-priced, some came back for repairs. He also found that he could cut his costs by buying movements and cases and assembling them. So, on April 1, 1887, he advertised in the Chicago *Daily News* for a watchmaker who could furnish his own tools. The applicant who received the job was Alvah Curtis Roebuck. He had been born on January 9, 1864, in Lafayette, Indiana. At twenty-three, he was earning $3.50 a week and his board by running a watch-repair shop in a delicatessen store in Hammond, Indiana.

Thus began a famous alliance. Roebuck was a tall, unusually thin man, whose black suit and high collar caused some to think of him as a Methodist minister. He was gentle and unaggressive. Sears was a handsome, mustached, restless young man of ingratiating personality, boundless optimism and incredible energy. Of him an admiring banker once said, "He could sell a breath of air!"

In addition to watches, the firm sold jewelry and diamonds, the last available on installment payments. Every article was "warranted exactly as represented," some of the watch movements were guaranteed for six years and anybody dissatisfied could have his money back. A small catalog was printed and the wares advertised in magazines. A branch was established in Toronto.

Sears had doubts early in 1889 about the permanence of it all. At twenty-five, he sold the Chicago business for $72,000 to what became the Moore and Evans Company. For $2,950, he sold Roebuck and another employee a half interest in the Toronto branch and a little later, for $5,190, the remaining half. Sears talked of becoming an Iowa banker and, in his mother's name, did invest $60,000 in Iowa farm mortgages. But in a few months he returned restlessly to the mail-order jewelry business.

As he had agreed not to do business under the Sears name for three years, he reopened in Minneapolis under his middle name as the Warren Company. But in 1891, Sears invited Roebuck to rejoin him, and on April 6, 1892, the business was incorporated as A. C. Roebuck, Inc. Of 750 shares, Roebuck held 250, Sears 499 and his sister, Eva Sears, just one. Sears was president and Roebuck secretary-treasurer; the three made up the board of directors.

In addition to jewelry, silverware and pistols were sold. On September 16, 1893, the three-year ban on the name having expired, the firm became Sears, Roebuck and Company.

An enlarged catalog of 196 pages, nearly all written by Sears, appeared at this time. In addition to watches, jewelry and firearms, it offered sewing machines, furniture, dishes, wagons, harnesses, saddles, buggies, bicycles, shoes, baby carriages, musical instruments and a little clothing. Prices were guaranteed "below all others" for the same grade of goods, and anybody

unhappy with his purchase was assured his money back. During
the two succeeding years, the catalog was enlarged to 322 and
507 pages respectively, despite a serious business depression.
To obtain better shipping facilities, the firm returned to Chicago.

Roebuck worried about the chaotic nature of the business.
There was little system in filling orders. Sears sometimes advertised items without adequate stocks. Net sales increased from
$276,980 in 1892 to $388,464 in 1893 and $393,323 in 1894,
but profits did not increase and the firm's debts grew. This was
too much for Roebuck's nerves. He insisted on selling his
interest. Sears paid him $25,000 and looked for another partner.

Roebuck allowed the firm to use his name and continued for
a time as head of the watch department. He then formed a
company that made stereopticons, motion-picture projectors and
later typewriters for Sears, Roebuck and others. In 1925, he sold
out for $150,000 and entered the real-estate business in Florida.
When this boom collapsed, he returned to Chicago and in 1933
again went to work for the company that bore his name.

He was employed in writing a history of the beginnings of the
company in 1934 when a manager asked him to make an appearance at one of the company's retail stores. The event was a
success; some customers traveled a hundred miles to shake his
hand. The next year, he was made a Kentucky colonel. He sometimes named Sears leaders and the money they made, punctuating
each with "He's dead" and concluding, "Me, I never felt better."
He continued happily to greet visitors in Chicago and to visit
stores until his death at eighty-four in 1948. His contemporaries
amassed great fortunes, but Roebuck outlived them all.[7]

The partner whom Sears sought, meanwhile, walked in the
door in the person of Aaron E. Nusbaum. He had made $150,-
000 from an ice-cream concession at the Chicago World's Fair
in 1893 and had invested some of it in a firm making pneumatic
tube systems. He hoped to sell Sears one of these, and the firm
eventually installed an elaborate one, but Nusbaum first found
himself talked into investing in the company. More important,

Nusbaum brought in his brother-in-law, Julius Rosenwald, who had been supplying some men's clothing.

The son of a peddler from Westphalia who established a clothing business in Springfield, Illinois, Rosenwald learned the business from the bottom up. He served an apprenticeship with his uncles who ran Hammerslough Brothers in New York. In 1885, he and a cousin started the manufacture of men's suits in Chicago, and in 1890 he married Nusbaum's sister Augusta. In 1891, their first son, Lessing, was born.

When the firm was reincorporated under Illinois law on August 23, 1894, with a capital of $150,000, Sears held 800 shares, representing $80,000. He was still president. Nusbaum and Rosenwald each held 350 shares worth $35,000. Nusbaum was treasurer and general manager. Rosenwald was vice president. But Sears sold more of his shares to the two until on April 12, 1898, each of the three partners owned 500 of the firm's 1,500 shares.

With his partners expertly handling phases of administration that bored him, Sears had more time for the advertising and selling, for which he had an extraordinary talent. The addition of rural free delivery to the mail service in 1896 helped the firm. Sales soared from $800,000 in 1895 to $11 million, a volume greater than Montgomery Ward's, for the first time in 1900. But it was not a happy partnership. Sears and Nusbaum were different types. For example, Sears issued suggestions rather than orders and believed in praising employees. Nusbaum thought criticism more effective.

The crisis came in 1901. Sears demanded of Rosenwald that he join him in buying out Nusbaum or that the two brothers-in-law buy the Sears shares. It was an agonizing decision for Rosenwald. He was bound to Nusbaum by many ties. On the other hand, the business had been built largely on Sears' understanding of the American farmer, his needs, his hopes, his suspicions. Neither of the other partners had this understanding.

Rosenwald sided with Sears. Nusbaum agreed to sell his third interest for a million dollars and at the last minute demanded a

million and a quarter. Sears and Rosenwald were furious but
agreed. By 1903, the full amount had been paid and Sears and
Rosenwald were free to deal with other problems.

Country storekeepers and their friends opposed the mail-order
business with slander and calumny as bitter as any in the history
of commerce. The goods were denounced as shoddy. They were
said to arrive damaged and late. In the race-conscious South, it
was rumored that Montgomery Ward and both Sears and Roebuck were black.[8] When Rosenwald included Negroes in his
philanthropy, the rumors began anew. Under the pressure of
local merchants, many newspapers refused to sell advertising to
the mail-order houses and joined in the derision at their operations.

Where a storekeeper also was the postmaster, it took courage
to accept the delivery of a Sears catalog, buy money orders in
the firm's name and later pick up the merchandise all under his
scornful eye. A man ran for mayor in Warsaw, Iowa, on the
pledge that he would discharge any municipal employee buying
from a mail-order house. In some small towns, children were
given ten cents each or admission to movie theaters for every
mail-order catalog that they produced. The catalogs thus collected sometimes were burned publicly.

The net effect may have been to advertise the mail-order
houses, to move the curious surreptitiously to send off orders.
In the 1903 catalog, the firm offered to send goods without the
name of the shipper appearing and promised to keep "every
transaction with us strictly confidential." It countered the
charges that its executives were colored by publishing their
photographs.

There was also persuasive propaganda, both planned and for-
tuitous, in behalf of the company. Customers were invited to
visit the firm when they came to Chicago. In the course of a tour,
a visitor lost a $5 bill. Richard Sears gave him another. A village
committee seeking funds to build a new church were told by a
local merchant to write to "Rears and Soreback." They did and
to the merchant's chagrin received $10.

An Ohio customer complained that the brake on a Sears bicycle ridden by his son had failed. In a pile-up into a tree, the boy's leg had been broken, a local doctor had set it improperly and the boy seemed destined to become a cripple. Richard Sears had the boy brought to Chicago at company expense. A famous surgeon reset the leg and the boy recovered.

As the company's operations became systematic, there were more satisfied customers. In 1905, these in turn were encouraged to make customers of their neighbors. It was one of Dick Sears' most successful ideas. In return for premiums in proportion to the resulting purchases, customers were asked to distribute catalogs to twenty-four friends. This was first tried in Iowa and produced such a flood of orders that the whole country was "Iowaized."

That winter saw the firm move into a new $5,600,000 plant constructed for it by the Thompson-Starrett Company on a forty-acre site at Homan Avenue and Arthington Street on Chicago's West Side. Railroad sidings eliminated much of the trucking previously required.

A remarkable "schedule" system of handling orders was worked out by Otto C. Doering, operations superintendent, and others. The mail was weighed as it came from the post office in the morning and hourly during the day to give the departments an idea of the work ahead. The first automatic mail openers ever to be devised slit letters at the rate of twenty-seven thousand an hour. Girls removed remittances, checked catalog numbers, typed out order forms, stamped a scheduled shipping item and shot them by pneumatic tube to stockrooms. From these, items moved by conveyor belts and gravity chutes to assembly points. There they were packed and dispatched by mail, express or freight. Some heavy items were sent direct from factories. Though filling and shipping an order involved twenty-seven steps, orders for a single item began to be filled in one day, and mixed orders, involving goods from several departments, moved out in two days. As there was a different-colored form for each day of the week, delayed orders were detected quickly. Henry Ford studied the Sears operation before setting up his famous automobile assembly line.

All of this required money. At the suggestion of one of Rosenwald's boyhood friends, Henry Goldman of Goldman, Sachs and Company, the firm was incorporated in New York on June 16, 1906. Lehman Brothers and Goldman, Sachs underwrote the sale of $10 million in 7 percent preferred stock and $30 million in common stock of the new corporation in return for $500,000 cash and $5 million in common stock. The preferred was marketed at $97.50 a share and the common at $50 a share.

Sears and Rosenwald received $4,500,000 each in cash in exchange for their previous stock. The latter advanced $90,000 to some senior employees to enable them to buy stock. The preferred, all retired by 1924, was listed at once on the New York Stock Exchange and the common was traded there beginning in 1910.

The timing of the recapitalization was fortunate. The year 1906 was one of prosperity. Sales of Sears, Roebuck for the year were more than $50 million, an increase of a third over the previous year. But in the fall of 1907, the Knickerbocker Trust Company closed in New York and a business panic followed. Sales of Sears, Roebuck for the fiscal year ending June 30, 1908, dropped by nearly $10 million to $40,843,866 and profits 37 percent to $2,034,796.

Dick Sears, who had been traveling in Europe with his ailing wife, returned and urged increased advertising and promotion as a means of meeting the crisis. In earlier years, he had spent 9 to 13 percent of sales profitably on advertising. For the fall of 1908, he suggested going as high as 17 percent. Rosenwald opposed increasing advertising or any other expense on the ground that customers simply didn't have the money to buy more goods. When two of Sears' own appointees, Louis Asher, the general manager, and J. Fletcher Skinner, the merchandise manager, reluctantly agreed with Rosenwald, the founder resigned as president on November 21, 1908.

He took no further part in the company's affairs though he

was board chairman for a time and continued as a director until November 26, 1913. He had worked such long hours and at such a furious pace that his health, as well as that of his wife's, was impaired. He spent his last years at Waukesha, Wisconsin, and died there in his fifty-first year on September 28, 1914, leaving an estate of $25 million and a legend as a Barnum of merchandising.

Under Rosenwald, who became president and later chairman of the board, the company entered a period of calm growth. Prosperity returned. Farm income increased. The company's first mail-order branch outside Chicago was established by Elmer L. Scott in Dallas, Texas, in 1906. Dallas has been important in Sears business ever since. Others followed in Seattle and Philadelphia. The start of parcel-post service in 1913 proved a great boon. Dubious patent medicines vanished from the catalog which became bigger but less flamboyant. It began to include automobile and electrical items, including telephones. A thirteen-year-old boy named Charles Franklin Kettering bought a Sears phone to dismantle and started his inventive career. From 1908 to 1911, an auto, the high-wheel Sears Motor Buggy, was sold at $445 to $495.[9]

More attention was paid to the development of reliable sources of supply. A testing laboratory was started in 1911 to insure the quality of materials. One of the early laboratory men, Donald M. Nelson, later rose to executive vice president of the company, and during World War II headed the War Production Board. While on a hunting trip, Dick Sears had noticed a $150 cream separator in a farm kitchen. He thought one could be made to sell at $50 and found a manufacturer able to do so. Thousands of separators were sold. This became the pattern for many other ventures.

During World War I, Rosenwald became a dollar-a-year man for the government and left Sears, Roebuck in the able hands of Vice President Albert Loeb, as de facto president. This gentle and able lawyer had been with the company since drawing the documents for Rosenwald's purchase of an interest in the firm and contributed greatly to its success.

While serving as chairman of the committee for the purchase of noncombat supplies, Rosenwald drew no salary from the company and allowed it to sell to the government only at cost. But he took along some Sears, Roebuck catalogs when he made a tour of American camps and hospitals in France as a representative of Secretary of War Newton D. Baker and the Young Men's Christian Association. Farm boys in hospitals found the catalogs a voice from home. As the only civilian in a party of generals, Rosenwald once introduced himself as General Merchandise.

The most dramatic service of Rosenwald came in 1921. In the fiscal year ending June 30, 1919, Sears sales reached a record $234,242,337 with profits of $18,890,125. A 40 percent stock dividend was declared. The next year, sales rose to $245,373,418 but profits dropped to $11,746,671. Prices of farm products began to tumble. Corn fell from $2.17 to 59 cents a bushel. Other prices followed and Sears was caught with millions of dollars' worth of merchandise bought at high prices. Many small mail-order houses failed. Lehman Brothers, Goldman, Sachs and four Chicago banks lent Sears, Roebuck $50 million on notes, but even this was not enough. Despite a reduction in the number of employees from 21,652 in 1920 to 18,144 in 1921 and other economies, the firm operated in the latter year at a loss of $16,435,469.

On December 29, Rosenwald pledged $20 million of his personal fortune, $4 million of it in cash, to aid the company. He gave the firm fifty thousand shares of its stock and paid the cash as down payment toward purchasing its Chicago real estate for $16 million if necessary. The cash enabled Sears to meet its bank debts. The stock rose eight points on the news. John D. Rockefeller, Jr., telegraphed his praise to Rosenwald, and C. W. Barron, the financial publisher, wrote: "I do not know of anybody in the United States in the mercantile line who today is held in higher esteem or sounder regard than you and your great enterprise." Business improved, profits the next year were $5,435,168, the debts gradually were paid and common-stock dividends were resumed in 1924.

Two important new executives joined Sears that year. To become president, Rosenwald brought in Charles M. Kittle, executive vice president of the Illinois Central Railroad. While working in Washington, Rosenwald had been impressed by the ability of rail executives to handle large affairs. Before settling on Kittle, Rosenwald had asked an employment agency to list the ten most outstanding railroad vice presidents under fifty years of age. At the same time, he added a new vice president, Robert Elkington Wood, a retired Army general with whom he had become acquainted in Washington and who lately had been working for Montgomery Ward.

Kittle was without experience in merchandising but did not shrink from bold decisions. He supported the building of additional mail-order plants in Kansas City, Atlanta, Memphis and Los Angeles. More important, he and General Wood in 1925 took the company into the retail-store business, beginning with one in the corner of the Chicago mail-order plant. In that year, Sears' sales of $258,318,000 came 95.5 percent from mail order and 4.5 percent from retail stores. The store figure grew steadily and from 1931 onward accounted for more than half of the firm's volume. Kittle did not live to see this. He died on January 2, 1928.

General Wood was then picked as president by Rosenwald, still the largest stockholder. Two older vice presidents, who may have expected the post, then resigned. They were Otto C. Doering, operations, and Max Adler, merchandising. Adler built the Adler Planetarium on the Chicago lakefront in 1930 at a cost of some $600,000. He was succeeded by Donald M. Nelson and Doering by the chairman's son, Lessing Rosenwald.[10] In 1932 on the death of his father (who left $17,415,000 after giving away $63 million), Lessing became chairman and on his retirement in 1939 was succeeded by General Wood. Replacing him as president were Thomas J. Carney, who died in 1942; Arthur Barrows, who retired four years later; and Fowler B. McConnell, who thirty years earlier had started to work as a Sears stockboy. But until his own retirement in 1954 in favor of Vice Chairman Theodore V. Houser, a veteran merchandiser, it was General Wood who led Sears. In 1955, he became the first living person elected to the Retailing Hall of Fame in Chicago.

He brought to Sears a background of colorful military experience. Born in Kansas City, Missouri, on June 13, 1879, he studied engineering at West Point, where he was graduated in 1900. After service as lieutenant of cavalry during the Philippine Insurrection, he worked for a decade on the Panama Canal, handling supplies both for the canal and the Panama Railroad. He retired in 1915 but returned to active service during World War I, became a brigadier general under his old Panama chief, Major General George W. Goethals, who was a Quartermaster General, and earned the Distinguished Service Medal as well as British and French decorations.

In 1919, Wood became vice president in charge of merchandising at Montgomery Ward. One of the first to see clearly the changes in American life heralded by completion of the Lincoln Highway and the increasing number of automobiles, he urged the establishment of retail stores to which farmers could drive. He also interested himself in automobile tires and put Ward far ahead of Sears in these items.[11] But differences with the president of Ward, culminating in a letter suggesting he resign, sent Wood to Sears. Four years later, incidentally, Houser, who was Wood's eventual successor as chairman, joined Sears after ten years at Ward's.

What Wood and Houser had done for automobile tires at Ward's, they also did at Sears. Wood drew specifications for a greatly improved tire and contracted with Goodyear to make it. Cash prizes totaling $25,000 were offered in a contest to name the new tire. One of the 937,886 entrants, Hans Simonson, an art student of Bismarck, North Dakota, won $5,000 for the name "Allstate." In 1929, Sears sold 4,300,000 Allstate tires, 3,000,-

000 of them in retail stores, and was far ahead of Ward. Goodyear gave Sears such favorable terms that the contract drew a Federal Trade Commission complaint and was a factor in the passage of the Robinson-Patman Act. The complaint came to nothing but the law caused Goodyear to cancel the contract and Sears returned to smaller tire makers.

The Allstate brand was applied also to automobile supplies and accessories and in 1931 to automobile insurance. Carl Odell, a Chicago insurance broker who handled some of General Wood's policies, suggested to him that the cost of automobile insurance could be cut by selling it by mail. With Odell as an officer, the Allstate Insurance Company was organized with $700,000 from Sears. Within a year, it was operating profitably.

In addition to selling by catalog and at booths in Sears stores, Allstate added branches and agents. In 1952, it began to write comprehensive personal liability, followed in the next few years by commercial and residential fire insurance and, beginning in 1957 through the Allstate Life Insurance Company, life insurance.[12] Commercial liability, personal health and group health and group life policies were added.

In addition, Allstate Enterprises, Inc., and its subsidiaries are engaged in the auto-finance, motor-club, insurance-inspection and safety-engineering businesses. Also, two separate subsidiaries act as distributor and as investment adviser, dividend disbursing agent and transfer agent for Allstate Enterprises Stock Fund, a mutual fund. Allstate Enterprises also owns a savings and loan association in California.

During 1971, Allstate exceeded the $2-billion mark in sales for the first time. Premiums written for all property and liability insurance lines increased to $2,254,304,000 in 1972, of which $1,646,839,000 were auto insurance premiums. Allstate Life Insurance operations added $2,059,000,000 of insurance that year, raising the total in force to $13,181,000,000. This mark has been achieved by Allstate faster than by any other life company.

Archie R. Boe, a thirty-one-year veteran of Allstate, succeeded Judson B. Branch as chairman and chief executive officer in 1972. Much of Allstate's dynamic growth in sales and earnings—$313 million to $2 billion and from $10 million to $113 million—was under the leadership of Branch, one of the firm's first agents, who served as its president from 1957 to 1966 and chairman from 1966 to 1972.

Everything, of course, was not a success. A notable failure was a line of high-fashion gowns styled by Lady Duff-Gordon. She gave each a name and one was called "I'll Come Back to You." This was prophetic, for every dress sold of that style was returned. The sale of groceries, a catalog item for years, was abandoned in 1929 in the face of A & P competition.

Then there was the *Encyclopaedia Britannica*. Because Julius Rosenwald golfed with Horace Everett Hooper, one of the proprietors who brought the venerable reference work to America, Sears first marketed a "handy volume" edition and then in 1920 bought the enterprise. When Sears needed money after the 1921 depression, it was sold back to Hooper with a loss to Sears of $1,848,000. But in 1928, Sears purchased control of the *Britannica* and attempted to make a success of it until 1943, when it was given to the University of Chicago. The *Britannica* was too costly and sophisticated for Sears customers.

Retail-store managers at first reported to branch mail-order plant managers who often had little understanding of the problems involved. In 1930, a committee of Sears executives, composed of T. V. Houser, J. M. Barker and E. J. Pollock, and an outside firm of consultants, worked out a more workable form of organization. While preserving central buying and fiscal authority in Chicago, it called for both retail and mail-order plants to report to territorial executives. The depression delayed its adoption but eventually it was carried out.

The stores proved so profitable and inventories were so well controlled that Sears came through the depression thirties, with a loss only in 1932, when the company was in the red by $2,543,-641. Salaries were cut 20 percent. The next year there was a profit of $11,249,295 on mail-order sales of $120,334,000 and retail business of $167,860,000. Totals for both rose steadily except in 1938, but the retail grew at a greater rate.

World War II, which saw many Sears factories converted to war work and some of its hard goods on priorities, slowed Sears' growth only a little. Sales soared past the billion-dollar mark in 1946 and the two-billion mark in 1948. By then, Sears had eight thousand suppliers turning out goods to its specifications and one thousand of them had been doing so for more than twenty years.

With the 1942 opening of a retail store in Havana, later expropriated by the Fidel Castro government, Sears started expansion into Latin America. As a young army officer in the Canal Zone, General Wood had invested profitably in a Panama City hardware store back in 1905 and realized the possibilities.

World War II interrupted the expansion, and it was not until 1947 that a big store was opened in Mexico City. Others followed in Guadalajara, Monterrey, Tampico, San Luis Potosí, Mérida and Puebla. Stores were opened two years later in São Paulo and Rio de Janeiro, Brazil. A crowd of 120,000 persons, including Papal Nuncio Carlo Chiarlo, who blessed the establishment, attended the opening of the latter. The first of six stores in Venezuela was opened in Caracas in 1950. Units followed in Peru and Costa Rica (1955), El Salvador and Panama (1956), Puerto Rico (1957) and Nicaragua (1965). In 1972, Sears had sales of $206,127,000 from sixty-one stores and thirteen sales offices in the ten countries.

All Latin-American stores of the company are staffed almost entirely with nationals of the country, and the bulk of their merchandise is manufactured locally to specifications from Chicago. Local customs are respected to the extent of closing some units from two to four for the traditional afternoon siesta. Sears is the largest advertiser in Mexico.

Sears moved into Canada in 1952 as a 44.3 percent partner of the eighty-year-old Robert Simpson Company, Ltd., the second-largest retailer in Canada. Each invested $20 million in a new company, Simpsons-Sears Limited, formed to sell by mail in

Canada and through retail stores. The new firm paid $48 million for the existing Simpson mail-order business and facilities. New stores were built in Ottawa, Vancouver, Hamilton, Moose Jaw, Kitchener, Calgary and elsewhere. In 1972, Simpsons-Sears had sales of $894,100,000 from 43 retail stores, four catalog-order plants, and 575 catalog-sales offices.

Without counting Simpsons-Sears establishments, Sears in 1973 had 837 retail stores, 12 catalog-order plants and 2,648 catalog-sales and telephone-sales offices. Of the stores, 289 were of the "A" type, a Sears designation for a complete department store with at least 100,000 square feet of selling space; 378 were medium-size department stores carrying extensive assortments of general merchandise; and 170 were hard-lines stores carrying major household appliances, hard lines, sporting goods and automotive supplies. All retail stores have catalog-order desks.

Much of Sears' growth in the sixties came from the expansion of soft goods and the introduction of fashion lines in women's and children's apparel. Women were cultivated in many ways. In 1963, Mrs. Claire Giannini Hoffman, daughter of the founder of the Bank of America, became the first woman on the Sears board of directors. Forty percent of the business that year was in soft goods. Letitia Baldrige, formerly Jacqueline Kennedy's social secretary, was employed to advise on teen-age merchandise.[13] In 1966, Lillian Jaffe, buyer of better furs for Sears, was chosen "Man of the Year" by the industry. Mrs. Hoffman retired as a director in 1970. Mrs. Eleanor P. Sheppard, a former mayor of Richmond, Virginia, served from 1971 to 1973. She was succeeded by Mrs. Norma Pace, a New York economist.

Public relations, advertising and employee relations became vital as the business grew gargantuan. Though Sears was not the primary target of the agitation against chain stores and for fair-trade laws, its operations were affected by both. The fair-trade measures caused the company to emphasize its own brands even more. Except for a few popular, well-advertised items, all fair-trade items were eliminated from the catalog. The anti-chain-store pressure impelled the company to systematize its public-relations activities in a department, headed since 1966 by William F. McCurdy, a vice president, and to identify itself with the communities in which it operated.

"Business must account for its stewardship not only on the balance sheet," said General Wood, "but also in the matters of social responsibility." Sears' first community activities naturally were in agriculture. As early as 1912, Julius Rosenwald gave $1,000 to each of the first hundred counties to employ a professional farm adviser. As many of its customers were part-time trappers who had trouble marketing their pelts, Sears in 1924 started a fur-marketing service without profit to the firm. Trappers sent in their furs and received money or merchandise as they wished. More than seven million copies of *Tips to Trappers*, a booklet by "Johnny Muskrat," were distributed. The Sears-Roebuck Foundation has supported education, youth activities and community improvement.

The company's newspaper advertising, which amounted to only $480,000 in 1925, has increased greatly. By 1972, it passed $275 million. In the space, often with colored ink, Sears advertised not only its retail offerings but often its purchasing in the locality. In addition, Sears advertising utilized circulars, radio and television and magazines under the direction of Gar K. Ingraham, national retail sales promotion and advertising manager. Many agencies are employed. As of 1973, these included Ogilvy & Mather, J. Walter Thompson Co., Foote, Cone & Belding; McCann-Erickson; Stern, Walters & Simmons; Marshall John & Associates; Smith/Greenland; Gerson, Howe & Johnson; and Vince Cullers. Most Allstate advertising, including a public-service campaign that resulted in anti-drunk driver legislation, has been handled by the Leo Burnett Co.[14]

The ubiquitous catalog, which is really two large and three smaller catalogs a year, appears in eleven regional editions. The contents vary, and some prices also may vary because of freight rates. Because of difference in climate, some items given space in one edition may be omitted in another. Items like tires and corsets appear in all, but woolen union suits and maple-syrup equipment are found only in the northern editions.

The biggest of the catalogs are the two general catalogs issued for the spring and fall seasons. Each contains about 1,700 pages, weighs more than five pounds and lists more than 140,000 items. A poll of customers found that the most popular cover ever to grace the big book was a landscape by George Inness. For the 1934 edition, the late Edgar A. Guest, the famous Detroit versifier, wrote a poem for the company entitled "The Catalog." There also are a summer book and a winter sale book as well as a Christmas-gift book of around 500 pages that appears in October. The catalogs cost from 50 cents to $2.00 each to produce and up to 16 million copies of the fall and spring books are distributed.

The expense of printing and mailing some 85 million catalogs a year is so great that much thought has been given to cutting their cost and increasing their attractiveness. In the early days, customers were asked to pay postage and it was sold briefly at $1. Free but judicious distribution proved the most effective. Anybody can ask for one, and in most cases, if he spends $25 in two catalog purchases during the next six months, will receive the next one without asking. The firm once toyed with the idea of letting noncompeting outsiders share costs. In 1931, Chevrolet and the Curtis Publishing Company were allowed to buy catalog pages at $23,000 each in a short-lived experiment. From 1903 to 1923, Sears did its own catalog printing. In recent years, R. R. Donnelley and Sons has done the printing and binding under great secrecy with prices set into type at the last minute. In 1972, Chicago-area customers were sent postcards inviting them to pick up catalogs at the nearest Sears store but offering to mail them if this was inconvenient.

Color printing, lightweight but improved paper and high-quality photography have enhanced the attractiveness of the catalog. From modeling for its pages, beauties like Gloria Swanson, Norma Shearer, Anita Louise, Susan Hayward and Joan

Caulfield moved to Hollywood. Some seven hundred persons, mostly in Chicago and New York, produce the catalog, art and copy. This must comply with the frequently revised two-hundred-page *Advertising Guide* and is a model of accuracy, simplicity, taste and forceful salesmanship in print. Exaggerated claims and unrestrained superlatives are forbidden. "Sweat" is preferred to "perspiration." For a certain hard-work garment, the word is "pants"; for dress, it is "trousers." The catalog itself explains: "Our descriptions are simple, honest, straightforward statements of facts." There is always the line: "Satisfaction Guaranteed or Your Money Back." When Julian Watkins, an authority on the subject, in 1939 chose "The 100 Greatest Advertisements," one was the Sears, Roebuck catalog.[15]

The catalog moves customers to telephone or send in orders by the thousands, as many as 100,000 a day to the Chicago catalog-order plant before Christmas. Each 100 pounds of mail contains approximately 3,500 orders for about $12 each, or $42,000 in business for each 100 pounds of mail. Most letters contain only order blanks but some are chatty missives informing the firm of the customer's activities, asking for advice on all sorts of problems or even ordering a mate. At least one such order was filled satisfactorily. A plea from a Montana rancher fell into the hands of a spirited girl clerk who was weary of Chicago. They were married and continued to buy from Sears, Roebuck. The catalog of "Shears Robust and Company" figured pleasantly in the hit musical show *Finian's Rainbow*.

Good employee relations began with Richard Sears, the founder. He was chary of using first names but was as considerate of his associates as of his customers. He did not summon men to his office but went to their desks. His approach was "What do you think?" or "Will you?" and he was quick to praise good work. The company began to publish an employee house organ, the *Skylight*, in 1901.

Elmer L. Scott, who rose from Sears' office boy to general manager, eliminated night and Sunday work, and began systematic employee training around 1904. Scott opened and managed the Dallas branch until 1913. After differences with Rosenwald, he resigned and devoted the remainder of his long life to welfare work, adult education and civic cultural activities. He was one of Dallas's most beloved citizens at his death there in 1954.[16]

Rosenwald also was concerned with employee welfare. Some of his activity was on the negative side. Of the sixty-two pages in a manual for new employees, twenty-eight were taken up with the evils of drink, the futility of smoking, the desirability of morality, diligence and thrift. He chased saloons from the neighborhood and the nearest put up a sign "First Chance."

The Savings and Profit Sharing Fund of Sears Employees, one of the company's greatest distinctions, was set up by Rosenwald on July 16, 1916. A stockholder, Mrs. Joseph T. Bowen, had suggested something of the sort to him in a letter a year earlier and he had been impressed by a plan started by the Harris Trust and Savings Bank of Chicago. It has since grown to be the largest fund of the sort in all industry.

To this fund, Sears employees of a year or more can contribute 5 percent of their annual salary but no more than $750.

Sears' contributions are figured on a sliding scale based on the company's consolidated net income before Federal income taxes and dividends. The percentage rises to a maximum of 11 percent on net income of $600 million or more. The maximum has been contributed for many years. Fund members are divided into four groups: Employees with less than five years of service; employees with more than five and less than ten years of service; employees with ten or more years of service; employees over fifty years of age with fifteen or more years of service. The company's contribution increases for each succeeding group. In 1971, the company contribution ranged to $2.40 for every dollar contributed by employees over fifty who had fifteen or more years of service.

Withdrawals can be made for emergencies. An employee, upon completing five years of service, who leaves the company for any reason receives all funds—his and the company's—credited to his account. Many old-timers pile up sizable amounts.

Meanwhile, in 1931 a central personnel department was established in Chicago, and it was decreed that no employee of five years' standing could be fired without its approval. Under Clarence B. Caldwell, a former store manager who rose to vice president in charge of personnel, systematic training programs, involving manuals, films and job rotation, were evolved. Promising college graduates, sometimes six hundred a year, began to be hired systematically. Since 1955, Sears has made a systematic effort to hire the handicapped for certain jobs and to aid them in other ways. Snack bars in forty Pennsylvania stores are run by the blind. W. Wallace Tudor became vice president in charge of personnel when Caldwell retired in 1956.

Following enactment of the equal pay law, Ray J. Graham was named director of equal opportunity in 1968 and Sears developed one of the first affirmative action programs "to employ, train and promote women and members of all minority groups." In 1973, Graham reported many women selling high-commission appliances and "a significant number" driving service trucks, working on repair benches and "generally reminding us that manual dexterity has no sexual boundaries." Despite this foresight, there were some complaints and Sears paid $50,282 to Kentucky women who claimed they were paid less than male salespeople and department managers. Sears auditors now check on equal pay compliance.

With an expanding organization and a rule that those earning $15,000 or more must retire at sixty-three, promotions are frequent at Sears. Regular estimates are made of future requirements. For senior assignments, these are made as much as five years in advance. The retirement of one senior executive may result in the promotion of fourteen persons.

Chairman Houser, termed "the greatest master of mass merchandising" by General Wood, was chief executive officer for four years, spending part of nearly every day systematically talking to distant Sears executives by telephone. He retired in 1958 and died in 1963. He was succeeded by Ohio-born Charles H. Kellstadt, who previously greatly expanded Sears' southern business. Practically "living" in the company airplane, he served as president from 1958 to 1960 and as chairman from 1960 until May 4, 1962, when he retired and was succeeded by Austin T. Cushman, previously vice president in charge of the Pacific Coast territory, where he directed all retail and catalog operations in nine states. Cushman was succeeded by Midwest Vice President Gordon M. Metcalf in 1967. Metcalf, who retired in 1973, continues as a director and as chairman of the board of trustees of the employees' profit-sharing fund.

Sears' current chairman, Arthur M. Wood—who was a close personal friend of but not related to the late General Wood— is teamed with President A. Dean Swift, an astute merchant and former vice president of the Southern territory. Arthur Wood joined Sears to organize the firm's law department and later served as company secretary, controller and vice president of the Far West and Midwest territories. He is a Princeton University and Harvard Law School graduate and is described as Lincolnesque and also as "a sophisticated, urbane intellectual with impeccable social credentials." "His appointment," *Business Week* reported, "reflects the changing nature of retailing and the necessity of having more than a buyer-and-seller of goods at the top. Today's merchant must have a broader grasp of government regulations and laws, finance, labor unions, real estate investment, consumerism and the host of other complex elements that populate today's retail environment."

Territorial vice presidents as of 1973 were Alfred I. Davies, Southwest; Culver J. Kennedy, Midwest; John G. Lowe, Far West; A. M. Prado, South; and Edward R. Telling, East.

President Franklin D. Roosevelt suggested that the best way to convince the Kremlin of the superiority of the American way of life would be to drop Sears, Roebuck catalogs over the Soviet Union. Something like this has been done. The Sears chapter of the first edition of this book was translated and published in both the Russian and Polish editions of *Amerika Illustrated,* the magazine of the United States Information Agency circulating behind the Iron Curtain.[17] The U.S.I.A. sends catalogs regularly to its overseas libraries. It may have had some effect. When Mrs. Nikita Khrushchev, wife of the Soviet Premier, visited San Francisco in 1959, she appeared at a Sears store before opening time. Roe Goisch, the manager, let her in and Titana Lysick, a Sears secretary who had been born in Siberia, translated for her and helped her shop. In an hour and a half, she bought a dozen of the best nylon stockings, many toys for her grandchildren and an armload of infants' clothing and paid cash—about $100.[18]

XVI
Lane Bryant

Maternity and Special-Size Fashion Pioneer

"Maternity dress, size 32, Amerika," wrote a young woman in Poland on an envelope. With only this address, her letter reached New York and was delivered promptly as the writer intended to the Lane Bryant store on Fifth Avenue at Fortieth Street, opposite the stone lions of the Public Library.

Today the company specializes in "fashions for big, beautiful women." Less than 1 percent of its record sales of $277,500,000 on which it earned $8,816,000 in 1972 were in maternity wear. But Lane Bryant has been so traditionally synonymous with maternity that the post office hardly could have done otherwise. No other company has done so much business in maternity wear.

The story of the enterprise starts with the birth of an indomitable girl named Lena Himmelstein in Lithuania, then part of Czarist Russia, in 1879. Her mother died ten days after her birth. As a child in the home of her grandparents, she witnessed cruel Russian persecutions. At sixteen, she gladly accepted the invitation of some distant relatives to accompany them via steerage to America.[1]

They delayed telling her that they were bringing her along as a prospective bride for their son. When she met the young man for the first time in New York, Lena wept. Rather than marry somebody she did not love, she joined her sister Anna, who had preceded her, and went to work at $1 a week in a sweatshop.

This was in Lispenard Street, where negligee and lingerie manufacturing was just beginning. "We made beautiful lingerie for fast women," the immigrant girl later recalled. Within four years, she learned to speak English, learned machine sewing, and advanced to the then high wage of $15 a week.

She gave this up to marry a man she did love. He was David Bryant, a young Brooklyn jeweler. Evenings she helped him in his store and they made brave plans for the future. But soon after their son, Raphael, was born on February 3, 1900, the husband became ill. Six months later he was dead of tuberculosis.

As the expenses of his illness wiped out the store, his twenty-year-old widow was left with only a pair of earrings set with small diamonds, his wedding gift, with which to face the future. She pawned the earrings for enough money to make a down payment on a Singer sewing machine and turned again to sewing as the only possibility of keeping her son with her and at the same time earning a living.

In a small apartment on West 112th Street, which she shared with her sister Anna, the young widow set up working quarters. It was the bicycle and shirtwaist era. The feminine ideal was the hippy and busty Gibson girl drawn by Charles Dana Gibson. Her waist was so tightly corseted that bosom and hips were accented. To achieve the popular hourglass figure, many women wore vestigial bustles.

The Gibson girl could buy blouses and skirts in stores of the day, but her dresses had to be made for her. If she was wealthy, they were imported from Paris. If she was in modest circumstances, she made them herself. If she was in between, she had her clothes made by seamstresses working either in her home or theirs.

Mrs. Bryant's skill and instinctive love for fine things attracted an increasing number of customers. Women came in carriages for her negligees and tea gowns made from delicate laces and fine silks. But there were difficult days. She delivered the finished articles herself and sometimes had to spend hours waiting for customers to pay. The diamond earrings had to be pawned more than once for the purchase of materials and supplies. She worked with her young son on her knee. One day while her attention was distracted he pushed a finger beneath the swiftly moving machine needle. For a time it was feared that the finger might have to be amputated.

In 1904, the year that New York opened its first subway, young Mrs. Bryant moved to 1489 Fifth Avenue. This was between 119th and 120th Streets and only a short walk from Mount Morris Park, where there was a playground for her son. For $12.50 a month, the household of three rented the first floor of a new six-story building. They lived in the rear and used the front room as a shop, hanging garments from the gas fixtures.

Enough trousseau finery was made to cause the place to be known as a bridal shop. An early sign misspelled it "bridle." But Mrs. Bryant soon earned more than a neighborhood reputation for fine work of all kinds, especially for women of unusual proportions. She estimated lengths by eye, ignored tape measures and patterns, kept few records but turned out better-fitting garments than many of her customers had previously worn. More carriages began to arrive at the door and the earrings made fewer trips to the pawnshop.

Into the modest shop one day walked an attractive young woman for whom Mrs. Bryant had previously done some sewing. After exchanging greetings, the customer announced: "I am going to have a baby, Mrs. Bryant. What shall I do?"

For an instant the young widow thought that her visitor was asking medical advice but this was not the case.

"You make all kinds of things," continued the visitor; "can't you make me something that will be both pretty and practical and in which I can entertain at home?"

While the Empress Eugénie of France had been recorded as having worn a maternity dress in the 1850s, such a garment was unknown in New York in 1904, but Mrs. Bryant met the challenge. She created a comfortable and attractively concealing tea gown by the simple device of an elastic band attaching an accordion-pleated skirt to a bodice. The result was the famous No. 5 maternity gown, so called because later it was given this number on a price list.

The first purchaser was grateful and enthusiastic. She was happy to pay $18 for the gown and praised it to her friends. She volubly told them about the ingenious little widow who made it. More expectant mothers ordered the tea gowns.

Word of Mrs. Bryant's talent and popularity reached the big downtown stores and two of them offered her jobs. But she preferred independence and the opportunity to rear her son. Her sister had married, and her new brother-in-law loaned the young widow $300 with which to open a bank account and to use as working capital for the purchase of fabrics.

Formalities required that Mrs. Bryant appear in the ornate quarters of the old Oriental Bank at 182 Broadway. She was so unaccustomed to the grandeur of the surroundings and the awe of having so much money that she filled out the deposit slip not as Lena Bryant but as *Lane* Bryant.

Thus was born Lane Bryant. The young widow was at first too timid to rectify the mistake and later grew to like the euphonious name. She used it when she opened a new shop in a loft at 19 West Thirty-eighth Street, a few yards off Fifth Avenue. There she employed a dozen girls. Mrs. Bryant was still not free from financial worries. She increased her balance in the Oriental Bank to $400 just in time to see the institution close in the financial panic of 1907. She eventually recovered the money. In the meantime the diamond earrings again served as collateral. But, despite the unbusinesslike methods, the little business grew.

Romance flowered again for Mrs. Lane Bryant soon after her move to Thirty-eighth Street. Through mutual friends, the twenty-seven-year-old dress creator met a handsome young engineer named Albert Malsin. He also had been born in Lithuania and they had many common interests. After being graduated as a mechanical engineer by the Polytechnic Institute at Gothen, Anhalt, Germany, Malsin emigrated to America and became associated with an engineering firm that constructed amusement parks all over the world.

Albert Malsin and Mrs. Bryant were married in 1909 and he adopted her young son, who thenceforth was known as Raphael Malsin. For a time, the engineer continued his work. Mrs. Malsin, however, soon began to wear her own maternity clothes. Three children, a daughter and two sons, were born to the couple within the next four years.

At first of necessity and later because he saw great possibilities, Malsin took an increasing role in his wife's enterprise. While she continued to design the dresses, he took charge of the business and began systematically to develop and expand it. Where his wife had worked without patterns and measurements, he instituted engineering exactness. Where sometimes she had set prices at the first figure that came into her head, he installed cost accounting.

To handle the financial end of the Lane Bryant business, which had grown to more than $50,000 annually, Malsin in 1910 enlisted an astute friend, Harry Liverman. For his task, Liverman had a remarkable background. As a youth he had sailed from England to Australia to seek his fortune in the gold mines. There he took part in civic affairs and served as both city councilor and mayor of Leonora, Western Australia. En route there after a vacation in England, he stopped off in New York and decided to remain. His experience and calm judgment proved invaluable to the Malsins.

One day Malsin and Liverman went walking and chanced to pass Crocker's, a store devoted entirely to the sale of mourning goods. This was possible because of the then rigid observance of mourning and a death rate that would now be considered high.

"This is a country of specialization," said Malsin, calling Liverman's attention to the mourning-goods store. Liverman agreed. They decided that Lane Bryant should specialize. The obvious first choice was maternity wear, to which the business already owed most of what success it possessed. Bridal finery was dropped.

The firm took the revolutionary step of designing maternity dresses for street wear. Up until this time expectant mothers had nothing appropriate to wear outside their homes and few ventured abroad in daylight.

At the same time, the earlier maternity gowns and dresses for indoor wear were varied and improved in construction. In addition to the original elastic, Lane Bryant employed drawstrings, snaps, hooks, buttons and other devices to adjust the garments to changing figures.

To obtain maternity dresses in quantity, the firm abandoned on-the-premises manufacturing and began to create a unique phase of New York's remarkable women's clothing industry. By mechanically cutting dozens of identical dresses at once and employing high-speed sewing methods, this industry began to produce dresses at lower costs than ever before. By 1910, it was large enough to support a newspaper and *Women's Wear Daily* was founded. Since then the manufacture of women's clothing has become New York's biggest industry and its products have made American women the best-dressed women in the world.

At a time when any kind of ready-to-wear dress was a novelty, the manufacture of maternity dresses presented more problems than the average contractor cared to face. More material and more work were required for a maternity dress than for an ordinary dress. Some also believed the maternity business would never be great.

Lane Bryant overcame these objections by supplying designs, patterns, materials and, in practically all cases, actually financing the contractors. Only then did the unique maternity wear begin to flow from the factory to the store. Once educated to the merits of the dresses, the suppliers helped work out more improvements.

One stumbling block remained. This was the refusal of newspapers, in keeping with the prudery that then existed, to accept advertisements for any kind of maternity clothing.

It was not until a memorable day in 1911 that the *New York*

Herald accepted a Lane Bryant advertisement for maternity dresses. The copy read:

> Maternity wardrobes that do not attract attention. It is no longer the fashion nor the practice for expectant mothers to stay in seclusion. Doctors, nurses and psychologists agree that at this time a woman should think and live as normally as possible. To do this, she must go about among other people, she must look like other people.
>
> Lane Bryant has originated maternity apparel in which the expectant mother may feel as other women feel because she looks as other women look.

The response to the advertisement was astonishing. More customers appeared than ever before. Malsin, Liverman and a boy working in receiving and packing had to help the two saleswomen wait on the eager throngs. By closing time, the store's entire stock of maternity dresses for street wear had been sold for $2,800. Mrs. Malsin, who was at home with her children, could hardly believe the figures.

Lane Bryant's fame for maternity wear and also its regular advertising date from this day. The business doubled within a year and was moved to still larger quarters in the same block at 25 West Thirty-eighth Street.

As expectant mothers were still shy and embarrassed customers, the side-street location was an advantage to the store. Some sensitive women left their carriages a block away and held veils over their faces as they entered the premises. Mail-order customers often insisted that their dresses be sent in plain wrappings.

Mail business even in 1910 was large enough for publication of Lane Bryant price lists illustrated by simple line drawings. A 1911–12 winter catalog of thirty-two pages was the first bound publication distributed. Though other garments were made, maternity wear accounted for the bulk of the business and a 1916 advertisement announced: "Society should not be abandoned by the mother-to-be. She needs the stimulus of the Opera, the Theatre, and other social functions."

The year 1916, which saw a woman elected to Congress for

the first time, also saw the business incorporated as Lane Bryant, Inc. Employees of the store subscribed to 25 percent of the capital stock. The company expanded its advertising from New York newspapers to *Vogue, Woman's Home Companion* and the *Ladies' Home Journal.*

World War I, like other wars, increased the birthrate. Young men marching the "long, long trail" of a popular song of the day and their wives wanted heirs. Lane Bryant's maternity business soared and the company's sales passed $1 million for the first time in 1917.

Lane Bryant for years did a large business in simple and elaborate layettes. When twins or triplets arrived, the additional layettes were free. They are no longer carried.

Maternity dresses for street wear were no sooner established than restless Albert Malsin, who always kept a T-square and a drawing board on his desk, turned his engineering talents to another specialty. Maternity clothing was a fine thing but its possibilities were limited. Not all women became mothers and those who did required maternity clothes only at intervals in a brief period of their lives.

Engineer Malsin began to study women's figures and found, as Shakespeare had observed of Cleopatra three centuries earlier, that they had an infinite variety. He began to chart feminine curves with the same thoroughness with which he earlier had planned the curves of scenic railways in amusement parks.

As a research tool, he invented a flexible yardstick for figure measurement. This device was of soft metal alloy that could be bent and twisted by slight pressure to conform precisely to the curves and angles of the human body. Springs held the metal in place while a tracing or other record was made. Release of the springs straightened the metal.

With this yardstick, Malsin measured the figures of 4,500 Lane Bryant customers. In addition, he obtained from a large insurance company the measurements of more than 200,000 women policyholders. He also studied population figures as to sex and age.

Malsin found that nearly 40 percent of all women were larger in some or all of their dimensions than the perfect 36 figure idealized by designers and artists. They were entirely healthy, normal and attractive women. Nature and inheritance simply had chanced to endow them with more flesh than their slenderer sisters.

Here were both the challenge and the opportunity that Malsin was seeking. Stouts were stout all of their lives and many became stouter as they became older. At the time, there was no ready-made clothing for women of larger sizes and most made-to-order clothing actually seemed to accent the size of the wearers. Some had even written letters to Lane Bryant begging that clothing be designed for them.

"Won't some ingenious man please take pity on us poor stout women?" read a typical appeal. "It seems as if some way should be found for us to walk into a store and buy comfortable and also stylish clothes as easily as our slimmer sisters do."

Malsin recognized the need and Mrs. Malsin began to design clothing especially for women requiring larger sizes. Dresses began to be made in a wide range of sizes to meet the needs of the three general types of stoutness that Malsin's research charted. These were the stout over-all type, the full-busted but normal-hipped type and the flat-busted but large-hipped type.

As a crowning psychological stroke, a size system was adopted which allowed a woman who requires a 42 elsewhere to fit comfortably into a Lane Bryant 40. More important, colors and lines were chosen that minimized the wearer's silhouette. Lane Bryant's designs for larger women borrowed both from the "height, slenderness and airy grace" of Gothic cathedrals and camouflage of World War I.

Camouflage is not the exclusive property of war [explained a company catalog], but has been used for years in architecture, in landscape gardening, in house furnishings and in the making of clothes. In camouflaging ships, for example, the idea was not to make the ships invisible, as many supposed, but to deceive the eye of the submarine observers as to the ship's size, its course and its speed.

Likewise, broad eaves are used to make a narrow house appear wider, and a striped wallpaper is used to make a ceiling seem higher. By the same principle, if correctly applied to the designing of one's clothes, the wearer may be made to appear smaller or larger, taller or shorter, as may be desired. Lane Bryant stout garments are not merely large sizes; instead, they are especially made with lines that create the optical illusion of slenderness.

So novel was the idea of styles for fuller figures when introduced by Lane Bryant that both manufacturers and customers were at first incredulous. The store had to finance its initial orders. Some of the customers thought that "stretched" maternity garments were being offered. Many 1916 advertisements headed "Appearing Stout Is Merely a Matter of Clothes" were required to convince shoppers that a distinct new line was being created.

Half sizes were first developed to eliminate excessive alterations for the average woman—this means the average American woman, who is actually five feet five or under. The half sizes are distinguished by the fact that the shoulders are cut narrower, waistlines are shorter, hips fuller and skirts shorter. The sleeves are fuller through the upper arm. They are generally young styles and close in fashion and styling to regular misses-size dresses.

In addition to negligees and dresses, Lane Bryant gradually introduced extra sizes in foundation garments, suits, blouses, sweaters, skirts, shoes, hosiery, both cloth and fur coats, gloves, sportswear and bathing suits until literally everything for the larger woman came to be stocked. Gloves are available in sizes up to 9½. Shoes are offered in sizes to 12 and 13 and in width to EEE. Even tent-size umbrellas are offered.

A salesman once attempted to sell a Lane Bryant executive a stock of reducing pills for sale to the store's stout customers.

"If these women reduced," objected the executive, "they wouldn't need our clothes."

"Don't worry," answered the salesman. "These pills don't work." Whereupon he was shown the door.

But even without pills Lane Bryant records indicate that larger American women are becoming more slender. Of the company's 38 to 60 sizes, 46 was long the largest seller. Today the average size is 44, with 42 a close second. Diet and activity are responsible.

The introduction of each of these articles in special sizes presented all the difficulties that had been overcome in maternity wear. Manufacturers were reluctant to manufacture them. Large-size coats and dresses demanded a great deal more material and work than in the usual sizes. The knitting of extra-size hosiery and the making of large shoes required additional machinery. In the case of almost all of these items, it was necessary for Lane Bryant to create an industry.

When fashion and artists like John Held, Jr., emphasized the slender, flat flapper figure in the twenties, Lane Bryant's service to fuller figures became doubly welcome. By the time of Albert Malsin's death in 1923, the store's larger-size sales had passed its maternity business in volume, despite steady increases also in the latter, and accounted for more than half of the $5 million annual business at that time.[2]

With such a background of success with the special-figure problems, it was only logical for Lane Bryant later to turn its ingenuity to two other important feminine groups with challenging figure problems of a different sort. These are tall women and chubby girls.

The average height of women in the United States is 5 feet 3⅙ inches. Thirty-six percent, however, are taller than 5 feet 4 inches; 20 per cent are more than 5 feet 7 inches; and there are enough six-footers to compose several tall-girl clubs.

Women of the latter groups are taller than most of the men with whom they come in contact and must dress carefully not to appear too towering. Dresses and accessories expressly designed to solve their problems are stocked by the Lane Bryant "Over

Five Seven Shops," started by George T. Palley, son-in-law of the founder, and now integrated in regular Lane Bryant operations. For the tall customers there are even suitably long necklaces, earrings and umbrellas.

The chubby customers are young girls and teen-agers who are plumper than their companions. The plumpness is usually a temporary condition, but while it lasts it may be a grave problem to sensitive youngsters. For these, Lane Bryant established the first special department in which sizes were determined not by age but by measurements. Here attractive dresses and coats designed to minimize weight are available, along with underwear and other articles in special chubby sizes. These range from 8½ to 14½ for girls and 11½ to 19½ for teens.

Lane Bryant for some years sponsored a Chubby Club but ended it when all teens became more sophisticated. Some also reported they "hated" and "loathed" the name.[3] Some of its activities are continued by the Teen Advisory Boards of the larger stores.

When Harry Liverman succeeded Mr. Malsin as president in 1923, Lane Bryant had stores in Manhattan, Brooklyn, Chicago and Detroit. Customers elsewhere were served by mail. Stores were established in Philadelphia and St. Louis in 1925 and in Baltimore in 1926.

Lane Bryant, in 1928, purchased two Midwest groups of stores, Newman Cloak & Suit Company and Benton's Coat & Cloak Company. These were combined as the Newman-Benton Stores and integrated by opening in them Lane Bryant departments selling special-size clothing.

As of 1973, there were 175 units in Lane Bryant, Inc.—126 Lane Bryant stores, three mail-order efforts, 14 Coward Shoe stores, nine Newman-Benton stores, 20 Town & Country discount department stores, most of them in Pennsylvania, and three new Smart Size shops in Germantown, Pennsylvania, Jersey City and Newark. These sell large, half-size and tall apparel at semidiscount prices.

Main-order operations were shifted in 1941 from New York to Indianapolis, where modern quarters provide four acres of floor space. There, nearly a thousand workers mail sixteen million catalogs a year. These are for Tall Girls, everything for women 5 feet 7 inches or taller; Hayes for half sizes and Minims for women 5 feet 3 inches and under; and the regular Lane Bryant catalog. Maternity catalogs are no longer printed. For maximum speed in filling mail orders, only right-handed girls are employed in the operation. Lane Bryant's mail business is the sixth largest in the nation and boasts a modern electronic plant.

Under the imaginative leadership of Raphael Malsin,[4] whose birth was a factor in the start of the business, the company more than doubled its sales and earnings in the 1963–72 decade and at the same time earned national fame for public service. He retired as chairman in 1972 and was succeeded as chief executive officer by his younger brother, Arthur Malsin, a Harvard-educated architect.

Arthur's first work for the firm was planning and designing its new stores as a partner in Sanders & Malsin. Upon the death of Theodore Malsin, the third brother, in 1964, Arthur became secretary of the company. He advanced to vice president in 1967, executive vice president in 1969 and became president in 1970.

The eight thousand employees of Lane Bryant for years have participated in a profit-sharing plan (they were among the first). This involves the annual distribution of a share of the company's profits before taxes. Employees share on the basis of length of service.

After one year, all employees are covered by an Employees Security Program, which consists of life insurance, Blue Cross hospitalization and major medical, surgical, health and accident insurance. All costs are borne by the company. Employees also participate in a company-financed pension plan. The pension fund, with assets of almost $18 million, guarantees a minimum of

$750 a year to retired workers in addition to their Social Security benefits. Employees of stores acquired by Lane Bryant are given pension credit for half of their previous service.

Employees may continue their education under the Albert Malsin Scholarships. These are administered by the company's Twenty-Five Year Club. The company contributes $100 to the club as each member joins, and the organization raises additional funds through contests and benefits.

After World War II, all Lane Bryant stores served as collection stations for maternity and other clothing for the devastated areas of Europe. Tons of clothing were collected and forwarded through various organizations to grateful women in a dozen countries.

Many Americans have vivid memories of aid from Lane Bryant in time of disaster. When explosion and fire devastated Texas City in 1947, the fifty-eight mail-order customers of Lane Bryant there received direct and through the Red Cross an offer to supply free new clothing to any whose wardrobes had been destroyed. The same offer was made in many other disasters, including Hurricane Agnes and the Rapid City, South Dakota, flood in 1972. A customer there wrote her local newspaper: "I am prayerfully grateful that I do not need to accept their generosity, of course, and forever when anybody says to me that big business is inhuman and heartless, I will always quietly say, 'perhaps, but let me tell you about Lane Bryant . . .' "

From 1948 to 1972, Lane Bryant gave annual awards of $1,000 and then $5,000 to an individual and to an organization in the United States "for distinguished volunteer service." A third award was sometimes given in the international field. In 1972, administration of the awards was turned over to the National Center for Voluntary Action. President Nixon spoke at the first presentation of what are known now as the Lane Bryant Prizes.

Senator Paul H. Douglas of Illinois, in an address at presentation of an early award to the Citizens' School Committee of Chicago, praised the company for "going back into the communities to search out and to recognize the groups of men and women who struggle unselfishly and without hope of reward to make our life better. . . . These awards may inspire others to start and to carry on similar works of unselfish citizenship." The awards earned an American Public Relations Association award for the firm.[5]

Such activities combined with conscientious service have made Lane Bryant a world-famous institution and increased the company's business far beyond the dreams of its founder.

Mrs. Malsin, a modest, gray-haired grandmother too small to wear any Lane Bryant garment, lived to see her modest venture become a great enterprise. Though her sons had directed the business for years, she still had an office in the New York store when she died at seventy-two of a heart attack on September 26, 1951. After bequests to her sister and twenty-one charitable and educational institutions, her will divided her $1,909,648 estate, $1,795,034 of it in Lane Bryant stocks, equally among her four children.

XVII
J. C. Penney Company

From Main Street to Shopping Centers

James Cash Penney, a twenty-six-year-old son of a minister, and two partners opened a tiny cash dry-goods store in Kemmerer, a frontier town in the southwest corner of Wyoming, on April 14, 1902. For his third, Penney, who ran the store, invested his $500 savings and a borrowed $1,500. His partners offered to lend him this amount at 8 percent but Penney found that his home-town bank in Missouri would let him have it at 6 percent. Thriftily and characteristically he obtained the money there.

He named the store the Golden Rule, and remembering his Baptist father's admonitions undertook to deal with the local coal miners and sheepherders in accordance with the Biblical injunction: "Therefore all things whatsover ye would that men should do to you, do ye even so to them."

Nearly all local trade was on credit at stores owned by the mining companies. Failure was predicted for Penney's store. It was only one room, twenty-five by forty feet, and off the main street. Penney and his young wife lived in the attic overhead. Their furniture was made from packing cases. Water had to be carried from a Chinese restaurant a few doors down the street.

With his wife as his only clerk at first, Penney went ahead undaunted. By liberally distributing handbills in advance and by staying open from sunrise to midnight, he managed to achieve first-day sales of $466.59. Thereafter, the store opened at 7 A.M. on weekdays and 8 A.M. Sundays and remained open as long as there was a miner or sheepherder on the street. Sales for the first year amounted to $28,898.11.

From this small beginning grew the great J. C. Penney Company, the nation's second largest retailer of general merchandise, which in 1972 racked up record sales of $5,529 million and record earnings of more than $162 million. Approximately a hundred million customer transactions are made every year in Penney stores, many of which are a result of the company's full-scale national advertising program that includes television and magazines as well as newspapers.

There are 1,643 J. C. Penney department and junior department stores containing 43,500,000 square feet of selling space. Thirty-nine new stores were built in 1972 alone, adding a net of 3,800,000 square feet to the chain's selling space. The Penney stores range in space from 2,500 square feet to 330,000 square feet and in annual sales from $15,000 to $24 million. A number of merchandise replenishment systems ensure up-to-date, pinpointed control of both fashion and staple merchandise.

For years, Penney has been the nation's largest seller of women's hosiery, sheets, blankets, cotton dresses, work clothes and men's underwear. More recently, it has spruced up its assortment of soft goods, adding designer dresses and youth-styled sportswear. It has done this by doffing its former T-shirt and coverall image and marching out in the direction of fashion merchandise.

From the beginning, profit sharing has been a keystone of the company's operations, with managers and store employees sharing in the earnings they have helped produce. There was once a $10,000 limit on all salaries at Penney, but this has long since been done away with.

The Penny Company has made such an impact on the public that its customers sometimes actually petition the firm to locate a store in their neighborhood. One unit in National City, California, for example, was opened in 1954 in response to a petition circulated by Mrs. A. H. Bolen, who had been a customer before moving there. About this time, a rancher drove fifty miles to the Penney store in Buffalo, Wyoming, and spent $910 outfitting his ten children.

The Penney merchandising philosophy was set forth by William M. Batten, chairman, when he said: "We are in the distribution business for any and all kinds of goods and services the great mass of people want. We will sell them anything for themselves or for their homes, in any way convenient to them, and for cash or credit, as they wish."

Many of the company's present policies trace back to the founder and his early associates in the little store that he opened in Wyoming in 1902. At that time James Cash Penney had a variety of experience behind him.[1]

He was born the seventh of twelve children on September 16, 1875, near Hamilton, Missouri, on the mortgaged farm of his father, an unsalaried Primitive Baptist minister. While keeping the farm, called Bluegrass for the Kentucky the parents had left, the father also bought and mortgaged a house in Hamilton to let the children go to school.

The family was poor. From the age of eight, Jim ran errands for money to buy his clothes. A number of childhood incidents made indelible impressions on him. For example, Jim learned a lesson in thoroughness one Sunday when he shined his self-bought $1 pair of shoes only in front and a neighbor named MacDonald called attention to them. Five boys of the MacDonald family later worked for the Penney Company, two becoming members of the board of directors.

When he was ten years old, Jim was in the pig business—at which time he learned a lesson in public relations after neighbors protested the odor. His father made him sell them at once, before they were fat enough for full value. Jim collected $60 and deposited it in two banks, lest one fail.

On graduation from high school, Jim began to grow watermelons on part of the family farm. When the county fair opened, he took a wagonload of watermelons to a spot just outside the entrance. He was doing a brisk business when his father ordered him home.

"You're disgracing the Penneys," said the minister. "Folks selling inside the fair pay for the privilege."

"But I wasn't inside the fair," Jim protested. "I was on the outside."

"Exactly," his father told him. "You were getting trade away from others without paying for the privilege." Jim never forgot this lesson in business ethics.

The boy's enterprise convinced his father that he had the makings of a merchant and a job was obtained for him at the J. M. Hale & Brother general store in Hamilton. The owner didn't need anyone at the time, but he took Jim on as a favor to his father.

Jim then went to work for Hale in 1895 for the salary of $25 for 11 months, or $2.27 a month. Though timid at first, he soon became a good salesman. In addition, he swept floors and sidewalks, sorted, dusted and kept the stock in order. He studied the stock so thoroughly that he could close his eyes and tell the grade, weight and price by the feel. By the end of the year, the twenty-year-old clerk who was laughed at by the other clerks for his dedication to his work, finished third in sales among the staff.

Jim's success in the store was a comfort to his father in the last days of his life. Shortly before he died, he said: "Jim will make it. I like the way he's started out."

Jim worked so hard at the Hale store that in three years' time his salary was raised to $300 a year. But he was also wrecking his health and a doctor warned him to get outdoors and out of Missouri. "Go to Denver at once," advised the doctor. "Otherwise you'll become a consumptive."

Jim did so. He worked briefly for two Denver stores, then went north to the small town of Longmont, where, with his entire savings of $300, he bought a butcher shop.

Longmont's leading hotel was his best customer. One day Jim's meat cutter told him that the hotel cook threatened to stop buying from them because they had neglected to send him a bottle of whiskey each week.

Jim bought the whiskey, sent it over and then, on second thought, regretted it. He remembered that, in Kentucky tradition, his grandfather and great-grandfather, although preachers, had each kept whiskey in their cellars. But his father had broken with that tradition. The more Jim thought about it, the more convinced he became that it was wrong to bribe the hotel cook. The following week he told the cook as much and promptly lost the hotel business. Not long afterward the shop failed.

Flat broke, Jim looked for another job. He found one at $50 a month with T. M. Callahan, who, with a partner, Guy Johnson, owned several stores in and around Longmont. On the strength of his $50 salary, the most he had earned until that time, on August 24, 1899 he married Berta Hess, who also had been sent to Colorado by a doctor.

It was with the backing of Callahan and Johnson that Penney opened his store in Kemmerer, a mining town, which then had a population of 1,000. He did so well there that when his partners decided to end the partnership in 1907 he was able to buy the Kemmerer store and two others for $30,000.

By this time Penney was the father of two sons and hoped to have a chain of six stores. He thought he could do it with $75,000. "It's shooting at the moon," he told his wife. She assured him he could do it and Penney agreed. "If I can find the right men for partners. Men who are capable of assuming responsibility, men with indestructible loyalty rooted in confidence in one another."

After interviewing fifty candidates, he found one such partner that same year in Earl Corder Sams, a restless man from Simpson, Kansas. Sams worked first as Penney's clerk in Kemmerer, then managed a store for him in Cumberland and, in his third year with Penney, became a partner in a new store opened in Eureka, Utah. Sams became increasingly important in the company's affairs.

Penney's goal increased to a chain of twenty-five stores. He already had fourteen and his expansion program was based on this plan: Enable a store manager to accumulate enough capital out of his earnings to buy a one-third partnership in a new store, provided he had trained another man to manage his former store. People later called Penney "The Man with a Thousand Partners."

Penney believed he had no right to be in business unless he could save his customers money on everything they bought. He confined his stores to small communities, refrained from expensive locations, had no fancy fixtures and handled only merchandise that created a general demand. This merchandise was piled on tables where customers could see and touch it, there was one price for all, cash was paid and purchases were carried home. If customers were not satisfied, they could return the merchandise and get their money back.

Penney prices in 1910 were unbelievably low. Children's underwear sold for as low as seven cents, ladies' fancy cloth coats cost $2.98, men's heavy suits were $4.98 to $6.90 and men's ties retailed for fifteen cents.

In 1910, the fourteen Penney stores had gross sales of $662,-331.16. Penney then had eight partners, all of them small-town men who had started with him as clerks. He had given up management of the Kemmerer store and set up headquarters in Salt Lake City, Utah.

Soon after this move, Penney and his wife planned a long-postponed wedding trip to Europe. But before they could leave Mrs. Penney developed pneumonia and died.

Penney plunged into his work and opened twenty additional stores in rapid succession in eight Western states. Finally, still beset with grief, Penney went to Europe alone. When he returned he changed the name on the store from the Golden Rule to the J. C. Penney Company.

Another change was made in 1913, when the company was incorporated under the laws of the State of Utah. Ten thousand shares of common stock with a face value of $10 each were issued. These were nonassessable, carried no dividends and were all issued to Penney as trustee.

Preferred stock, however, was issued to each of the partners in proportion to their individual store interests. Dividends were paid to the preferred stockholders on the basis of the earnings of each store.

By 1914, the chain extended to 48 stores and registered sales of $3,650,293.75. A central buying office was established in New York that year and Penney visualized a national chain with perhaps as many as 500 stores. Two years later there were 127 units doing an annual business of $8,428,144. When Penney went to the annual convention of partners in Salt Lake City in 1916, he nominated Earl Corder Sams as his successor. On January 1, 1917, Sams became president while Penney was elevated to chairman.

During World War I, when Penney corporate headquarters were moved to New York, the government had imposed heavy taxes on business. One of the first things President Sams had to do was to find new sources for borrowing to finance the rapidly expanding company.

New York investment bankers did not approve of the Utah articles of incorporation, and to win them over Sams and Penney agreed to change the preferred stock to a common issue. A board of directors was authorized to issue a limited amount of this stock for public sale to meet tax burdens.

This change satisfied the bankers and expansion went on with tremendous strides. Hundreds of new stores opened. In 1923 Penney bought the store from his first employer, J. M. Hale & Brother, in his home town. It was reopened as the five hundredth Penney store.

The company expanded further in 1927–29 with the purchase of 54 stores from F. S. Jones and Company, 20 stores from the Johnson-Stevens Company and 113 stores from the J. B. Byars Company and the J. N. McCracken Company. All of these were in the West and Middle West.

At the end of 1929, there were 1,395 stores and the company reported record sales of $209 million and more than $12 million in profits. Penney stock was listed on the New York Stock Exchange beginning October 23, 1929, just six days before the stock market crashed and the depression got under way.

Sales dropped to a low of $155,271,981 in 1932 but even then there were earnings of $5,082,672. Recovery began for the company the next year. With 1,466 stores, seven fewer than in 1932, sales soared to $178,773,965 and profits more than doubled to total $14,235,638.

Florida bank failures affecting his personal fortune and a sharp decline in the value of Penney stock at this time were a blow to founder Penney's personal fortune which was estimated at about $40 million. He successfully met the crisis by again rolling up his sleeves, going back to work full time for the company for a while and borrowing from five New York City banks. Jim Penney's health improved after a stay at a sanitarium and he traveled throughout the vast empire to stimulate his managers and salespeople. "I tried my best to put in a hard day's work every day," he recalled about that period.

In one of his books, *Fifty Years with the Golden Rule,* Penney described how he made it through that most trying period. "When I accepted the fact that that disastrous event had not destroyed any essential capacities of mine, I began to fight," he said. "Fighting kept me going on and going on kept me fighting."

The Penney Company was one of the first to recognize the strength of the movement against chain stores. From 1927 onward, the company directly and through trade associations fought antichain measures in courts, before legislative committees and in public forums. This activity was redoubled when Representative Wright Patman of Texas introduced his "death sentence" antichain bill which would have imposed additional taxes of $63,912,000 on the company at a time when its earnings were $13,739,160 a year.

As the first opposition witness at 1940 hearings of a Congressional subcommittee considering the bill, President Sams traced the history of his company and asked defeat of the measure for these reasons:

1. It would destroy the Penney Company or any other similar company.

2. It would destroy the finest field of opportunity that has ever existed in retailing for the young ambitious man born without family means.

3. It would add to the cost of living for every American family of limited means and would lower the American standard of living.

4. It would deal a staggering blow to the entire economic life of this country and would be especially destructive to the smaller cities and towns for the benefit of the larger cities.

5. It would hurt and tax this entire nation for the protection and enrichment of a small minority group of self-interested middlemen and of another small minority group of ill-advised marginal retailers.

Scores of witnesses, including spokesmen for farm, labor and consumer groups as well as the chains, followed Sams to Washington to condemn the bill and it was killed in committee.[2] No more states have enacted antichain legislation, and some of the earlier measures, such as those that were in force in California and Utah, have been repealed.

Proposals for mergers of Penney with Montgomery Ward and then Sears, Roebuck were considered seriously when the mail-order giants moved into the retail-store field, but negotiations came to nothing. There seemed to be no way to transfer goodwill and trained personnel.

Although Penney has had a tradition of leasing most of its stores, a flexible policy of ownership is now followed wherever savings in occupancy costs can be achieved over leasing. The stores owned by the company are financed internally, as are the warehouses owned by J. C. Penney Properties, Inc., a wholly owned subsidiary.

In 1960, the average new Penney store measured about 40,000 square feet. Five years later, the new stores constructed averaged 86,000 square feet.

The prototype of the "new" Penney department store was the

220,000-square-foot shopping center unit in King of Prussia, Pennsylvania. This two-level facility has 32 major departments, 238 separate subdivisions and parking in the plaza for 9,000 cars. Among the services offered in this store are a snack bar, an optical shop, a beauty salon and a portrait studio.

Penney deals with more than ten thousand merchandise suppliers throughout the world. But, unlike some other large chains that have a financial stake in many companies that manufacture their goods, Penney has no monetary interest in any of its sources.

There are Penney stores in every state except Rhode Island. California has the largest number of these stores with 169, and Texas is next with 130. There are Penney stores in Levittown, New York, and Levittown, Pennsylvania, in Anchorage, Alaska, and Honolulu, Hawaii, in the suburbs of Chicago and in downtown Denver.

In 1957, a 150-page merchandising character study following an intensive internal two-year survey of their company convinced Penney officials that sweeping merchandising and operational changes had to be made. The most serious problem found was that 96 percent of Penney's volume was in soft lines. This heavy preponderance of apparel and home furnishings meant that, according to one vice president: "We had no browsing areas for men while their wives shopped, like paint and hardware departments. We had nothing to attract the kids, like a toy department. We realized we needed to tend more toward the one-stop shopping idea."[3] As a result, the first full-line department store was opened in 1963.

While soft goods still predominate at Penney, hard lines—also with Penney private labels like Penncrest—are now very much in evidence. In those stores with appliance, television, hardware, furniture and other male-oriented departments, the ratio is 70 percent soft lines to 30 percent hard goods. Approximately 85 percent of all Penney's sales consist of private-brand merchandise, which the company calls "Always First Quality."

Another innovation has been the introduction of in-home

selling through Penney decorators who visit customers' homes to show samples as part of a complete decorating service. About 275 Penney stores sell a variety of home furnishings ranging from carpeting, curtains and drapes to decorative accessories and furniture. Tires, batteries and auto accessories have also been added at more than three hundred units to broaden the product base.

Shortly after the merchandising study, Penney engaged the management consulting firm of McKinsey & Co., to look into its management compensation program. Prior to that time, there was a $10,000 ceiling on salaries—which meant that some Penney executives had to borrow money during the year until they received their substantial year-end bonuses. In addition, the company's contribution to each employee's profit-sharing account was based on salary, resulting in relatively small amounts being added each year to the accounts of even the most senior executives. After an analysis of these problems by McKinsey, the ceiling was eliminated and salaries and incentives were established according to the skills and knowledge required for each particular job.

Penney has a savings and profit-sharing plan into which employees can deposit from 2 to 10 percent of their total earnings. Up to 6 percent of an employee's earnings are matched by the company at rates depending on profits each year. Any employee's personal deposits can be withdrawn in time of need or when he or she retires or leaves the company.

While Penney store buildings vary greatly, Penney men and women are usually the same everywhere—rarely flashy but always hard-working and trustworthy individuals who are assets to their stores and communities. Their company trusts them. The more than $2 billion that flows into its cash registers each year is largely in cash or the equivalent and managers bank it locally. But no Penney employee is bonded. While a Penney man goes wrong now and then, the loss is much less than the cost would be to bond all who handle money.

A "Penney-type" man, besides liking retailing, must know

how to be helpful to people and treat them fairly. He must know how to make money and build a business. He must know how to make a place for himself in any community where he may be sent.

The company has some 162,000 worldwide "associates"—the word "employee" isn't used at Penney. To train them and keep them abreast of new sales techniques, Penney uses sales courses on teaching machines that can be circulated from store to store.

Just like all other employees, the top Penney executives have started at the bottom. Even Earl Sams began as a clerk in the original Kemmerer store. After managing several other stores, he served as president from 1917 to 1946. He was then named board chairman until 1950, when he died at the age of sixty-six.

J. C. Penney retained the chairmanship of the company he founded until 1946. He took the post again after Sams died and held it until 1958, when he relinquished it to Albert W. Hughes.

Hughes's history with the company is typical of a successful Penney executive. When he was a young man, he tutored Penney's sons in Latin at the Hill School in Pottstown, Pennsylvania, and quickly decided that retailing would be more exciting than teaching a dead language. He began in a store at Moberly, Missouri—where Jim Penney told him, "If you can sell merchandise to a Missourian, you can sell anyone"—and managed stores in Utah and Georgia. Later be became head of the personnel department in New York, was elected a vice president of the company in 1937 and was named president in 1946.

William M. Batten, now the chairman of the board and the company's fourth chief executive, first worked for Penney as an extra salesman in 1926 while attending high school in Parkersburg, West Virginia. He washed windows, worked in the stockroom and then sold shoes. After graduation from Ohio State University in 1932, he joined Penney in Lansing, Michigan, in 1935 as a shoe salesman. He became assistant manager of the store and then joined the personnel training department in New

York. Batten moved up the ranks to the presidency in 1958 and the chairmanship in 1964. He now spends the bulk of his time concentrating on long-range planning and corporate affairs.

The president of the company is Jack B. Jackson, a native of Sherman, Texas, who started his career with Penney at its store in his birthplace in 1941. Although it took him eleven years to become a store manager, he moved quickly through the ranks afterwards. He came to the New York headquarters in 1970 on a special assignment to head a study group before becoming director of regional operations in 1971 and president and the man in charge of day-to-day operations in 1972.

Linking headquarters and store managers are five regional managers and some sixty-five district managers. These men spend most of their time visiting stores to counsel with managers on problems of all kinds, to detect new customer tastes and to help train store personnel. Zone and district men meet for a fortnight each December. There are also quarterly district meetings for managers, who in turn meet frequently with their department heads and clerks. There is free discussion at all levels—which Penney executives regard as a great source of company strength.

The store manager is the key man. He hires and trains his own help. If he runs a store in the Southwest, this may include such things as giving Spanish lessons. He decides what to do about local advertising and supporting local causes with money and manpower.

The store manager at Penney orders much of his merchandise from lists and samples sent him by headquarters but is not required to accept anything he thinks is unsuited to his climate or his customers' tastes. A number of automatic programs, especially in the fashion areas, have been instituted to shorten the time required to get new merchandise into the store. The manager can choose which central-office training, promotion and advertising aids best fit his needs. Ninety percent of the advertising expenditure is usually in newspapers but managers can use other media if they like.

In recent years, Penney has sharply increased its advertising budget as it has moved away from an almost complete reliance on local space to become a big-time national advertiser as well. Beginning in 1969, when it selected its first advertising agency, McCaffrey & McCall, the company has stepped up its advertising program to include local and network television.

In 1971, for example, Penney spent $3,254,500 for spot television commercials on stations throughout the country. In 1972, its expenditures on television exceeded $8 million, including more than $5 million for its initial involvement on the networks. Part of this went for attention-grabbing election-night commercials on all three television networks in that Presidential year.

Fashion as well as value is now stressed in Penney apparel offered as part of a general trading-up policy, although the $4 housedress can still be found in many Penney stores. A semiannual publication, *Fashions and Fabrics,* reports fashion news and forecasts trends for the home sewer. Fifty thousand copies of this magazine are given away to home-economics teachers and others as part of the company's public-relations program. This program also includes the circulation of motion-picture films on Penney operations to schools and colleges.

Most Penney buying is done in New York, although buying offices in Dallas, Miami, Los Angeles, the Far East and Europe cover the ready-to-wear and similar industries in those areas. While the company once owned its own corset and brassiere factory, everything is now purchased, partly in the open market but primarily from manufacturers with whom buyers work closely to plan articles of definite quality to sell at predetermined prices. The International Silver Company, for example, created silverware of a special pattern for both the Penney twenty-fifth and fiftieth anniversaries.

In recent years, the company has taken steps to upgrade its hard-goods lines to the same prominence as its apparel and home furnishings. Some of the country's leading durable-goods manufacturers—among them the Hotpoint division of General Electric

Company, the Goodyear Tire & Rubber Company and the SCM Corporation—now produce merchandise under Penney's private labels.

All of this, says Chairman Batten, is a part of the company's basic strategy: "The broadening of merchandise assortments to include a greater representation of hard goods . . . and two, the introduction of services such as charge accounts and catalog shopping to make shopping at Penney's easier."

Credit, which was introduced at Penney only in 1958 and expended to the whole chain in 1962—all against the wishes of the founder, whose middle name, after all, was Cash—accounts for slightly more than a third of the company's total sales. Catalog selling, which began in the Midwest when Penney bought the General Merchandise Company of Milwaukee in 1962, was extended into the Southeast in 1965 and Columbus, Ohio, in 1974.

Penney's goal is to have a nationwide catalog service, à la Sears, Roebuck and Montgomery Ward. Catalog selling is already profitable for the company, with more than 1,200 sales centers, principally in Penney stores, and a total volume at the centers and through mail order of $388 million.

At the time it acquired General Merchandise, Penney also bought that concern's Treasure Island discount store. This type of merchandise outlet has since become important in the company's overall operations, with twenty-three of these units— now called the Treasury—containing three million square feet in key market locations.

In recent years, the chain that began with a one-room store in Wyoming has expanded widely into other fields, retailing and nonretailing, both at home and abroad. In 1969, Penney bought the Thrift Drug Company—now containing 205 drugstores and nineteen health and beauty-aid departments, primarily in the Northeast. The following year, it purchased Supermarkets Interstate, Inc., which now operates forty-six food supermarkets in Penney and in other stores.

Great American Reserve Insurance Company, with its life

and health and accident insurance capability and other financial services, also came into the Penney fold in 1970 as a means of taking a strong position in still another industry. And toward the end of the last decade, Penney moved into Europe—a thus far unprofitable trans-Atlantic journey but a necessary beginning for a projected international base—with the acquisition of the 87-store Sarma chain in Belgium and the opening of four stores under the Penney name in Italy.

In 1964, Penney moved its executive headquarters and buying offices from an eighteen-story building on Manhattan's west side to 1301 Avenue of the Americas. This move to a $40-million structure constructed by the Uris Building Corporation, which was then named the J. C. Penney Building after its prime tenant, was another symbol of the changing face and dynamic activity at the company.

Penney leases thirty-six of the forty-five floors of this building, representing 850,000 square feet of its total of 1,150,000 square feet. Furthermore, it occupies the entire 270,000-square-foot addition built later to accommodate the overflow of staff at the growing corporation. Twenty-five hundred company employees made the move following the completion of what was then the largest lease of commercial office space in real-estate history.

The Penney Building is a single sheer tower set back more than thirty feet from the building line, thus creating room for a spacious landscaped street-level plaza and a second, sunken plaza offering access to lower-level shops. Pedestrian walks on side streets bring the total plaza area to nearly 30 percent of the entire site.

Penney has set aside seventeen merchandise floors on which a huge assortment of goods is displayed for evaluation by its buying staff. Display and storage facilities, many of which are automatic, provide easy access to a wide range of sample merchandise. In the shoe department alone, there are racks capable of holding forty to fifty thousand pairs of shoes.

Inside the building too is Penney's highly regarded and well-equipped product-testing laboratory, its Merchandise Testing Center. The extent of the equipment in this laboratory run by sixty-five people can be seen from its electronic testing section, where machinery in use is similar to that utilized in space installations. It even has its own closed-circuit television station that can broadcast signals in both black-and-white and in color.

A complete data-processing center is part of the New York complex. Here computers quickly translate sales information received from the Penney stores into stock orders and statistical reports.

All of these twentieth-century tools are necessary, says Chairman Batten, for Penney's future development. "If we are to continue to grow and prosper," he believes, "then our methods must change, our merchandise mix and customer services must adhere more closely to mass market demand and the environment in which our customers shop must be on rising levels of convenience and taste comparable to those which they are achieving in their daily lives." Another executive adds, "We don't make things cheaper, we make them better."

James Cash Penney, who kept a close relationship with the company throughout his lifetime—including a memento-filled office on the forty-fifth floor of the new headquarters building —died in 1971 at the age of ninety-five, leaving an estate of $35 million. This twentieth-century merchant prince, who had received among his dozens of accolades the prestigious Tobé Award in 1953 for contributions to retailing, had kept five full-time secretaries busy until his death with a voluminous correspondence with Penney retirees, young people seeking his advice and others who wrote him in connection with his charitable and religious endeavors.

There is still a Penney store in Kemmerer. It is better located, more attractive and bigger than the one in which everything began, and it does many times the business of the founder in his remarkable first year.

XVIII
Broadway-Hale

Colossus of the West

Just before the turn of the century, Arthur Letts, an unschooled native of England who moved to the then young city of Los Angeles, opened a small dry-goods store there with assets of less than $10,000. Now the company, of which that little store was the precursor, is a billion-dollar retailing organization headed by Edward W. Carter, a graduate of the Harvard Business School. The changes that have taken place at Broadway-Hale Stores, Inc., in the years between the Letts and Carter regimes symbolize the progress of the American West as well as the development of its largest and most significant group of stores.

For today's Broadway-Hale is not only the largest department store organization in the West, it is also an amalgam of distinguished specialty stores with outstanding reputations and sales records. In addition to the fifty-five full-line department stores operating under the Broadway, Emporium, Capwell's and Weinstock's names in California, Arizona and Nevada, there are three apparel specialty store groups in the corporation that epitomize fashion, taste and quality.

These groups are the nineteen Holt, Renfrew stores in Canada, the five Neiman-Marcus stores in Texas and Florida and the one and only Bergdorf Goodman in New York City. Also under the Broadway-Hale wing are the Walden Book Stores, which the West Coast company pushed from a $7-million annual business to a $50-million bookselling empire during the three years of its ownership, and Sunset House, a novelty mail-order company.

Despite these vast national and international operations, Broadway-Hale is best known as a California company. Just as the Broadway division dominates Los Angeles retailing, Emporium and Capwell dominate the San Francisco Bay area and Weinstock's is a major power in California's central valley around Sacramento.

And as if to symbolize the rebirth of downtown Los Angeles where Broadway-Hale has its corporate headquarters, the company and Ogden Development Corporation built a major metropolitan commercial center there called Broadway Plaza. Not only does this $75-million center contain a 250,000-square-foot Broadway flagship store—the first new downtown department store built in Los Angeles in fifty years—but it also has a shopping center, a 500-room hotel, a 32-story office building and a 2,000-car parking garage.

The tremendous growth of Broadway-Hale took place in the years after World War II, when California and the entire West grew at a rate far in excess of the national average in population, employment and per capita income. But its foundations were laid in 1896 by the brilliant merchant Arthur Letts, who founded its first store in downtown Los Angeles on South Broadway, which accounts for the first half of the company's present name.

Letts, then thirty-four years old, was born in Northamptonshire, England, and apprenticed at the age of fourteen to a dry-goods—or drapery, as it was known there—business. He worked in London long enough to pay his passage to Canada and informed his parents of his departure only when he was aboard ship.

After working for a while in Canada, he moved to Seattle and opened his first store in a tent. This store went bankrupt in the panic of 1893 and Letts moved to Los Angeles, after paying his creditors thirty-five cents on the dollar.

One day in 1896, he walked along Broadway and saw a little store on the corner of Fourth Street, with a sign "The Broadway Department Store," that had been closed because of failure. Letts purchased the bankrupt stock of merchandise for $8,167—$80 more than the next highest bid—and took over the store.

Letts' first slogan was "All cars transfer to Fourth and Broadway" because the electric trolley cars all came past his new store. By maintaining fixed prices for all merchandise (a rarity for that day), by pioneering odd-cent prices and by offering a liberal exchange and refund policy, the store prospered.[1]

Beginning in 1902, as he obtained excess funds from the business, Letts started repayments to all of the creditors in his Seattle bankruptcy and paid them in full three years later. In 1906, when many of the San Francisco-based apparel manufacturers and wholesalers that had sold to him during his pre-bankruptcy period were hit by a damaging earthquake, he sent out additional checks to each one covering 6 percent interest for each year of the delay.

Letts was also responsible for the establishment of Bullock's, when in 1906 he invested $250,000 and placed two of his most trusted employees in charge of the new department-store venture three blocks from the Broadway. They were two young Canadians—John Gillespie Bullock, for whom the store was named, and Percy Glen Winnett—who developed the downtown unit and later its branches into keen competitors with the Broadway (see Chapter XXI).

The largest and most profitable division of Broadway-Hale is still the Broadway, where the Broadway-Hale store began. Its first suburban store opened in Hollywood in 1931, followed by another in Pasadena nine years later. One of the nation's first planned shopping centers was developed by the Broadway in Crenshaw, California in 1947 and became a prototype for the industry. There are thirty-two stores in the division, operated out of a 1.8-million-square-foot central office and warehouse in

Los Angeles and run by a regional management team that controls all of its buying, advertising and accounting from a central headquarters location.

Weinstock's, which operates nine department stores in central California and Reno, Nevada, traces its origins back to 1876. That was the year when Hale Bros. Stores (which accounts for the second half of the corporate name) was acquired and two years prior to the establishment of Weinstock, Lubin & Co., also now part of the amalgamated firm.

To obtain a foothold in northern California, Broadway-Hale acquired the Dohrmann Commercial Company in 1956. The key aspect to this purchase was not the small retail operations or the hotel-supply company owned by Dohrmann—which have since been sold off—but rather its 24 percent interest in the Emporium Capwell Company.

Over the next fifteen years, Broadway-Hale bought additional stock in Emporium Capwell, which began in 1897 as the Emporium & Golden Rule Bazaar. But for this entire period, it did not attempt to merge because, in Carter's words, "The management there didn't want it; we had a good working relationship with the management and we weren't going to force them."

By 1970, however, Emporium Capwell was finally in favor of a link-up with Broadway-Hale, which then acquired the remaining 50 percent of the stock. Today Emporium Capwell has fourteen department stores, with nine in the San Francisco area and five on the Oakland side of the Bay.

Thus today's Broadway-Hale is a major retailing complex whose name is known far from its California home. Among department-store merchants, the company ranks among the top ten. In 1970, its sales reached $680 million; in 1972, they topped $900 million; and by 1973, they neared the $1-billion mark that Ed Carter set his sights on decades before.

For Carter, who joined the company in 1946 at the age of thirty-four as its boss, had originally hoped to reach $1-billion in sales just about the time of his expected retirement around

1976. Now with his company firmly entrenched as the biggest in the Western region and its acquisitions reaching throughout the United States and even Canada, he is shooting for $1.5 billion for 1976. Incidentally, the 1946 volume figure of Broadway-Hale, when Carter started his expansion moves, was less than $40 million.

One of the first department-store organizations to eliminate its basements ("We can't be all things to all people," said Carter) and one of the few department-store groups that have refused to set up a discount-store subsidiary ("There's not enough profit potential"), the company is looking ahead to European retailing operations and other domestic expansion that meets the competitive requirements of the Federal Trade Commission. And sitting atop this colossus is Carter, the Maryland-born retailer who came to California at the age of nine.

"We seek dominance in anything we go into," he has said. "And we're going to continue concentrating on the very broad middle segment of the population. We want to have stores in each center of population in the West. We want to be where most people are."[2]

In addition to Carter, who became executive vice president and chief executive officer of Broadway-Hale in 1946, president in 1947 and chairman in 1972, the senior officers in the company's top management include Prentice C. Hale, chairman of the executive committee; Philip M. Hawley, president; Eaton W. Ballard, executive vice president; J. Hart Lyon, chairman of the Broadway; and Ardern R. Batchelder, chairman of Emporium Capwell.[3]

XIX
Neiman-Marcus

The Pride of Texas

The famous Neiman-Marcus Company of Dallas was acquired as an autonomous, wholly owned subsidiary by Broadway-Hale Stores, Inc., in 1969 in exchange for convertible preferred stock worth $39 million. Neiman-Marcus sales were then more than $62 million a year. The deal, in President Edward W. Carter's words, added "the luxury element" to the big merchandising complex and assured Neiman-Marcus of capital to accelerate expansion outside of Texas, where it then had two stores in Dallas and one each in Fort Worth and Houston.

Bearded Stanley Marcus continued as chief executive of Neiman-Marcus and became a corporate vice president of Broadway-Hale. He and his brother, Edward, were elected directors of the parent company. The Marcus family collectively became the second largest stockholders of Broadway-Hale.

While the negotiations were being concluded, a Neiman-Marcus fur buyer outbid rivals to pay the highest price in history for mink skins at the Hudson's Bay auction in New York—$2,700 each for forty skins of new Emba's Kojah mink. This effectively answered rumors that the Broadway-Hale might change Neiman-Marcus prices and quality. The skins were made into a single coat that sold for $150,000.[1]

Early that year the Houston operation moved from an unpromising downtown location into a new $10 million store designed by Gyo Obata, a noted Japanese-American architect, in the suburban Post Oak-Galleria shopping center. Managed by Lawrence Marcus, now executive vice president of the firm, it outsells a fine locally owned Sakowitz shop across the street in what has been called "a lovely war."[2] A \$5-million store designed by Herbert Johnson was opened in 1971 at Bal Harbour, north of Miami Beach, Florida, the first expansion outside Texas.

An Atlanta store, designed by John Carl Warnecke & Associates, followed in 1972. Stores were announced for Frontenac, a suburb of St. Louis, and in Northbrook Court, near Chicago. The latter is planned as a two-level \$6-million project of Homart Development Co., a subsidiary of Sears, Roebuck, which will have a store there. Chicago's Michigan Boulevard and Washington, D.C., will have Neiman-Marcus stores.

"Mr. Stanley" was one of the first merchants from the United States to be invited to the Canton Trade Fair in China following President Nixon's visit to that country in 1972. Marcus made the trip in May and wrote an account of his adventures for the *New York Times*.[3] He spent \$250,000 for antique porcelains, jewelry, mandarin robes and acupuncture dolls. Everything was snapped up as soon as it arrived. He made a second trip in November, this time to Peking, becoming the first American merchant to reach that city on a buying trip in a quarter of a century.

On his return he assumed the title of chairman, while continuing as chief executive, and promoted his thirty-four-year-old son, Richard Marcus, to president. A graduate of Harvard like his father, Richard had been executive vice president in charge of the Dallas and Fort Worth stores. At the same time Neal Fox and Bernard Newberg were named senior vice presidents.

One reason for the success of Neiman-Marcus is the talent for showmanship of Mr. Stanley and his staff. The company attracts newsmakers as customers and makes news itself. When a fortnight's strike of pilots threw American Airlines stewardesses out of work, the store hired forty of them as models and salespeople. They earned their money and spent much of it in the store. Neiman-Marcus garnered two pages in *Life* and newspaper publicity throughout the country.[4]

Though she had lived in Washington, D.C., for many years, Mrs. Lyndon B. Johnson on January 20, 1965, wore to the five inaugural balls marking her husband's new term as President a gold-colored evening dress purchased from Neiman-Marcus. It had been designed to order in New York by Texas-born John Moore. Her daughters, Luci and Lynda, also danced that evening in gowns from the Texas store. Mrs. Johnson has had a Neiman-Marcus charge account since her student days at the University of Texas and had worn a Neiman-Marcus dress to her husband's inauguration as Vice President. He had given friends hats from the store.

When Luci Baines Johnson and Patrick J. Nugent were married on August 6, 1966, in the most spectacular wedding in White House history, Neiman-Marcus supplied her gown and trousseau, the Adele Simpson-designed yellow silk dress of her mother and the pink dresses of the twelve bridesmaids. Mrs. Priscilla Kidder of Boston, who made Luci's white organza gown, was present to help with the train. As friends of the Johnsons, Stanley Marcus and his family were among the seven hundred wedding guests.

Considerable salesmanship had also been employed by the store in outfitting Mrs. Dwight D. Eisenhower with a pink Nettie Rosenstein gown and a Hattie Carnegie suit for the 1953 inaugural festivities. The story of the gown and the suit began three years earlier. While on a European buying trip, Stanley Marcus was introduced to General Eisenhower at Supreme Headquarters in Paris. Marcus expressed his admiration for the general and recalled the latter's residence in Texas.

"I hope you win the nomination," said the merchant as he departed. "If you are nominated, I hope you win the election. As you were born in Texas and served in Texas, I hope you'll remember there's a store in Texas that would like to dress Mrs. Eisenhower for the inauguration."

General Eisenhower laughed and nodded. When the votes were counted and the Eisenhowers were deluged with proposals of all kinds, Marcus reminded the general of the conversation in Paris and submitted a number of sketches. Mrs. Eisenhower chose the Rosenstein number.

To Miss Kay Kerr of Neiman-Marcus' New York office, Mrs. Eisenhower wrote: "I have so many things for which to thank you—your patience, your courtesies, your helpfulness, your excellent opinions and judgment. . . . I can imagine what difficulties were imposed upon you where fittings were concerned by my nasty cold. . . . That you accomplished so much under handicaps is a tribute to your patience and efficiency. . . ."

The store was founded by three remarkable individuals, Herbert Marcus; his sister, Carrie; and her husband, Abraham Lincoln Neiman. Herbert and Carrie were born in Louisville, Kentucky, and had moved to Hillsboro, Texas, where a brother had a grocery, and thence fifty miles north to Dallas. There Herbert sold women's shoes and was promoted to boys'-department buyer for Sanger Brothers. Carrie followed him and became an assistant buyer at A. Harris & Co. When Al Neiman, as he was called, a promoter of department-store sales from Cleveland, conducted a sale at the latter store in 1905, he met Carrie and they were married.

At this time, Herbert Marcus, married and the father of a newborn son named Stanley, demanded a raise at Sanger Brothers, then the largest as well as the oldest of Dallas stores. The raise was granted but only for $1.87 a week. He quit and joined Neiman in opening an advertising agency in Atlanta, Georgia.

They succeeded so well that two years later they had the choice of selling it for $25,000 cash or trading it for Coca-Cola stock and a Missouri franchise for the soft drink. They spurned the latter option (which quickly became worth millions), took the $25,000, returned to Dallas and started Neiman-Marcus. This decision once caused son Stanley to remark that the store was founded "on bad business judgment."

The capital was $22,000 from Neiman and $8,000 from the Marcuses. Herbert was then twenty-nine and Carrie twenty-three. The trio rented at $9,000 a year a 5,000-square foot, two-story building and spent $12,000 on red-mahogany fixtures and luxurious carpeting. Neiman was an able financial man. Marcus was a born merchant who even in his last blind years could accurately judge the quality of leather by its feel. Carrie Neiman's contribution was the most important of all— unerring taste and a shrewd judgment of style.[5]

To avoid merely duplicating existing Dallas retail operations, they undertook to make Neiman-Marcus a specialty store of style and quality for customers who did not need to haggle over pennies. Carrie Neiman spent $17,000 in New York for an initial stock and in the fall of 1907, with a page of the *Dallas News,* the new firm announced:

On September Tenth will take place the formal opening of Neiman-Marcus Co., the South's finest and only exclusive ready-to-wear shop, the most elegantly equipped storeroom in the South. . . . It shall be the policy of Neiman-Marcus to be at all times leaders in their lines and to give buyers in Texas something out of the commonplace. . . . With these aims in view, exclusive lines of high-class garments have been secured, lines which have never been offered before to the buyers of Dallas. . . . We will miss a sale rather than have a garment leave the establishment which is not a perfect fit. . . .

Carrie Neiman and Herbert Marcus were ill on opening day, the latter with typhoid fever, and failure of the Knickerbocker Trust Company in New York precipitated a business panic the next month. Nevertheless, within a few weeks the stock of "demi-costumes, modish waists, dress and walking skirts, better coats and millinery" was sold. There was money from cotton and also from oil in Texas even in 1907. Within three years, Carrie Neiman was making buying trips to Paris. In addition to women's clothes, the store began to sell accessories, infants' wear, girls' clothing and eventually men's wear and many other items.

In 1913, the firm had a $20,000 profit on a $380,000 sales volume despite a fire that destroyed the store. Neiman-Marcus then moved east to its present site at Main and Ervay Streets, but not without difficulty. The owner declined to sell but was agreeable to a ninety-nine-year lease on condition that a building costing at least $100,000 be erected. As the firm's capital amounted only to $80,000, Al Neiman sold five blocks of stock at $10,000 each to New York manufacturers. One has held his stock through the years and seen it increase to $700,000 in value. With additional funds borrowed, the firm built a $192,000 structure.

By 1916, Neiman-Marcus customers were becoming familiar with names like Callot Soeurs, Lanvin, Revillon Frères and Martial and Armand. Sales reached $1,260,046 in 1918 and $2,191,911 in 1919 as more oil fields were discovered in Texas.

Herbert Marcus, whose formal schooling ended at fifteen, helped raise money to launch Southern Methodist University. He gave Miss Hockaday's School for Girls $100,000 for a fine-arts building and served as a trustee. He helped found the Southwestern Medical Center. He helped bring grand opera to Dallas. He owned canvases by Renoir and Sir Thomas Lawrence. He encouraged his sons in similar tastes.

Neiman-Marcus's reputation was built by the free-spending customer. Perhaps the most famous was Electra Waggoner Wharton Bailey Gilmore, heiress to land and cattle fortunes, who bought as much as $20,000 worth of merchandise in a single day —and returned the next day for another $20,000 she had forgotten. The store continued on its luxurious way during the twenties and sales reached a peak of $3,600,000 in 1929, but the firm had gone through a crisis the previous year.

After twenty-three years of marriage, Al and Carrie Neiman were divorced. Marcus bought Al's interest in the firm and Neiman moved to New York. There he remarried, founded his own merchandising firm, Neiman Associates, and outlived both his former partners. Though Herbert Marcus became blind in

1946, he continued active in the store almost until his death from hypertension at seventy-two in 1950. His sister, by then "Aunt Carrie" to many, died three years later.

Stanley Marcus, Herbert's eldest son, who joined the store as a floor man in 1926 after earning a master's degree in business administration at Harvard, stepped into many of Neiman's duties. In 1928, he became secretary, treasurer and a director, also merchandise manager of the sports shop. The next year he was promoted to merchandise manager of all apparel divisions. In this role, he met Mary Cantrell, a pretty buyer in the store's sportswear shop. In 1932, he married and retired her. "Mr. Stanley," as he was soon known in the store, became executive vice president in 1935, and, after the death of his father, president. As they grew up, his three brothers also joined the store.

According to the organization chart, Mr. Stanley is supposed to deal only with top executives, but actually he deals with everything and everybody. It was Mr. Stanley who first believed the store could attain national stature. He began to advertise Neiman-Marcus in national fashion magazines when such advertising was almost unknown. Many of the dramatic promotions have been his ideas. In addition to everything else, he personally has sold more than $5 million worth of fur coats.

The two sides of Stanley Marcus's personality make him both an intellectual and a hard-driving merchant. His library includes works on art, china, brass and silver. He collects primitive masks and sculpture and is a serious student of typography. He has served as president of the Dallas Art Association, a trustee of the Dallas Museum of Fine Arts, president of the Dallas Symphony Orchestra and an overseer of Harvard University. He is also a fellow of the Pierpont Morgan Library and a trustee of Southern Methodist University.

Wherever there is a customer who might be interested in Neiman-Marcus merchandise, Stanley believes in going to the customer. In fact, Stanley Marcus once flew a fashion show to Australia and continued around the world with it. A show toured through Mexico and South America. Women in Detroit have been subjected to the temptations of a Neiman-Marcus fashion show, and when Stanley once heard of a woman in St. Louis who wanted a fur coat, he took the coat to her.

During the depression, the store lost money for two years. Though it was in 1930 that the great East Texas oil field, the biggest the world has ever known, was brought in, there still weren't enough big spenders even in Texas for Neiman-Marcus to grow large with just the expensive lines of its early years. Some of this "new" oil went for as low as ten cents a barrel, and while it served to cushion the money panic that was about to paralyze the rest of the country, the store could no longer depend exclusively on high-priced merchandise.

Neiman-Marcus decided to split its personality and cater to the moderate income as well as to the wealthy. New lines of lower-priced though well-edited merchandise began to appear. The store went after the under-$20,000 income group in earnest. This policy increased sales between 1942 and 1953 almost five-fold. The store's first suburban branch, a $2-million Preston Center store, was opened in 1951. A $5-million expansion of the downtown store was completed in 1953. A Houston branch was acquired with purchase of Ben Wolfman, Inc., in 1955 and a $1-million expansion there was completed in 1959. In that year, the store offered 133,800 of its 598,800 family-owned shares to the public at $19.50 a share. The $2,600,000 offering was snapped up in a day and within a week the stock was selling for $21.

A $4-million branch was opened in the Ridglea area of western Fort Worth in 1963. A new $4-million North Park store with twice the floor space replaced the Preston Center branch in 1965. That autumn, the Neiman-Marcus Greenhouse, a $2-million spa for improving the health and beauty of thirty-six women able to spend $850 a week for its luxurious services, was opened at Arlington, midway between Dallas and Fort Worth.

An unusual promotion was the Neiman-Marcus cookbook, *A Taste of Texas*, produced by Marihelen McDuff and Jane Trahey in 1949 when they were respectively in charge of the store's public relations and advertising.

They asked notables to contribute their "favorite or most tantalizing" recipes. Many did so. Paul Gallico, the writer, retorted with a letter saying he was planning to start a store and would like Neiman-Marcus to send him free "your favorite or most successful pieces of merchandise" and particularly "a fur evening wrap for a small blonde woman, about size 14, solid gold cuff links, a fine rod and reel for deep sea fishing, a pair of diamond and sapphire clips. . . ." The editors published his letter as a recipe for "Specialty Store à la Gallico." Six printings of the book have been sold.[6]

Authentic Egyptian mummy cases were featured in the 1971 catalog, at $16,000 for the pair. They were sold to a museum on the West Coast. A $35,000 one-day cruise of the Caribbean for six hundred was bought by the Crippled Children's Society of Miami. The 1972 Christmas catalog advertised an emerald ring for $150,000 and a sable cape for $42,000. One year Neiman-Marcus had a page captioned "How to Spend $1,000,-000 at Neiman-Marcus." Several sable capes have been sold, and one-of-a-kind jeweled chess sets for $165,000 found a buyer.

Stanley Marcus takes great pride in his sales personnel and fashion models. He was furious when their morals were aspersed by U.S.A. Confidential, a book published in 1952. A suit for $7,500,000 was instituted against the authors, publishers and printers. The publishers and printers made public apologies in coast-to-coast newspaper advertising.

Neiman-Marcus employees are well treated and well trained and, in the words of the late author George Sessions Perry, "are to ordinary clerks as statesmen to politicians."[7] They have a profit sharing-retirement plan open to all who have been with the store for two years. The various benefits amount to about 23 percent of the payroll dollar. In big or little crises, the employees respond with enthusiasm and ingenuity. A big-game hunter from Dallas called Neiman-Marcus for help with a lion's head she had shot and had mounted for her fireplace. She felt the lion's mane was too skimpy, so Neiman-Marcus made a dynel wig for it, matching its own mane exactly. When a jubilant football fan fell afoul of the law after a Texas-Oklahoma game, the store posted $250 bail for him and charged it to his account.

Employees performed miracles after a five-alarm fire swept most of the main store early on December 19, 1964, a Saturday, at the height of the Christmas shopping season. Damage was more than $10 million. President Johnson telephoned to express his sympathy. Wedding dresses for ten brides, some being married that day, were destroyed.

The store rented a suite in the nearby Statler-Hilton Hotel and at once began to fit them in gowns flown in from Houston and trucked from Fort Worth. One wedding was scheduled for 4 P.M. At 2 P.M. a wedding gown arrived at the hotel by truck from the Neiman-Marcus store in Fort Worth. A fitter measured the bride-to-be and the dress there and at 2:22 P.M. rushed it off to the Preston Center branch. There three seamstresses made the alterations in an hour and at 3:40 P.M. the fitter delivered it to the church, where the bride was waiting in her underclothing. That wedding began on time and so did the other nine. The bride in one was Ginny Lou Martin, a Baylor University senior chosen by *Glamour* as one of the ten best-dressed woman students in American colleges.[8]

For several years Stanley Marcus has written an open letter in answer to one he has received, which is published in an advertisement each Monday in cities with Neiman-Marcus stores. In these letters he responds to complaints and compliments and discusses many subjects, such as correct dress in Ethiopia or in the Alps, a recent trip abroad, the best education for a merchandising career, dress lengths, urban problems, new books, films or plays, government regulations and gift suggestions.

One of Neiman-Marcus's big promotional achievements is the annual presentation of the Neiman-Marcus Awards—the fashion "Oscars" for "distinguished service in the field of fashion." Instituted in 1938, the presentation is the climax of a five-day celebration that includes fashion shows, lively Western-style parties and sometimes a Champagne Ball.

Awardees have included internationally famous personalities. Madame Helène Lazareff of Paris, editor of *Elle*, and Dr. Francis Henry Taylor, director of the Metropolitan Museum of Art, have shared honors with Norman Hartnell of London, dressmaker to the British royal family; Hattie Carnegie, Elsa Schiaparelli, Lilly Daché, Adrian, Anne Fogarty, John Frederics, Jacques Fath, Pierre Balmain and many others. The 1973 awardees were Levi Strauss & Co., Hanae Mori, Rosita and Ottavio Missoni, Jean Muir and Ralph Lauren.

In 1966, the year of the disastrous flood in Florence, all who received awards—Fiamma Ferragamo, Valentino, Lydia de Roma and Giancarlo Venturini—were Italian, and a special award was presented to the Artisans of Florence, accepted by Emilio Pucci. All Neiman-Marcus Award expositions are benefits, and proceeds from the balls and luncheons are donated to civic and cultural organizations.

More important have been the "Fortnights" devoted to promotion of the products of a country or a region. These involve infinite planning, the obtaining of official and community cooperation and the investment of thousands of dollars by other interests as well as the store. Stanley Marcus chanced to visit Nordiska, Stockholm's leading department store, in 1955 when it was holding a French exposition. A French chef was preparing food. There was French décor and French merchandise. On his way home, Stanley stopped in Paris and visited the Comité des Foires, which stages French fairs and expositions throughout the world. He arranged for one for Neiman-Marcus in 1957. It was the first held in America.

Twenty buyers scoured France for merchandise. Nine months before the event, Stanley Marcus invited Dallas leaders to lunch and obtained their cooperation. The Dallas Museum of Fine Arts exhibited French paintings. The Memorial Auditorium showed French tapestries. Theaters showed French films, nightclubs booked French entertainers, civic clubs booked French speakers. Advertising supplements in *Vogue* and the *Dallas Times-Herald* advertised the event.

The mayor of Dallas and French Ambassador Hervé Alphand officially opened a round of gala balls and festivities. Some two hundred French visitors came by Air France charter, the first to land at Dallas. They included the mayor of Dijon, an eighty-year-old priest; businessmen; industrialists; designers; artists; models; authors and actresses. The French Fortnight was so successful that before it was over, British interests asked the store to do one for Great Britain the following year.

It did so and what had been planned as a one-time event became an annual one. For the British Fortnight, the Old Vic Repertory Company was brought to Dallas for performances at the State Fair Music Hall. A South American Fortnight followed in 1959 and an Italian one, actually a whole month, in 1960. For this the store imported an opera company from Palermo. The Fortnight was American in 1961, Far Eastern in 1962, Swiss in 1963, Danish in 1964, Austrian in 1965. Dr. Bruno Kreisky, the Austrian Foreign Minister, visited and spoke in Dallas for this. In 1966, the store Fortnight returned to France to celebrate the tenth anniversary of the programs.

In 1967, the Fortnight returned to Great Britain, with a personal appearance by Princess Alexandra of Kent and her husband, Angus Ogilvy, and in 1968 Italy was chosen again. In 1969, the theme was East Meets West. In 1970, an imaginary country, Ruritania, was honored in a gigantic spoof. A slight departure in 1971 brought the Fête des Fleurs, a massive display of flowers and flower-inspired merchandise, and a visit from Princess Grace and Prince Rainier of Monaco. France again was visited in 1972 and England for a third time in 1973.

Many other stores now stage similar events, but few are as successful in enlisting the support of their communities. In addition to profits, they have earned an array of foreign decorations and honors for Stanley Marcus and suggestions that he be appointed an ambassador.

XX

Bergdorf Goodman

Opulence on the Plaza

Of all the moves taken by Broadway-Hale during its modern surge of growth, none has attracted more attention than the purchase in 1972 of Bergdorf Goodman. Considered by many fashion-conscious women to be the leading specialty shop in the nation, the Fifth Avenue store which looks out on to Central Park, the Plaza Hotel and the General Motors skyscraper—and which registered some $36 million worth of sales in 1972—had long been one of the most sought-after operations by the giant national and regional retaining groups.

When the store was sold by the Goodman family for about $11 million in Broadway-Hale stock—plus a minimum of $1.1 million in annual rentals for the eight store buildings between Fifty-seventh and Fifty-eighth Streets—a new era began for Bergdorf Goodman. But the old era of elegance in merchandising maintained its impact on the elaborate store.

There is still a custom fur salon where women purchase sables for up to $30,000 and the salesperson may be a grand duchess in exile or her descendant. There is a continuing appeal to the opulent, as in the time when Bergdorf's offered all 282 issues of the extinct magazine *Vanity Fair* for $1,000. There is a Givenchy Nouvelle boutique where the designs of the French designer reach the New York market. There is a new men's clothing department where suits made by Oxford Clothes and Hickey-Freeman range up to $450. And there is all over the store the aura of elegance, service and authority.

Of course, there are changes from the days when Bergdorf

Goodman was first and foremost a custom salon for luxury merchandise in which ready-to-wear became an added—and profitable—appendage. The Miss Bergdorf salon for junior-size merchandise in 1955, the Bigi shop for teen-agers in 1964 and the Mallett's of London antique shop in 1970 are examples of the new image established by Bergdorf Goodman in appealing to a younger and broader segment of the population.

The president of Bergdorf Goodman since 1951 has been Andrew Goodman, son of the man who established the enterprise. Number 2 man at the store is Leonard Hankin, executive vice president who began his career at the store in 1935 in the fur-storage department. Since 1972, the top team has been augmented by Gordon P. Franklin, who became vice president and general merchandise manager shortly after leaving the presidency of Saks Fifth Avenue.

All three are involved in the opening of Bergdorf's first branch store, in White Plains, New York, a 120,000-square-foot unit located between Saks Fifth Avenue and B. Altman branches there. But all three men are equally devoted to maintaining the traditions that have won "Bergdorf Goodman on the Plaza," as its label proudly proclaims, thousands of loyal customers throughout the world.

These traditions are an outgrowth of a tiny New York women's tailoring shop that began in the nineteenth century at 870 Broadway, offering dresses and suits for $50 each. The store was first known as H. Bergdorf and was owned and run by Herman Bergdorf, a hard-working Frenchman who, despite his diabetes, began his day at 4 A.M.[1]

The shop later became Bergdorf and Voight and in 1901 was changed to Bergdorf and Goodman. The Goodman in the name was Edwin Goodman, son of a Lockport, New York, merchant. Edwin was an enterprising man who had come to New York City and gone to work for Herman Bergdorf two years earlier to learn the tailoring trade. When he purchased a half interest in the business from Bergdorf, the Bergdorf and Goodman name was placed outside the store and remained the official title of the corporation until the purchase by Broadway-Hale, even though the store long had been called Bergdorf Goodman by its customers.

The store moved to 32 West Thirty-second Street in 1903, while Goodman was on his honeymoon, and a year later Herman Bergdorf sold out his interest to his younger partner. In 1914, the location was changed to 616 Fifth Avenue, where it remained until 1927, when work on construction of Rockefeller Center encompassed that site. During these years, Bergdorf's owner developed a reputation as an austere and tyrannical perfectionist, and wealthy women throughout the city flocked to Edwin Goodman's doors for their gowns, suits, coats and furs.

Goodman, who was searching desperately at that time for a property in which his $3-million-a-year store and manufacturing workrooms could be located, finally found one on the west side of Fifth Avenue between Fifty-seventh and Fifty-eighth Streets. Frederick Brown, a real-estate man, had purchased the Vanderbilt mansion there for $6 million, torn it down and erected seven individual white marble buildings for retail use on the Avenue, running back 125 feet.

Goodman chose the Fifty-eighth Street and Fifth Avenue corner, even though Fifty-seventh Street was then considered to be the avenue's northernmost retailing outpost. He developed the slogan "Where fashion starts and ends," and his customers agreed. When Bergdorf's opened there in March 1928, sales of such merchandise as sixty-dollar hats and thousand-dollar wedding gowns helped to earn it the appellation of one of the most prestigious stores in town. The Fifty-seventh Street corner was occupied by the prominent hatter Dobbs, while the buildings in between were taken by Mosse Linens, Tecla Pearls, Louis Sherry Confectionery and Grande Maison de Blanc, a specialty store.

In the midst of the depression, Bergdorf Goodman purchased part of this property and expanded to the south. It bought the remainder of the block facing Fifth Avenue in 1948, and in 1967 took over 53,000 square feet more in the Fifty-seventh

Street area when it acquired the lease held by another specialty store, the Tailored Woman.[2] Some of this area has been used to establish for the first time a men's tailored clothing division, which opened with considerable fanfare in 1973.

Andy Goodman joined his father in the store in 1926, although he later admitted that retailing was not his original choice. "I wasn't much interested in retailing when I was young," he says. "But I was young at the time when it didn't matter much what I was interested in. It was what my father was interested in that counted . . . and he was most interested in my taking over at the store."

Since the store on the plaza was built, the Goodman family has lived in a sixteen-room penthouse apartment above the sales floors and workrooms. At one time, Edwin Goodman was listed as the janitor of the property because city regulations would not permit anyone but the superintendent to live in a building where manufacturing occurred.

The third elevator in the main bank of elevators serves the apartment, and customers and salespeople have long been used to seeing members of the Goodman family ride up and down from their home. When the store's elevators were run by operators, there was a rule in the store that members of the family were to be taken immediately to whatever floor they wished, even if passengers had to go in a reverse direction from which they were heading. Most customers were understanding, but one wrote angrily, "Why don't you Goodmans wait until 5:30 when the store is closed? Then you can ride up and down that elevator all night as far as I'm concerned."

The paternal feeling that the Goodmans have long fostered at their store ends with "Mr. Andrew," since his son and two sons-in-law, who were once executives at Bergdorf Goodman, have departed voluntarily.[3] Now executives at the store talk about expansion over the next decade and about investments from Broadway-Hale of $40 million to $50 million to open three branches ranging from 100,000 to 200,000 square feet: including the White Plains store, another New York suburban store and a third in a city along the Eastern Seaboard.

But the coziness and warmth that have characterized Berg-dorf's store in New York's most fashionable retail district form one of its most valuable assets and will certainly be maintained by the professional managers who will run it in the future. "Our goal is to make it a lot of fun for people to spend a lot of money dressing themselves," says Hankin. And Andrew Goodman, who became one of New York's leading merchants despite his original misgivings, observes, "We have always concentrated on our role and known where we wanted to go—to have the finest store in the world. And we can't have too much living in the glories of the past."

XXI
Bullock's and I. Magnin

California's Glamour Pioneers

Boastful Californians spend their increasing wealth in all manner of stores, but many take the greatest pride in the spacious and beautiful establishments of Bullock's, Inc., and I. Magnin & Co. At these stores, fashion, décor and service are combined with a high degree of elegance to offer the most pleasant of shopping experiences.

The warmth of Bullock's relationship with its customers is perhaps best illustrated by the grade-school composition of a Los Angeles girl named Janice McCoslar. When she and her schoolmates were asked to list what they liked best, Janice wrote: "1. Birthdays. 2. Bullock's. 3. Home. 4. School." The store heard about it and sent Janice a doll. Her mother acknowledged this with a note ending, "Anything I buy from now on until the year 2000 will be from Bullock's."

Both Bullock's and Magnin are noted for dignity and taste. Advertising is restrained and often entirely institutional. The store buildings are famous in architectural circles for their adaptation to the sunny climate, the luxury of their interiors and the prescience with which provision was made for automobile traffic in a state that now leads all others in automobile registrations.

The company is named for John Gillespie Bullock, a Canadian of Scotch ancestry who brought to his business all the Scotch virtues of energy, frugality and integrity. He was born on January 14, 1871, in Paris, Ontario, and his father, a railroad employee, died two years later. When he was eleven, the boy went to work for two dollars a week delivering groceries for Munn & Co., a tiny local store.

"We kept open until midnight Saturdays," he recalled years later, "so Mother used to come down and fetch me, so I wouldn't be afraid of walking home in the dark." All his life he treasured a picture of the little store and a penny notebook in which he wrote orders.

He moved on to Rheder's, a dry-goods store that was the largest in town, but at twenty-five he was not earning enough to marry. So, when two uncles who were mining in the West wrote back about the wonders of California, his widowed mother staked him to a railroad ticket to Los Angeles and lent him $150.

His sister packed some clothes for him and he reached Los Angeles in January, 1896, with all of the $150 intact. He deposited this in the Citizens National Bank and drew it out at the rate of a dollar or two a week while he read newspaper advertisements and looked for work.

"It was a time of unemployment and I walked the streets in vain until late in February," Bullock once said. "Then I read in a newspaper that a bankrupt stock was to be sold the next day in a store at Broadway and Fourth. I was there early but the man in charge said he needed no more help. Still I waited around with the crowd for the store to open. It was soon filled and the front door had to be locked until some of those inside left by a rear door. I went in that way and told the man it looked like he could use me. I was hired—at $12 a week."

Bullock's employer in the busy little forty-foot store was Arthur Letts, who had purchased the bankrupt stock for $8,167 with borrowed money. In September, when Bullock was beginning to do some of the men's-wear buying, Letts hired another Canadian as cashboy. He was fifteen-year-old Percy Glen (Jack) Winnett, a youth in short pants who had come to California from Winnipeg with his parents. By then there were twenty-six employees at the Broadway store, which later became the keystone of Broadway-Hale Stores, Inc. (see Chapter XVIII).

Letts pioneered odd-cent prices in Los Angeles and it was

the job of the new $2-a-week cashboy to handle the pennies. He was short a penny one day and was scolded, an experience that he never forgot.

Bullock spurned offers of jobs with a bakery and another store. He was soon making $75 a month and married his Canadian sweetheart. Winnett advanced from errand boy to wrapper in the men's furnishing department when Bullock became the buyer. Between packages, Winnett worked behind the counter and learned what he could from Bullock. Both learned from Letts.

As the Broadway store grew, Letts made Bullock superintendent and gave him the responsibility for all hiring. Young Winnett succeeded Bullock as men's-furnishings buyer after five older men had failed in the job. He later bought women's and children's knit underwear and hosiery.

As the salespeople disliked bothering with the complicated sizes. Winnett found the children's end neglected and returns of merchandise high. He established a children's section and placed a woman in charge with firm instructions not to leave her post in order to sell any women's garments. Her attention and specialized knowledge made the section a great success and convinced Winnett of the merit of what later became unitization —a term that he coined.

The big opportunity came for Bullock in 1906. Some Eastern merchants had planned a department store at the northwest corner of Seventh and Broadway. With the steel framework for seven stories erected, the death of one of them halted the venture and E. T. Earl, the builder, offered the unfinished structure to Letts. It was three blocks outside the shopping area at that time but appealed to Letts as an alternative site for his Broadway department store if he could not renew the lease there on favorable terms. He signed a fifty-year lease with Earl, who completed the building.

To utilize the new structure until the time that it might be required for the Broadway store, Letts gave Bullock $250,000 and the task of establishing an additional store. Winnett, who at twenty-six held an important merchandising job, asked to be allowed to join the new venture and Letts somewhat reluctantly consented. A third executive from the Broadway, William A. Holt, also went along.

They planned to call the new store Bullock's Department Store but Winnett argued for a shorter name like Macy's and it was shortened to Bullock's. Bullock was made president and Winnett vice president and general manager of the new company. Letts gave them complete freedom to operate on their own.[1]

They set up an office in the Lankershim Hotel across the street and hired a staff of four hundred, who sat on beds as they were interviewed. H. M. Bigelow, who had just sold his general store in Grundy Center, Iowa, walked in and was employed as floor manager. Buyers were sent to market.

On the night of March 2, 1907, Letts and the public saw the new store at a nonselling preview. Thousands crowded through the brightly lit buildings to listen to bands play on the lower floor and to see a pony show in the roof garden. In later years, Easter services were conducted in this roof garden.

But rain, something of a rarity in Los Angeles, fell when the store opened for business on March 4 and customers were few. "You could shoot a cannon through the aisles without hitting anyone," Winnett recalled. Those who came found a beautiful store, singing canaries and violets. Bullock's gave away violets every March 4 for many years.

Unexpectedly, the finer-quality merchandise sold more rapidly than the inexpensive goods. Buyers replaced their stocks with better goods and the "mistakes" were cleared in the first of the August sales. Bullock's was opened as a strictly cash store but within a few months established charge accounts and devised a coat of arms with the legend SUPREMA REGNAT QUALITAS, Latin for "Quality reigns supreme."

Troubles came when the panic of 1907 hit in October. Two other Los Angeles stores that were started at the same time as Bullock's did fail, but Bullock's struggled ahead. The store's six immaculate horse-drawn delivery wagons were sent out whether there were packages in them or not. Some shelves were filled with empty cartons and one floor was closed off.

Nevertheless, Bullock and Winnett counted sales of $1,310,-725 in 1907 and $1,511,650 in 1908, and operations became profitable. Letts, meanwhile, renewed the Broadway store lease and decided to continue both stores. Bullock's sales reached $2,031,408 in 1909 and $4,746,024 in 1912. In that year began expansions that eventually spread the big store over a good portion of the Broadway, Hill, Sixth and Seventh Street block. A street dividing the block, called St. Vincent's Court after a college once on the site, was bridged.

Bullock's also grew in character and prestige. While other stores were advertising $25 men's suits for $15, Bullock's startled the community by offering $15 suits for $15. Thousands laughed but they bought the suits. The store's policy of constant but dignified advertising was born. Bullock's was one of the first stores to use color in newspaper advertising and claims the distinction of publishing the first "three-dimensional" store advertisements, a series in the *Los Angeles Times* that had to be read with colored glasses.

A customer was once so moved by Bullock's annual Christmas institutional pages that she decided to embroider a sampler of it. So the store obligingly had the engraver make proofs of it on nylon, rayon and cotton and sent all three to the lady.

Bullock kept this motto on his office wall: "The ideals of this business must not be sacrificed to gain." Like many other executives, he gave every employee a copy of Elbert Hubbard's "A Message to Garcia." A reminder from Winnett said, "Nothing much counts in the retail game until somebody sells somebody something."

There was little that Bullock's would not do for a customer. In his usual wing collar, Bullock was once at the door bidding customers good-by the evening before St. Patrick's Day, when a lady expressed her regret that she had found no clay pipes for an Irish party the next day in Santa Monica. He noted her address, had the city scoured for clay pipes that night and had them delivered to the amazed customer in Santa Monica.

One Saturday at 11:30 P.M., a night watchman answered the phone in Bullock's. A customer complained tearfully that a set of chinaware, purchased as a golden-wedding gift, had not arrived and that the anniversary was the next day. The watchman called an executive, who called a packer. The executive delivered the china himself on Sunday morning in time for the celebration.

During a holiday season, a Bullock's employee overheard a conversation about how a doll and a toy truck that a widowed mother had purchased to come from Santa Claus had been delivered too early and had fallen into the hands of the children. Without charge, the store sent some more toys as coming from Santa Claus.

Once a motorcycle messenger was dispatched 150 miles to Trona with an evening dress required by nightfall. A special trunk required by a customer was delivered to him, also by messenger, in Paris. Southern California's growing population, especially the segment connected with the movie industry, greatly appreciated such service.

Sales reached $7 million in 1918, and Bullock's increased its buying facilities by becoming a charter member of the Associated Merchandising Corporation. Volume passed $10 million the next year, and soon after Letts died in 1923 sales were running at more than $22 million a year.

To finance the purchase of the store from the Letts estate, the bank in which Bullock had deposited his mother's $150 when he first arrived in Los Angeles was happy to extend him a credit of $6 million. A new corporation, Bullock's Inc., was organized and $4 million in bonds and $4.5 million in preferred stock were subscribed in an hour in the first public store financing in California.

On September 26, 1929, Bullock's Wilshire was opened in a beautiful new building, fronting three hundred feet on Wilshire Boulevard, that cost $6 million to build. It quickly became a high-fashion showplace and established a new shopping area.

Sightseers still come to view its pink-marble foyer, its style shows, its glass-walled porte-cochere rear entrance and its ceramic birds for sale at $1,350 a pair. One of the features is a children's barbershop patronized by the sons and daughters of many Hollywood notables.

Investors in the new company received dividends from the start. Though sales dropped from a peak of $27 million in 1930 to a low of $18 million in 1933, Bullock's earned profits all through the depression. Bullock's Palm Springs was opened in that California desert resort in 1930 and Bullock's Westwood in 1932.

One of the happiest days in the life of John Bullock came in 1930 when he returned with his daughter to his birthplace of Paris, Ontario. Henry Rheder, the merchant for whom he had worked as a boy, and the board of trade gave a dinner in his honor. Mayor Stewart, once a schoolmate of Bullock's, presided. Present even was Mr. Penman, the big millowner whom Bullock as a boy never hoped to know socially. A scroll was presented to the local boy who had made good. Solemn toasts were drunk: "His Majesty the King," "the President of the United States" and "John G. Bullock."

Bullock died of a heart attack on September 15, 1933, leaving an estate of $2,587,559, mostly in the stock of his store. Mrs. Bullock presented two sets of bells to the Little Country Church of Hollywood in his memory. A bronze bust of the founder, the work of Helen and Holger Jensen, stands in Bullock's Downtown with a plaque: "This memorial testifies to our love for a friend and our loyalty to a leader whose spirit still lives and to whose ideals this business remains dedicated and devoted."

His successor both as president of Bullock's and as a local civic leader was the tireless P. G. Winnett, who had shared the responsibility for the store from the first. Bullock's famous Collegienne shops, where women young in years or ideas find everything conveniently gathered, for example, were started because of the interest of his own daughters in such merchandise.

To finance the modernization and expansion of the downtown

and branch stores, Bullock's increased its capital in 1945. The common stock was split three for one and 237,775 additional shares were sold. Eighty thousand shares of a new issue of 4 percent preferred stock were sold at $103. Bullock's received a total of $13,515,334, used $6,640,757 to pay bank loans and retire the previous 5 percent preferred stock and had new capital of $6,874,577 for additionad facilities.

The bulk of this went into a new Bullock's Pasadena branch, widely acclaimed for its beauty and revolutionary architecture. Planned by Welton Beckett and Associates, the building is a merchandising machine specially designed for the optimal functioning of the sixty individual shops. "Inside and out," said one observer after the opening on September 10, 1947, "it looks more like a club than a store—and a rather expensive club, at that."[2]

On the topmost of the three levels is a terrace café called the Coral Room. It provides a fine view of the mountains and is the scene of a daily fashion show. The middle level contains a series of men's shops that can be reached without passing through the lingerie and other feminine areas on the same floor. On the bottom level are the home-furnishing shops and service facilities. The store is so much the domain of the motorist that there is only a single entrance for pedestrians.

President Winnett became chairman of Bullock's in 1950 and was succeeded by his son-in-law, Walter Candy, an affable, outgoing retailing man. With the exception of three years of war service as a commander in the Navy, Candy, a native of St. Louis and a graduate of Princeton, had been with the firm since joining Bullock's Wilshire as a merchandise manager in 1935.

Another key executive at the company for many years was Mahlon E. Arnett. A soft-spoken but perceptive merchant, he joined the concern in 1929 as chief accountant and rose in the ranks to the most senior positions at Bullock's.

With the I. Magnin & Co. merger in 1943, Bullock's acquired one of the best-known women's specialty-store organizations in the world. It was founded by Mrs. Mary Ann Magnin, a tiny energetic woman of unerring taste in high fashion. Born in Scheveningen, Holland, she married Isaac Magnin, a Dutch wood-carver, in London and together they migrated to San Francisco. There Magnin became a decorator and Mrs. Magnin in 1876 opened a shop.

She began by making and selling fancy baby clothing and notions. Later she made trousseaux. She moved her business from shop to shop as the fashionable retail trade centers shifted and acquired an exclusive clientele who relied on her for the latest and finest gowns and accessories from Paris.

The name Magnin became a synonym for elegance and its showings of new models by famous Paris designers were soon important events for California society. As the business grew with California, Magnin's became the largest buyer in the high-priced wholesale dress market and acquired exclusive West Coast representation of some of the greatest names in fashion. It earned profits continually except in 1906, when earthquake and fire destroyed the San Francisco store, and 1932.

"People want more than 'thank you' in this world," said Mrs. Magnin as she explained her quest for the finest in apparel. She yielded management of the business to her sons beginning in 1903 but continued to interest herself in its affairs. A remarkable personality, she lived on in the St. Francis Hotel, celebrating her birthday each April with a big party, until she died there on December 15, 1943, at the age of ninety-five.

A few weeks later, President Winnett of Bullock's and two of Mrs. Magnin's sons, E. John and Grover, who had entered the business around the turn of the century, quickly worked out the merger. Magnin stockholders received one Bullock's share in exchange for three and a half shares of the stock of their company.

Hector Escobosa, a well-known fashion expert of Spanish descent, was chosen to head Magnin on the retirement of Grover Magnin at the end of 1950. Though a native of San Francisco, Escobosa had been for some years executive vice president and general manager of Frederick & Nelson, the Seattle department store owned by Marshall Field & Co. When Escobosa died in 1963, the Magnin presidency went to William P. Keeshan, who had been a merchandise manager at Bullock's Wilshire store.

Bullock's-Magnin was involved in one of the hottest proxy battles of 1964 over a proposal to merge it into Federated Department Stores, Inc. On one side was Mr. Winnett, the largest individual stockholder, who vehemently opposed affiliating with Federated. On the other side were eleven of the twelve Bullock's-Magnin directors, headed by Mr. Candy and cheered by Ralph Lazarus of Federated. They cited the higher market price of Federated common stock even at the proposed 1.4-to-1 share exchange ratio, the greater dividend income their stockholders would receive, the promise they had received of complete autonomy and the strength of the entire Federated corporation that would be available to Bullock's.[3]

When the sound and the fury subsided, 70 percent of the shares (slightly more than the required two thirds) were voted for the merger and Bullock's-Magnin Company was made a division of Federated in August 1964. Mr. Winnett quickly retired from active management but visited a company store each afternoon until his death in 1968 at age eighty-five.

Under Federated, Bullock's "unitization" under which departments were autonomous, was replaced by conventional centralized store organization. I. Magnin was made a separate division and expanded to Chicago's Michigan Avenue in 1971. Bullock's expanded to Palo Alto in 1972 and later to Walnut Creek. A Bullock's North Division was established in 1973 with B. Paul Heidrick, president, and Richard Crafts, executive vice president.

Howard Goldfeder, a former May Company executive, was then chairman and Herbert R. Bloch, Jr., president of what is now Bullock's South. Ross F. Anderson was chairman and chief executive officer and John Schumacher president of the I. Magnin division.

XXII

L. L. Bean, Inc.

Sporting Goods by Mail from Maine

Motorists following U.S. Highway 1 through the "Down East" section of Maine come eighteen miles north of Portland to the old village of Freeport. It is a pleasant tree-shaded community of 5,000 which was famous in early Maine history as the place at which documents were signed giving the state its independence from Massachusetts.

Freeport is now famous as the home of L. L. Bean, Inc. This unique firm sells annually more than $15 million worth of sporting goods to hunting and fishing enthusiasts all over the Western hemisphere. To it, letters addressed merely "Bean, Maine" and "Mail order sporting goods house in a small town in Maine" have been delivered without delay. Signs lead the traveler to a store and offices on Main Street and huge frame buildings to the rear housing workrooms, warehouses and shipping facilities.

Regardless of the day or hour, you will find the place open and somebody on hand to sell you a hunting or fishing license or any of several thousand items for the sport, dress or comfort of outdoor sport enthusiasts. This twenty-four-hour service is an example of the consideration of customer needs that enabled Leon Leonwood Bean, who died at ninety-four on February 5, 1967, to build this remarkable business deep in Maine and to stamp his colorful personality on it.

"We have thrown away the key to the place," the bronzed, booming-voiced founder used to say. "A lot of our customers drive up from New York and Boston. Many leave right after work and are so eager to start hunting or fishing that they drive all night. This often brings them through Freeport in the middle of the night or even on Sunday. Where else can you get a hunting or fishing license on Sunday?"

Hundreds of places sell nonresident Maine hunting and fishing licenses, but L. L. Bean, Inc., is one of the two top outlets. The firm collects the usual thirty-five-cent fee on each, but more important is the traffic it brings to the store.

"Only about one person in twenty-five who comes in for a license goes out without buying something else," says an executive. "When they leave home, they don't worry about being short something. They say, 'We can always get it at Bean's.' " And they can. The best year's business under the founder was $3,857,000 in 1966. Under his grandson and namesake, Leon A. Gorman, products are lighter, more colorful, and sometimes even fashionable. Sales soared to $15,750,000 for the year ending February 28, 1973.

The store stocks all the hundreds of items offered in the famous Bean mail-order catalog, plus several hundred more, including items like ammunition which cannot be sent through the mails.

The merchandise ranges from twenty-cent shoe laces to $340 canoes. A very popular item is "Bean's Chamois Cloth Shirt" priced at $8.35 in 1973. It is made also for women and *Playboy*[1] once pictured a "playmate" wearing nothing else. The founder wore it hunting and fishing. It may be the most popular sportsman's shirt in the world. One of the founder's ideas, Bean's Field Coat, with a game pocket that lets down to serve as a waterproof seat, is described by gunners who previously had to sit on a frosty log as one of the greatest inventions since the wheel.

The firm is the largest outlet in the United States for the famous Hudson's Bay Company's woolen blankets. There are scores of sporting accessories. But the backbone of the Bean business is in its own boots and shoes. These are stitched by sewing machines or made by hand in Freeport. In fact, the enterprise grew out of a special hunting shoe devised and made by Bean on a financial shoestring.

Bean was born October 13, 1872, on a farm near Greenwood, Maine, an Oxford County town that no longer exists. He was the fourth of six children, five boys and a girl.[2] The family is descended from the Scottish Highland Clan MacBean, sometimes spelled MacBeane. Its coat of arms shows a wildcat, a dagger and a glove, with the motto "Touch not the cat bot (without) a glove." Three brothers came to America and their descendants shortened the name to Bean. George Warren Bean, a Union soldier in the Civil War, died a Confederate prisoner and is buried at Andersonville, Georgia. His second son, Benjamin Warren Bean, was the merchant's father.

"My father lived on a farm," Bean once recalled, "but he was really more of a hunter and trader." Lennie, or L. L., as he became known, inherited both of these interests. When he was eleven and the family moved to Milton Plantation, his father gave him the choice of going to a fair at Norway, Maine, or using the money to buy five muskrat traps the boy had been wanting. Young Bean settled for the traps. When he was thirteen, both parents died. He grew up with relatives at South Paris. His first big business deal was transacted at sixteen. L. L. went hunting and shot a good-sized buck. An empty-handed hunter offered him $12 for it. With the money, Bean bought some bread and salt pork and a pair of mittens, returned to the woods and went trapping in earnest. When he came out three weeks later, he was carrying five sables, plus a wildcat and most of the twelve dollars.[3]

In 1912, after many jobs and ventures, L. L. became a partner of his brother Guy in a small clothing store in Freeport. It was just across Main Street from the present location of the firm. Some old newspaper advertisements attest that they sold overalls and shirts at thirty-nine cents each and some handkerchiefs at one cent apiece and ten cents a dozen. They once attracted a big crowd by closing the place up mysteriously for several days and then having a big sale.

Bean eventually bought out his brother, and the latter, who was one of the few Democrats in Maine, became Freeport postmaster. As his brother was the biggest user of postal service in Freeport (70 percent in 1934 and 85 percent in some later years), Postmaster Guy Bean put the post office on the first floor under the L. L. Bean office. It moved in 1962 to a new building two blocks east of Main Street but a rent-free substation continues in the space. In consequence, a simple conveyor system takes packages from Bean's downstairs to the substation for mailing.

L. L. was so much more interested in hunting and fishing than in shopkeeping that the clothing store kept going only through the tolerance of his creditors and customers. Then in his forties, Bean was considered an easygoing failure until he began to discover business opportunities as well as personal happiness in his sport.

His success began when he came home with sore feet one day from a hunting trip. Woodsmen's shoes were then heavy and stiff. After being wet, they dried into torturing shapes. Bean sought something more comfortable. Next time out, he tried wearing rubber overshoes with three pairs of wool socks around the uppers.

He found this comfortable, but at the end of a day's hiking had a "flat-footed" feeling. The wool socks also were not substantial enough for tops. He remedied the first by contriving an inner sole with a steel arch. Instead of the socks, he had Ted Goldrup and Dennis Bibber, local cobblers, cut and sew leather tops to the rubbers. He tested the new hybrid shoes in the woods and found them light, waterproof and comfortable. Thus was born Bean's famous Maine Hunting Shoe.

When some of his friends also liked the shoes, Bean borrowed $400 from the local bank and began to have them made in the basement of his store. By way of advertising he sent holders of hunting licenses a single blue-sheet circular showing the shoe and describing it as "designed by a hunter who has tramped the Maine woods for the past eighteen years." Orders came in and a pair of these shoes were in the first parcel-post package mailed from Freeport when the service began in 1913. A tag on each guaranteed absolute satisfaction. Ninety of the first hundred pairs came back. The rubber had been too light and had torn away from the uppers. Bean made good on all and the shoe was improved.

By 1915, he had moved the business across the street. The clothing store faded out and, with stationery resplendent with ducks and fish in color, Bean became a manufacturer of "leather and canvas specialties." As he sold more and more shoes, he began to add related items, of similar quality and utility, starting with socks. While his formal education had included only grammar school and a short commercial course, he described his goods with persuasive simplicity.

With some patented improvements, more than 1,620,000 pairs of the Maine Hunting Shoe have been sold. General Matthew Ridgway, a regular Bean customer, wore them in Korea. Rear Admiral Donald Macmillan, a native of Freeport, outfitted an Arctic expedition with them. Supreme Court Justice William O. Douglas has hiked in them. Big-game hunters like Richard Sutton have worn them all over the world. U.S. Marines took them to Iceland. They suddenly became popular with women in 1972 and some had to be custom-made for size 5 feet.[4]

The fame of the shoe led the government to employ Bean as a consultant and contractor during World War II. By inducing the Army to use boots with twelve-inch instead of sixteen-inch tops, he lightened the burden of many a soldier and saved millions in costs. He also designed for the Navy a nonskid boot for wear on aircraft-carrier decks that could be removed quickly in the sea.

"For hunters who go just before the first snow," explained a catalog note on the Maine Hunting Shoe, "it is next to impossible to find footwear that is adaptable to both bare ground and snow hunting. For bare ground, its lightweight cushion inner-sole keeps it from drawing feet, while the crepe rubber sole keeps it from slipping. Outside of your gun, nothing is so important to your outfit as your footwear. You cannot expect success hunting big game if your feet are not properly dressed. The average hunting shoe weighs about four ounces more than ours. As big game hunters walk about seven miles (or 18,480 steps) a day they lift 2310 pounds more than necessary."

Bean's sales passed the $100,000-a-year mark in the early twenties and attained $1,000,000 for the first time as the business celebrated its thirtieth anniversary in 1937. Spurred by important notice in national magazines[5] and the spread of the shorter workweek, which gave more men leisure for hunting and fishing, the business doubled again in less than a decade.

With growth came an increase in number of employees to more than one hundred, and incorporation in 1934.[6] L. L. was president until his death in 1967. He was succeeded by his son Carl, who died eight months later in the same year. Leon A. Gorman, a grandson of L. L., now heads the company as president and treasurer. William E. Griffin is vice president and Daniel A. Lord controller. These and J. T. Gorman, Jr., and Mrs. L. L. Bean are directors.

While the mailing list is now on magnetic tape and a computer is used, the firm has preserved the friendly informality that charmed customers like Presidents Calvin Coolidge and Franklin D. Roosevelt, Babe Ruth and many other notables. The spring and fall catalogs have grown to 120 pages. There also are sixty-page summer and Christmas circulars. The firm mailed 1,200,000 copies of the 1972 fall catalog. On the cover was L. L.'s favorite painting, "The Old Country Store," by P. B. Parsons. Mrs. Edith Williams, once the founder's secretary, is advertising manager.

In addition to its direct mail, Bean's buys advertising space in the *New York Times* and some eighty national publications in all, including the *New Yorker, Field and Stream* and *Outdoor Life*.

Sales have quadrupled under President Gorman, who was only thirty-two when he became head of the family business. He was born in Nashua, N.H., in 1934; grew up in Yarmouth, Maine; was graduated from Bowdoin in 1956; and was a destroyer officer in the Navy from 1957 to 1961. After a brief training period at Filene's in Boston, he joined the firm. He is quiet and mild-mannered but everything is orderly and efficient. A high speed machine opens mail. Orders are dispatched by an automatic writing machine and data-processing system installed by Singer's business machines division. There are more than four hundred employees. The business has expanded into several buildings, and parking lots are larger. But reminders of the founder are much in evidence.[7]

Largely to save himself time in answering questions, Bean in 1942 wrote and published a small book, *Hunting-Fishing and Camping;* into 100 pages, he packed a world of practical advice based on his own game bag. This included, incidentally, thirty-six deer, two moose, one bear and a caribou, as well as all sorts of small game and fish ranging from brook trout to tuna.

"To my mind," he wrote, "hunting and fishing is the big lure that takes us into the great open spaces and teaches us to forget the mean and petty things in life." He advised on what to wear, what to carry, where to go in Maine and how many to include. "A perfect trip," he warned, "may be ruined by one person who does not fit. I recommend small parties, not over four. Two make a good party."

"No one should enter the big woods without being posted on Chapters 3, 13, 14, 15, 16," warns Bean. These, respectively, are How to Dress a Deer, Safety Rules, Signals for Hunters, How to Use a Compass and How to Find a Lost Hunter. He also included advice on bobcat hunting and camp cooking recipes. The initial printing sold out promptly at $1 a copy. Since then twenty-two additional editions have been published, each with a map of the kill of deer and bear in Maine, and more than 139,000 copies have been sold.

Customers like to trade ideas with the firm, and frequently send suggestions for improving one product or another. Some of the ideas adopted include a sheepskin-lined bottle holder that enables a bottle to be tossed about without breakage, and a decoy with a movable head that permits more lifelike attitudes.

An impressive number of celebrities have visited the store. Jack Dempsey, Lauritz Melchior, Kenneth Roberts and Mrs.

Eleanor Roosevelt have been among the many who have stopped by on vacation trips to Maine. Famous autographs are to be found in Bean's letter files. Mail customers include Captain Alan Bean (no relation), who walked on the moon; John Wayne, Lee Marvin, Gregory Peck, Walter Cronkite, Lowell Thomas, Mrs. Ethel Kennedy, Amy Vanderbilt, Robert McNamara and Ralph Edwards.

One winter day when the New York Telephone Company needed forty pairs of snowshoes for its repairmen in an upstate emergency, Bean's got them off within an hour. Nearly all orders are shipped the day received.

Because the salesroom is continuously open, it serves as the fire-alarm reporting center for Freeport. Fires are reported on a special telephone there and the answering clerk dials the appropriate signal into the alarm system to muster Freeport's volunteer firemen.

Among the letters that Bean cherishes is one from a Minneapolis man saying: "Enclosed find check for which please send me one Bean's Pack Basket one Pack Basket cover. Outside of my wife, this is the handiest piece of equipment a man could take to the woods." The same year, a customer named Otto Loeffler wrote: "For several years Miss Jean Hulbert, 606 Oakmont Ave., Erie, Pa., and Otto Ford Loeffler, 305 Poplar St., Erie, Pa., have been receiving your semi-annual catalogues. . . . Effective today, kindly remove Miss Hulbert's name from your mailing list, because she is Mrs. Loeffler now. The common interest in the items listed in your catalogue helped greatly to bring us together."[8]

Bean's prescription for success is: "Sell good merchandise at a reasonable profit, treat your customers like human beings, and they'll always come back for more."

Just how much more they come back for is evidenced by an order from a man in St. Mary's, Pennsylvania. The sportsman wrote that it would take "too damn long to fill out the list he wanted," and instructed Bean's to send him every item in the catalog on pages 8 through 64 inclusive.

XXIII
Ohrbach's, Inc.

"A Business in Millions, a Profit in Pennies"

High style at low prices has been the announced goal of count-less retailers of women's apparel, but none have achieved it more convincingly than Ohrbach's, Inc. Its slogan, "A business in millions, a profit in pennies," is a literal statement of its suc-cess. By faithful adherence to an economical, low-markup oper-ation devoid of frills, the firm has expanded from a small outlet on New York's Fourteenth Street to eleven stores in the New York and Los Angeles areas. In 1954, moreover, Ohrbach's astonished the retailing world by transferring its headquarters store to the Thirty-fourth Street store formerly occupied by McCreery's, thereby coming into head-on conflict with the Herald Square and midtown Fifth Avenue department and specialty stores.

The firm was founded by Nathan M. ("N.M.") Ohrbach, an early-rising self-made merchant who for decades opened the doors of his store each morning to greet his customers. A man who never smoked and who drank only rarely, he worked for years at an ultramodern kidney-shaped desk in a glamorous book-lined office with paintings by Thomas Gainsborough, John Constable and Thomas Hart Benton lining the walls.

The Ohrbach's credo of merchandising was once expressed succinctly by the soft-spoken founder: "The housewife likes to feel that her favorite stores are not selling to her—they are buying for her. She is paying for a service, simply defined, to locate in the markets of the world those items which will best serve her wants, requirements and pocketbook."

Ohrbach, who built what has been called the Rolls-Royce of low-margin retailing, was born in Vienna on August 31, 1885. The Strauss waltzes were being composed there at the time, but the pleasures of the Hapsburg capital were not for the Ohrbachs. When Nathan was two, his parents took their share of the family's few gulden, derived from a tollgate and a small salt mine thirty kilometers from the city, and migrated to America, without improving their fortunes.

Nathan and his three brothers grew up in the Williamsburg section of Brooklyn. He attended elementary schools there and De Witt Clinton High School. At fourteen, he went to work for $3.50 a week "running errands and sweeping out" for J. M. Tobias, a wholesale coat and suit house. By the time he was seventeen, he had been a traveling salesman. He was also briefly a Coney Island lifeguard and a delivery boy for Macy's.

At twenty, even though he had originally wanted to be a lawyer, he became a buyer and "assistant to the president" of the First Co. of Jersey City at $25 a week. He was also a buyer for Berlin's in Brooklyn, Erich Brothers in Manhattan, and Brager's in Baltimore. By 1907, his prospects were bright enough for him to marry Matilda Kane of Brooklyn, a sister of two of his business acquaintances.

In 1911, he opened a small specialty shop selling women's coats, Bon Marché, Inc., on Fulton Street in Brooklyn and later one in Manhattan on teeming Fourteenth Street between University Place and Fifth Avenue. He also acquired some small stores in Pennsylvania towns. All sold low-priced ready-to-wear clothing in small quarters but managed to attract crowds with a table of fast-moving merchandise just inside the door. This latter became a basic Ohrbach sales device.

By 1923, he had saved some money and had spent eighteen of his thirty-eight years in retailing. This experience convinced him that success for a retailer lay in either of two different directions. One was in providing customers with every imaginable service and charging them accordingly. The other was in cutting services to bare essentials and sharing the savings thus effected with the customers. He chose the latter course, a move that spawned the development of numerous other low-price apparel stores in the years ahead.

He then interested Max Wiesen, a dress manufacturer, in joining him in a new store to sell ready-to-wear—in the form of job lots, seconds, manufacturers' overstocks and irregulars—in large volume at low prices. Each invested $62,500 in a partnership and Ohrbach made a careful search for a high-traffic location accessible both by subway and surface transportation.

He settled on a narrow dingy, fire-gutted structure on Fourteenth Street not far from his own small shop. Across the street to the north was Union Square, where orators of all political and economic persuasions voiced their visions. A few yards to the east and across the street was "S. Klein, On the Square," Sam Klein's famous cash store that within a few years was to claim to be the largest women's-wear shop in the world. To the west were several other big stores.

The site chosen by Ohrbach was historic ground. In the nineteenth century it had been the home of General Bronson Winthrop, law partner of Henry L. Stimson. On March 4, 1903, Adolph Zukor opened a penny arcade there, and the first motion pictures were shown in penny machines. The pennies rolled in so fast that a small car mounted on a track was required to haul them to the basement, where a shooting gallery also contributed to the profits. On the second floor, Zukor built the world's first nickelodeon. To entice New Yorkers upstairs, he made the steps of glass, installed an electric-lighted waterfall underneath them and called the place Crystal Hall.

It continued in business for two decades until it was badly damaged by fire a few months before Ohrbach decided to make a store of it. The partners spent $70,000, more than half their capital, repairing it over a period of many weeks.

The two floors and basement were stocked with dresses to sell at $1 and coats at $5. Ohrbach, then and later, contended that there was nothing wrong with pricing items in round, or even, figures.

"In the early days of the cash register," he once explained, "the odd price was developed by retailers as a method of compelling clerks to ring up sales. If an item sold for $1, and the customer gave the salesperson a dollar bill, the clerk might hand over the merchandise and put the dollar bill elsewhere than in the register. But if the item sold for 95 cents and the customer presented a dollar bill, the salesperson would be much more likely to ring up the sale on the register in order to get the necessary change. In certain lines, women's gloves, for example, the odd price has become firmly established in customers' minds, but I unhesitatingly brand the general worship of the odd price as rank foolishness.

"I believe strongly that every retailer should experiment in this matter of odd prices. Profits in retailing are made in pennies, and the difference between profit and loss in more than one store might be found by refraining from throwing away profits in the form of smaller markups due to the fanatical worship of odd prices." Incidentally, with sales taxes, in effect in most states and many municipalities, pushing most sales prices above the even dollar marks, odd pricing is less appealing to retailers now than it was in 1923.

A "grand opening" was scheduled for October 4, 1923, for the new store. A huge sign announced "Ohrbach's, a bonded word for savings. . . . More for Less or Your Money Back." Ohrbach and his brother-in-law, Jack Kane, were at work in the store the evening before the opening when they recognized Sam Klein, the patriarch of the "On the Square" store, peering through the door.

They invited him inside for what proved to be the only meeting of Ohrbach and Klein—rivals until Klein's death many years later. Klein, a poor Russian immigrant who had made a fortune with pushcart methods, shook hands and looked around with amusement. "Such long counters," he said. "Such high ceilings! It's a joke!" He took his leave and announced, "I'll give them just seven months!"

Klein proved completely wrong about Ohrbach's. The opening-day crowds of 20,000 that Thursday—still considered a lucky day of the week at Ohrbach's—overwhelmed the store's fifty employees. A score of persons were cut and bruised and the police were summoned. Additional merchandise had to be rushed in that night to fill the bare racks.

The store was a success from the start and never had a loss. In 1924, sales amounted to $1,600,000 and profits totaled $119,000. As business grew, the original frontage of twenty-seven feet was expanded by taking over adjoining buildings.

A "Miracle Day" sale, a duplicate of the opening-day event, was held at the end of every month for the next three years with slow-moving coats, suits and dresses drastically reduced in price. Then, however, an internal crisis threatened the store. Wiesen and Ohrbach disagreed over how the business should be run. When Wiesen refused for a time to sell out, Ohrbach leased quarters nearby and announced plans for a second store (all earlier Ohrbach stores by then had been sold, one of them to his brothers). The move brought Wiesen to terms, and in January 1928 he accepted $650,000 for the interest that had cost him $62,500 less than five years earlier.

At this time, Ohrbach abandoned special sales, forbade the use of loss leaders and undertook to make every day a sale day. He then coined the slogan "A business in millions . . . a profit in pennies." Ohrbach's markups were lower than the typical department store's and his prices reflected this difference.

He also added men's and children's furnishing and accessories. Most important, he began to "trade up" his women's merchandise and to offer garments of a higher style and quality than had been previously available regularly in the neighborhood. This caused some other merchants there to call the store "the fancy pants of Fourteenth Street." Ohrbach was always out on the floor greeting customers and moving the merchandise around.

Ohrbach also formalized his policies of no price advertising, a minimum sales force, no alterations, no deliveries, cash and carry and no comparative price promotions.[1] This helped Ohrbach's open a branch in Newark in 1930 and pass triumphantly through the depression, even earning 16 percent on invested capital in the difficult year of 1932. A few years later, Ohrbach's wrested the Fourteenth Street sales leadership from S. Klein by a margin of many millions.

Ohrbach's today is a bargain hunter's paradise. Its management has blended daring buying and merchandising with conservative operations policies, and in so doing has wooed women of all income levels into its doors. Until recently, all of its advertising was institutional and contained no prices of merchandise.

"A customer," says Ohrbach's manual for its employees, "may state that she has seen an article like ours for less in a competitive store. When this happens, call your department manager at once. Someone from our comparison department will shop the article to determine whether the quality and workmanship are equal to ours. If the customer is proven right, our item is marked down. If the customer has paid the higher price, she is given a rebate for the difference."

The company has always operated under the philosophy that the customer is a lot smarter than many merchants suspect. Once, as an experiment, Ohrbach put one hundred handbags on sale at a low price—ninety-two of high quality and eight shoddy purses. At the end of the day, he was gratified to discover that four of the six bags left were the "dogs."

At Ohrbach's, there are probably more women's coats sold each year than at any other store in New York City, if not in the nation. Vice President Sydney Gittler is known in Europe and on Seventh Avenue as "the coat and suit king" for the styling ideas and merchandise volume he has been able to create during his long tenure at the store. Rose Wells, another vice president, has also become an important figure in New York's merchandise world.

Some of Ohrbach's low markup is made possible by its buying methods. As most ready-to-wear, however, is produced on the same sewing machines by members of the same union, the International Ladies' Garment Workers Union, the possibilities in this direction are limited. Nevertheless, the store has developed special suppliers and often induces manufacturers to make additional runs of their products at trimmed prices without labels or under an Ohrbach label. The company buys as much as $45,000 worth of a single suit style at a time, compared with the $1,500 worth that another store might purchase.

The real economies, however, are in the store's selling operations. Fair-trade merchandise is avoided entirely. Selling is semi-self-service. This enables Ohrbach clerks to cover more customers and sales areas than clerks in stores where the merchandise is less open.

One favorite story of the Ohrbach's people is about a genteel lady who was caught up in a crush around a glove table and was pushed squarely into another woman. "Oh, I do beg your pardon," she said sweetly. "I simply could not help myself." The other woman looked down at her and muttered, "If you're so damn polite, why aren't you shopping at Altman's?"

There is no alteration service at Ohrbach's. If garments don't fit, customers must alter them or find a seamstress to do it. There is no delivery service but packages will be wrapped for mailing if the customer desires. Employees, who in other stores receive discounts of as much as 30 percent, get only 20 percent at Ohrbach's.

Ohrbach's low-markup policy is a firm one. An executive of the Newark store, who once telephoned with the suggestion that the price of umbrellas be increased because it was raining, received a severe lecture from Nathan Ohrbach. Any change in price is supposed to be downward.

"Promotion is like taking dope," asserted the founder. "You use one dose of it and you have to have another and another and another. The only price that matters on an item is the price for which it can be bought. The people who advertise $89 values for $19.95 simply insult the customers' intelligence. If you advertise dresses at $12.95, formerly $16.95, you are simply saying to women: 'Dear customer, we thought we could sell these garments to you at $16.95, but you were too smart for us.

You have decided they are worth no more than $12.95, and that's what we are pricing them.' "

Some Seventh Avenue manufacturers use Ohrbach's as a sensitive barometer of what will sell and what will not. One technique they use is to place two dozen dresses of a new style on sale at the store. If eighteen or more have been bought by the end of the first day, the manufacturers will begin cutting several thousand, confident that a best seller is in the making.[2]

No sales slips are written at the store. Each item bears a single price ticket. As Ohrbach's attempts to turn over its merchandise about fifteen times a year, more than twice as often as many other similar stores, markdowns come fast if merchandise fails to move.

Style, adroitly advertised and publicized, as well as price, has figured in Ohrbach's success. As Ohrbach once said: "It is essential that the retail novitiate recognize the utter and absolutely autocratic sway of Dame Fashion and her satellites, style and design, over the world of merchandise." He classified women shoppers in these four categories:

A. The woman who is highly style-conscious and whose purse is able to withstand the onslaughts of high style. Price is no consideration to her. She wants to be among the first to sport the new.

B. The woman who likes style but not to the exclusion of price. Her desire for fashion first may be as keen as that of the other woman. But she must, perforce, keep a weather eye on her purse. She will not buy at the very start of the season. First she must assure herself that the fashion trend is set—she cannot afford to buy a fashion flivver. Second, she must assure herself that the price is not exorbitant.

C. The frugal woman, who is style conscious but who, through habit or necessity, must bide her time. She is quite eager to be up to the fashion. But she must watch her dollars carefully, and therefore she waits until the season is well on before starting to shop. She, also, represents an important group—and an individual pricing problem.

D. Our final type is the woman who buys only when clearances are featured. Women in this group may or may not be fashion conscious—the fact is that few women, these days, do not know the basic style trends. But for economic or other reasons these women buy only when prices are at bedrock.[3]

Women of the last three classes are Ohrbach's regular customers. And for many years the store has aspired to the "Class A" women too with lower-priced, line-for-line copies of creations by French, Italian and Spanish designers. Nathan Ohrbach was made a Chevalier of the Legion of Honor in recognition of his heavy promotion of French imports beginning in 1948. Originals by French and Italian designers like Dior, Givenchy, St. Laurent, Chanel, Valentino, Balenciaga, Fabiani, Simonetta and Capucci have been purchased by Ohrbach's on trips to Europe to copy for mass distribution.

Adroit publicity and advertising attempt to keep customers aware of Ohrbach's fashion achievements. For example, the store's publicity director, Mark Klauser, a former *New York Times* sports writer, once arranged a fashion show for a Ladies' Day crowd of sixty-five thousand attending a Yankee-Red Sox baseball game at Yankee Stadium. Fifteen jeeps carried models wearing sunsuits, bathing garb and other summer wear about the field. This stunt helped push Ohrbach's sales above $30 million and its profits over the $1-million mark for the first time shortly after World War II.

Another way that Ohrbach's keeps its name before the public is by furnishing fashions for use on television programs and theatrical productions. Daytime and evening shows with a total of over 175 million viewers a week run the credit line "Fashions by Ohrbach's" at the end of the show. Musical and industrial shows in many cities are also costumed by the New York store.

Five years after Ohrbach's was founded, its advertising was entrusted to Grey Advertising, Inc. When William Bernbach and others handling the account there formed their own agency, Doyle Dane Bernbach, Inc., in 1949, Ohrbach's went along with them as their first account.

Unusual, gay illustrations, ample white space and short, often humorous copy have characterized Ohrbach's distinctive advertising. Many early advertisements of the store were one-panel cartoons depicting the adventures of a big-eyed, curvaceous young lady called Melisse who always snared her man. This series attracted national attention and the original Melisse, Mildred Oppenheim, the artist who created the character, went into business for herself.

Several paintings from a notable collection of New York scenes commissioned by Ohrbach were used in the store's advertising. This collection of sixty paintings, by ten artists working without restrictions, also was exhibited at the Museum of the City of New York and attracted much favorable criticism in art circles. The artists were Thomas Hart Benton, Aaron Bohrod, Adolf Dehn, George Grosz, Peter Hurd, Fletcher Martin, Paul Sample, Georges Schreiber, Lawrence Beall Smith and Frederic Taubes. Later some abstract illustrations by Erik Nietsche were used in Ohrbach's advertising and proved so abstract that it was suggested that they be repeated upside down.

Humorous drawings by Peter Arno and Paul Rand followed and gave way to equally amusing photographs, sometimes published awry or in fragments. Though copyrighted, one captioned "Don't walk your legs off," and showing a young lady apparently doing so, was copied widely. Another showing bearded men dueling was captioned, "I'd rather die, sir, than give up a woman who shops at Ohrbach's."

In last couple of decades, the whimsical approach in both art and copy—developed by some of the same Doyle Dane Bernbach personnel who have worked on this Ohrbach's account since the agency's inception—has been featured. Perhaps the ad that drew the greatest attention was the 1958 one headlined "I found out about Joan."

This advertisement, which appeared only once, pictured a saucy cat wearing a hat and smoking a cigarette in a holder. The copy consisted entirely of comments by a catty woman explaining how her neighbor Joan dresses well by shopping at Ohrbach's. Thousands of requests for copies of this ad have been made by people from all over the world and granted by the agency.[4]

"We're telling the consumer in all of these ads," says Bernbach, "that no matter what you want, you'll get good quality merchandising at Ohrbach's at a good price. I think that we have built the understanding in the public's mind that you will always get fashion merchandise at a good price at Ohrbach's."

Some idea of the originality and effectiveness of Ohrbach's advertising was revealed by a classroom survey in the Julia Richman High School of New York. With names and addresses deleted, twenty full-page advertisements of big Manhattan and Brooklyn stores from Sunday editions of the *New York Times* were shown to students. Eighty percent of them remembered and identified the Ohrbach's advertisement. Only one other advertisement was recognized by as many as 50 percent. The pages of three stores were identified by 25 percent, eight pages had a smaller score and the remaining seven pages were entirely unrecognized.

It wasn't until 1966 that Ohrbach's moved from the strictly cash-and-carry policy that had guided the store since its origin to the availability of charge accounts. Its executives reached the conclusion that modern electronic data-processing equipment sharply reduced the cost of record keeping and thereby eliminated a major reason for no credit: heavy expenses that would have to be passed along to the customer. With the introduction of charge accounts, Ohrbach's turned away from its founder's aphorism, "The more billing, the less cooing," and gained thousands of new customers who preferred to use credit.

Ohrbach's expansion to California came as result of the growth of the fashion industry there. The firm employed the services of a buying office in Los Angeles as early as 1939 and in 1945 opened one of its own.

Three years later, it leased three floors and the mezzanine in a wing of the glittering new Prudential Insurance Company building on fashionable Wilshire Boulevard's "Miracle Mile."

Into the 150,000 square feet of floor space went fixtures and decorations, including some mural paintings, costing $2,500,000 and merchandise valued at the same amount.

Lured by newspaper and radio advertising of the same institutional type that had proved successful in New York, thousands were on hand for the initial day's business. Nine minutes after the doors were opened, they had to be closed and, as in the case of the Manhattan opening in 1923, police had to keep order. By afternoon, spot announcements on local radio stations were saying: "Please don't come to Ohrbach's today; come tomorrow or next week." Customers buying bargain nylons, handbags and similar items overwhelmed the store staff, and twenty-five additional cashiers were flown from New York to handle the rush that continued for days.

So well received was the firm in the West that in 1953 it purchased Milliron's, a downtown Los Angeles store dating back to 1905, and spent $1 million modernizing its eleven-story quarters. Using golden scissors, Mrs. Nathan M. Ohrbach cut a ribbon to formally open the refurbished store. A crowd of seventy-five thousand rushed in for opening-day bargains. The store was so crowded at midday that newcomers were admitted only as those inside departed. However, the opening-day aura didn't last long at this branch and, after first shutting down five floors of the building as an economy move, Ohrbach's closed the Milliron store in 1959 because of an unsatisfactory merchandise mix as compared to the other Ohrbach's stores'.

Since then, Ohrbach's has opened ten more stores, five in the East and five in the West. In the New York metropolitan area, units were opened in Queens, Westbury, and in Paramus, Wayne, and Woodbridge, New Jersey. Southern California stores are in Los Angeles, La Mirada, Torrance and Cerritos —plus a new Wilshire Boulevard store into which Ohrbach's moved its operations from the original site. When criticized for this relatively late entry into the booming branch-store business, Ohrbach's said, "I'd rather be right than first."

Many glamorous shoppers became customers at the Ohrbach's

stores in and around Los Angeles. Present at one fashion show, for example, were the Baroness d'Erlanger, Gene Tierney, Lady Lawford, Princess Pignatelli and many others. Linda Christian told the store how she paid $10 for a coat at Ohrbach's, wore it awhile and then sold it to a thrift shop for $15.

When the Wilshire Boulevard store sold the bankrupt Merry Hull stock of costly children's clothing at a 70 percent markdown, Mrs. Alfred Vanderbilt bought $600 worth of the garments and Lauren Bacall purchased $800 worth.

In 1954, Ohrbach's undertook its boldest move—from the six seventy-five-year-old buildings that had been put together to form the Fourteenth Street store to the heart of New York's busiest shopping area on West Thirty-fourth Street off Fifth Avenue, just across the street from the Empire State Building. This opportunity to trade in both location and merchandise came when the venerable James McCreery and Sons store, immortalized in *Life with Father*, closed its doors after becoming unprofitable.

Undaunted by the fact that any store in this location must compete with Macy's and Gimbels to the west and such famous fashion stores as Lord & Taylor, B. Altman & Co., and Arnold Constable nearby on Fifth Avenue, Ohrbach decided to take over the site. A ninety-year lease was arranged and Ohrbach's took possession of the property early in 1954. At a cost of $2,500,000, all eleven floors of the old 501,000-square-foot building were rebuilt and remodeled under the direction of designer Raymond Loewy.

Around 100,000 persons crowded into the store, swamping the 2,000 employees on opening day, August 26, 1954, and spent $500,000. "If you live through this, you are ready for Macy's," said the latter in an advertisement welcoming its new neighbor. Just about all the stores in the area benefited from the Ohrbach's move.

The advent of the 1960s brought on a change in the ownership of Ohrbach's, Inc. The company stock had always been closely held by the Ohrbach family, so corporate information has not been made generally available. But enough details have been pieced together for us to come up with this sequence of events:

It had become obvious to Nathan Ohrbach that his only son, Jerome Kane Ohrbach—a Cornell University graduate who rose from assistant buyer to president of Ohrbach's—was not interested in taking over completely the reins of the company. Jerome Ohrbach had many other outside interests, was well known in Wall Street as a large investor and was actively connected for many years with the Dreyfus Corporation, which markets the closed-end Dreyfus Fund.

Therefore, in January 1962, about half of the stock in the Ohrbach corporation was sold to the Dutch-American Investing Company, Inc., an affiliate of the Holland-based C. & A. Brenninkmeyer Co. The Brenninkmeyers—who built a European mercantile empire that began in 1841 and now consists of almost two hundred stores in the Netherlands, West Germany, Great Britain and Belgium—are even more close-mouthed about their personal affairs than are the Ohrbachs.

At that time, Nathan Ohrbach retained the chairmanship of Ohrbach's, Inc., and Jerome Ohrbach continued as president and treasurer. Changes, however, were not long in coming. Jerome Ohrbach resigned in July 1963 and was succeeded by Elmar Brenninkmeyer. Anthony Brenninkmeyer, his cousin, became a vice president of Ohrbach's. And in 1965, when he reached the age of eighty, Nathan Ohrbach retired from the chairman's post, so that today the entire ownership of Ohrbach's is within the Brenninkmeyer empire.

In 1967, Anthony Brenninkmeyer took over as president, succeeding his cousin. Two years later, the presidency of the specialty store group was returned to an American when Kermit G. Claster was named to the job and Anthony Brenninkmeyer moved up to chairman of the board and chief executive officer. And in 1973, Robert J. Suslow was appointed president of Ohrbach's.

Suslow joined Ohrbach's in 1972 as executive vice president

after spending four years at G. Fox & Co. in Hartford, Connecticut, as vice president and general merchandise manager. Previously, he had spent fourteen years at Bloomingdale's in New York in various merchandising positions.

The executive vice president and general manager of the West Coast division of Ohrbach's is Richard Rubin. Rubin, a ready-to-wear veteran, was vice president in charge of men's and boys' wear at the May Company in Los Angeles before joining Ohrbach's in 1973.

Ohrbach's reached a peak sales level well over $150 million in 1972. The East Coast stores contributed about two-thirds of the total, with the remainder derived from those on the West Coast.

Morale is high among Ohrbach's four thousand employees. Practically all executives have risen from the ranks. Dining rooms and cafeterias serve good food at low prices. There are sick benefits, life insurance and pension plans. All regular employees receive a week's winter vacation after five years of service in addition to two weeks' vacation in the summer. The company has a revolving loan fund on which employees can draw in financial emergencies.

Ohrbach clerks are given careful instruction in courtesy and grooming but are allowed more latitude in dress than in many other stores. In the summer, for example, salesgirls are permitted "leg makeup properly applied" in lieu of stockings. An Ohrbach girl is supposed to look "crisp and well-put-together." She is instructed: "Don't go in for slouching or slinking, walk naturally—don't rumba."

Employees are invited to make suggestions for the improvement of the store and its operations, and a "suggestion committee" distributes cash prizes for those accepted. Employees also are rewarded for the detection of shoplifters.

"A customer owes you nothing," the store tells its employees. "You owe her courtesy by the very fact that she is in your store. It is our aim to make every Ohrbach customer a satisfied one— satisfied not only with any merchandise that she might purchase here but also with the friendly, courteous treatment she receives from each and every employee whom she chances to contact in the store. A customer should never be made to feel that she must buy; she should know that she is perfectly welcome to shop."

Nathan Ohrbach always believed that the retail leaders of the future will be college graduates. Thus he had been interested for many years in the New York University Institute of Retail Management, the Fashion Institute of Technology, the Laboratory Institute of Merchandising and the High School of Fashion Industries. He also had been chairman of an advisory committee that arranges part-time jobs for retailing students at the College of the City of New York.

Ohrbach died in 1972 at eighty-seven after a long illness. He was eulogized by government leaders, former employees and competitors in retailing. Many of them remembered his philosophy of retailing, which he frequently repeated. "Retailing," he said, "when stripped of all its details, is found to be the art of pleasing people. Brains, imagination, courage and all the other attributes of youth are demanded by retailing as by no other single industry."

XXIV
Webb's City

"The World's Most Unusual Drugstore"

Since science, beginning with the sulfa drugs in the 1930s, found medicines that actually cure major diseases and prevent costly hospital stays, the drugstore has become the most important store of all. One of the most amazing of American institutions, it is the heir of both the itinerant "medicine man" and the ancient apothecary shop. Physicians of Greece and Rome compounded their own prescriptions, but in A.D. 754 an Arab named Abu Coreisch Isa el Szandalani, at the instance of the Caliph of Baghdad, opened in that city probably the world's first apothecary shop. Developments followed in England, Germany and France, and immigrants brought these skills to America.

Elias Durand, who had been a pharmacist with Napoleon's army, opened a shop in Philadelphia in 1825. It was the first to boast a soda fountain. As early as that date, pharmacists of Philadelphia and Boston were attempting to stabilize retail drug prices. "One evil where there is a difference in price," one of the latter noted, "is that the purchaser either thinks that the one who charged high wronged him as to price, or that the one who charged low wronged him as to quality." It is not surprising that like-minded merchants, through the National Association of Retail Druggists, advocate fair-trade (price-fixing) legislation.

Other drugstore owners believe it more profitable and perhaps even their duty to cut prices. There are differences as to what a drugstore should sell. Lascoff's in New York and at least four hundred others carry on in the apothecary tradition, selling only drugs, sometimes only drugs prescribed by physicians. A great many more sell many other items as well and may be notable for their customers. One such drugstore is Schwab's in Hollywood, where film folk still gather. In tiny, isolated Wall, South Dakota, Ted Hustead's colorful drugstore and its concrete dinosaur attract a million tourists a year, attracted by mileage signs to Wall posted even in the Eastern Hemisphere. The seventeen Sanborn stores in Mexico are famed for food and silver gifts as well as their prescriptions.

But it is in St. Petersburg, Florida, a pleasant city with so many senior citizens that the curbs are sloped for wheelchairs, that the world's largest and most extraordinary drugstore is located. By bargains and ballyhoo, it has attained a sales volume of more than $30 million a year and does the largest retail cash business in the South. For years it has advertised widely as "Webb's City, the World's Most Unusual Drug Store."

It might also be called "The World's Most Unusual Meat Market," or "The World's Most Unusual Barbershop"—distinctions all supporting its boast of being America's first "one-stop shopping city." The complex is open from nine to nine weekdays and from twelve to six on Sundays. It sprawls over seven city blocks and has seventy-seven busy stores, including one selling women's ready-to-wear. There are two restaurants, a beauty shop, a gasoline station and a supermarket. Twelve parking lots provide space for 2,500 automobiles. Buses stop 450 times a day and Webb's City sells bus tokens at a discount. All this attracts around 45,000 customers a day in a city where the 1970 census counted only 216,232 residents.

But the heart of the operation is the drug department with which Doc Webb originally started. Ten registered pharmacists, aided by twenty-four typists and clerks, compound more than nine hundred prescriptions a day in immaculate quarters. The main floor is a super drugstore, and despite the growth of other departments, drugs, the huge soda fountain, cosmetics, and related sundries account for a fifth of Webb's huge volume. Ninety-nine percent of all purchases are paid for in cash but the BankAmericard is accepted.

The main building is four stories high with a basement cafeteria. Across the street is a seven-floor furniture store and Webb's professional building, housing optical and hearing-aid shops. Nearby is the Trading Post, a super service station that boasts selling more gasoline than any other station in America. The Post also sells automotive supplies, sporting goods, paint and hardware.

A second huge store, expected eventually to add $22 million to Webb's volume, was opened in the fall of 1972 at Pinellas Park, ten miles to the northwest, where the firm had a sixteen-pump gasoline station. This was continued, and on a floor as big as two and a half football fields the venture began with drugstore, supermarket, garden-supply, restaurant and related operations. The manager of the main floor is H. C. Friedrich, previously grocery manager at the main store. The gigantic second floor of this new store will house a complete department store.

Webb also has a service station in Largo and plans others in western Florida. On the boulevard to Tampa is another branch, Webb's Outpost, marked by a five-story electric sign. This is a small supermarket and souvenir shop and fountain restaurant that gives tourists information about St. Petersburg and Webb's. Road signs, some of them 750 miles away, also direct motorists to the place.

Responsible for it all is James Earl "Doc" Webb, who had been aptly described as "a peculiar blend of merchant prince and leprechaun."[1] His portrait in oil hangs in the store over the escalator. Of slight stature but immense energy and with a great flair for showmanship, he is a cocky bantam who has found fun and fortune in running a store like a circus. He was born August 31, 1899, in Nashville, Tennessee, of Scotch, Irish and English descent. His formal education ended after the seventh grade but his business education already had begun.

"My father—he was a contractor—had been injured by a truck," Doc once recalled. "Mother and I took over the family. I began making money when I was nine years old. I raised vegetables and sold them. I put on backyards shows, sold lemonade and later peddled both morning and afternoon papers." In his teens he worked around drugstores. "I was manager of a retail drugstore with twelve adults working under me by the time I was twenty," he says.

He was in Knoxville by this time and here earned his informal title of "Doc" by developing a venereal-disease compound which was known through Tennessee and Kentucky as "Webb's 608." Profits enabled Webb to buy a Rickenbacker automobile.

After seven years in Tennessee drugstores, where he learned a lot but never bothered to qualify as a registered pharmacist, Webb at twenty-six decided to go into business for himself. Because he liked the climate and he found a real-estate boom there, he chose the west coast of Florida. But, just as he arrived in St. Petersburg with $5,000 and a partner, the boom collapsed and stores began to close.

Undaunted, he opened a tiny cut-rate drugstore with four employees in rented space seventeen by twenty-eight feet. It was in an old building at the south end of the business area adjoining the slum district, and between the Seaboard and Atlantic Coast Line railroad tracks. The spot is now more than occupied by Webb's cigar and magazine department, but a museum replica of the original store is to be found on the fourth floor. The tracks have since been removed and there is a big Webb's parking lot on the site of the Seaboard station.

The first year's receipts amounted to $38,990.45. With $6,000 in bills unpaid, Webb and his partner then parted and the latter eventually received $18,000 for his interest. Webb says his partner was "too conservative." The next year sales reached $90,000. By shrewd purchasing, ruthless price cutting and spectacular promotions, Webb began to lure crowds to the out-of-the-way location. Sales passed $1 million in 1936 and $2 million in 1939.

One of his most spectacular loss leaders was the three-cent

breakfast with which he introduced his basement cafeteria. For this price, you received one egg, two strips of bacon, three slices of toast, grits and ham gravy. After six months, during which the cafeteria became well known, the price was advanced to fourteen cents. Later, during sales, this was cut to nine cents!

Cheeses weighing four thousand pounds have been cut up and sold in a single day. Webb also has sold fifteen tons of bananas and fifty-two thousand pounds of chickens in one day. He sold a freight car of cantaloupes for two cents each, moved a carload of canned peaches in a day and even staged a carload sale of cigars. With sidings on two railroads, he found it easy to handle such shipments. When butter was at seventy-nine cents a pound, Webb's sold some at nineteen cents and once marketed $17 automobile tires for $9.95. A cigarette war with a rival store ended with Webb's giving away two packs to each customer.

At times, Webb's posts the sale advertisements of rival drugstores with an additional line: "10 percent off these prices at Webb's." But the height of this sort of thing probably was the sale of two thousand $1 bills at 95 cents each, later the sale of twenty-five hundred more at 89 cents each, and the repurchase a few days later of the "cheap" money at $1.35 per greenback. Mobs jammed the store.

"Any merchant," Webb believes, "should have the right to sell any item in his store for whatever price he decides." His tactics brought him into conflict with the fair-trade laws and at one time he had six legal firms defending him. He was successful in having Florida statutes invalidated, with the Florida Supreme Court ruling that inflexible price arrangements "are not in line with our traditional concepts of free competition." This was years before consumer advocates pressed the issue nationally, and the Pathmark chain profited in the Northeast with Webb's tactics.

When a "quality stabilization act" was proposed in Congress in 1963, he sent a representative to Washington and bought space in the *Washington Post*[2] to show how he believed the measure would increase the prices of drugs and appliances. "Please kill the quality stabilization act for All America," he asked. It was defeated.

The Florida Poster Girls were Doc Webb's most durable publicity venture. Each year eight girls were chosen from several hundred on the basis of "beauty, character, talent and charm." Clad in bathing suits and other Florida products, they staged fashion shows throughout the country and otherwise publicized Florida, St. Petersburg and Webb's. During some years, they even invaded Hollywood in a Florida-versus-California beauty competition.

Doc Webb's markups have been so low that at times he has been short of cash. In 1940, he needed $200,000. When local banks couldn't accommodate him and underwriters wanted 10 percent, Webb decided to sell $100 preferred shares over the counter. He filed the proper papers, obtained a broker's license and put a big advertisement in the local Sunday paper. It concluded, "You have 7 days to buy these securities. . . . Come now! See J. E. Webb." A Monday page said, "Today is the Day."

On Tuesday morning, he advertised "$73,400 of stock sold and paid for," on Wednesday, "$126,600 sold and paid for." On Thursday, a horrified representative of the Securities and Exchange Commission arrived to explain that securities could not be advertised like drugstore bargains. But the advertisement that morning simply said, "Thank you." All the stock had been sold.

"At that time," recalls Doc Webb, "I found that we need never fear to be in the hands of the people."

This preferred stock subsequently was retired. Doc Webb owns a majority of the company's common stock and with his officers controls 70 percent of it. The other 30 percent is owned by some 1,500 persons, many of them employees or customers. Doc Webb pays himself a salary of only $15,000 a year.

Sales increased from $3,693,945 in 1941 to $12,305,000 in 1947, $18,218,837 in 1951 and $24 million in 1954. Sales passed $29 million in 1959 and soared past $30 million in the sixties. Though perhaps a hundred important shopping centers now encircle the area, Webb's sales continue at this level. Profits increased from $219,833 in fiscal 1971 to $343,440 in 1972.

The Walgreen Company, biggest of the drug chains ($863 million sales from 564 stores in 1972), closed its St. Petersburg outlet in the face of Webb's competition but has other stores in western Florida. Several of the more than 260 Florida drugstores of the Jack Eckerd Corporation, called "the most profitable major drug chain in the U.S." by Value Line in 1973, are in the area. In the nondrug field, Webb's competes with Sears, Roebuck, J. C. Penney, Safeway and many other huge retailers but nevertheless continues to meet all prices.

The name "Webb's City" denotes the operation conducted by Webb and his associates. The business is citylike in that more than seventy-seven separate operations are carried on principally under one roof and all the necessities and many of the luxuries of life can be procured in the various "stores." Each store has its own manager who is responsible for purchasing goods and selling them quickly at a modest profit, which Doc Webb says averages between 1 and 2 percent in a typical year. The discount for paying cash is sometimes the only profit on an item. Supervising the store managers are six division managers, most of whom are vice presidents.

Alabama-born Fred B. Scott is executive vice president and general manager. He joined Webb's City in 1951 after Air Force service, A & P experience and management of a Dunlap chain department store. Senior vice presidents are B. E. Webb, Doc's brother, and J. C. Holley. Also vice presidents are Thomas P. Johnson, Sam J. Harrington, L. A. Claffey, Seymour Handy, and H. F. McIntyre. Over everybody is Doc Webb, President.

"This is not a department store operation at all, though one of the seventy-seven stores is a department store," Doc Webb points out. "Every manager is in charge of his own store and has responsibility for its operation with help as needed from his division head, Mr. Scott, or from me. Before World War II this was essentially a one-man operation—I had the ideas, planned the remodeling, made the rules and regulations. Now we have more of a team system."

The seventy-seven store managers are almost independent operators, for they hire and fire their own help, act as purchasing agents and are everything that their title implies. According to the season, the number of employees varies between 1,200 and 1,500. A bonus is paid each May and there is incentive pay in some departments in the form of weekly commissions to augment salaries. There are also paid vacations, sick leave and an insurance-participation plan. Webb is proud of his employees and says that someday he is going to build a country club and swimming pool for them "and my customers." There are many ten-, fifteen- and twenty-year and several thirty-year employees in the organization.

"Most businesses start with one man and I started Webb's," Doc says, "but somewhere along the line you have to have help and I am lucky to have my staff. You can't build a business staying in an office. The greatest failure in the world came when America's banks closed in the early thirties. If those bankers had been out in front meeting people and talking to them, the depositors wouldn't have taken out their money."

Doc Webb doesn't get to the store and "out in front" until the afternoon, but he has not been idle. The home that he shares with his attractive wife, Aretta, a businesswoman in her own right, has seven telephone lines, three to Webb's City, and there are telephone outlets in every room. Doc does most of his business by telephone. When he does arrive at the "office," he probably will breeze in wearing a white suit, one of the 150 that he owns.

After an hour or sometimes less, Webb usually darts restlessly out of the office to do something more exciting. He may grab a microphone and over the public-address system announce a sudden bargain as if he were back selling medicine in the Tennessee mountains.

"Hear this, hear this!" he'll chant. "For the next thirty

minutes, the next thirty minutes only, we will sell in the appliance department $25 electric toasters for $9.95 apiece. Hurry, hurry, *hurry!*" A mob will converge on the department and all the toasters probably will be sold in a few minutes.

If there are circus acrobats performing, as sometimes is the case, Webb may strip to the waist and get into the act. He likes to jump up and down on mattresses. In his mid-seventies, he is a wiry and active athlete and still plays tennis three times a week. With a partner, he once won the veteran doubles championship of Florida and had no difficulty obtaining a $500,000 insurance policy on his life for the benefit of the store.

Traffic builders for Webb's include a branch post office, second only to the main St. Petersburg office in volume, and a check-cashing service where telephone and all other utility bills may be paid. At any time in the day, there will be a line at the check window. Checks totaling more than $30 million a year are cashed. This service costs Doc Webb $20,000 or more, but it is cheap advertising. Bankers' hours are unheard of at Webb's, and, check cashing goes on day and night. Losses from bad checks are infinitesimal—and the few persons who write them are relentlessly pursued. "We cash more checks than most banks," Doc Webb claims proudly, and he doesn't have to add that a lot of the cash is spent in the store. While competitors have gone largely to credit and premium stamps to increase volume, he has gained without them.

Doc Webb doesn't believe in setting aside any fixed percentage of income for advertising. "There isn't any yardstick you can apply—you just have to spend what is needed," he declares.

The advertising budget is around $750,000. Everything possible in the way of "push money" and advertising allowances is obtained from suppliers. To Doc Webb, advertising means first a schedule of full-page and double-page ads in local newspapers; it means five hundred roadside signs extending as far north as Knoxville, where he used to live; it means a cross-country tour for the Poster Girls in their specially designed bus; it means entertainment of many kinds at Webb's during business hours.

Webb also uses radio and TV time, but Doc's major confidence is in black-and-white newspaper advertising with emphasis on the big black letters and figures that announce his bargains.

Many things keep traffic flowing. A summer special is the managers' sale, in which the various store managers try to outdo each other in bargains. Entertainers perform five times daily. Sometimes there is a topsy-turvy day, in which the drug department may sell avocados, the cosmetic department may feature gallon cans of motor oil and the bakery may offer hardware items. The big stage on the main floor has also been the scene of unusual events. For example, a reptile expert has milked rattlesnakes of their venom, aerial acts have performed, boxing matches have been staged and magicians have done their stuff.

On the No. 1 parking lot, just outside the store, there have been free elephant rides, clowns have cavorted, people have been shot from cannons and lion acts have been staged. Here, too, Doc Webb has invited his customers to participate in a "Country Fair," which exhibits hobbies, crafts and foods—and the exhibitors were invited to sell their cakes, their bedspreads or whatever, even when competing with Webb's merchandise.

Doc Webb takes an active role in civic affairs, supporting projects he likes and opposing those he thinks unwise. He bought newspaper space to defeat an urban-renewal project that he considered impractical. He has received a "distinguished service to the community" plaque from the Chamber of Commerce, a "citizenship medal" from the Veterans of Foreign Wars and other honors. On one occasion, the *St. Petersburg Independent* said: "As if reclaiming and building up an entire area of the city, once low-rated, and advantageously supplying millions of customers, were not enough, Doc Webb has also made his impress on the area in civic directions. It was he who devised the now commonly accepted term 'Sun-coast' to describe the whole Gulf Coast area— in this even antedating the naming of the big Tampa Bay bridge 'Sunshine Skyway'—and he who was the major factor in setting up new and better quarters for St. Petersburg's senior citizens."[3]

Webb says solemnly that two miracles have occurred at Webb's

City in recent years "even though we may not be the best of Christians.

"Right after the war when we were expanding faster than we could borrow money, we just about came to the end of our rope. Our building program was well along, but we had stretched our finances too far. . . . We were actually praying for divine help when we went home from the store one night.

"In the next morning's mail was a check for almost exactly the amount we needed from the U.S. Treasury. We had been trying to get a refund on taxes and thought this $40,000 had been returned to us from the Internal Revenue people. Actually, the check had been mailed to us by mistake. But we used the money at the time for our building and it was four years before we had to pay it back, and we could afford to do it then. That has always seemed like a miracle to me.

"The other was a different sort of miracle. Webb's ran a highly profitable liquor store for many years—in fact it grew to a place where it had a $2,000,000 gross volume and was providing about half of our gross profits a few years after the war.

"Then I got to thinking that we were having to fire some of our people because they were drinking, and yet we were tempting them to drink with our liquor store. I didn't think that was fair and I could tell our employees didn't think it was right, so I decided to eliminate the liquor store. We did cut it out and here's the miracle—we had a bigger volume of business the next year and our profits were $75,000 greater.

"I have always had a feeling that gold shouldn't be the master in any business, and I thought we ought to get out of the liquor business before it got too strong a hold on us. Some of our people didn't agree at the time; they felt that sale of liquor was legal and that there was nothing wrong with our liquor store. But I couldn't hear and read about people getting in trouble because they had been drinking and still feel right about selling it. And we're better off today for being out of that business. A store's principles are just like a person's; they've got to be good or you'll go down. . . ."

Some analysts figure that Doc Webb's success hinges largely on the fact that St. Petersburg is populated by a bigger than average number of oldsters who are looking for an interesting place to spend their pension money. Doc scoffs at this idea, though he is proud that "a lot of people with small incomes are able to live well because they shop at Webb's."

"I just run a fundamentally sound business," Webb declares, "and I could do it just as well in Egypt or Paris if the state would let me operate without interference. The United States is the last country where there is free enterprise, and it's a battle to have it here because of the chain stores and the fair-trade laws.

"But I've whipped 'em on prices and I've whipped 'em on this fair-trade thing. It's nobody's business what I sell an item for after I buy it, and I'm going to keep giving my customers the lowest prices they can find anywhere."

XXV

The Discounters Arrive

Korvettes, K-Mart and Their Rivals

"Do you know what discounting is?" the head of a major retail chain once asked.

Then he answered his own question. "It's nothing more than selling inferior merchandise on Sundays."

This facetious comment was untrue when it was expressed and is certainly untrue today. But it symbolizes the feeling that many people, both in and out of retailing, have about discount houses, despite their enormous development since World War II.

Discount stores had total sales of a whopping $33 billion in 1972, an estimated $3 billion, or 10 percent, more than the preceding year. Their growth, moreover, has been equally spectacular. Sales of discount stores have advanced from less than $3 billion in 1960 to the current level, an increase of more than 1,000 percent. Between 1967 and 1972 alone, volume more than doubled. Discount sales have been rising at the rate of some 15 percent annually, about four times as fast as retail sales in general. By mid-1972, about 150 major discount chains and 4,720 discount stores were in operation, with 376 new units being added during the most recent year.[1]

Yet, as big as discounting is now, the origins of many discount stores are humbler than those of most giant retailing establishments. E. J. Korvette got its start as a small luggage shop in a second-floor Manhattan walkup. The Two Guys chain began in an eight-hundred-square-foot store next to a New Jersey diner. Other major discounters began in factory buildings, in warehouses and in other offbeat locations.

Department-store executives in the past have called discount stores everything from "a malignant cancer" to "an unsound method of distribution" that "takes it out of the hide of the consumer." Whatever they are called, though, discounters believe that they have succeeded in spurring traditional retailers to do a sharper job of merchandising.

As an industry, discounting has few certainties. First, there is no general agreement on exactly what a discount house is. The name itself indicates a store that sells merchandise for less. But what merchandise? And for less than whom?

A good definition of a discount house is a store of more than 10,000 square feet, largely self-service, that operates at a lower average markup than conventional stores selling the same types of merchandise. Another definition, this one by Perry Meyers, a retailing consultant, calls a discount house "any store which operates on a low-expense, low-markup basis and which emphasizes competitive pricing as a main attraction to win customers." Kurt Barnard, executive vice president of the Mass Retailing Institute, a trade association of discount stores, calls his members "self-service retailers selling general merchandise."

But in the discounting field, definitions are rarely all-encompassing. For example, do the above definitions apply to Korvette, an early giant of discounting, which has upgraded its merchandising and fixturing to such an extent that it calls its units not discount stores but promotional department stores?

How about such well-known New York stores as Alexander's and Mays? These stores were in business and selling apparel at discount prices long before discounting came into vogue. They term themselves "underselling" stores.

With this confusion over definitions, it is not surprising to find that there are no precise figures to describe the size of discounting. Perhaps because of this very confusion, the Department of Commerce does not compile monthly and yearly sales figures for discounters as it does for department stores and other retailing categories, so that even the best estimates of volume are simply that.

Furthermore, food as well as nonfood sales of discounters are usually included in estimates of their annual volume. Although food sales currently represent between 15 and 20 percent of total discount industry volume, they are generally under the control of independent lessees, while nevertheless adding to total volume figures.

Discount houses have frequently been termed revolutionary developments, but they can more precisely be described as evolutionary. For their development has been a gradual one that began long before the present-day versions were conceived.

Since the early years of the twentieth century, neighborhood and downtown stores have conducted sales, either periodically or occasionally, when discounts were offered even though the name was not used. "Loss leader" merchandise—where the discounts are so large that the selling price is pushed below the cost to the merchant in order to stimulate traffic in his store—has long been found in department and specialty stores.

For many years, R. H. Macy—the epitome of the traditional department store—told the world that it would "save our customers at least 6 per cent for cash." And then there is the old slogan "Nobody but nobody undersells Gimbels." Another development in the evolution of discount stores was the supermarket. This method of retailing, particularly the very popular self-service aspects, brought food, and later related items, swiftly and efficiently to the consumer.

With all of its precursors, the discount house as it is now known got its start shortly after World War II. There were, to be sure, some discounters operating in the late 1930s, such as the first Masters store in a New York City loft opened in 1937 with borrowed capital of $500 to sell radios. But it wasn't until the opening of the outlet stores in New England, "the cradle of discounting," in abandoned textile mills or old warehouses that discounting began making rapid strides. One of the earliest of these stores was Ann & Hope, founded in 1953 by Marty Chase in an old Cumberland, Rhode Island, mill and later visited by many of the discounting pioneers as they were learning their trade.

The discount-house image at the outset was based on un-adorned shelves, plain pipe racks, simple wooden tables, few salespeople ("no service is better than bad service" was the theory), no deliveries and a complete lack of frills. Since they were called "houses" instead of "stores," many people considered these outlets a place to buy only seconds, factory close-outs, irregulars and similar merchandise.

By and large, the situation has changed significantly. Dis-counters now sell goods in all general-merchandise categories, have attractive lighting and landscaping in and around their stores and feature extensive, easily accessible displays. Most of their stores today are one-level units in the nation's major metro-politan areas, located in shopping centers and along roadside strips.

Discounters have also helped to force traditional prices down, stimulate Sunday selling, provide the convenience of late-hour shopping and move big-city style selection to all markets. By 1973, they had captured 47 percent of all full-line store sales. Almost from the start, the hard-goods discounters found them-selves battling with national-brand manufacturers, who cited fair-trade laws in an attempt to prevent them from price cutting their merchandise. But as these manufacturers saw discounting take on an increasing percentage of their total retail sales, many began to sell to discount stores.

Nowadays discount houses sell brand-name merchandise in profusion at prices generally below the "list," where there is a legitimate one. In fact, the erosion of the list price in many metropolitan centers has been largely due to the constant price pressure of the discounters.[2]

Few manufacturers of television sets, refrigerators and other appliances, including many of the very same companies that initially refused to sell discounters directly, can move their merchandise to the consumer without using discount stores. All of the staple items—toys, hardware, paints, etc.—are carried as a basic part of the inventory of most large and small discount houses.

Discount merchandising has also emerged from a hard-goods emphasis to a more balanced operation that sells both durable and nondurable goods. Some discounters have even grown up specializing in soft goods and have won new customers by offering apparel for men, women and children at apparent discounts. Between 25 and 40 percent of a typical discounter's volume is currently done in soft goods.

The discounters have proceeded still further into the province of department and general-merchandise stores. They have added such extras as service (beauty salons, watch repairing, etc.), tire and battery centers and audio equipment, gaining new customers for their older departments in the process.

What propelled discounting to its present position in the American economy? Perhaps the most important factor was the growth of the suburbs after the end of the Second World War.

As families in even the lower-income brackets moved away from the center of cities and towns, and as the automobile became an essential in many areas for even the simplest shopping tasks, a new type of market was created. The discounters, who moved quickly to those places where new communities developed and who brought new merchandising ideas that had not been tried before, found an audience that welcomed them with open arms.

Moreover, most of the department-store branches that were built for the suburbs usually didn't include the "basement" or "budget" store that the same companies successfully ran downtown. Many department stores thus virtually abdicated the lower-income portions of the suburban market to the onrushing discounters at first.

Discount centers provided special attractions for their customers. Large adjacent parking areas with spaces for thousands of cars, night hours almost every day of the week and even Sunday openings in some communities were features that brought out larger and larger crowds of shoppers. Because self-selection was the vogue, merchandise was individually packaged for convenient customer handling and inspection.

The bazaarlike atmosphere—with such appurtenances as loud-speaker announcements of "fifteen-minute specials," pretzel and popcorn vendors outside the front doors and nearby carousels and other amusements—made shopping at many discount houses equivalent to a family outing.

As the discounters expanded, many of them utilized the services of concessionaires, or operators of leased departments. Leased departments are nothing new in retailing—some department and specialty stores have long been using them for certain departments like millinery, shoes, health and beauty aids and fine jewelry—but the concept was carried much further in discount houses.

One reason for the growth in the number of lessees was that, with them, discounters were able to reduce the amount of capital investment required to get started, since less inventory had to be purchased by the store owner. Another is that lessees brought a degree of merchandising experience and sophistication in their fields that a large number of store owners originally needed and were willing to pay for. Food lessees, usually big supermarket chains, were taken in as the complete food and nonfood one-stop shopping idea gained momentum among discounters.

The trend toward the use of lessees has abated considerably. Leased-department operators who suffered financially when certain stores in which they had concessions went bankrupt have become more cautious, while the discounters—continually gaining more experience and anxious to obtain better control over merchandising and advertising policies—have taken over more departments that had formerly been leased out to others. Today leased departments are at a minimum.

In 1962 and 1963 came discounting's biggest shake-out, with many undercapitalized, poorly merchandised discounters falling by the wayside. Another series of discounting projects took place in the early 1970s. Most of those units that have remained, at least the big ones, are in a stronger position than they were in the early 1960s,[3] even though discounting failures are by no means a thing of the past.

Three of the most recognizable characteristics that differentiate discount houses from other retailers are:

1. Lower markups. From the outset, discounters have operated at lower gross margins than department stores because their costs of construction, personnel and overall operations have usually been lower. While the differential has narrowed in recent years as discount stores added some of the services they originally disdained—like credit plans, carpeting and expensive fixtures in certain store areas and a greater selection in certain merchandise categories—there generally is still a sizable gap between the two. The typical large department-store markup, figured as a percentage of the selling price, is about 45 percent. In contrast, average markups of discount stores generally range between 30 and 35 percent.

2. Higher turnover. Inventory turnover, or the number of times each item of merchandise is sold during the year, is generally acknowledged to be greater among discounters than among department stores. Executives of discounting organizations say that they can turn over their stocks close to four times a year, compared with the typical department-store stock turn of well under four.

3. More self-service. Self-service is one of the keynotes of discount houses. With central checkout counters to serve many departments and fewer salespeople in the stores, discounters have been able to reduce tremendously the personnel costs of manning their stores. Consumers have become accustomed to fending for themselves in discount houses and in most cases manage to do it successfully. Thus while payroll costs of depart-

ment stores amount to 19 percent of sales, those of discounters are 11 percent.[4]

No organization has been more identified with discounting than E. J. Korvette, or, as it is now called, Korvettes. From a small second-floor luggage store in New York opened in 1948, Korvettes has gone on to become the nation's best-known discounter with more than fifty units throughout the country. It had sales in 1972 of well over $600,000,000. The sharp growth of the company without adequate financial controls in the 1960s led to its merger in 1966 into Spartans Industries, Inc., an apparel manufacturer and retailer. Four and a half years later, Spartans itself was merged into Arlen Realty and Development Corporation, a real-estate company. But the Korvettes name continues as a leading light among the nation's discount stores.

The man who created E. J. Korvette and coined its unusual name is probably the most unorthodox merchant in the United States. He is Eugene Ferkauf, a shy, wiry native of Brooklyn who, while ignoring the shibboleths of retailing from the outset, nevertheless succeeded in being elected, in 1962, to the Retailing Hall of Fame at the Boston Conference on Distribution. At one point during Korvette's pre-merger peak, Ferkauf was listed in a highly regarded compilation as one of the six greatest retailers in American history.

In 1968, Gene Ferkauf resigned from all his associations with Korvettes and Spartans, whose chairman, Charles C. Bassine, had succeeded him as chief executive officer. The later merger into Arlen created a new top-management hierarchy with Arthur G. Cohen as chairman and chief executive of the combined corporation, Marshall Rose as president and David Brous as president of Korvettes. But while these executives have restored Korvettes to financial health, reorganized its management and established sound systems for future growth, they have not captured the public's imagination to the extent that Ferkauf and his "boys" did in the early post-World War II years.

For Ferkauf broke many of the long-cherished traditions of the retailing fraternity—and for a long time was enormously successful in doing so. Not only did he spark the discount revolution; he also refused to conform to the attitudes and formalities that had become standard among prosperous merchants.

He had no private office, no secretary and no personal files. His closest business associates were his high-school buddies who joined him when he began opening discount stores and stayed with him long enough to become rich men. He usually wore an open-collared shirt, moved around the room rapidly and used his instinct rather than research reports on major decisions. Although he founded Korvettes, was its major stockholder and always served as chief executive in actual fact, he had no formal title until 1955, when his investment bankers insisted that he take one. Even then, Ferkauf chose the nebulous-sounding title of chairman of the executive committee to leave himself free to visit his stores and take whatever freewheeling actions he desired.

A disarmingly uncomplicated man, Ferkauf loved to go out on the sales floor to wait on customers and learn what they were thinking. He once claimed that Korvettes has "done more to stretch the buck than anyone in American distribution. I don't know by what percentage we've increased the purchasing power of the American dollar, but I know it's significant."[5]

By the mid-1960s, the lack of tight financial management and the problems inherent in too rapid trading up overtook the mercurial Ferkauf. Management shakeup followed management shakeup as he sought to bring into his company executives who could convert the merchandising skills of the E. J. Korvette buyers into a well-organized and profitable entity. But Ferkauf—who readily admitted "I love to go to the marketplace"—could not find the right man until Bassine, a successful businessman for many years and an old friend, stepped into the picture in 1966.

Bassine immediately took charge, slowed the vast expansion program until stability had been restored and reassured the financial community about Korvettes' future. And Ferkauf, who was happy to spend many of his days at his Douglaston, Long Island, store overseeing the 5,600-square-foot art gallery there, recognized that he was no longer needed at Korvettes and departed two years later from the retailing empire he had built.

The story of Korvettes' development is one of merchandising know-how coupled with close attention to an old retailing principle: get the customers in the store with low prices and keep them coming by giving them value for their money. Whenever it departed from the formula—as during the years it concentrated more on fashion than on prices—it ran into trouble. But by keeping its eye on its original promise of discounting, or promotional selling, Korvettes has achieved the distinction of being the most newsworthy new merchandiser to emerge in the United States since the end of World War II.

"It doesn't take any special mental processes to become a retailer," Ferkauf frequently said, to the consternation of the retailing establishment. Yet how many men could take a thousand-square-foot luggage store, add small appliances and jewelry and from that base build a national chain of fifty-two department stores in major metropolitan cities?

The average Korvette store contains around 200,000 square feet and does an annual volume of $15 million to $20 million in all hard and soft lines. From its base in New York, the company has spread west to Chicago and Detroit and south to Baltimore and Washington. All but five of these stores are located in suburban or regional shopping centers.

The Korvettes success formula can be broken down into these components: Pick good locations. Choose executives for their character and general intelligence. Maintain a close relationship with all employees. Provide customers with the best possible quality and value. Give service only if it is wanted but charge a fair price for it. And convince the public that substantial storewide savings are offered.

Perhaps nowhere is the change that has come over discounting better exemplified than in the E. J. Korvette store on Fifth

Avenue and Forty-seventh Street in Manhattan. When Korvettes first came to the royal row of American retailing in 1962 to occupy the store formerly used by the well-known W. and J. Sloane furniture retailer, skeptics gasped with disbelief. Plain pipe racks on Fifth Avenue?

Korvettes, however, knew otherwise. It opened a seven-story, crystal-chandeliered store that had carpeting, many higher price lines and fashion apparel ranging up to expensive fur coats and stoles. It built up an elaborate soft-goods operation (that later spread to other Korvettes stores), using private-label merchandise and brand-name clothing without the manufacturers' labels when they would not sell to Korvettes openly, just as it had done in earlier years with hard-goods lines like television sets and refrigerators. As a result, the Korvette Fifth Avenue store topped $30 million in sales its first year and has since become a New York tourist attraction.

A similar public reaction occurred when Korvettes came to Manhattan's Herald Square in 1967. For by taking over the Thirty-fourth Street site vacated by Saks-34th Street, Korvettes opened its doors right in between two of the city's leading traditional department stores, Macy's and Gimbels. The ten-story, marble-clad store quickly became an important factor in New York's retailing picture as it reached the $30-million sales level and brought thousands of additional shoppers to the retail hub of the city.

These merchandising advances are a far cry from the beginnings of Korvettes. Eugene Ferkauf, born in Brooklyn in 1920, graduated from Tilden High School and went directly to work in his father's two small luggage shops near Grand Central Station called Rex Luggage Company. There he learned what retailing was all about and was exposed to his father's principles of merchandising, which included the theory "If you're good to a store, it will be good to you."

After World War II service as a sergeant in the Signal Corps, Ferkauf returned to his father's stores but became quickly discontented. He wanted to test his theory that he could boost sales substantially by chopping the conventional 40 percent markup in half. And so, on a $4,000 investment (partially supplied by his father), Ferkauf rented a second-floor walkup on East Forty-sixth Street and began selling luggage at a discount. He called his store E. J. Korvette—"E" for his first name, "J" for Joseph Zwillenberg (one of his early close business associates) and "Korvette" for the small warships that were spelled with a "C" instead of a "K."

Almost as an afterthought, Ferkauf decided to stock some then hard-to-get small electrical appliances and jewelry and priced them at cost to draw traffic. When he saw that he sold these appliances as fast as he got them into the store, he added small markups—and they still sold.

By plowing all the profits back into Korvette, Ferkauf found himself running a $2-million business only two years after he started. In 1951 there were three stores, in 1955 there were eight and the expansion program was well under way. Sales totaled $36 million in 1955, $71 million in 1957, $180 million in 1961, and advanced to $622 million in 1964 in a virtually unparalleled record of retailing growth. Not since the first five-and-ten-cent stores did a chain enjoy such sudden success.

By 1966, Korvettes, then the biggest volume discounter, was pushing ahead toward the magic billion-dollar sales figure. But Ferkauf's magic touch finally grew cold as inadequate coordination and a confused operational image took its toll. Sales slumped, profits fell sharply—and the merger with Spartans had to be arranged.

What has happened to Gene Ferkauf since he left Korvettes in 1968 at the age of forty-seven? A restless man who could never remain idle for very long, despite the great wealth he had accumulated, Ferkauf soon became involved with new retailing ventures. First he started a group of giftwear boutiques called Parsons Utopia—named after two thoroughfares near his home in Queens—which were sold to the Bohack's supermarket chain. Then he became a co-founder of stores selling imported china and crystal called Bazaar, which was converted in 1972 into a chain called DeFabio and Stein. This fledgling company consists of five small stores in New York and New Jersey under the Don DeFabio and Al Stein names, selling men's and women's wear in addition to the china and crystal.

For Ferkauf, these stores are just the first step toward what he hopes will be another merchandising empire. Yet even if his dreams for a new mercantile adventure do not work out, Ferkauf won't be forgotten among students of retailing, because he was the man who first put the discount house squarely on the map of American retailing and made every other merchant take notice. For this, he earned the title of "Duke of Discounting" and the high regard of the other discounters who followed in his footsteps.

Korvettes has long since been surpassed as the No. 1 discounter by K-Mart, the giant chain of discount stores owned by the S. S. Kresge Company. By the end of 1972, after only a decade of discounting, Kresge had opened 580 K-Marts, which contributed $3.3 billion of the corporation's $3.8-billion volume. Ninety-five K-Mart stores with eight million square feet were opened in 1972 and a similar number were planned for the next few years to maintain the same rapid pace of expansion.

Unlike Korvettes, K-Mart did not begin from a standing start. Its parent, Kresge, was founded in Detroit in 1897 by Sebastian S. Kresge, who had entered the dime-store business two years earlier in partnership with another well-known variety-store merchant, J. G. McCrory. By 1912, the Kresge chain was the nation's second-largest variety store group, and over the next fifty years it grew to become one of the giants among the general merchandise chains.

By the mid-1950s, though, its management realized that the patterns of retailing were changing fast and undertook a study of new selling methods. Harry B. Cunningham—a former cub reporter, then general vice president of the company and later president, chairman and chief executive officer in the period of K-Mart's most explosive growth—was in charge of this study in 1957 and 1958 and recommended the entry into discounting. Kresge got its feet wet in 1961 via a defensive marketing program by opening three small discount stores called Jupiter in unprofitable downtown variety stores. This move turned out well enough for the first K-Mart to be opened in a Detroit suburb in 1962, followed by seventeen more that year and hundreds of others in the years to come.

Cunningham said afterwards about the outset of this fast-paced expansion program, "The Kresge organization was our ace in the hole. I knew that our people could undertake any kind of new venture and perform admirably." Ranging in size from 75,000 to 95,000 square feet, with most in the middle of this range, the K-Marts today have a full line of hard goods and soft goods and carry primarily nationally advertised brands.

In addition to the K-Marts, Kresge operates mini-K-Marts of 40,000 to 65,000 square feet, 116 Jupiter stores that have been converted from variety stores and, of course, the standard variety stores on which the company was created. Heading Kresge today are Robert E. Dewar, chairman and chief executive officer; Ervin E. Wardlow, president and chief merchandising and operations officer; and Walter H. Teniga, vice chairman and chief financial and development officer.

Other large discount department-store chains started their business in more modest surroundings. For instance, the Two Guys chain, operated by Vornado, Inc., had its genesis in a small hard-goods discount house in a twenty-by-forty-foot diner.

The company was founded with capital of $28,000 in 1947 by two brothers, Herbert and Sidney Hubschman, who opened their store in the town of Harrison, New Jersey. The empty diner, owned by Herbert and vacated when he opened a tobacco and card concession, was across the street from a vacuum-tube plant of RCA Corporation, to which the brothers used to run coffee.

They began in the discount business by selling, on a cash-and-carry basis, cut-price television sets, refrigerators and washing machines for $5 to $10 above their cost, with a six-man staff and customers writing out their own orders. Because of their low markup, profits came from the service contracts they sold. The name they chose for their store was Two Guys from Harrison, which stuck for many years until widespread expansion beyond the confines of New Jersey and the closing of its last store in Harrison made it wise to contract the name to the first two words.

The original name, by the way, was based on a competitor's comment about the Hubschmans when he found out that they were underselling him by 25 percent. "Those two bastards from Harrison," he said, and the words—with a slight modification—were taken for the corporate name.

At one time, the company had ten buses in use as mobile showrooms around Woodbridge, New Jersey. Later came a rash of tiny "pup," or, as they are also called, "acorn," stores in New York City and New Jersey.

Today Two Guys is no longer in the pup category. With 64 discount stores containing some ten million square feet of retail space along the East and West Coasts, Vornado is now a major factor in discounting. Its sales in 1972 were close to $800 million and its earnings topped $11 million. In addition to its discount stores, Vornado operates more than three dozen Builders Emporiums, two Sutton Place catalog showrooms and the franchising company for Foster's Freeze drive-ins.

The company derived its present corporate name after a 1959 merger between Two Guys from Harrison, Inc., and the O. A. Sutton Corporation, an appliance manufacturer that used the Vornado brand. The Hubschmans held the two top executive posts until Sidney left the company in 1963 after policy friction and Herbert died in 1964.

Currently the management of Two Guys is under the direction of Frederick Zissu, a Wall Street lawyer who joined the company in 1949 and now serves as Vornado's chairman and chief executive officer, and Sol Rogoff, a former lessee, who is president.

Another early discounting company is Interstate Stores, Inc.

Here is an instance where a company did a complete about-face from an outright reliance on conventional merchandising to an emphasis on discount retailing—and in so doing became one of the leaders of that field. In recent years, its earnings have sagged badly and it had a $40-million deficit in 1972 but sales topped half a billion dollars.

Sol Cantor, chairman and chief executive officer of Interstate and long a dynamic spokesman for discounting, was running a conventional forty-eight-unit department-store chain in smaller cities whose roots went back to 1928. In 1957, he visualized the advantages of discount merchandising and tried out an experimental unit in Copley, Pennsylvania, outside Altoona.

It worked so well that the next year he opened his first new discount store and found it to be much more profitable than his other stores. In 1959, therefore, he bought the two-store White Front in Los Angeles, and the following year he took over the ten-store Topps chain in the East. He was on his way.

"We are rebels in the retail field," Mr. Cantor has said, "and we must continue to think of ourselves that way."

By thinking of himself as a rebel, Mr. Cantor has created a retailing empire that even after a divestiture of unprofitable units consists of about seventy-five discount stores, under the White Front name on the West Coast (Los Angeles) and the Topps name in the East (Baltimore) and Middle West (Chicago, Ohio, Michigan). There are still thirty-one successful conventional department stores operated by Interstate as well as forty-five Toys-R-Us toy supermarkets, the fastest growing segment of the company. Robert E. Fogley, a former management consultant, is president of Interstate. Walter Craig is president of the discount-store division, while Charles Lazarus is president of Toys-R-Us.

The growth of Interstate, according to Mr. Cantor, "is due to the fact that we are attracting customers from the middle and upper income brackets. Bare pipe racks are out; we are going more and more to chandeliers, carpets on the floor and chrome display devices."

The list of discounters who are attracting wider groups of customers can be extended much further. Stores run by King's Department Store, Inc., the Zayre Corporation, National Bellas Hess, Daylin, Inc., and other big companies in the field have become important elements in the overall retailing pattern throughout the country by merchandising all kinds of goods for all elements in their communities.

There has been, moreover, an increase of entries into discounting by other types of merchandisers. As these companies, which have already won their spurs in retailing, gain more experience in discounting and realize its benefits, their interest in and enthusiasm for discount stores can be expected to grow.

In this category, for example, are the department-store chains that have developed discount-store divisions. Included here are May Department Stores, with its Venture stores; L. S. Ayres & Co., with its Ayr-Way stores; Rich's Department stores, with its Richway chain; Allied Stores Corporation, with its J. B. Hunter and Almart stores; Federated Department stores, with its Gold Circle stores; and the Dayton Company, with its Target stores.

Many variety-store chains also have discount divisions. In addition to Kresge's K-Mart, the following are among the former dime-store organizations with discount divisions: the F. W. Woolworth Company, with its Woolco stores; J. J. Newberry Company, with its Britt stores; Neisner Brothers, Inc., with its Big-N stores; and M. H. Fishman Co. with its Mason's stores.

Finally, many of the supermarket chains are involved in discounting to a large extent. Besides operating as lessees in discount stores run by others, food chains have started discount divisions of their own. The Grand Union Company operates Grand-Way, Food Fair Stores owns J. M. Fields, the Kroger Company purchased Thriftown, Stop & Shop has Bradlees; and Jewel Tea Company runs Turn-Style.

As other retailers move into discounting and as the discounters develop into major merchandising organizations, a lot of the clear-cut differences between department stores and discount houses have disappeared. Discounters are offering additional amenities to make shopping more pleasant, while department stores have met low-margin merchandisers on their own ground by offering discounts in certain categories themselves.

Despite this blending—or perhaps because of it—the discount store shows every indication of continuing as a potent force on the retailing scene. The big K-Mart, Woolco, Zayre, Korvette, Two Guys, White Front and similar stores in the suburbs are betting on an uninterrupted growth in the affluence, purchasing power and standard of living of middle-class Americans. Few retailers are betting against them.

XXVI
Retailing in the Future

Some Predictions for 2000 and Later

What about retailing in the future? Developments have come so fast in the second half of the twentieth century that many talk of "the revolution in retailing." This is more alliterative than accurate. By definition, a revolution is a complete overthrow, or a complete change of a system. This has not happened and is not likely to happen in retailing.

New forms and variations in selling goods to consumers are evolving constantly despite the obstacles and harassments thrown in their way by those with vested interests in older forms. The new when it emerges usually proves neither as problem-solving as its enthusiasts predict nor as destructive as its foes fear. The same fears that are now being voiced about franchising, discount houses, vending machines and shopping centers in the past have been shouted about department stores, mail-order houses, trading stamps and chain stores.

Automation is swifter than hand operations. The new is more profitable than the old but the two continue to exist next door to each other in many communities. Most retailers, or business-men in general for that matter, are not eager for the new but they can be persuaded. One of the early buyers of the new electronic computer terminal cash registers in 1973 was Flah's, an Albany, New York, group of clothing stores that had done business since 1914 without ever installing mechanical registers.[1]

One of the strongest trends as of 1973, that of merchandisers ensuring quality in products by planning and, in some cases, manufacturing them, is a return to a virtue of the oldest retailers. The divergent approaches of selling everything or special-izing continues. There are drugstores and supermarkets that sell soft goods and hardware. At the same time, there are shops that sell only clothing and shoes for tall girls or only women's wigs.

But shifts in population, the advent of the telephone, the automobile, broadcasting, changes in transportation and traffic, and more recently the computer and electronic data processing have affected greatly the pattern of retailing. Cable television may also spur change.

Since 1964, big retailers have sold more goods in suburban and outlying stores than downtown. Some famous stores have closed. Others have thrived. In thirty years, shopping centers increased their sales from little or nothing to about $140 billion. The trend in shopping center design is to the enclosed mall with multilevel units, sometimes with levels underground. In 1960, the eight general merchandise-variety chains had 37 percent of their stores and 14 percent of their sales in shopping centers. In 1970, the figures were 68 and 60 percent. For 1980, they are projected at 73 and 85 percent.[2]

It is interesting and challenging to speculate further ahead, especially to the magical, millennial year 2000. One eminent commentator on the future, Daniel Bell, the Harvard sociologist who is chairman of the Commission on the Year 2000, warns against expecting really startling developments: "A complex society is not changed by a flick of the wrist. Considered from the viewpoint of gadgetry, the United States in the year 2000 will be more *like* the United States in the year 1967 than *dif-ferent*. The basic framework of day-to-day life has been shaped in the last fifty years by the ways the automobile, the airplane, the telephone, and the television have brought people together. . . . It is highly unlikely that . . . impending changes in tech-nology will radically alter this framework. . . . The problem of the future consists in defining one's priorities and making the necessary commitments."[3]

A provocative study, "The Future of Retailing to the Year

2000," presented by Dr. Leo Bogart of the Bureau of Advertising, keynoted the 1973 convention of the National Retail Merchants Association. A little later the Center for the Study of Democratic Institutions issued a report on "social futures" for 2000. Earlier, in its hundreth-anniversary issue, the *American Druggist* published a collection of forecasts about "the next 100 years."[4] In 1969, the Chamber of Commerce of the United States issued a report with many retailing implications titled "America's Next 30 Years: Business and the Future."

Some uncanny predicting was done as early as 1887 by the writer-reformer Edward Bellamy. He wrote prolifically but is remembered for his Utopian novel, *Looking Backward 2000– 1887*. It sold 200,000 copies the first year and has been in print ever since.[5] In it a young man is hypnotized in Boston and after sleeping "exactly one hundred and thirteen years, three months, and eleven days," awakens on September 10, 2000. He finds a more attractive Boston; homes equipped with "musical telephones" very like radio sets; beautiful women who have attained political and economic equality. They wear attractive paper clothing, usually trousers, available for ten or twenty cents a garment and discarded after use.

Women and men work part of their lives in the industrial army of a cooperative state. A benign government controls production and distribution of goods. Attractive stores containing samples of everything are in each ward of the city "so that no residence was more than five or ten minutes' walk from one of them." There a shopper chooses articles, pays for them by having a credit card punched and they are delivered promptly by pneumatic tube to his home or near there.

Paper apparel is available today—especially women's underpants, hospital and laboratory gowns and uniforms. Elisa Daggs of New York for some years designed fashion items in paper, including bathing suits and wedding dresses, but prices had to be six to fourteen dollars, not ten or twenty cents, and it proved uneconomic. Pneumatic tubes carried first-class letters and small packages swiftly underground in New York for many years. But fragile and bigger packages could not be handled, and in 1953 Postmaster General Arthur E. Summerfield, who had a background in automobile dealership, ended the service. But improvements on New York's Roosevelt (formerly Welfare) Island call for pneumatic removal of refuse.

Catalog showrooms envisaged by Bellamy are everywhere. Some believe they will be replaced or augmented by closed-circuit television devices that will permit Mrs. Consumer to see and buy without leaving home. "Two-way cable television, with its multitude of channels," said President Edward S. Donnell of Montgomery Ward & Co. in 1973, "makes in-home electronic selling feasible. A miniature, up-to-date, flexible and economically practical electronic catalog already is foreseeable."[6] Professors Alton F. Doody and William R. Davidson of Ohio State have proposed a closed-circuit device that will picture merchandise. By pushing buttons the customer can order it and also pay for it by automatically transferring money from her bank account to the city-wide shopping service.[7] Bonwit Teller in 1973 had a Picturephone shopping service in Chicago between its Oak Brook and Michigan Avenue stores. New Century Town in north suburban Vernon Hills near Chicago is to have cable television in every home and store. Half of all U.S. households are likely to have this by the early 1990s and may use it in buying items that do not require "fitting" or "feel."

Free enterprise is so deeply ingrained in America that any government takeover of distribution such as described by Bellamy is fanciful. But government actions will continue to affect retailing, directly and indirectly, and increasingly so. In the centennial issue of the *American Druggist,* several pharmaceutical leaders predicted an end to the corner drugstore, with pharmacists becoming part of a government-directed national health service. Many government safety requirements simply formalize precautions that responsible retailers have long taken to see that products do not poison, hurt or incinerate their customers.

Mail-order houses are at the mercy of the postal service. What government at all levels does about crime, mass transportation, traffic and other problems affects everyone. If food prices are allowed to go so high that necessities take all of most people's income, stores that sell luxuries are in trouble. Taxation, too, affects everybody.

Because of the complexities of government, there is a trend for big retailers to choose as chief executives men with legal training as well as merchandising experience. "The Bar Association seems to have gone retail," said a 1973 *Women's Wear Daily* headline.[8] At that time, to name only a few of them, chief executives with law-school backgrounds included: Arthur M. Wood, Sears, Roebuck and Co.; Thomas M. Macioce, Allied Stores Corp.; Donald D. Smiley, R. H. Macy & Co.; Robert E. Dewar, S. S. Kresge Co.; Sol W. Cantor, Interstate Stores; Frederick Zissu, Vornado; Charles G. Rodman, Grand Union Co.; and Leonard H. Straus, Thrifty Drug Stores.

Fewer babies are being born, and so families will be smaller. The economic growth rate, which has been 4.5 percent, probably will drop to 3.8 percent in 1980–90. Lane Bryant has closed the lounge for "expectant fathers" in its New York store and no longer distributes *Stork Facts* or a maternity catalog. The majority of families will have only one or two children. This does not mean an end to or even a drop in sales of baby cribs. In most families these are bought for the firstborn and passed along to later arrivals. What would have been spent on other children will be spent on other things.[9]

While families will be smaller, their incomes will be larger, and retail sales will pass a trillion dollars by 1985. The average hourly wage, which was $2.82 in 1970, will average $7.50 by the year 2000. There also will be more leisure, shorter workweeks, more three-day weekends and longer vacations. More people will be traveling, and traveling farther.

As a corollary and consequence, the use of national credit cards will expand as an advantage for both customer and retailer. They probably will eventually carry the photograph and the fingerprints of the card owner. The use of these cards originally cost a retailer 7.5 or even 10 percent in charges, but this has been halved by some cards and sometimes effects great savings in accounting expenses.

More women, some of them mothers with small children, will be earning and spending their own money. It will be advantageous for stores, as some do already, to provide day care centers for children of their customers and of their own employees. In 1972, for the first time, a majority (51 percent) of women aged eighteen through sixty-four were employed, many of them in retailing. With equal-rights laws requiring equal treatment for them in training and promotion, retailing can be expected to produce more women like Mildred Custin of Bonwit Teller, Geraldine Stutz of Henri Bendel and the late Dorothy Shaver of Lord & Taylor.

There will be more old people in the population—a great many of them if some of the forms of cancer are conquered before 2000, as many forecasters predict. Shortly after the turn of the century, half the people in the U.S. will be over fifty, and one out of three fifty-four or older. "The individual will live longer and face the problem of renewed education and new careers," says Daniel Bell.

There will be more franchising. The spectacular losses of General Foods and others in hamburgers showed that this is not an easy road to riches for all, but interest has revived and growth has been resumed. As this is written, there is talk of a nationally franchised chain of Masters and Johnson type sex clinics.

"To take care of our customers in the 1980's and 1990's," says Albert Sussman, executive vice president of the International Council of Shopping Centers, "we will need almost to triple our present retail facilities. We will need at least 25,000 more shopping centers of all kinds. We will have to expand existing centers, and we will have to upgrade them."

While the advent of automation typified by the computer-terminal electronic cash register is eliminating clerical tag-sorting jobs in retailing, there are more interesting merchandising, buying and promotion jobs in the field than ever. When she retired in 1973 after forty-two years of recruiting retail executives, Alice Carol Groves said:

"Retailing is the greatest profession for young, well-adjusted people. It offers more and faster rewards for diligence and high performance than any other field. For every executive, there is a yardstick of profit contribution that is lacking in other businesses."[10]

Retailing is a great field for all sorts of people; men and women; the young and the old; the trained and the untrained; the part-time and the full-time worker. This will be true in the future. Working conditions are improving and discriminations declining. There are no onerous apprenticeship or educational requirements for entry but special knowledge or experience may bring high rewards. The future is especially bright for alert merchants able and willing to follow customers in their migrations and swiftly to adapt hours and inventories to changing life styles.

Notes

I. PEDDLERS TO PALACES

1. H. Gordon Selfridge, *The Romance of Commerce* (London, John Lane, the Bodley Head, Ltd., 1918), pp. 121–38. Also H. Pasdermadjian, *The Department Store* (London, Newman Books, 1954).
2. Caroline Bird, "Macy's of Moscow," *Coronet,* March 1959. Also J. E. Evans, "Russian Retailing," *Wall Street Journal,* November 19, 1956, pp. 1, 21; Audrey R. Topping, "On Sale at GUM, Moscow's Super Shop, *New York Times Magazine,* July 28, 1963, pp. 13, 46–48; Associated Press, "A Store in Russia Hard on Shoppers," *New York Times,* Oct. 7, 1973, p. 56.
3. Philip W. Whitcomb, "Class with Mass," *Christian Science Monitor,* May 5, 1970, p. B7.
4. Philip Shabecoff, "Pretty Girls Adorn Tokyo Store," *New York Times,* Nov. 4, 1968, p. 69. Also Crocker Snow, Jr., "Japan's Incredible Department Stores," *Boston Globe,* Aug. 30, 1972, p. 18.
5. *Forbes,* Jan. 1, 1973, p. 168.
6. Phineas T. Barnum, *Struggles & Triumphs* (Buffalo, 1883). See also Gerald Carson, *The Old Country Store* (New York, Oxford University Press, 1954).
7. Leonard Sloane, "G. Fox: Bit of Hartford History," *New York Times,* Dec. 23, 1965, pp. 27, 33.
8. Leonard Sloane, "Iowa's Younkers: Friendly Store," *New York Times,* April 11, 1966, pp. 55, 59.
9. Leonard Sloane, "Brigham Young's Store Moves with Times," *New York Times,* April 8, 1966, pp. 37, 42.

10. Joseph H. Appel, *The Business Biography of John Wanamaker* (New York, Macmillan, 1930), p. 52.
11. Lawrence B. Romaine, "Benjamin Franklin the Father of the Mail Order Catalog," *American Book Collector,* December 1960, pp. 25–28. Also, earlier, *Direct Advertising.*
12. Samuel Feinberg, *What Makes Shopping Centers Tick* (New York, Fairchild, 1960), pp. 41–43.
13. Emerson Chapin, "Japanese Shops Go Underground," *New York Times*, May 24, 1964, VIII, pp. 1, 16.
14. Tom Mahoney, "Shopping Centers—the Big Success Story," *Rotarian*, January, 1964, pp. 34–37, 57. See also Gurney Breckenfeld, "Downtown Has Fled to the Suburbs," *Fortune*, October 1972, pp. 80–86, 156–162; and Martha Weiman Lear, "A Master Builder Sights a Shopping Mall (An Account of Edward J. DeBartolo)," *New York Times Magazine*, August 12, 1973, pp. 12–13, 57–84. *Shopping Center World* and *National Mall Monitor* are devoted to the field and publications like *Chain Store Age* and *Women's Wear Daily* give it increasing attention.

II. THE HUDSON'S BAY COMPANY

1. These are definite distinctions of the venerable company, according to A. R. Huband, its secretary. The oft-applied phrase "oldest trading company in the world" must be weighed with the fact that Stora Kopparbergs Bergslays AB, Sweden's oldest industry and the oldest stock firm in the world, was chartered in 1347. Its activities include mining, iron and steel, pulp and paper.
2. Richardson was born in Winnipeg in 1924, the son of Muriel (Sprague) and the late James Richardson, and is a graduate of the University of Manitoba. He is president of James Richardson & Sons, Ltd., and senior partner in Richardson Securities of Canada. He had been named deputy governor in May 1970.
3. *A Brief History of the Hudson's Bay Company* (a fifty-page

booklet published by the company) includes a bibliography of more than eighty volumes on its history. The most scholarly of all is E. E. Rich's *Hudson's Bay Company 1670–1870* (Toronto, McClelland and Stewart Ltd., 1960), 3 vols. The Hudson's Bay Record Society has published twenty-five scholarly volumes of papers covering events before 1870, and half of the company's magazine, the *Beaver*, is devoted to history. For a concise account see "The Bay: Into the Fourth Century," *Time,* May 18, 1970, pp. 10–11, and for a humorous account: Ronald Searle and Kildare Dobbs, *The Great Fur Opera, Annals of the Hudson's Bay Company 1670–1970* (Toronto, McClelland and Stewart, 1970).

4. The early struggles of the Hudson's Bay Company supplied material for many novels. A young Scot, R. M. Ballantyne, a nephew of Sir Walter Scott's publisher, joined the company as a clerk in 1841. After six years at York Factory, Norway House and other posts, he quit and wrote eighty books based on his adventures. Many a later Hudson's Bay man has confessed that he joined the company after reading Ballantyne's *The Young Fur Traders* or *Hudson's Bay.*

III. BROOKS BROTHERS

1. Leonard Sloane, "John Wood Marks 20th Year at Helm of Brooks Brothers," *New York Times*, April 16, 1966.
2. Maurice C. Carroll, "A Stylish Robbery at Brooks Bros.," *New York Herald Tribune*, Jan. 22, 1964.
3. Jerome S. Kriska, "Brooks Bros.' Russell Tucker," *Daily News Record*, Oct. 21, 1970.

IV. TIFFANY'S

1. The article, "There's Only One Tiffany's," by Tom Mahoney and Mort Weisinger, was published in the October 1952

issue of *Coronet*, several months ahead of Henry La Cossitt's "Treasure House on Fifth Avenue," authorized with restrictions by the old Tiffany management, in the Jan. 24 and 31, 1953, issues of the *Saturday Evening Post*. The stock was held for a few years and sold at a 100 percent profit.

2. "Hoving Raced by Plane to New Hampshire for Needed Tiffany Stock," *Wall Street Journal*, Aug. 22, 1955. Hoving was born on Dec. 2, 1897, the son of a Swedish surgeon and a Finnish opera singer. He was graduated from Brown University and had been a successful executive of R. H. Macy & Co., Montgomery Ward, Lord & Taylor and Bonwit Teller.

3. Letitia Baldrige, *Of Diamonds and Diplomats* (Boston, Houghton Mifflin, 1968), pp. 89–146. She was recommended for the job by her former employer, Ambassador to Italy Clare Boothe Luce, who chanced to sit next to Walter Hoving at a dinner soon after he took over Tiffany's.

4. Causing a Nashville, Tennessee, newspaper to carry the headline "General Shoe Buys Tiffany's." Actually General Shoe increased its holdings of Hoving Corporation stock to 65 percent.

5. *New York Times, New York Herald Tribune, New York Journal-American*, Sept. 10, 1965.

6. Charles Lewis Tiffany wrote an account of the American Jewelry trade in Chauncey M. Depew's *One Hundred Years of American Commerce* (New York, D. O. Haynes, 1895), pp. 589–94.

7. The careers of all members of the Tiffany family are detailed in Joseph Purtell, *The Tiffany Touch,* New York, Random House, 1971. A June 27, 1967, *Look* picture feature by John Peter and Douglas Jones on the William Pahlmann-decorated Hoving appartment in New York's River House had the same title. Interest has revived in recent years in Tiffany glass. See Robert Koch, *Louis C. Tiffany, Rebel in Glass* (New York, Crown, 1964).

8. Samuel Feinberg, "Walter Hoving: Autocrat of Taste," *Women's Wear Daily*, Sept. 19, 1973.

V. THE SINGER COMPANY

1. Tom Mahoney, "The Machine That Sews Everywhere," *Reader's Digest*, January 1951. In the preparation of this article at the time of Singer's hundredth anniversary, the author interviewed President Milton Lightner, Vice Presidents Otto Myslik and Alvin K. Aurell and many other Singer executives and had access to the company's nineteenth-century letter books. These have since been given to the University of Wisconsin.

2. For a detailed account with genealogical charts of Isaac Singer's remarkable personal life, his twenty-four children and their heirs, see Frank J. Manheim, "The Singer Saga," *Town & Country,* December 1941, January and February 1942. Also, John Kobler, "Mr. Singer's Money Machine," *Saturday Evening Post*, July 7, 14, 21 and 28, 1951.

3. Bourne reported the sewing-machine industry in Chauncey M. Depew's *One Hundred Years of American Commerce* (New York, D. O. Haynes, 1895), pp. 525–39.

4. Annual reports. Also Edmund K. Faltermayer, "It's a Spryer Singer," *Fortune*, December 1963, and "Singer," *Forbes*, Oct. 15, 1964. Identified as "The International Manufacturing Company," Singer cooperated with Assistant Professors Bruce R. Scott and William D. Guth in nine 1964 Harvard Business School case studies of the company's 1958–1963 decisions.

VI. FILENE'S

1. Tom Mahoney, "Fabulous Filene's," *Future*, July 1947, and *Reader's Digest*, August 1947. The author interviewed Lincoln Filene, Harold Hodgkinson, Stacy Holmes and other Filene executives at length. Holmes in 1958 wrote *A Brief History of Filene's* and revised it in 1972. It is an excellent summary of the firm's "firsts." For many years Holmes has

authored Filene's famous topical Christmas poems appearing as full-page advertisements in Boston newspapers. Some 1972 lines:

"Gather ye, Wencelaus, armsful of fuel
For Wellesley's new President, Barbara Newell . . .
At Harvard please trundle a gift-laden barrow
To Nobel economist, Kenneth J. Arrow."

2. Federated does not announce sales figures for its units.

3. Paul M. Mazur and Myron S. Silbert, *Principles of Organization Applied to Modern Retailing* (New York, Harper, 1927).

4. Mary La Dame, *The Filene Store* (New York, Russell Sage Foundation, 1930), pp. 273–74. The book presents a detailed account of employee relations.

5. Filene's basement has been described many times, as in "Filene's Automatic Bargain Basement," *Retail Management,* March, 1945. Also Madeleine Blais, "Filene's Basement: The 9th Wonder," *Women's Wear Daily,* June 14, 1973.

6. Since being acquired by Associated Dry Goods, L. S. Ayres is no longer a member of the group.

7. A. Lincoln Filene, *A Merchant's Horizon* (Boston, Houghton Mifflin, 1924), p. 11, and Edward A. Filene, *The Way Out* (New York, Doubleday, 1924), pp. 178–79, gave their statements on need of a business plan for the future, the latter saying: "A businessman is a failure, although he makes millions of dollars, if he creates a business so dependent upon his personal administration that it disintegrates after his death." Edward A. Filene also wrote *More Profits from Merchandising* (A. W. Shaw, 1925); *The Model Stock Plan* (New York, McGraw-Hill, 1930), a book still used; *Successful Living in This Machine Age* (New York, Simon and Schuster, 1931); *Next Steps Forward in Retailing* (New York, Harper, 1937). Lincoln Filene wrote *Unfair Trade Practices—How to Remove Them* (New York, Harper, 1934), and, with Ralph E. Flanders, Morris Leeds and Henry Dennison, *Toward Full Employment* (New York, Whittlesey House, 1938).

8. One of his sons, Lincoln E. Kirstein, became famous as a supporter of the ballet and liberal publications, notably the

Nation. See "Public Balletomane No. 1," *New York Times,* March 30, 1966.
9. Gerald W. Johnson, *Liberal's Progress* (New York, Coward-McCann, 1948), pp. 21–35.

VII. F. & R. LAZARUS & COMPANY

1. According to the Value Line, forty-one funds held about 2,300,000 shares on June 30, 1973.
2. Tom Mahoney, "When FDR Juggled Thanksgiving," *American Legion Magazine,* October 1964. Details from Fred Lazarus, Jr., and voluminous files on the affair in the Franklin D. Roosevelt Library, Hyde Park, N.Y. President Roosevelt also wanted to change Thanksgiving from Thursday to Monday but abandoned that feature when Protestant church leaders objected. Instead of warning the Ohioans as had been planned, he announced advancing of the date on Aug. 14, 1939, at Campobello, New Brunswick, in the course of a vacation fishing trip.
3. Walter Peck, "Lazarus Launches Indiana Beachhead," *Women's Wear Daily,* Feb. 21, 1973.
4. *Fortune,* February 1947.
5. *Business Week,* May 14, 1955.
6. *New York Times,* Dec. 31, 1963; "The Man at A & S," *New York Post,* Feb. 18, 1965.
7. *New York Times* and *Women's Wear Daily,* Jan. 12, 1966, had lengthy biographical articles recounting his achievements.

VIII. MARSHALL FIELD & COMPANY

1. Leonard Sloane, "On State Street It's Still Marshall Field," *New York Times,* December 21, 1965, pp. 55, 63.

2. Tom Mahoney and Rita Hessian, *Public Relations for Retailers*, (New York, Macmillan, 1949), p. 9.
3. Leonard Sloane, "Halle's of Cleveland Keeps Personal Touch," *New York Times*, March 30, 1966.
4. Lloyd Wendt and Herman Kogan, *Give the Lady What She Wants* (Chicago, Rand, McNally & Company, 1952). Literature on Field's also includes John Tebbell, *The Marshall Fields* (New York, Dutton, 1947); Emily Kimbrough, *Through Charley's Door* (New York, Harper, 1950); Robert W. Twyman, *History of Marshall Field & Co.* (Philadelphia, University of Pennsylvania Press, 1954). This book quotes Field archives and lists fifty books and more than 150 shorter works with references to the store.
5. Peg Zwecker, "Chicago's All-Out Welcome for Philip," Chicago *Daily News*, March 18, 1966, p. 22.
6. *Women's Wear Daily*, April 11, 1966.
7. Tebbell, *op. cit.*, pp. 136–37.
8. "Marshall Field, the Store," *Fortune*, December 1945.

IX. BRENTANO'S

1. "Collier Holders Score Store Deal," *New York Times*, April 6, 1962.
2. Bennett Cerf, "The Story of Brentano's," *Saturday Review*, March 4 and 11, 1950.
3. While Kroch's & Brentano's has been advertised as "the world's largest bookstore," this distinction seems to belong to Foyle's of London, which has nine acres of floor space and more than four million volumes. See George Kent, "The World's Biggest Bookseller," *Saturday Review*, Oct. 7, 1950, pp. 14–16.
4. Stanton Griffis, *Lying in State* (New York, Doubleday, 1952), pp. 62–72.
5. Jean F. Mercier, "Walden Book Company: HQ is still back of the tracks but Walden is opening #200," *Publishers Weekly*, Oct. 2, 1972.

6. Susan Wagner, "Leonard Schwartz," *Publishers Weekly*, Feb. 19, 1973.

X. R. H. MACY & CO., INC.

1. Margaret Case Harriman, *And the Price Is Right* (Cleveland and New York, World, 1958).
2. Ralph M. Hower, *History of Macy's of New York 1858–1919* (Cambridge, Harvard University Press, 1946).
3. Curtiss S. Johnson, *The Indomitable R. H. Macy* (New York, Vantage Press, 1964).
4. Curtiss S. Johnson, *America's First Lady Boss* (Norwalk, Conn., Silvermine Publishers, 1965).
5. Leonard Sloane, "A Fourth Generation Retailer," *New York Times*, June 23, 1963. Also, *Time* cover article, January 8, 1965.

XI. THE FOOD GIANTS

1. "Supermarket Sales Hit Record High," *Chain Store Age,* Stores Edition, July, 1973.
2. Eleanor Johnson Tracy, "How A & P Got Creamed," *Fortune*, January 1973.
3. J. C. Furnas, "Mr. George and Mr. John," *Saturday Evening Post*, Dec. 31, 1938.
4. Daniel Henninger, "A Big Price War Interrupts Rising Food Costs," *National Observer*, Aug. 5, 1972.

XII. RICH'S

1. Tom Mahoney, "The Store That Married a City," *Saturday Evening Post,* Dec. 3, 1949, pp. 34, 176–80. Also Professor

Henry Givens Baker, *Rich's of Atlanta* (Athens, University of Georgia School of Business Administration, 1953).

2. Among the many honors received by Neely was the 1952 Gantt Medal of the American Management Association. In 1962, he received an honorary Doctor of Laws degree from Mercer University, and the Georgia Institute of Technology named its Nuclear Research Center for him.

3. Dick Rich received an honorary Doctor of Laws degree from Emory University in 1965. He has served as trustee of Young Harris College and been active in more than forty civic, religious and charitable organizations. He was Georgia's "Citizen of the Year" and received the Rotary Club's Armin Maier Cup for outstanding community service in 1953 and the National Retail Merchants' Association Gold Medal in 1963. He served as chairman of the Atlanta Arts Alliance, Inc., formed to raise funds for the Atlanta Memorial Cultural Center, a complex housing an art gallery and performing-arts facilities. It honors the memory of 122 members of the Atlanta Art Association killed June 3, 1962, in a plane crash at Paris.

4. Celestine Sibley, *Dear Store, An Affectionate Portrait of Rich's* (Garden City, Doubleday, 1967), pp. 119–127.

XIII. F. W. WOOLWORTH CO.

1. Carl Rieser, "What's Come Over Old Woolworth?," *Fortune,* January 1960, pp. 92–98, 212–18. Don Wharton, "See What's Happened to the 5 & 10!" *Reader's Digest*, February 1962, pp. 241–44. "The Old Five-and-Ten Spreads New Wings," *Business Week*, Nov. 14, 1964, pp. 58–67.

2. John K. Winkler, *Five and Ten, The Fabulous Life of F. W. Woolworth* (New York, Bantam, 1957), pp. 7–9. Winkler had access to company records.

3. *Woolworth's First 75 Years* (published by the company, 1954), pp. 22–26.

4. She married Prince Alexis Mdivani, Count Kurt von

Haugwitz-Reventlow, Cary Grant, Prince Igor Troubetzkoy, Porfirio Rubirosa, Gottfried von Cramm and Prince Doan Vinh Na Champacak of Thailand.

5. Winkler, *op. cit.*, p. 233.
6. Isadore Barmash, "Woolworth Changes the Guard," *New York Times*, Dec. 11, 1969.
7. Robert E. Bedingfield, "Woolworth Recruits F.B.I. Man," *New York Times*, June 7, 1970.
8. John S. Roberts, "Effective Employment of Minorities Is Considered Essential to Business and to the Lives of All Americans," *NAM Reports*, May 24, 1971.

XIV. DAYTON'S AND HUDSON'S

1. Oscar Webber, "J. L. Hudson, The Man and the Store," reprint of a November 8, 1954, address to the Newcomen Society of North America. Besides much little-known family history, this includes the only public statement for many years of the store's sales figures. Also, Tom Mahoney, "Hudson's of Detroit," *Coronet,* October 1955, pp. 67–69.
2. Leonard Sloane, "In Detroit—Hudson's," *New York Times*, Dec. 10, 1965, pp. 73, 80.
3. William T. Noble, "Joseph L. Hudson, Jr., Detroit's Merchant Prince," *Detroit News Pictorial Magazine*, September 12, 1965, pp. 7–16.
4. "History of the Men's Wear Industry 1890–1950," *Men's Wear,* Feb. 10, 1950, pp. 206–249.
5. "The hardest hit city was Detroit," writes Caroline Bird in *The Invisible Scar* (New York, McKay, 1966). "The unemployed auto workers could not pay their rent; landlords could not pay taxes; banks could not realize on mortgages; the city could not pay on its municipal bonds, and so could not borrow money to keep relief going." Pp. 103–104.
6. "Artists Paint Michigan," *Life*, Aug. 23, 1948.
7. "Men Make Their Own Dignity," *Detroit Free Press*, March 10, 1961.

8. Leonard Sloane, "Dayton's Strikes a Dominant Key Among Stores of Upper Midwest," *New York Times*, Nov. 19, 1966.

XV. SEARS, ROEBUCK AND CO.

1. According to the Value Line, 32 funds held 2,387,767 shares as of Sept. 30, 1972. Ten funds held 320,100 Sears shares at the end of 1954, according to Arthur A. Werfel, *Women's Wear Daily*, June 28, 1955.
2. Used as a headline by *Changing Times*, October 1950, in summarizing *Catalogues and Counters, A History of Sears, Roebuck and Company,* by Boris Emmet and John E. Jeuck (Chicago, University of Chicago Press, 1950), a 788-page volume that gives the history of the enterprise in great detail.
3. *Detroit News,* Oct. 15, 1965, p. 7-C. Two Sears employees, Daniel Kleczkowski, twenty-four, and Mark Rebrovich, eighteen, trailed the bandits, hailed a police car and were given principal credit for recovery of $9,780 and the arrests.
4. James C. Worthy, Sears personnel department, in *Harvard Business Review*, January 1950. Also Harvey E. Runner, *New York Herald Tribune*, Jan. 18, 1950.
5. A 1932 Calvin Coolidge letter, catalogued in 1954 by Paul Hoag, Gilmanton, Massachusetts, autograph dealer, advised a contractor that "Sears are sending" some building supplies by freight and instructed him to haul them to his Vermont farmstead, which he was then modernizing.
6. "How Giant Sears Grows and Grows," *Business Week*, Dec. 16, 1972, pp. 52–57.
7. Kenneth McKenna, "Forgotten Men of Business," *New York Herald Tribune*, March 9, 1961.
8. In its "50 years ago" department, *Printer's Ink* of Aug. 27, 1948, reproduced an advertisement headed "An Infamous Lie" offering $100 reward for detection of the man who started the story that "Mr. Ward is a mulatto Negro."
9. Made from 1908 to 1911 by the Lincoln Motor Car Works,

Chicago. It had five forward speeds and was popular on Texas farms. One preserved by Frank Stokes, Covina, California, was pictured in *Horseless Carriage Gazette,* January–February, 1954, p. 14.

10. In his retirement, Lessing Rosenwald assembled one of the world's greatest collections of prints at Alverthorpe, his estate at Jenkintown, Pennsylvania. He has enriched the National Gallery of Art and the Library of Congress with gifts of rare books and prints.

11. John Reddy, "The General Who Built the World's Largest Store," *Reader's Digest,* January 1964, pp. 181–85.

12. An earlier effort to sell life insurance through a Hercules subsidiary from 1934 to 1938 was less successful and it was sold.

13. John McDonald, "Sears Makes It Look Easy," *Fortune,* May 1964, pp. 120–27. Includes a listing of ten critical decisions that have led to the company's success.

14. *Advertising Age,* Aug. 28, 1972.

15. Julian Lewis Watkins, *One Hundred Greatest Advertisements in History* (New York, Dover Publications, 1959), p. 199. "No book on great copy would be complete without this most famous of all salesmen in print," said Watkins. "More than a thousand pages of the strongest selling copy ever written—any page, any item, any year."

16. The *Dallas Morning News* obituary of April 21, 1954, described Scott as one "who cared more for people's welfare and culture than for a personal fortune."

17. *Amerika Illustrated,* Issue No. 41, 1959.

18. *Wall Street Journal* and other newspapers of Sept. 22, 1959.

XVI. LANE BRYANT

1. Details of Mrs. Bryant's early life were obtained from her by Tom Mahoney in a series of interviews for a magazine article, "$49,000,000 Business in Round Figures," *Inde-*

pendent Woman, October 1950, and condensed as "Maternity Mart—The Story of Lane Bryant," *Reader's Digest,* November 1950.

2. "Lane Bryant, Lord of the Outsize Market," *Clothes,* May 1, 1967.

3. Angela Taylor, "They Admit to a Problem—But Don't Call Them Chubby," *New York Times,* Nov. 30, 1972.

4. Raphael Malsin was probably the only head of a retail company in America to be a member of both Phi Beta Kappa and Sigma Xi, honor-society distinctions that he earned at Yale. He was a secretary of Arthur Brisbane, the famous Hearst journalist, and worked as a newspaper reporter on the *New York Mail* and *Evening Journal* before joining Lane Bryant in the merchandising office. He became advertising manager, then general manager. He served with the Lend-Lease administration in North Africa during World War II.

5. Alfred Lief, *People Who Care* (New York, Appleton-Century-Crofts, 1967) gives detailed accounts of a dozen winners. Recipients of the individual award have included Mrs. Lester G. Auberlin, Detroit; Dr. Jessie Royer Greaves, Paoli, Pa.; Danny Kaye, Beverly Hills, Calif.; Rev. W. L. Buffington, Augusta, Ga. Among others, group awards have gone to the Henry Street Settlement, New York; League of Women Voters, Des Moines, Ia.; Parents and Friends of Mentally Retarded Children, Bridgeport, Conn.; American Field Service and Harlem School of the Arts, New York.

XVII. J. C. PENNEY COMPANY

1. James C. Penney, *Fifty Years with the Golden Rule* (New York, Harper, 1950).

2. Godfrey M. Lebhar, *Chain Stores in America 1859–1950* (New York, Chain Store Publishing Corporation, 1952).

3. Alfred Law, "From Overalls to Fashion Wear," *Wall Street Journal,* October 22, 1964.

XVIII. BROADWAY-HALE

1. William H. B. Kilmer, *Arthur Letts, A Biography* (Los Angeles, privately printed, 1927).
2. Leonard Sloane, "Coast Chain Follows the Crowd," *New York Times*, March 21, 1967.
3. Isadore Barmash, "Merchant from the West," *New York Times*, June 6, 1971.

XIX. NEIMAN-MARCUS

1. Isadore Barmash, "$2,700 a Skin Bid for New Mink," *New York Times*, Feb. 27, 1969.
2. Wendy Haskell Meyer, "O What a Lovely War!!!" *Texas Monthly*, February 1973, pp. 40–43. Also "The Showdown at Post Oak" *Business Week,* Feb. 28, 1970.
3. Stanley Marcus, "Marcus Polo at China Trade Fair," *New York Times*, June 4, 1972.
4. "From Skies to Store," *Life,* Aug. 30, 1954, pp. 14–15.
5. Frank X. Tolbert, *Neiman–Marcus, Texas* (New York, Henry Holt, 1953), and many others. The store has a lengthy bibliography of everything published about it.
6. *A Taste of Texas* (New York, Random House, 1949).
7. George Sessions Perry, *American Cities* (New York, McGraw-Hill, 1947).
8. Charlotte Curtis, "Neiman-Marcus and the Last of the Big-Time Spenders," *New York Times*, Sept. 16, 1965.

XX. BERGDORF GOODMAN

1. Booton Herndon, *Bergdorf's on the Plaza* (New York, Knopf, 1956).

2. Leonard Sloane, "Bergdorf Goodman Plans Expansion," *New York Times*, Nov. 15, 1967.
3. Stephen Birmingham, "But the New Generation Doesn't Want to Mind the Store," *New York Times Magazine*, Sept. 26, 1971, pp. 16–17, 65–82.

XXI. BULLOCK'S AND I. MAGNIN

1. *Op. cit.*
2. "A Store for the Motorized Carriage Trade," *Architectural Forum*, May 1948.
3. Leonard Sloane, "Retailers in Hot Proxy Fight," *New York Times*, July 5, 1964.

XXII. L. L. BEAN, INC.

1. *Playboy*, May 1963, pp. 119–20.
2. Genealogical records of many generations of Beans are listed in L. L. Bean, *My Story, The Autobiography of a Down-East Merchant* (Freeport, Maine, 1960), pp. 34–35, 78–79. Some are pictured.
3. This and most of the other details of this chapter are from a 1954 interview by Tom Mahoney with L. L. Bean at Freeport, supplemented by correspondence, especially a long letter from him dated Oct. 12, 1965, the day before his ninety-third birthday.
4. Rita Reif, "A Rustic Store That Became Awfully Chic," *New York Times*, Nov. 25, 1972.
5. Important national notice began for the business with the Oct. 13, 1941, issue of *Life* which published a four-page

picture feature, "Maine's Bean Outfits Sportsmen Every-where." The December 1941 issue of *Reader's Digest,* pp. 112–15, condensed Webb Waldron's "Bean, the Happy Hunter," from the *Kiwanis Magazine* of the same month. The *Saturday Evening Post* published Arthur Bartlett's "The Discovery of L. L. Bean," Dec. 14, 1946, pp. 30–31, 92–99.

6. Except for ten shares each given three employees, all stock was held in the family at incorporation in 1934. Carl Bean and the late John T. Gorman, a son-in-law, were named vice presidents in the first election of officers Nov. 16, 1934. Mr. Gorman died in 1959.

7. The workings of L. L. Bean have been the subject of a case study by the Harvard University Graduate School of Business Administration; also of articles in *Business Week* (Sept. 6, 1952, pp. 46–49) and *Sales Management* (September 1955).

8. Dated June 2 and Oct. 29, 1954, respectively. Published as *My Story,* p. 103.

XXIII. OHRBACH'S, INC.

1. Selma Robinson, "Even the Rich Love Bargains," *McCall's,* June 1964.

2. Herbert Brean, "High Style Cash-and-Carry," *Life,* Jan. 26, 1953.

3. Nathan M. Ohrbach, *Getting Ahead in Retailing* (McGraw-Hill, New York, 1935).

4. Leonard Sloane, "Ohrbach's Offbeat Approach," *New York Times,* Jan. 26, 1964.

XXIV. WEBB'S CITY

1. Hyman Goldberg, "Million-Dollar Medicine Man," *Cosmopolitan,* February 1953, pp. 104–111. Other accounts of the

rise of "Doc" Webb include: Paul Gardner and Allan Gould, "Pink Pills and Pin-Ups." *Collier's*, Nov. 22, 1947, pp. 97–98; *Fortune*, January 1948, pp. 92–95, 124–128, condensed by *Reader's Digest*, pp. 109–112, as "The World's Most Unusual Drugstore." Tom Mahoney, "The Drug Store That Became a City," *Pageant*, April 1955, pp. 110–14.
2. *Washington Post*, Aug. 8, p. D20, and Aug. 20, 1963, p. A14.
3. *St. Petersburg Independent,* Jan. 21, 1960.

XXV. THE DISCOUNTERS ARRIVE

1. *Discount Store News*, Dec. 11, 1972.
2. Walter Henry Nelson, *The Great Discount Delusion* (New York, McKay, 1965).
3. E. B. Weiss, *A Reappraisal of New Rental Trends* (New York, Doyle Dane Bernbach, Inc., 1964).
4. Leonard Sloane, "Discount Stores Broaden Inroads," *New York Times*, July 19, 1964.
5. "Everybody Loves a Bargain," *Time*, July 6, 1962.

XXVI. RETAILING IN THE FUTURE

1. *Women's Wear Daily*. Jan. 15, 1973, p. 22.
2. *Chain Store Age*, Jan. 15, 1973.
3. Daniel Bell, "The Future as Present Expectation," in *The Futurists*, Edited with an introduction by Alvin Toffler, (New York, Random House, 1972), pp. 257–63.
4. July 13, 1970.
5. Edward Bellamy, *Looking Backward 2000–1887* (New York, Modern Library, 1951). Originally published by

Ticknor, Boston, in 1887. More than a million copies have been sold in many languages.

6. To a National Shoe Fair industry breakfast, *Women's Wear Daily*, March 13, 1973.

7. *American Druggist*, Nov. 6, 1967; also *Harvard Business Review*, May–June, 1967, pp. 4–20.

8. March 14, 1973.

9. Caroline Bird, *The Crowding Syndrome* (New York, Mc-Kay, 1972), pp. 172–75. Also "Gearing Up for Near Zero Growth," *Signature*, March 1973, pp. 29–31.

10. Samuel Feinberg, "Alice Grove Compares Retailing to Hollywood," *Women's Wear Daily*, Feb. 23, 1973.

Index